"*Unleashing A Wild Hope* is an important book for all people of faith who want to do more than just lament the great environmental, economic, political, and spiritual problems in our world."

JIMMY CARTER
39TH President

"In his latest book, Tom Sine has written more than a Christian version of *Megatrends*; he has penned a sweeping description and Christian prospectus for the coming years, and this *Wild Hope* will surely become an important text for discussion among interested Christian leaders and laymen."

MARK O. HATFIELD
United States Senator

"The looming date *2000 A.D.* has brought forth numerous efforts to catalogue the past and weigh what it portends for the future new era. Some of those efforts are authored by people of faith and are directed toward the churches. Standing with one foot in traditional evangelicalism and the other in ecumenical liberalism, Tom Sine speaks both appreciatively and critically to each. Few authors attempt such empathetic bridging, and that makes this book doubly valuable. Furthermore, it not only gathers significant data on most of the key issues and challenges of our times, but indicates what is being done—and ought to be done—by the churches to confront them."

PEGGY L. SHRIVER
Staff Associate for Professional Church Leadership
The National Council of Churches of Christ

"*Wild Hope* is an extraordinary study that will challenge every preconceivable idea for ministry fervently embraced by most Protestants and Roman Catholics. Tom Sine brilliantly connects historical information with present and future trends that bring us back to our missiological drawing board. This is a powerful volume for all who compassionately participate in God's world and God's salvific activity."

MANUEL ORTIZ
Professor
Westminster Theological Seminary

"*Wild Hope* is essential reading for any Christian leader in North America who wants to operate from a comprehensive grasp of the world we may be trying to reach with the Christian gospel in the years ahead."

TOM HOUSTON
Executive Director
The Lausanne Committee for World Evangelization

"With comprehensive precision, Tom Sine chronicles the current state of the earth and the challenges that face us if we are to have a future. He outlines how the American dream has become a nightmare for both the environment and human relationships, but he doesn't leave us in despair. He offers inbreaking signs of hope, a compelling vision for the future, and practical advice on how to get there. Sine's new vision is rooted in the old vision of the Christian Scriptures, God's promises of justice and healing, and new creations. And he invites us, as we pursue it, to embrace the 'wild hope' that is necessary to keep us going into the 21st century."

    JOYCE HOLLYDAY
    Associate Editor
    Sojourners Magazine

"*Wild Hope* gives me hope that the alternative vision of the churches, the vision of the gospel, can guide us through the perplexing moral, social, political, and technological challenges of the future. Humans have never been capable of doing so much. Yet without an appreciation of our role in God's creation, our great capability is for naught. *Wild Hope* is a clear, compelling, and convincing call to all church people to prepare for a future in which we will need to preach the gospel with great clarity, compassion, and foresight."

    ARCHBISHOP RAYMOND HUNTHAUSEN
    Catholic Archdiocese of Seattle

"This book is vintage Tom Sine, only better. With this book, Sine's vision is clearer, his analysis more sure, his prescriptions more focused. This is a richly crafted chronicle of American culture that is must reading for anyone concerned about making a difference in the years ahead."

    WILLIAM E. PANNELL
    Associate Professor
    Fuller Theological Seminary

"*Wild Hope*—an interesting, reader-friendly presentation of issues facing the human community on the threshold of the third millennium. Tom Sine offers stimulating suggestions for ways the church could help meet the challenge."

    ARIE R. BROUWER
    Former Deputy General Secretary
    The World Council of Churches

WILD
HOPE

WILD HOPE

TOM SINE

WORD PUBLISHING

Dallas · London · Vancouver · Melbourne

WILD HOPE

Scripture quotations marked RSV are from The Revised Standard Version of the Bible, copyrighted 1946, 1952, © 1971, 1973 by the Division of Christian Education of the National Council of the Churches of Christ in the U.S.A., and are used by permission. Quotations marked NIV are from The Holy Bible, New International Version. Copyright © 1973, 1978, 1984 International Bible Society. Used by permission of Zondervan Bible Publishers. Quotations marked PHILLIPS are from *The New Testament in Modern English* by J. B. Phillips, published by The Macmillan Company,© 1958, 1960, 1972 by J. B. Phillips.

Library of Congress Cataloging-in-Publication Data:

   Sine, Tom
      Wild Hope / by Tom Sine.
        p.   cm
      Includes bibliographical references.
      ISBN 0-8499-3131-2
      1. Christianity—21st century. 2. Christian life—1960—
   3. Church and social problems. I. Title.
      BR121.2.S555 1991
      270.8'29—dc20   91-30031
                                       CIP

Printed in the United States of America

1 2 3 4 5 9 RRD 9 8 7 6 5 4 3 2 1

*To the Christians
in mission all over the world—
Catholics, mainline Protestants,
Mennonites, evangelicals, charismatics—
with whom I have had the privilege to work.
You have all stretched me and enriched my life
in ways I could never have anticipated, and
I am fortunate to count you as my friends.
I pray that together we will experience
a renewal of the Wild Hope of God
in response to the challenges
of a new century.*

contents

acknowledgments

Typically, people who write comprehensive books on the future have teams of researchers who work with them. In writing this impressionistic analysis of the future I have not had access to these kinds of resources. As a consequence, I have relied on the kind help of a number of persons with widely divergent areas of expertise to help complete this book.

First, I want to acknowledge those who have been most directly involved in providing support to me and this project, including my parents, Tom (who passed away 14 December 1990) and Katherine Sine; my sons, Wes and Clint; a few close friends; and the Board of Mustard Seed Associates. The friends who read, challenged, and supported this struggling effort include Greg and Eydie Cowley, Evvy Hay, Shirley Hein, Liz Knott, Theron and Robin Miller, Mark Mayhle, Donna Ring, Arek and Lorraine Shakarian, and Sue and Andy Wade.

I am particularly indebted to Anne Christian Buchanan for her tireless editing of a manuscript which, of necessity, kept changing with the maelstrom of global change over the past four years. The strong support of the executive staff of Word Books, especially Kip Jordon, David Pigg, and Dan Rich, is particularly appreciated. The literary guidance and thoughtful insight of Roy Carlisle was essential to the completion of this project. JoAnne Whitney labored endless hours in word processing not only on the original manuscript but its many revisions with a commitment for which I am very grateful. And Marie Lanier spent many hours researching important parts of this manuscript.

Numbers of scholars, activists, and church leaders have been extremely generous in sharing their time and expertise in the development and critique of this manuscript. They include: Martin Abbott, Gordon Aeschliman, Mark Amstutz, Bishara Awad, Jerry Bacharach, Gerald Barney, Carla Berkedahl, Craig Blomberg, David J. Bosch, Arie R. Brouwer, Charles Burgess, James A. Caporaso, James Dator, Reed Davis, Calvin B. DeWitt, Elward Ellis, Samuel Escobar, Tom Getman, Os Guinness, Steve Hayner, Peter J. Henriot, Paul Hiebert, P. J. Hill, Don Holsinger, Tom Houston, Archbishop Raymond Hunthausen, Carl Kreider, Karen Latea, Kathy Lee, John D. Mason, Charlie Mays, Douglas Meeks, Arlin Migliazzo, Marlin

Miller, Caesar Molebuts, Jürgen Moltmann, Don Mosley, Steven Mott, Richard Mouw, Kara Newell, Manny Ortiz, David Ortman, René Padilla, Bill Pannell, David Rozen, Vinay Samuel, John Scott, Terry Shea, Peggy Shriver, Ron Sider, James Skillen, Andrew Steer, John Stott, Jean Stromberg, Jim Wall, Richard Watson, Bob Wauzzinski, Edward Wenk, and Jun Vencer.

Finally, my thanks to David Willis, who stumbled upon the phrase "wild hope" in *The Last Battle,* by C. S. Lewis. He runs recreational and environmental treks under that name out of his base in Southern Oregon Wild Hope—Sierra Treks, Littlefoot Expedition—15187 Greensprings Highway, Ashland, OR 97520.

1

Receiving a Wake-Up Call from the Twenty-First Century

As we crossed the threshold of the final decade of the twentieth century, we found ourselves inundated with images of dramatic change and flickering hope . . . images of young people dancing on the Berlin Wall . . . children singing in the streets of Soweto at the release of Nelson Mandela . . . Hungarian students crowding into churches to pray . . . and Jews and Arabs searching for lasting peace in the wake of a devastating war.

In an amazingly short period of time, the Warsaw Pact has been dismantled. Troops have been pulled back. The Soviets have instituted reforms. The Cold War has come to an end. East and West Germany have been unified. And there are unprecedented opportunities to see the end of apartheid in South Africa and the beginning of peace in the Middle East.

Less visible but no less significant is the widespread renewal of the church throughout the world, including parts of Eastern Europe. Romania's Reverend Laszlo Tokes, for example, is widely regarded by many as his country's real liberator. His courage and that of his congregation was widely credited as the initial spark which led to the liberation of Romania in 1989.

I strongly affirm that these flickers of hope are neither random nor isolated. The jubilant dancing on the Berlin Wall is the dance of God. The songs of freedom sung exuberantly by South African children are the songs of God. The ardent prayers of East European young people are the prayers of God. And the longings for peace in the Middle East are the longings of God. Our God is alive and well— and not found only in the songs of celebration. Our God can also be heard in the cries of pain in the prisons of El Salvador, the scenes of desperation in the urban wastelands of the United States, and the mounting famine in the Horn of Africa. Our God fully participates in both the pain and the hope that fills our world.

But many in focusing on the future are more aware of the convulsions of pain than the flickers of hope. And they have little difficulty finding evidence to support their predictions of apocalypse and catastrophe—including warnings about a disintegrating ozone layer, reports of continuing human-rights violations in Central America, and predictions of massive deterioration in American cities.

"Doom," a nonreligious apocalyptic organization, predicts the imminent end of the world unless radical action is taken to address urgent environmental and economic crises. And religious apocalypticism is also on the rise, particularly in connection with events in the Middle East. As war with Iraq loomed in 1990, for instance, former presidential candidate and religious broadcaster Pat Robertson told his television viewers that the nations of the world were "going up against Israel" and that in these latter days the Middle East is "going to explode. It's exactly as the Bible said."[1] (Remarkably, while many view the growing international pressure on Israel to resolve the Palestinian issue as a promising sign, Mr. Robertson believes it will set the stage for the Battle of Armageddon.)

Regardless of whether we view the future with optimism or fatalism, most will agree we are living in a time of turbulent change. Not only are we poised at the threshold of the last decade of the twentieth century and the third millennium since the coming of Christ. We are also living in a world which is changing at blinding speed.

Only once before have church and society gone through such a major millennial shift—the year 1000. In the tenth century, Europe was under siege. Nomadic horsemen from Asia invaded what is now Germany, Italy, and France. Saracens sacked villages in the Italian peninsula, and the Norsemen repeatedly plundered coastal communities in the British Isles.

These events and many others were confirming signs to many that they were indeed living in the "last days." In fact, a number predicted that crossing the threshold into the year 1000 would be the "evening of the world." Although the church didn't officially sanction the many different apocalyptic visions, numbers found them persuasive. As the year 1000 approached, apocalyptic visions began to increase, and there was "a groundswell of belief that the world was drawing to a close."[2]

> In the last night of the year 999, crowds of people singing and praying, waving torches and palm branches filled the streets and squares of Rome. Their flickering brands performed a ghostly dance in the darkness, and the

incantations of numberless men and women sounded like a swarm of giant bees. High above, the church bells of the papal city began to toll, not for the new year but for the final one. They carried a terrible message: "I praise the true God, I call the people, I assemble the priests, I mourn the dead, I put Satan to flight and I ring in the last judgment."

When the fatal hour struck the crowd remained transfixed, barely daring to breathe, "not a few dying from fright, giving up their ghost then and there," but when the moment passed and the earth did not open to swallow church and worshippers, and when no fire fell from heaven, all stirred as if awakening from a bad dream. Then amid much weeping and laughing, husband and wife, servant and master embraced. Even reconciled enemies hailed each other as friends and exchanged the kiss of peace, and the bells of every church on the seven hills of Rome began to ring with a singing voice. The bitter cup passed, the ancient chroniclers relate, and the world was reborn.[3]

In light of that last millennial transition, as well as the fact that societal turbulence typically increases at the end of any century, it is reasonable to expect that crossing the threshold of the third millennium will likely bring a major time of societal change and destabilization. But added to that "normal" unrest is the fact that many of the challenges we now face are unprecedented and mounting at a rate unknown in previous centuries. Many of these will require decisive action in this decade if we are to avoid a calamity.[4] So you can be sure that prophecies regarding the end of the world will increase as we approach Millennium Three.

Pope John Paul, in stark contrast to various endtimes prophets, looks forward to the third millennium with renewed hope. Almost from the beginning of his pontificate, he has shared a passionate vision for the reunification of the entire church. He believes that in the third millennium God may well reunify the Orthodox, Catholic, and Protestant communions.[5]

As we race toward a new millennium, some are looking forward to the future with apprehension, some with optimism, and a few with humor. For a number, the accelerating rate of change is terrifying. These people simply refuse to read their newspapers because they can't deal with the tremendous number of events tumbling over one another and daily reshaping our world. They assume the classical ostrich stance, hoping somehow that none of this will touch them.

Then there are the optimists. But recent surveys indicate these people may be trying to hide from the realities of change, too. George Gallup reports, "Most Americans see a better life for themselves in the 1990s. But those rosy expectations often don't extend to society as a whole."[6] This survey indicates many people may not want to face how intimately our personal futures are bound up with the future of the larger society.

A few understand a little more clearly how their personal aspirations relate to the serious changes we are facing. A couple of these people wrote, from the perspective of 1999,

The world is bigger than it was—and smaller. There are 10 billion of us now, but pizza can be delivered thousands of miles in a few seconds. New countries have sprung from the ocean; others have melted. Global warming has tropicalized the tundra. Skiing and L. L. Bean down parkas are things of the past. But earthlings are the same. They hustle round our world lost in wonder, searching for Eldorado, squabbling over oxygen rights. And it hardly rains any more. Tell us this isn't still the best planet in the whole _____ universe."[7]

Of course, we are all most aware of that change that impacts us directly. It's impossible to ignore! We pay twice as much as we used to for cars, only to sit still twice as long on gridlocked streets and freeways. We are urged to use more sunscreen, consume less cholesterol, exercise more (but not out of doors during air pollution alerts). We buy electronic products our parents never dreamed of—VCRs, CDs, laptop computers—and are chronically frustrated over how quickly they become obsolete and how little time we have to enjoy them. We work longer hours for money that doesn't go as far. We rush our kids around—to school, to the mall, to the park, even to church—and still don't have time to enjoy one another. And we feel guilty if we don't make an extra trip to the recycling center! When you add all this to news of the tremendous national and international changes confronting us through the media, life in the nineties can be more than a little overwhelming.

WAKING UP TO TAKING THE FUTURE SERIOUSLY

The message of this book is if we don't begin in our lives, professions, and churches to anticipate both the new challenges and the new opportunities the twenty-first century brings us, we will quite literally be buried alive in the onrushing avalanche of change. No longer can we drive headlong into the future with our eyes fixed on our rear-view mirrors. We must learn to take the future seriously in every arena of life.

Our entire society is reeling from the global changes and conflicts that are filling our newspapers and flooding our television screens. In other days, events in other parts of the world seemed remote and disconnected from our lives. But now, not only does the rate of change seem to be accelerating, but the impact of world events on our lives seems to be increasing as well. In an increasingly interdependent, interconnected world, we are rapidly discovering that events happening elsewhere can have a very direct impact on our lives.

In 1990, for example, the residents of Vancouver, British Columbia, were awakened to the reality that a remote event half a world away could change their lives decisively. Apparently, it never occurred to the residents of Vancouver, B.C., that the tragic repression in Tienanmen Square in June 1989 could have any significant impact on their future.

Had they made an effort to anticipate the consequences of that event on their lives and community, this story might have had a very different ending. All they had to do was ask themselves three questions: (1) What impact is the Tienanmen Square massacre likely to have on Hong Kong—a region that is slated to become a part of the People's Republic of China in 1997? (2) If residents of Hong Kong were motivated by this repressive action to emigrate, where would they be likely to go? (3) If Vancouver, B.C., became one of the major destinations of thousands of Chinese immigrants, how would this change be likely to affect the Vancouver community?

Virtually no one in Vancouver made any effort to anticipate how this seemingly remote event would impact their community. Now, after the fact, they are trying to pick up the pieces.

The Tienanmen Square massacre did indeed trigger a wholesale exodus of residents from Hong Kong. And because the largest Chinese settlement outside of Asia is Vancouver, B.C., that city became a major destination for the waves of immigrants. These new residents immediately started buying up homes and apartments, totally disrupting not only the real estate market, but the lives of many long-term Canadian residents. Housing prices jumped over 24 percent in three months, making it impossible for many Vancouver residents to purchase homes in their own communities. Many of the wealthy immigrants who bought apartment buildings converted them into condos, displacing other Vancouver residents and driving up rent prices.

Now the government, business community, and churches of Vancouver must seek to ameliorate not only the problems caused directly by the unexpected immigration, but another problem as well. Many Vancouver residents are showing increased animosity toward all people of Chinese ancestry—including those who have lived in Canada all their lives.

In a world changing as rapidly as ours, we all have a growing responsibility to anticipate the change that is likely to fill our future.

Corporations attempt to take the future seriously. When I worked with the Weyerhaueser corporation, for example, we used futures research and planning extensively to help start new business ventures. Most of the Fortune 500 companies have in-house forecasting capabilities. The remainder use the services of one of some three dozen futures consulting agencies such as the Hudson Institute and the Futures Group. You know that corporations wouldn't spend money anticipating change if such anticipation wasn't beneficial.

Some state governments take the future seriously as well. A number of states from Maine to Hawaii have, in the past two decades, conducted state futuring projects. In 1974, a small group of us persuaded Governor Daniel Evans of Washington state to run the first statewide participatory futures process involving citizens from all over the state. We secured helpful input from Alvin Toffler, and the Brooking Institute ran the process. Regrettably, Governor Evans' successor didn't follow up this innovative process.

On occasion, even the federal government has been known to take the future seriously. The White House under Jimmy Carter provided significant leadership in futures research and planning by commissioning *The Global 2000 Report to the President,* which also became an important resource for those of us working in international planning.[8]

Often, when I do futures consultations with denominations, religious organizations, and churches, I ask two questions at the beginning of the presentation.

Question number one is: "What were some of the unexpected happenings of the sixties, seventies, and eighties?" Typically, they list items like the Vietnam war, student protests, the drug scene, the counterculture, the values revolution, the civil rights movement, the discovery of poor people in the United States, global famine, women's rights, abortion, and the AIDS epidemic.

Question number two is: "How effectively did the church respond to these challenges?"

Invariably the response is, "We didn't do very well." And one of the reasons we didn't do very well is that we really didn't expect the future to be different.

Every denomination and religious organization I have worked with does long-range planning. Ironically, they do long-range planning as though the future will simply be an extension of the present. Anyone who has survived the last three decades or the last three years knows better. Yet it is the unusual religious organization or church that makes any effort to anticipate tomorrow's needs, challenges, or opportunities. As a result, we are chronically surprised by change. In the future, we can no longer afford this luxury.

Let me be clear. In spite of our best efforts to anticipate the rapidly changing contours of the future, we are still going to be surprised by change. Attempts to anticipate the future are fraught with peril.

One has only to reread Herman Kahn and Anthony Weiner's *The Year 2000,* published in 1967, to realize how far their optimistic forecasts missed the dislocations of the seventies and eighties. Charles A. Reich's classic, *The Greening of America,* which predicted we would ride the wave of the sixties' counterculture into the twenty-first century, missed the yuppies by a mile. And not a single secular futurist anticipated the emergence of the religious right which played such a dominant role in shaping much of life and culture in the United States in the eighties. (Perhaps as a result of this major oversight, some of these authors are beginning to discuss religion in their books.)

Our track record of attempting to project how the future will be different from the present is littered with failures. But we really only have two choices when it comes to anticipating change. Either we can make our best effort, knowing some of our predictions will be wrong. Or we can let ourselves be totally surprised and attempt to cope with calamities as they happen—usually too late and with ineffective resources.

You can be sure that in this book the forecasts will sometimes be off the mark. Although a number of the predictions in my 1981 book, *The Mustard Seed Conspiracy,* were right on target, I missed a few as well. But the intention of *Wild Hope* is not to predict all of the changes that will confront us in coming decades, but to begin a discussion of how we can more responsibly, creatively, and effectively engage the escalating challenges of tomorrow's world.

WAKING UP TO A WILD HOPE

Wild Hope is written to sound a wake-up call that "business as usual" will not begin to respond to the escalating challenges of a new millennium. The only way we can live responsibly in a rapidly changing world is by learning to take the future much more seriously.

Wild Hope is particularly written for those on the cutting edge—decision makers who must constantly struggle to make sense of tomorrow's world. And it is intended specifically to enable church leaders to engage the challenges of a new century more creatively, compassionately, and effectively. Because the church's response to the future is a fundamental part of my quest, I will attempt to answer the critically important question, "Given the church's own projected changes in demographics and funding and its immersion in the values of a secular culture, how likely is the church to engage tomorrow's escalating challenges?"

I ask this question with full awareness that "the church" in twentieth-century America is far from monolithic. It is made up of many groups and denominations with different emphases and, often, contradictory stands. There are many different ways I could describe these many facets of church life. In my experience, however, most American Christians tend to identify with one or the other of two general camps.

First, there are those Christians who identify themselves with some of the historic denominations that first settled the shores of this country. Those in this group tend to focus their attention on broader societal issues such as peace and justice concerns, inclusive language, and funding for social reforms such as AIDS research and care. They are generally committed to greater ecumenical union, supporting the World Council of Churches and similar groups. This group tends to be more liberal politically and to place a very high value on tolerance toward persons with divergently different values and behavior. I will, in this book, refer to these Christians as *mainliners* or *ecumenical Christians.*

The second group of Christians may have roots in some of the more historic churches or even belong to mainline denominations. More often, however, these people are connected to churches that have their origin on this continent. They tend to focus their attention on the more private, pietistic, and relational dimensions of faith. And they tend to be conservative—not only theologically, but politically and economically as well. When they focus on societal issues, these Christians typically give their energy to "prolife" and "profamily" concerns. They tend to place a very high value on issues of personal morality. And they are often very suspicious of ecumenical organizations such as the World Council of Churches, identifying instead with the National Association of Evangelicals. I will refer to this group as *conservatives* or *evangelicals*.   SOME don't even fit here!

There are problems with such broad categorizations, of course. Many Christians do not fully identify with either group. And while most major denominations lean toward one camp or the other, these groups often cross denominational lines. (Generally, I find that Catholics tend to align themselves with ecumenical Protestants on most issues other than abortion.) Nevertheless, as I work with both groups, I find the two general categories both helpful and accurate in understanding the attitudes and approaches of different Christian groups. I use the terms with full knowledge of their shortcomings.

In general I have found that each of these groups tends to be highly critical of the other camp but much less critical of itself. In this book, therefore, I will challenge both groups to examine much more carefully the assumptions on which they premise life, faith, and action.

Wild Hope is written, therefore, to begin a conversation about how we in our personal lives, communities, and churches can learn (1) to *anticipate* tomorrow's changing landscape; (2) to examine and clarify our *vision* for a better future; and (3) to respond more *creatively* to the anticipated challenges in a way that gives expression to our vision.

I have already illustrated why, in a world that is changing as rapidly as ours, it is essential that we learn to take the future more seriously. In the first seven chapters I will overview some of the environmental, technological, economical, political, societal, and religious change that is likely to fill our future as we enter a new century. Specifically, in chapter 7, I will assess how effectively the church is likely to respond to these challenges.

Wild Hope is written not only to help us anticipate something of the changing contours of the future and our response to those changes, but also to challenge us to examine much more critically the visions and values to which we have given our lives and devoted our institutions. The visions and values to which we have given our allegiance will, I believe, largely determine both the ways we respond to the escalating challenges and the effectiveness with which we respond. If we are content to allow the dominant culture to continue defining our vision for a better future, then we had better be ready to accept the consequences that accompany that choice.

In chapter 8, therefore, I will evaluate the dominant cultural model—modernization—and the future to which it aspires—the Western Dream. The Western Dream, which was born out of the ferment of the Enlightenment, defines the better future largely in terms of ever-increasing levels of economic growth and technological progress. The American Dream, a variation on the theme, also defines the better future in largely economic and materialistic terms. I will use the two terms somewhat interchangeably because they share common roots, a common commitment to modernization, and similar goals for the future. My primary concern is that both ecumenical and evangelical Christians seem to have uncritically embraced modernization as well as the visions and values that go with it, apparently oblivious to the consequences for the future of the church or the larger society.

But this book does not simply offer a critique of the dominant cultural vision. In chapter 9, it offers an alternative—a biblical vision of the future that is of God. It is premised on the wild, outrageous hope that the God who created all things will write the final chapter and make all things new. I argue that it is possible to know something of God's intentions for the future. And this knowledge provides not only a premise for hope, but a basis for both life and action—a platform from which to respond to the growing challenges of the coming decades.

Finally, *Wild Hope* offers, in the last three chapters, a spectrum of creative ways in which we can, in our lives and institutions, live out the Wild Hope of God so that we are able to engage the challenges of a new century. While I won't attempt to address all the issues raised earlier in this book, I will suggest some beginning points. In conducting futures creativity workshops with Christian organizations, we at Mustard Seed Associates[9] are continually amazed at people's creativity. This book is written to enable the reader to burst out of the wineskins of the conventional and create new possibilities to engage a new future.

WHY ANOTHER BOOK ON THE FUTURE?

As we near the twenty-first century, we are seeing an explosion of books on the future. They range from optimistic predictions of technological progress and economic expansion to endtimes warnings of decline and destruction.

John Naisbitt and Patricia Aburdene's *Megatrends 2000*,[10] written primarily for the corporate crowd, is buoyantly optimistic—*Time* magazine described its dominant mood as "mega-euphoria." *Megatrends 2000* bases its hope on an unquestioned confidence in the marketplace, on science and technology, and on the aspirations of the human spirit. It scarcely looks at possible dislocations. In fact, Naisbitt and Aburdene devote a single page to environmental issues, concluding simply that mounting environmental challenges will provide a wonderful opportunity for us to work together in the coming decade.

Other futurists, also writing primarily for the American corporate community, follow suit. They include Marvin Cetron and Owen Davies, whose book, *American Renaissance*, offers us a very upbeat view of America's economic future.[11] The late Herman Kahn, who for years was the leading technological optimist in the United States, typified this view.

Given the inherently secular worldviews of this category of authors, it isn't surprising that God plays little role in their visions for the future (though they are beginning to give a little more coverage to religion). As Peter Drucker asserts in *The New Realities*, "the belief that religious faith could create the city of God on earth" has disappeared from serious discussion or become irrelevant.[12]

Another group of writers—some recognized futurists like Willis Harmon, who wrote *Global Mind Change*,[13] and some lesser known New Age religionists—take a more spiritual approach to the future. Like those writing for the corporate community, they are basically optimistic, but they base their optimism neither on the marketplace, expansive technology, nor human rationality. Their hope for the future is premised on a sense of their own inner divinity and their belief in the inherent beneficence of the larger natural/spiritual world. But this more spiritual approach to the future doesn't usually include a Creator God who is able to act within history and to be encountered personally.

A third major category of books on the future consists of Christian "prophecy books." Perhaps the best known of this group is Hal Lindsey's *The Late Great Planet Earth*, which sold over nineteen million copies in the seventies. Another, more recent, offering is John F. Walvoord's *Armageddon, Oil and the Middle East Crisis*.[14]

While undoubtedly sincere in their intent to help Christians interpret the events of "these last days," these books typically reflect a very superficial understanding of complex societal change and a fatalistic view of God's ability to act in history. Unwittingly, they tend to infect adherents with a deterministic view of history and a fatalistic view of the future. This makes it almost impossible for many to believe they or the God they serve can make any significant difference in the world around them.

I seriously doubt, for example, that these good people ever prayed—or imagined—that the Berlin Wall would come down. And they were so convinced by their own endtimes speculations about Soviet Marxism—that the Soviets were going to take over the world and institute a "one world" atheistic society—that they are in a bit of disarray over the decline of the Soviet Empire. Regrettably, a number of prophecy hobbyists are looking to the Middle East to find a substitute "evil empire"; this trend could further fuel anti-Arab sentiments in the West.

I have found a number of people throughout the United States, in Canada, and overseas who are looking for another kind of book on the future. They want a book that helps them make sense out of the future without the naïve optimism of the technological optimists and the New Agers or the unrelenting pessimism of the prophecy buffs. They find the secular books on the future inadequate because these books discuss the future with no recognition of God's presence or activity. And they find the prophecy books frustrating because they are usually written as though

God were impotent to act within history . . . as though God were captive to prophecy charts and a dispensational determinism.

Wild Hope offers an alternative view of the future. It attempts to examine some of tomorrow's challenges candidly and realistically. But it proceeds with sure faith that the God who created us invites us to collaborate in responding to the urgent new challenges of the twenty-first century, in anticipation of that day when all things are made new. It is rooted in the firm confidence that the Creator God is alive and well and able to act within history . . . and will write the final chapter.

WAKING UP TO THE POSSIBILITY OF HOPE

Pierre Teilhard de Chardin once said that "the world belongs to those who offer it hope." Where can we find a hope that is based on neither ignorant naïveté nor whistling in the dark? Such a hope must take into account the reality of suffering and pain. How else can it be meaningful for a world that in a single century has experienced two world wars, the calculated extermination of millions, nuclear destruction of entire cities, famine that has decimated entire tribes, and the adaptation of modern technology to purposes of mass destruction.

Elie Wiesel, a survivor of Auschwitz, forcefully reminds us that while we all struggle to grasp hope, most of us have little understanding of the brutal suffering and anguish so many have experienced.

> Accept the idea that you will never see what they have seen—and go on seeing now, that you will never hear the cries that rent their sleep. Accept the idea that you will never penetrate the cursed and spellbound universe they carry within themselves with unfailing loyalty.
>
> And so I tell you: You have not experienced their anguish, you do not speak their language, you do not mourn their dead, think before you offend them, before you betray them. Think before you substitute your memory for theirs.[15]

One is humbled and overwhelmed when reminded of those who struggle, with much more travail than most of us will ever know, to find a shred of meaning or hope in their existence. But Esther Bejarno, another Holocaust survivor, who deals with issues of tragedy and hope in her music, suggests part of the answer to the quest for hope: "We will live despite the world is burning." In other words, we must live with a tough realism that confronts the stark issues of our world today and tomorrow with a compassion and a determination born of hope.

And such realism must include a recognition of the presence and power of evil in the world. The apostle Paul reminds us that we do not "wrestle against flesh and blood, but against principalities and powers." Hendrik Berkhof, in his seminal work, *Christ and the Powers*,[16] declares that there are powers manifested in all cultures and times through the structures of human society. And these powers are not subject to God. Rather, they demand to be recognized as the ultimate reality. They insist on setting the agenda for all human life. And they seem intent on undermining all that God intends for the created order and human society.

Evil is no more illusory than God is. The powers influence the visions and values to which we give our individual lives. But their influence also pervades the economic, political and technological structures that undergird our global society and even the church.

Nevertheless, *Wild Hope* affirms that God is not only present in the songs of hope and the cries of despair. God has taken initiative in history to unmask and destroy the "principalities and powers," to restore all that God intended for the created order. In the crucifixion and resurrection of Jesus Christ, the powers have been defeated and evil dethroned.[17]

We live in an in-between time. In Jesus Christ, the powers been defeated. God's promised future of peace, justice, and righteousness has truly broken into the world. And yet, obviously, neither we nor the world we live in has been fully changed.

In this in-between time, we are called to be co-workers with our God in unmasking the powers. First, we must unmask their influence in our lives, families, and congregations. And then we are called to expose their influence in the economic, political, and technological structures of our world.

In their place, we reaffirm our allegiance not only to God, but to all that God purposes for the human future—a wild, outrageous hope that all things will be made new. This is the hope that will enable us to live "while the world is burning." Only this type of hope can motivate the people of God to respond compassionately to the unprecedented challenges we are facing as we enter the third millennium. We follow a God who dances on walls until they crumble, a God who sets captives free, a God who responds to the prayers of the oppressed.

The prophet Isaiah compellingly described the unswerving purposes of such a God:

> The Lord Almighty has sworn,
> "Surely as I have planned, so it will be,
> and as I have purposed, so it will stand. . . .
> [The] yoke will be taken from my people,
> and [the] burden removed from their shoulders."
> This is the plan determined for the whole world;
> this is the hand stretched out over all nations.
> For the Lord Almighty has purposed, and who can thwart Him?
> His hand is stretched out, and who can turn it back?
> Isaiah 14:24–27, NIV

part one

A Wake-Up Call

2

Waking up to an Environmental Ultimatum

It took Ed Yamamoto and eleven other Maui Community College students an hour and a half and fifty oversized garbage bags to remove the huge heap of trash from the white sand beach on that shimmering Hawaiian morning.

It was Earth Day—22 April 1970. The twelve students had decided to spend part of the nationally proclaimed day of environmental awareness picking up cans and bottles on that strip of beach near their college in Kahului. But their agenda changed immediately when they found the mountain of garbage piled at surf's edge near a luxury hotel. Apparently the hotel was routinely disposing of its waste by dumping it near the water's edge for the waves to carry away—and no one had ever questioned this practice.

Today, however, the students carried their fifty bags of hotel garbage right into the center of the plush lobby. Then they sat down beside the towering heap of debris and settled in for a long stay.

When the hotel manager emerged from his office to find the mountain of trash and the twelve resolute students, he exploded. Red-faced, he ordered them to get that trash out of his lobby and never come back. But these normally docile students held their ground. Ed Yamamoto said they would not leave until the manager gave his word that the hotel would never again dump its garbage on the beach.

Over the next two-and-a-half hours, the hotel lobby was the scene of a stormy confrontation—the manager screaming, Ed and the other students quietly refusing to cave in. Finally the manager realized his guests were becoming annoyed by the whole event. Reluctantly, he gave in to the students' demands and promised to stop trashing the beach. They promptly left, taking the garbage with them.

This was just one of more than three thousand environmental initiatives taken by people nationwide on and following Earth Day 1970. These initiatives represented a dawning environmental awareness—a grassroots realization that wasteful, careless lifestyles were endangering the very planet that sustains us.

The environmental movement of the sixties and seventies was essentially a young people's movement. It was also surprisingly effective—and well publicized. Young environmental crusaders like the Maui students with their mountain of garbage awakened public awareness and influenced passage of important legislation. In the intervening years, however, environmental issues have often been shoved to the back burner.

Now, as we prepare to move into a new century, the environment has once again become a front-page issue. People are realizing that ignoring environmental issues has not made them go away. Instead, the environmental problems that concerned so many Americans in the early seventies have now reached crisis proportions. As Denis Hayes, the organizer of Earth Day 1970, observes:

> Twenty years after Earth Day, those of us who set out to change the world are poised on the threshold of utter failure. Measured on virtually any scale, the world is in worse shape than it was 20 years ago. How could we have fought so hard, and won so many battles, now to find ourselves on the verge of losing the war?[1]

Even as we celebrated the twentieth anniversary of Earth Day on 22 April 1990, it became clear that we weren't just celebrating the past; we were anticipating the future. For more and more people from all walks of life—young and old, Republican and Democrat, in the United States and worldwide—are hearing an urgent environmental wake-up call from the twenty-first century. It is, in fact, an ultimatum: clean up our act or pay the consequences—possibly the breakdown of the very systems that support planetary life as we have known it. I believe at a maximum we have ten to fifteen years to begin reversing the trends of environmental degradation—or suffer the consequences.

But there are signs of hope in this growing awareness. At the beginning of the nineties, we seem to be at the threshold of a new environmental movement. The focus of environmental concern will not be on a day this time, but on a decade—a decade of education and action. I believe we will be able to look back from the year 2000 and remember the nineties as the Earth Decade. The question remains: Will we be able to do enough to reverse the destruction of our habitat?

In this chapter I will briefly summarize the journey from that first Earth Day in 1970 to the present beginning of Earth Decade. I will outline some of the challenging new environmental issues facing us in the nineties and beyond. I will also share some signs of hope. And then, in conclusion, I will examine our responsibility as the people of God to participate in God's purpose of "making all things new"—including the created order.

A Glance Back—A Bittersweet Recollection

Rachel Carson's *Silent Spring* appeared unobtrusively on bookstore shelves across the United States in 1962. A few voices branded this small treatise on the dangers of pesticides and herbicides as "extremist," but it gradually gained a following. For many it became a first introduction to an ecological view of their world—a consideration of the intricate interaction between organisms and their environment. Today, of course, one would be hard pressed to find anyone who views Rachel Carson's classic as "extremist."

The dawning ecological awareness of the sixties and seventies gave rise to a number of environmental groups that passionately promoted a broad spectrum of environmental legislation to clean up air and water and to assess the environmental impact of our many human activities. Along the way they won some important victories, although they lost some battles, too. An impressive array of environmental legislation was signed into law. And the United States began the harrowing task of cleaning up the enormous amount of garbage our upscale lifestyles had generated over many decades.

The Environmental Protection Agency, created in 1970, was given responsibility for enforcing much of the new environmental legislation. The EPA's record on enforcement has been mixed, but there have been important successes. Lead levels in urban air are down 87 percent from 1977. Sulfur dioxide levels have been reduced 37 percent, and particulates are lower by 23 percent. More than 127 million Americans are served by sewage treatment systems, compared to 85 million in 1972. The use of certain pesticides, such as DDT, has been abolished, and some struggling efforts are underway in the field of comprehensive waste management.[2]

Remarkable gains were made during the seventies as individual Americans learned to conserve resources, recycle materials, and view their world more ecologically. Americans learned how to adjust their thermostats, recycle newspaper, drive smaller cars to conserve gasoline, and develop alternate energy sources such as the sun and the wind. But many environmental challenges remained, and now we are facing new ones—from radon to electromagnetic fields.

"Don't Worry; Be Happy"

But as we entered the eighties, the emerging ethics of conservation began to give way to a new ethic: the pursuit of affluence. Forces appeared in the eighties that were intent on rolling back environmental regulations and subverting their enforcement in the name of recovering economic prosperity.

In *The Mustard Seed Conspiracy,* written in 1980, I predicted that economic concerns would be given increasing priority over environmental ones. "In the future we can anticipate a further slackening of environmental regulations, with increasing health problems and contamination of the air, water, and food supply as part of the hidden price tag for attempting to stimulate the economy."[3]

In large measure, that prediction was accurate. But I didn't anticipate the extent to which we would be urged to *forget* about environmental problems. Instead of being encouraged to continue taking specific steps toward preventing or undoing environmental damage, we were given a new message, summarized by the title of a popular song: "Don't Worry; Be Happy." We were encouraged not to worry about the environment, but to trust the "magic of the marketplace" to resolve all our problems. And we were repeatedly assured that if we gave the market its head and supported supply-side economics, all dislocations from unemployment to environmental problems would take care of themselves.

Herman Kahn and Julian Simon wrote *The Resourceful Earth,* for instance, to challenge many of the assumptions underlying the environmental movement. The authors argued that the only way to a better future is to grow our way out of our problems—again, trusting the market to take care of the dislocations.[4]

Most Americans seemed to succumb to this appeal. In the eighties, as a whole, we concerned ourselves much less with environmental issues, felt less responsibility, and focused more on our personal lives. We hoped that somehow the marketplace would assume responsibility for larger issues such as the environment. Many of us chose to look at our world in narrowly economic terms, to forget about consequences, and to work for our own economic self-interest. Detroit began building bigger cars again, and many of us began ignoring our thermostats, just as before. And belatedly we discovered that the high economic growth of the eighties didn't solve our environmental problems; it compounded them.

AWAKENING TO EARTH DECADE

We were all abruptly awakened from our environmental neglect by a series of events in the late eighties. In fact, in 1988, *Time* magazine devoted an entire issue to the "Planet of the Year." The lead article read:

> This year the earth spoke, like God warning Noah of the deluge. Its message was loud and clear, and suddenly people began to listen, to ponder what

portents the message held. In the U.S. a three-month drought baked the soil from California to Georgia, . . . raising fears that . . . global warming . . . might already be underway . . . and on many of the country's beaches garbage, raw sewage and medical wastes washed up. . . ."[5]

That was just a beginning. Hurricanes ripped the Caribbean and the United States. In Soviet Armenia, the earth convulsed with terrifying power, killing fifty-five thousand and leaving many more homeless. San Francisco, too, was shaken by a violent quake. Northern Iran and the Philippines have been shaken by violent quakes. And Bangladesh in 1991 was devastated by a huge typhoon and tidal wave that may have killed over one hundred thousand people. Clearly, the earth has gotten our attention again.

National Geographic editor Wilbur Garret, writing in a special issue on the future of the planet, warned, "Environmental apocalypse is now. We've borrowed the earth from our children and unless we come around very quickly, we are going to give it back to them in very bad shape."[6]

There were other forebodings of environmental disaster. In the U.S. it was revealed that federal weapons-making plants had recklessly and secretly littered large areas with radioactive waste. The further depletion of the atmosphere's ozone layer . . . testified to the continued overuse of atmosphere-destroying chlorofluorocarbons. . . . Perhaps most ominous of all, the destruction of the tropical forests, home to at least half the earth's plant and animal species, continued at a rate equal to one football field a second.[7]

Then, in 1989, the tanker *Exxon Valdez* ran aground in Alaska's Prince William Sound, spilling over ten thousand barrels of oil, the largest oil spill in America's history. Since then, Exxon and its fellow companies have treated us to encore performances in other parts of the country.

But these disasters are far from isolated; reports of large-scale pollution all over the world appear in the news with frightening regularity. As the Iron Curtain lifted, unbelievable levels of environmental devastation in Russia and Eastern Europe came to light. And the ecological consequences of the 1991 war in the Persian Gulf may outweigh political or military ones. The burning of vast Kuwaiti oil fields and the deliberate dumping of oil into the Gulf has endangered not only the region itself—through air and water pollution—but may well accelerate global warming and other negative trends. This kind of eco-terrorism places the entire planet at risk.

Suddenly thoughtful Americans were rudely awakened to discover that our worst nightmares had become true. Our earth home is facing unprecedented catastrophes unless we act intelligently and decisively to change how we live on the earth. Never has there been such widespread and growing recognition by both leaders and those at the grassroots that we must clean up our act. The magic of the marketplace won't fix the environmental havoc we have wrought.

It is true that this sudden environmental awakening is not universal. Strongly entrenched resistance to any further environmental reforms still exists. And the arguments are usually couched in economic terms. Near the end of the eighties, pollster Louis Harris reported that those opposed to environmental initiatives inevitably put the question this way: "You can take your pick: if you want your jobs then you have to slow down environmental cleanup, and if you want to end pollution, make up your minds that it will cost you your jobs."[8] Such threats as job loss or a weakened economy were the chief means the resistance forces could employ to dampen enthusiasm for environmental reform. But times are changing. The polls clearly indicate that environmental preservation is no longer a liberal nor a conservative issue, but an issue of growing concern for all people.

For example, in 1986, 93 percent of the American public was convinced that pollution of lakes and rivers by toxic substances from factories is a serious problem. The intensity of the public outcry over Exxon's devastating oil spill in Prince William Sound underlines the strong convictions reflected in Louis Harris's surveys. According to Harris's polls, 92 percent believe disposal of hazardous wastes is a serious issue. Another 86 percent are convinced that contamination of drinking water is a matter of serious concern. And 79 percent feel that pollution by radioactive wastes is a serious problem.

The public was directly asked, "Do you think a factory whose pollution is clearly dangerous to human health should be granted an exception from this requirement for any reason—such as jobs will be lost, the factory will be shut down, or the company will lose money? Or should a factory whose pollution is clearly dangerous to human health be strictly required to install the best antipollution systems available?" And the result was an overwhelming 81- to 15-percent majority who answered that no exception should be granted,[9] according to Louis Harris.

EARTH DECADE: A NEW ACTIVISM

With the dramatic increase in media attention to environmental issues and the growing public conviction that we can't ignore the well-being of our earth home, I believe it is fair to say that Earth Decade has begun. A whole new environmental movement is in the process of being born.

Earth Decade will not be an instant replay of the environmental movement of the sixties and seventies. As I have indicated, this time it will be global instead of national. It won't just be a young people's movement this time. People of all ages and all walks of life will get involved. Its goal will be not just the creation of new laws, but more serious enforcement of laws already on the books. I suspect (and hope) a growing number of people will not only rediscover the ethics of conservation, but will create whole new forms of interdependent self-reliance, seeking to live more lightly on the earth. Already this movement shows evidence of being more spiritually oriented than the movement of the sixties and seventies.

I foresee a growing grassroots activism among the new environmentalists. Environmental groups such as the Audubon Society, Friends of the Earth, Earth First, and Greenpeace will probably enjoy growing support. And on the horizon we are already witnessing the emergence of a whole new generation of environmental activists that range from aerial crusaders to environmental martyrs.

Lighthawk, a Santa Fe-based group of pilots and volunteers, have played a key role in a recent string of environmental victories. For example, Lighthawk helped expose the single largest source of sulfur-dioxide emissions in the United States—the Phelps-Dodge Copper Smelting Plant in Douglas, Arizona. Lighthawk pilots used their planes to fly journalists, political leaders, and scientists over the remote site to evaluate the situation. As a consequence, in part, of Lighthawk's assistance, the plant was closed in the late eighties. George Frampton, president of the Wilderness Society, declared that "Lighthawk is one of the most important and effective conservation efforts in the U.S. today."[10]

Chico Mendes, a Brazilian rubber worker, never intended to become an environmentalist. As he once put it, "we became ecologists without even knowing that word."[11] He certainly never planned to become the target of savage attacks and eventual martyrdom because of his work to save the Amazonian rain forests. For ten years he served as the leader of the National Council of Rubber Tappers, an organization representing some 150 thousand people who earn their income from the rain forests in Acre Province in Brazil. And Chico Mendes unwittingly began to place his life in peril from the moment he started to organize his fellow rubber workers to protect the forests from which they derived their livelihood.

Chico's work achieved results. Undoubtedly his greatest achievement was the negotiation of four "extractive reserves" in Acre and eight other Amazon states. These reserves will protect more than five million acres for rubber extraction, nuts, resins, and other forest projects.

But this work to prevent destruction of the forests raised the ire of wealthy landowners of Brazil who profit from destroying the forests. Three days before Christmas 1988, Chico Mendes was gunned down in his yard after having survived five previous attempts on his life. A local landowner who was benefiting by cutting down the rain forest confessed to the brutal murder and was finally tried and convicted.

This tragic assassination has already inspired people around the world to join in the important work Chico Mendes left behind.[12] Such a legacy of positive activism will undoubtedly inspire others throughout the nineties.

EARTH DECADE—A NEW AWARENESS

The message the earth is sending us couldn't be clearer. We can't go on like this! From the jungles of the Amazon to the farmlands of Kansas, there is a dawning realization that the way we treat the earth could threaten our common future. There are hidden and escalating costs for all our irresponsible treatment of God's creation. And we will have to pay those high costs and answer to our God for the ways we have unwittingly collaborated with "the powers and principalities" to compromise the created order. In this section we will look at the costs to rain forests, atmosphere, land, and water and at the specific threats represented by the proliferation of garbage—especially nuclear and toxic waste.

Waking Up to the High Costs to Rain Forests

The Amazon rain forest that Chico Mendes was trying to save is a case in point. Already six percent of the Amazonian forest has fallen to the chain saw and the torch. In 1988, an area the size of Indiana went up in flames. In recent years, smoke from burning the forests has forced the frequent closure of major airports all over Brazil.[13]

Twenty million acres of virgin rain forest are burned each year around the globe. This destruction has resulted in the wanton murder of thousands of indigenous natives. And the future of those that do survive is seriously threatened by the rapid destruction of their habitat and their way of life.

But rain-forest dwellers are not the only ones threatened by the decimation of these great forest regions. The World Commission on Environmental Development states:

> If deforestation were to continue in Amazonia at present rates until the year 2000, but then be halved completely (which is unlikely), about 10 percent of plant species would be lost. Were Amazonia's forest cover to be ultimately reduced to those areas now established as parks and reserves, 66 percent of plant species would eventually disappear, together with almost 69 percent of bird species. All these forests (in Africa, Asia and Latin America) are threatened, and if they were to disappear, the species loss could amount to hundreds of thousands.[14]

Such a potential loss is not only a concern to scientists, but to all of us. Since we don't even know the role that many species play in our fragile global ecology, it is impossible to place a dollar value on this wholesale destruction of the world's forests. We do know that we will experience significant loss in major fields such as medicine. Many of our newest medicines are directly derived from new plants we are still discovering in the jungles of the Two-Thirds World.*

*Throughout this book, I use the term *Two-Thirds World* rather than the more common term *third world* to refer to poor and underdeveloped countries. *Two-Thirds World* more accurately represents the demographic reality that the poor nations make up the larger portion of the world's population.

Waking Up to High Costs to Our Atmosphere

Of course, the loss of huge forested areas of our planet not only threatens the extinction of thousands of plants and animals; it threatens our fragile atmosphere as well. It represents a tremendous loss of trees, which both absorb enormous quantities of carbon dioxide and produce vast amounts of oxygen on which other life depends.

In 1989, Great Britain's Meteorological Office and Department of the Environment completed a three-year simulation study on the Amazon Basin. They concluded that if the entire rain forest were converted to pasture land, there would be a 20 percent reduction in rainfall, and the region would be "substantially" hotter. That change, in turn, would likely alter the climate throughout the hemisphere.[15]

More important, the destruction of the forests is likely to contribute to the so-called "greenhouse effect," a global warming trend based on an increased amount of carbon dioxide in the atmosphere. In the heat of the summer of 1988, we discovered that there is a probable link between the massive burning of Amazonian jungles and the increase in atmospheric carbon dioxide. This, together with the CO_2 produced from burning fossil fuels, is likely to accelerate global warming trends.

> Using the midpoint of this range and combining the two sources yields a total discharge of roughly 7 billion tons. Even without any additional carbon dioxide buildup, scientists believe these changes ensure another one degree increase during the next few decades, enough to make the earth far warmer than at any time since civilization began.[16]

Some climatologists dispute the greenhouse theory, and their viewpoint is being given strong support by the business community. As this book is being written, even President Bush is leaning in their direction. But recent "direct measurement of atmospheric heat and water vapor have confirmed for the first time a fundamental feature of the theory that is central to predictions of global warming."[17]

Scientists are in general agreement that if the greenhouse effect—probably more accurately called the "heat-trap effect"—is valid, it could have a broad range of negative effects on our society. Such a warming trend could increase the risk of forest fires, cause major droughts in farming regions, and even cause the oceans to rise. Since the potential impact of the heat-trap effect is so significant, would it not be reasonable to take the threat seriously until the theory is either disproved or fully substantiated?

The threat of global warming is not the only reason to reduce air pollution, of course. Pollution in the atmosphere also is responsible for acid rain, which poses a serious threat to forests in Canada, the United States, and Europe. For example, in a forest near Hof, Germany, more than half the trees are dying, and one in five is already dead. Across the border in Czechoslovakia, 30 percent of the trees are dying from acid rain and from the direct results of air pollution.

Of course, air pollution is worst in industrialized regions and crowded cities. It is already a problem in many large American cities. But it is much worse in many Two-Thirds-World cities and cities in Eastern Europe, where breathing the air is literally a life-threatening activity. For example, air pollution in Budapest, Hungary, is thirty times higher during rush hour than is considered even minimally safe. And there is little indication that cities like Manila, Calcutta, Budapest, or Bucharest will be able to take necessary steps to reduce pollution. In fact, every indicator suggests that in many of these cities in the nineties the air pollution will become even more deadly, rendering some cities almost uninhabitable.

As a result of the environmental initiatives in the sixties and seventies, the United States passed some legislation to begin cleaning up the air. But even in the United States we are discovering that our air quality is still seriously at risk. And laws passed in the seventies did not even address the issue of acid rain or many of the chemicals we dump in the air. Even laws passed by the United States Congress in the early 1990s are not adequate to address the problem. And the Bush administration, despite paying lip service to protecting the environment, has proved unwilling to bite the bullet on a range of new environment issues.

In fact, at the economic summit meeting in Paris in July 1990, Bush blocked an important new international environmental initiative. German Chancellor Helmut Kohl strongly lobbied for the world's seven richest nations to set limits on gases that contribute to global warming. Mr. Bush vetoed this proposal and lashed out at environmental organizations who challenged his position, insisting later that "he had defended American jobs from the assault of a radical fringe."[18]

Bush's environmental commitment seems to be to try to provide modest benefits "in an economically efficient way." I believe his primary loyalty to business will likely continue to outweigh his concern for the environment. But both parties need to wake up to the reality that voters and consumers evidence an increasing desire for environmental action.

Yet another threat to our atmosphere, a direct consequence of our rapid industrial growth, is the dangerous thinning of the ozone layer—the life-protecting atmospheric "shield" that normally envelops the earth.

> Newly analyzed data revealed that since 1969 the ozone layer has thinned by as much as 3 percent in the latitude spanning much of the United States, Canada, Western Europe, the Soviet Union, China and Japan; the loss was more than six percent over parts of Alaska and Scandinavia in winter months. The findings were three times worse than expected.[19]

By releasing ozone-depleting chlorofluorocarbons (CFCs) into the atmosphere through air conditioners, aerosol spray cans, refrigerators, and industrial processes, we have clearly placed our global future at risk. Degrading the ozone shield allows ultraviolet rays to reach the earth's surface, where they are absorbed by living organisms, causing skin cancer in humans and interfering with the genetic structures of plant and animal life on this planet. The increase in the amount of ultraviolet radiation reaching the earth has also been blamed for an increased incidence of cataracts, suppression of the immune system, decreased crop yields, and disruption of the aquatic food chain. (Such disruption of the productive capacity of the ocean could have disastrous ramifications for all of us, since we depend on the ocean for much of our food.)

In 1988, in response to concerns over depletion of the ozone layer, "the U.S. Senate voted 83 to 0 to ratify an international accord to cut world use of chloro-fluorocarbons . . . in half by 1999."[20] But even though twenty-nine nations, including the United States, ratified this agreement, called the Montreal Protocol, it won't immediately solve the problem.

Over one hundred nations attended a follow-up conference in London on 27 June 1990. It was reported that there was an unexpected 6 percent reduction of the ozone layer in the northern latitudes during the winter. This report brought growing pressure to bring the ban into effect by 1997. Former British Prime Minister Margaret Thatcher declared at that meeting, "We should be warned by that experience that the northern hemisphere trends could also accelerate . . . affecting heavily populated areas of the world."[21] Again, the United States has resisted following the European lead to address this issue decisively. In fact, the solid fuels used in NASA space-shuttle launches are a major factor in the United States' contribution to ozone depletion. And by the year 2000 we will pick up the price tag for destroying this life shield . . . hundreds of thousands of Americans dying of skin cancer.

Waking Up to High Costs to Lands and Water

As we approach the year 2000, our forests and atmosphere are not the only environmental areas at risk. Agricultural land and water supplies worldwide are also in danger of both depletion and pollution—and the two problems are closely intertwined because of the use of chemicals and technology.

Environmentalist Lloyd Timberlake asserts that the land on which six-tenths of the world's people rely for food, water, and income is becoming poorer. Huge tracts are being lost to encroaching desert (desertification), erosion, and overfarming. "According to U.N. studies, one fifth of the planet's surface, over half of all its arid and semi-arid land, is under direct threat of becoming worthless desert."[22] Most of this desertification is caused by overuse of lands as a result of excessive population growth. Changing weather patterns and global warming may also play a part.

In Africa we are seeing growing numbers of environmental refugees, people fleeing from regions no longer habitable. The seas around Haiti are brown from topsoil washing down the limestone mountainsides. The tropical forests of the Philippines have been ravaged, in part to provide disposable chopsticks for the Japanese. And entire regions in Bangladesh, Nepal, and East Africa are in danger of total environmental collapse. These fragile ecosystems simply cannot sustain the present level of human growth and activity.

We in the United States are struggling with many of the same problems of land and water depletion and pollution as those in the Two-Thirds World. While the net loss of topsoil worldwide is 25.4 billion tons annually, we in the United States lose 1.7 billion tons each year to erosion.[23] And as we approach the year 2000, the United States, along with other parts of the world, will have difficulty finding adequate water for agriculture. In many parts of our country, water tables are already falling, and regional disputes between the haves and have-nots are increasing. Further, more and more Americans are drinking water polluted with chemical and industrial runoff. The availability of safe, clean water will doubtless be a growing issue in America in the nineties and beyond.

Our production of agricultural chemicals in the United States rose fifteenfold from 1945 to 1985. And although certain pesticides and herbicides have been banned, approximately 70 percent of all cropland (not including hay and alfalfa and range land) still depends on some use of chemical agents. And although pesticide use has significantly increased agricultural yields that improved America's diet and its economy, it has had some undesirable side effects. Ground water in at least thirty states, for instance, has been polluted with more than fifty different kinds of pesticides.[24]

The hazards of chemical pollution to land and water are real for the United States and Europe, but they are even worse for the Two-Thirds World. They are reportedly much worse in the Soviet Union and former Warsaw Pact nations than almost anywhere else on earth. Eighty percent of the rivers in what was East Germany and virtually all the rivers in Russia are seriously polluted. In Poland, 65 percent of the rivers are too polluted for industry to use. You can be sure the people in these areas are having to pay a very high hidden price for uncontrolled industrial growth in their countries. And if these nations ever get their economies turned around, they will have an enormous bill for environmental clean-up waiting for them.[25]

Waking Up to the High Costs
of Living in Our Technological Waste

An even larger—and more rapidly growing—environmental hazard is evident. Population growth, technological proliferation, and "throwaway lifestyles," especially in the United States, are resulting in ever-increasing amounts of waste. Traditional methods of handling that waste are becoming less and less effective, and some are downright dangerous. Our growing awareness of an environmental ultimatum includes realization that, unless we take significant and responsible action, we may literally be suffocated in our own garbage—if we aren't poisoned first by our hazardous waste!

For example, the "downwinders" who live downwind from the Hanford nuclear site in the state of Washington recently got some bad news. They discovered that Hanford had, over a number of years, released low levels of radioactivity into the air. The "downwinders" were repeatedly exposed, without their knowledge, to levels of radioactivity significantly in excess of levels now considered safe. They claim that those who live downwind from Hanford have a much higher incidence of cancer than the general population and they are seeking compensation from the government.[26] In addition, belatedly, the Atomic Energy Commission is revealing that thousands of Americans working at or near other nuclear plants have been exposed to unsafe levels of radiation over the past four decades.

The United States has the somewhat dubious distinction of being by far the largest producer of garbage among Western countries. And we Americans consume twice as much energy and resources as our European counterparts, who have roughly equivalent lifestyles.

> At a distance, the yellow granulated mounds rising 250 feet over Staten Island might be mistaken for sand dunes—if not for the stench. Fresh Hills is the largest city dump in the world, home to Gotham's garbage—24,000 tons each day brought round the clock by 22 barges. "It was a valley when it started [in 1948]. Now it's a mountain." By the year 2000, Fresh Hills will tower half again as high as the Statue of Liberty.[27]

Our modern way of life mandates that we constantly create new consumer appetites for whole new lines of products and thus constantly increase our levels of consumption. In response to our penchant for convenience, we have become the premier disposable society of all time. We consume huge quantities of disposable razors, disposable diapers, and even, increasingly, disposable furniture and appliances, designed for very rapid obsolescence. And this trend will continue unless we rise and say enough! Unless producers of all kinds—and American consumers as well—are challenged to be more responsible, the nineties will be the Garbage Decade instead of the Earth Decade.

As a direct consequence of our conspicuous waste, our landfills are bursting at the seams. By 1992, half of the nation's landfill sites will be full. Philadelphia's cost of garbage disposal was only $20 a ton in 1980. By 1987 it had increased to $90 a ton—an increase of more than 400 percent. And you can be sure the price is going to continue to escalate as we run out of landfills and space to put new ones. The United States may wind up spending an incredible $100 billion a year on waste management by the year 2000. It's just beginning to dawn on us when we talk about throwing something away—"there is no real 'away' at all."[28]

Mounting piles of garbage are not only a nuisance; they are hazardous as well. In fact, we are sitting on a toxic time bomb because, until recently, there has been no monitoring of waste disposal—particularly disposal of toxic chemicals and radioactive materials. Numbers of Americans have been placed at serious risk from irresponsible or inefficient methods of disposal, and most of them don't even know it.

It wasn't until after the Love Canal disaster in 1978 that the government began to show an interest in toxic waste disposal and instituted a "superfund" to clean up abandoned toxic-waste dumps. Presently the EPA has identified more than a thousand priority cleanup areas—Love Canal is nowhere near the most dangerous. (And unbelievably, houses are beginning to sell at Love Canal again.)

The cleanup work is going very slowly. Only thirty-five of the original list of 1,212 have been cleaned up enough to be considered safe. The fact is, the EPA doesn't have enough money to begin cleaning even half the sites. And many people who live on or near hazardous waste sites don't know they are at risk.[29]

Surprisingly, one of the major culprits in illegal hazardous-waste disposal is the United States military. According to *The New York Times*, "military bases show up prominently on the EPA's national priority list. Currently, 41 military bases are proposed for inclusion on the list." Congressman John D. Dingell, who is chairman of the House Energy Committee, was quoted as saying: "Our investigation suggests that military facilities are among the worst violators of our hazardous waste laws. They have caused extensive soil and ground water contamination both on their installations and off. The Defense Department's attitude varies between reluctant compliance and active disregard for the law."[30]

The images of tens of thousands slowly dying from an accident such as the Chernobyl nuclear explosion in 1986 add urgency to mounting concerns about the hazards of nuclear technology. And this includes not only the risk of tragic accidents such as Chernobyl, but the disposal of radioactive waste from the defense industry, nuclear power plants, and hospital radiation. Bruce Piasecki and Peter Asmus of *The Christian Science Monitor* estimate that just cleaning up the waste generated by the nuclear arms race (excluding the peaceful uses of nuclear power) will cost the United States in the neighborhood of $130 billion. To place that figure in perspective, the United States spent $160 billion in 1987 on all domestic discretionary programs, from law enforcement to health research. It seems unlikely that we will find that kind of money unless there is significant public pressure. And it seems even more unlikely that the administration will allocate that kind of money for nuclear waste disposal as the economy struggles.[31] There is every likelihood, therefore, that coping with our nuclear waste will be yet another task that falls to our children and grandchildren.

Not only are unwitting citizens in peril because of improper disposal of toxic or hazardous waste, there is danger from ordinary garbage as well. The rapidly swelling landfills give off huge quantities of methane gas which traps heat in the atmosphere twenty times as powerfully as does carbon dioxide—thereby hastening planetary warming. Responsible waste management, therefore, requires finding new ways to dispose of our garbage—particularly nuclear waste—and to clean up the toxic waste sites. It also means taking timely action to harness the methane being generated by landfills and to slow our slide toward planetary warming.[32]

In light of all of this, it shouldn't be surprising that waste management has become a big business. Giants such as Chemical Waste Management saw their profits for legal waste disposal zoom from $25 million in 1985 to $115 million in 1988. But since landfill sites are rapidly disappearing and incineration is strongly opposed by some environmental groups, the price of waste disposal is dramatically increasing. And these escalating costs have motivated a growing number of institutions to seek illegal options for handling their waste. This explains in part the hospital wastes (such as syringes) on our beaches and corroding barrels of chemicals dumped in vacant lots. Perhaps more disturbing is the fact that increasingly we in the United States are paying countries in the Two-Thirds World to accept our waste—at serious risk to the health of their own people.

In 1980, Alvin Toffler asserted that for years we had been treating the rest of the world as though it is our "gas pump, garden, mine, quarry and cheap labor supply."[33] Now we can add garbage dump to Toffler's list. As the waste-disposal problem in the United States and Europe has escalated, there has been an unbelievable explosion of schemes to transport our dangerous wastes surreptitiously to poor nations that need our money—but not our garbage.

There have been some moves to stop the practice of dumping American garbage on Two-Thirds-World countries. A recent meeting of the Organization of African Unity condemned the dumping of waste in any African nation as a "crime against Africa and a crime against humanity."[34] But it isn't clear that this declaration by OAU will actually stop the flow of our waste to Africa. And other Two-Thirds-World nations don't appear to be addressing this serious issue at all.

Waking Up to the Return of the Energy Crisis

Twenty years ago, the Organization of Petroleum Exporting Countries brought the United States to an abrupt awareness of our energy vulnerability. A dramatic increase in the price of oil caused global inflation to soar. Many of us learned to wait in gas lines. President Jimmy Carter called for a program of energy independence to reduce our consumption, develop energy alternatives, and thus reduce our national vulnerability. And as a nation, we responded to the call to reduce our energy consumption. As noted earlier, we turned down our thermostats. We bought smaller, more fuel-efficient cars. And we invested millions of dollars in researching and developing wind, solar, and geothermal energy sources.

Then, in the high-growth days of the eighties, we forgot about our vulnerability, backed down on our commitment to conservation, and scrapped most of our research on alternative energy sources. My 1980 prediction that we were headed back toward a much more energy-extravagant lifestyle came true with a vengeance.[35]

Now, as a direct result of our failure during the Reagan years to develop and implement a national energy policy, we are once again vulnerable. And we have gone to war in the Middle East to protect "our" strategic oil interests.

It is likely that, in the aftermath of the Persian Gulf war, leaders will be inspired once again to call us to conserve energy and develop energy alternatives. The least expensive energy available today, of course, is the energy we save through conservation, by constructing more energy-efficient buildings, homes, and transportation systems. And most alternative energy systems both use renewable energy (such as wind and solar energy) and they pollute far less. Remarkably, however, Bush's energy proposal following the 1991 Persian Gulf War called upon us neither to conserve nor to develop energy alternatives. It simply sought to increase domestic production and support the United States's oil interests.

EARTH DECADE: AN AGENDA FOR RESPONSE

As both society and the church look toward the twenty-first century, clearly we are going to be faced with a broad spectrum of environmental challenges that call for our involvement. Let me briefly summarize the challenges we have discussed in this chapter—challenges that will require serious attention.

- preserving the tropical rain forests—plant and animal species and human inhabitants—from unbridled exploitation,

- protecting Northern forests as well from irresponsible harvesting and acid rain,

- protecting the atmosphere from levels of pollution that cause global warming and depletion of the ozone layer and that threaten human health,

- maintaining the ecological balance in parts of the world threatened by desertification and environmental breakdown and extinction of species,

- relocating the growing numbers of environmental refugees,

- ensuring the safe marketing and application of chemicals and pesticides,

- promoting ecologically sound farming practices to reduce soil depletion and water pollution,

- cleaning up running water, ground water, rivers, lakes, and oceans that have been polluted by agricultural runoff and industrial waste,

- cleaning up toxic waste sites and nuclear dumps to reduce the cost of health care and economic costs to the next generation,

- reducing production of disposable consumer goods and unnecessary packaging to reduce pressure on dwindling landfill sites,

- recycling to reduce waste stream flow and limit landfill impact,

- reducing consumption of unnecessary consumer items and purchasing only those items built for durability,

- conserving energy and switching where possible to alternate, nonpolluting energy sources,

- creating affordable energy alternatives for the poor.

As inhabitants of this good earth, we have, I believe, ten to fifteen years at the outside to address these mounting environmental challenges. After that, I believe we will be in danger of losing control of the processes of environmental degradation.

The church in all its traditions must provide spiritual and moral leadership for this new environmental movement. If we shirk this responsibility, you can be sure that others with very different values will step into the breach. Therefore, those of us in the church who believe we are called by our God to be earthkeepers need to be in the forefront of this new movement for the protection and the restoration of the created order. We must join thousands of others in finding creative new ways to respond to this environmental ultimatum.

EARTH DECADE: SIGNS OF HOPE

As we stand at the threshold of both a new century and a new millennium, we have been forcefully reminded again of the vulnerability of our earth home and human life on the planet. My intention in raising these issues, however, is not to create a heightened sense of fear, but a heightened sense of responsibility for ourselves, our families, and God's entire created order. Our whole way of life has been called into question, and we realize we must act. We must be a genuine part of the Earth Decade.

Thankfully, there are signs of hope. Nationwide and worldwide, people and organizations are already acting both decisively and creatively to care for the earth. Let's look at just a few examples.

One of the hopeful signs is a renewed interest in nonpolluting alternatives to fossil fuels as a primary energy source. The state of California has been a leader in this respect. When Jerry Brown was governor of California during the seventies, he took action to lead his state onto the "soft-energy path." At the time, he was widely criticized for his windmills and solar collectors. But times have changed and so have attitudes.

In the mid-eighties, California was running an energy shortfall. Now, thanks to Governor Brown's foresight, the use of wind plantations, solar collectors, and geothermal energy has contributed to an energy surplus—and California leads the nation in development of alternative energy sources. In the nineties, it will be essential that we all learn new ways both to conserve energy and mount major initiatives to develop energy alternatives for the future that are both renewable and nonpolluting.

There are also signs of hope in the preservation of the forests. The national preserve Chico Mendes fought for is one example. Another is Costa Rica's attempt to slow the assault on its forests by creating six "megaparks." They are designed for research and education and aimed at reaching foreign "ecotourists." It is estimated that by using megaparks for research, education, and tourism the land will generate 4.7 times as much cash as if it were used for ranching and agriculture.[36]

World Concern, a Christian relief and development agency, in cooperation with the Kaleheywat church in Ethiopia, was recently involved in a major reforestation project. The unemployed were hired in a food-for-work program to plant thousands of trees on barren hillsides near the church. Not only has this effort significantly reduced erosion and provided work for the hungry; in two years, the trees will be harvested, the hillside replanted, and the wood sold to make furniture. The profits from the sale of the wood will be used to construct an orphanage and school for the growing numbers of orphans in Ethiopia.[37]

Recycling efforts are springing up nationwide. The city of Seattle, for instance, has set the goal of 70 percent waste stream reduction through a community-wide recycling effort. It has contracted with several recyclers to experiment with different methods of collection. Essentially, the city collects glass, metal, paper, and plastics once a week. Seattle now leads the nation in reducing the waste stream. And a whole new industry is springing up in Seattle and elsewhere to recycle plastics, since they do not break down in the environment as other resources do. The recycled plastics are used for construction materials and drainage gutters in Europe, septic tanks in Thailand, and fill for sleeping bags and parkas in the United States.[38]

And churches are getting into the act, too. In Knoxville, Tennessee, for example, some members of the Episcopal Church of the Ascension have organized as the Environmental Evangelists as an expression of concern for stewardship of the earth. Their efforts began with a wash-up brigade to eliminate foam cups at Sunday-morning coffee time and have continued with a number of educational and action efforts—including involving Sunday school children planting trees and releasing ladybugs on Earth Day 1991. Now they are making plans to join with other denominations to establish a regional grassroots environmental effort. As we stand at the threshold of Earth Decade, it is essential that all Christians and churches follow the lead of such innovative groups in finding creative ways to be caretakers of God's creation.

EARTH DECADE: A NEW BEGINNING

We are receiving a wake-up call from the twenty-first century. The environment is issuing an ultimatum: clean up our act or suffer the consequences. This is Earth Decade. And if we heed the warning, if we join others in taking serious action to change our direction, there is still time.

There is still time to develop and implement international policies to protect the atmosphere and oceans we share in common. There is still time for nations to take action to reverse degradation of land, air, and water. And there is still time for individuals, congregations, and communities to develop new ecological strategies to respond to the new challenges.

I would propose, however, that the first step in responding to this unprecedented environmental challenge isn't the development of new global policies or even radical changes in our personal lifestyles. The first step is a critical appraisal of the visions, values, and assumptions on which our modern society and our lives are based.

Earth Decade: A Christian Response

As we awaken to the unprecedented environmental challenges of the nineties and beyond, the role the church will play in meeting these challenges is unclear. As I have mentioned, the new environmental movement shows signs of being much more spiritual in its character than the last one, but it is too early to tell how much of that spirituality will reflect a Judeo-Christian perspective.

Concern for the environment is being expressed from a broad range of religious perspectives, including Hindu philosophy, New Age eclecticism, latter-day animism, and reawakened interest in various fertility cults. This variety of religious expression means that those of us coming from a Judeo-Christian heritage need to be very clear about the nature of our biblical mandate. We need to ask, "What is our responsibility for the care of the earth, and how should we be involved in this new environmental movement?" To help clarify these issues, let us briefly examine how mainline and evangelical Christians responded to environmental issues in the seventies and eighties and then discuss our prospects for the nineties.

In the seventies, those from the evangelical tradition published two important books on environmental issues. Loren Wilkinson, working with colleagues at Calvin College, produced a provocative book entitled *Earthkeeping*.[39] Wesley

Granberg Michaelson, who now monitors both environmental and societal issues for the World Council of Churches, authored a very thoughtful work, *Worldly Spirituality*.[40] Regrettably, neither book seems to have received much attention in either the evangelical world or the larger church.

In the eighties, the majority of evangelicals aligned themselves with the Reagan agenda and Mr. Reagan's priorities for society. And as we have already pointed out, concern for the environment was not terribly high on President Reagan's list of priorities. (For that matter, the environment was not a particularly high concern for most Democrats in the eighties, either. By the end of the decade, there was greater grassroots concern for the environment than reflected by either political party.)

You might remember that Reagan's Secretary of Interior, James Watt, "indicated to the House of Representatives committee concerned about our forests and rivers that he did not worry much about the destruction of earth's resources because 'I do not know how many future generations can count on them before the Lord returns.'"[41]

Regrettably, many conservative American Christians share Mr. Watt's eschatological viewpoint. A similar attitude probably kept large numbers of evangelicals disengaged during the last environmental movement—and threatens to keep them absent this time around as well.[42]

At the evangelical gathering on the mission of the church called Lausanne II (Manila, 1989), there was scarcely a mention of the environment. Thankfully, the topic is showing up occasionally in the evangelical press with authors and lecturers like Calvin B. DeWitt, but it still seems to stir very little interest in the larger evangelical population. (The Southern Baptists, who have come out with a strong environmental emphasis, are a welcome exception.)

Evangelical leaders need to remind their people that God hasn't removed our responsibility given in Genesis 1 to be caretakers of creation. And we need to recover a biblical vision of a God who plans to make "all things new," including creation. One of the greatest needs in the evangelical movement today is to recover a redemptive theology that includes God's created order.

During the sixties and seventies, a number of mainline Christians were involved in environmental issues. But in the eighties, the majority of mainliners seemed to set aside their ecological concerns in favor of concerns for the nuclear freeze campaign, inclusive language, and political conflicts in Central America and South Africa. These issues are important, of course, but it is regrettable that they were allowed to obscure vital environmental concerns during this critical decade.

As we were preparing to enter the nineties, more and more ecumenical Christians began linking their other priorities with the issue of the environment. In 1987, the Pontifical Academy of Sciences of the Roman Catholic Church issued a document that recognized for the first time the unprecedented threat to our planet's life system. Other mainline churches have also begun to respond to environmental dangers. This reawakened care for creation has the potential of being much more influential than similar advocacy in the past.[43]

Perhaps one of the most encouraging signals regarding the church's response comes from the Roman Catholic Church in the Philippines, whose bishops have called preservation of the environment "the ultimate pro-life issue." They have issued a pastoral letter entitled, "What is happening to our beautiful land?" It was written as a complement to Pope John Paul's call for "authentic human development." The letter asserts that the ecological crisis

> lies at the root of many of our economic and political problems. To put it simply, our country is in peril. All living systems on land and in the seas around us are being ruthlessly exploited. The damage to date is extensive and, sad to say, it is often irreversible.[44]

On 5 December 1989, Pope John Paul brought his first papal message solely focusing on the environment. He used uncommonly strong language, sparing almost no one. He attacked the industrialized nations as the "privileged few" who selfishly squander valuable resources, while millions live in impossible squalor. But he added that while poverty in some countries explained their unsound ecological practices, poverty was no excuse. One of the most significant suggestions was that the United Nations add to the Universal Declaration of Human Rights the "right to a safe environment."[45]

The World Council of Churches held a historic conference on "Justice, Peace, and the Integrity of Creation" in Seoul in March 1990.

> The destruction of the planet has approached an order of geological magnitude. The soil is eroded, 70 percent of the reefs where the fish breed are gone, the rivers are polluted from mine trailing, the forests reduced to bare ground. The world's people are wounded.

It was against this backdrop of concern that the delegates struggled to find compelling Christian responses not only to the environmental challenges, but also to the human needs that will fill tomorrow's world.[46]

While ecumenical Christians are in the forefront of those providing leadership for the new environmental movement, I am not sure they have truly counted the cost of their concern. This war will not be won with denominational task force resolutions or comfortable conferences on ecology. It will require Christian leaders, for instance, to consider serious lifestyle changes that model "living more lightly" on the earth. It will require denominations to take a critical look at travel and conference costs as they seek to conserve energy resources. If mainline Christians are to provide leadership for this movement, they will have to begin by taking another look at their fundamental values and their spirituality.

Calvin B. DeWitt observes,

> A global crisis of environmental and cultural degradation is enveloping the earth. While we know more today about how the world works, we have become largely unthinking participants in a system that produces this degradation; it is a system that fosters a contagious and consuming belief system that feeds upon human arrogance, ignorance, and greed. The destruction that has become increasingly apparent around us and around earth is compelling us to look anew at ourselves, our values, and our beliefs.[47]

And that's where we must begin: critically reexamining "ourselves, our values, and our beliefs." We need to take a hard look at many of the fundamental assumptions underlying modern culture, especially our assumptions about what constitutes a better future. For much of the environmental degradation we are now experiencing is a direct by-product of seeing the better future in largely economic and materialistic terms . . . of ever-increasing consumerism. But as the church awakens to the emerging ecological crisis, I will be very surprised if leadership of any Christian tradition critically examines these assumptions. I am afraid what is more likely to happen is that we will continue to enjoy all the "perks" of our modern consumer culture while railing against the unpleasant side effects.

Working for the renewal of God's created order, therefore, must begin with fundamentally calling into question the Western Dream of conquest and consumerism. It also demands we discover and embrace a new dream based upon a biblical vision that includes the restoration of the created order. And it requires the recovery of a vital spirituality and a reexamination of our relationship to all created life.

This is where we begin to run into trouble. Most conservative Christians envision the future of God in a nonmaterial realm—somewhere "up in the clouds." Many of them have little idea that Scripture has anything to say about the redemption of the created order.

Few ecumenical Christians, on the other hand, have difficulty viewing the creation as a part of God's future and therefore a part of our responsibility today. But a growing number of ecumenical Christians are embracing a "creational" theology that is more Hindu in its assumptions and that tends to dismiss the need for God's redemptive initiative to restore the created order.

The biblical word *shalom* summarizes the biblical vision of a future in which all things seen and unseen are united within the reign of the Creator. And that union can only take place when all that is twisted is made straight and the broken made whole. It is a nonhierarchical vision in which we live in harmony with the Creator God and all created life forever. Wesley Granberg Michaelson states it this way:

> Shalom finds its full expression in Jesus. The reign of God which he announced fulfilled the hope that creation's brokenness would in all ways be

healed. The New Testament sees the principalities and powers defeating the rebellion that threatens all God intends for the world.[48]

Only as we recover a new biblical vision of a world restored through the initiative of the One who created it do we have a premise for a new environmental initiative. We are looking forward to much more than simply the survival of the ecological system as it is. We are looking forward to what God intends it to become . . . a completed creation, a "new heaven and a new earth."

Wendel Berry, a priest and a widely respected environmental prophet, affirms God's redemptive purposes in Christ for creation and reminds us of the responsibility that is ours.

The whole creation, as St. Paul says, is suffering and in need of redemption. If it is to be redeemed, that is because God loves it, not on the condition it be redeemable, but as it is now. If he loves it as it is now, we make it worse at our own peril.[49]

Only when we find such a biblical vision for our lives and communities do we have a premise from which to develop a new environmental initiative. Only as we begin to act out this new vision in our lives can we, with integrity and spirituality, help fashion a new ecological strategy for the preservation and restoration of God's good creation.

Questions for Discussion

1. Up to this point in history, what are the environmental battles that have been won? Which battles have been lost? Are you aware of any important developments since this book was written?
2. What are some of the groups who are most active in addressing the environmental issues? How would you evaluate their effectiveness and their strategies?
3. What are the major threats to the planet's rain forests? To the extinction of species? What can be done to moderate these threats?
4. What are the major threats to the planet's atmosphere? What must be done to protect our atmosphere?
5. What are the major threats to land and water? What must be done to renew farmlands and waterways?
6. What are the threats posed by toxic and nuclear waste, and what can be done to moderate them?
7. What are the threats posed by our throwaway lifestyles? What needs to change?
8. What are some of the religious groups who want to provide spiritual influence for the new environmental movement?
9. How has the church been involved in environmental issues to this time? In what specific ways can the church provide leadership in addressing environmental issues during Earth Decade?
10. Why is it important for Christians to examine the visions and values of modern culture critically and to seek a new biblical vision?

3

Waking Up to
the Intimate Machine

As the robot came toward me, I stopped dead in my tracks. At the last moment it turned away. A small group of curious travelers surrounded it. I watched in amazed silence as the robot introduced itself to this intrigued assemblage, shook hands, and began to carry on a conversation. In my many trips through Chicago's O'Hare Airport I had seen many strange sights, but nothing to ever rival this.

Elmo was, I would estimate, about five foot ten. He moved smoothly down the concourse on a wide base with motorized wheels. The base tapered upward into something that looked very much like a human torso encased in an aluminum skin. Elmo had a brown travel bag slung casually over his right shoulder. His robotic arms saluted passersby, while his head turned toward anyone who spoke to him.

Elmo's head consisted of what appeared to be two very large video camera eyes. Metal eyelids blinked when he talked—his voice coming from a small speaker located in a mass of wires right beneath his eyes.

I must have followed Elmo at a distance for more than half an hour. Every ten yards he would stop and engage another group of travelers. And every time he stopped, a smiling crowd gathered. With eyes blinking and hand extended, he would always introduce himself, then begin his line of banter and repartee. He took on all comers. As one young man swished by, Elmo called after him, "Hi there, cutie."

To this day, I have no idea who was operating Elmo. I never spotted anyone with a remote control. But as I watched him disappear down the concourse, gathering crowds as he went, I was reminded how much we as a people love novelty, particularly technological novelty. Every day we welcome new technological novelties into our lives with the same level of noncritical delight that travelers at O'Hare welcomed Elmo into their midst.

In many ways the scene at the Chicago airport could well be a metaphor for our future. In the coming decades we will be introduced to an incredible array of new technologies that will be at least as intriguing as Elmo. And as we welcome these new technologies into our world and our lives we will, I predict, seldom stop to ask from whence they have come or where they might take us.

Undeniably, we have all benefited in a myriad of ways from the scientific and technological progress of the past two centuries. Most of us in industrialized countries are significantly better fed, sheltered, and clothed than those who have gone before us. Many in Western countries have access to high-tech health care. Most of us take advantage of modern transportation and communication systems. And our consumer technology allows us to choose from more goods than we can possibly consume.

But as we mentioned in the last chapter, we are belatedly discovering that there is no free lunch. We are waking up to the reality that we are having to pay twice for much of what we enjoy in our modern consumer society. First, we pay the asking price for the amazing array of goods and services available to us. And we pay a second time in terms of a seriously polluted environment, soaring health-care costs, mounting psychological stress, and heightened spiritual estrangement as well. And we are only beginning to question the hidden costs of our first "Nintendo war" in the Middle East.

The Creator God has placed us in a bountiful garden called earth and has called us to be caretakers of that garden. As we saw in the last chapter, instead of caring for the garden, we have often been complicit in the rape and plunder of God's creation. And we have carried out part of this assault through an expansive technology that too often has been uncritically accepted and advanced. As a culture, we have invited the machine into the garden, and we are only now beginning to wake up to the consequences of our invitation.

Now, we are at the threshold of a major scientific and technological lift-off. The next fifty years will see an unprecedented number of scientific breakthroughs and technological advances. These innovations will promise to extend our life, heal our genetic defects, connect us to a global information system, and enable us to colonize space. In this chapter, we will anticipate a few of these changes. But in addition to anticipating these remarkable developments, we will also ask what hidden price we will be asked to pay for them. Will the promised benefits outweigh the costs—all the costs?

In particular, this chapter will focus on the implications and possible consequences of our growing and largely unexamined intimacy with our technology. In fact, this chapter will be organized to reflect my concern for this growing intimacy and its implications for the human future.

We will begin by recalling briefly how the machine was first invited into the New World garden and the ways it began to decisively change the American landscape. Then we will discuss the likely consequences of inviting the machine into the final frontiers of stellar space, ocean space, and the frozen continent.

We have more recently invited the machine into the intimacy of our human community. We will question how our growing intimacy with technology is likely further to change the way we relate to one another. And now we are at the threshold of inviting the machine into the intimacy of life itself through genetics, eugenics, and bionics. We will explore the possible consequences of this growing involvement for the human future.

We also will briefly summarize at the end of the chapter, the major technological challenges facing us, list some signs of hope, and discuss our Christian response to these new challenges.

Welcoming the Machine into the New World

From the beginning of the American experience, there were those who were reluctant to allow the emerging technology of the European factory system to get a toehold on this continent. Thomas Jefferson was in the forefront of the resistance to bringing the factory system to the New World, even after he left the United States presidency in 1809. In his trips abroad he had seen the brutal side effects—the urban wastelands, the human degradation, the environmental pollution—and he wanted none of these things for the new republic.

Jefferson was quite content to allow Americans to import their manufactured goods from Europe—that is, until the War of 1812. Then he suddenly realized that in order to be politically viable, the new nation had to become self-sufficient in terms of manufactured goods.

Jefferson explained, "Manufacturers are now as necessary to our independence as to our comfort. How are circumstances changed!"[1] So the recalcitrant Jefferson totally reversed himself and welcomed the machine into the New World. But he did so determined to provide for the social management of the new factory technologies. And initially, our factory system was more humane than its European counterpart.[2] But eventually we, too, lost control, creating the same kind of urban blight Jefferson had so wanted to avoid.

While those first factories were being constructed along the Eastern Seaboard, the potent power of steam was being unleashed to conquer a continent. In 1819, for instance, the Yellowstone expedition embarked on a specially designed steamboat called the *Western Engineer* to expand the white immigrants' knowledge of and control over the Western lands.

One public official exulted,

> See how those vessels, with the agency of steam, advance against the powerful currents of the Mississippi and the Missouri! Their course is marked by volumes of smoke and fire, which the civilized man observes with admiration, and the savage with astonishment.[3]

It wasn't long before steam was harnessed on the land as well as on water. Initially, the locomotive was seen as an alien monster, too, breaching the virgin countryside of the new land. But it didn't take long until, through song and story, both the steamboat and the steam locomotive were incorporated in the American mind as a part of our pastoral landscape. The machine became seen as an integral part of the New World garden.

WELCOMING THE MACHINE INTO THE FINAL FRONTIERS

Once we invited the machine into the garden, we discovered that it seemed to have an insatiable appetite to master all environments and conquer all frontiers. Now, our technology and those who control it are ready to mount an assault on those frontiers that in the past have resisted our total conquest. We are still in the early phases of colonizing and exploring space, the "high frontier." In the nineties we will also probe more deeply into both ocean space and Antarctica. And the conquest of these final frontiers will be made possible through the essentially expansive nature of Western science and technology.

Welcoming the Machine into the High Frontier

As we enter the twenty-first century, we will witness a new space race. And this time it won't be limited to the United States and the Soviets. Already some forty nations—from Italy to China—have joined the contest. Europeans have created a consortium of thirteen nations called the European Space Agency to coordinate their ventures into space. The major emphasis of the new space race is likely to be the colonization and development of space. The ultimate vision is for the establishment of large-scale space colonies, "terraforming" new living environments on other planets, solar sailing in our own galaxy, and even exploring deep space through the use of robotic crafts.

But before these grander visions can be seriously considered, more immediate projects need to be undertaken. The National Commission on Space, for example, has set the goal of having a permanent lunar base by 2005. It is projecting a human outpost on Mars by 2016 and a full Mars base by 2030. There is no assurance these goals will be reached, but given our present technology they are possible.[4]

Remarkably, preparation is already underway for long-term life in the alien environment of space. Biosphere II, a totally self-sufficient environment, has been created on 2.25 acres north of Tucson, Arizona. Under a superdome of glass and steel there is a sheltered rain forest, a savanna, a desert, and an ocean. All food is produced on a twenty-thousand-square-foot farm which grows everything from corn and lettuce to papayas and figs. Eight scientists were trained to live in this miniature earth for two years, beginning in 1990. I suspect that what they learn from this very creative venture will not only have application for communities in space but on earth as well.[5]

Nevertheless, there is a down side to the dream of developing the high frontier. First, it is likely that efforts to develop space will compete directly for funding with efforts to develop the poorer regions of the planet. And at any rate, the dream of exploiting the high frontier will not be equally accessible to all nations. Many Two-Thirds-World countries, for instance, will be unable to afford access to communication and weather technology satellites.

And there are more direct dangers as well. Even as funding for the Star Wars defense system is cut, some military planners are still intent on taking the arms race into space. And much of the most useful space technology now being developed has great potential for abuse—including satellite surveillance.

Finally, space exploration is far from being a "clean" activity. The European Space Agency estimates that between thirty thousand and seventy thousand fragments of space debris exist as a direct by-product of taking the machine into space. Planetary policy makers are just beginning to explore how to deal with the dramatic increase in space junk.[6]

The exploration and development of the high frontier is not an unalloyed technological "good"; it raises important ethical questions. To my knowledge, virtually no Christian organizations are monitoring these important issues or having direct policy input into the development of the high frontier.

Welcoming the Machine into the Deep Frontier

Human beings have always maintained a very intimate and nurturing relationship with the sea. The oceans of the world have been highways, protective boundaries, sources of food, and places of adventure. And yet the oceans remain in many ways an unexplored frontier. New technologies, for example, are making possible the exploration and mining of the ocean floor and are even making it possible to live in the deep frontier.

Long-term undersea habitation has moved from the realm of pipe dreams to reality. For example, marine scientists increasingly use underwater habitats to study biology and geology of the world's oceans. New under-sea habitats will allow scientists to live below the ocean's surface for months at a time and in relative luxury. . . . This could lead to "special interest" colonies staffed entirely by chess players, compulsive gamblers (complete with their own casino), young single men and women, musicians, or others with like interests according to a report from International Resource Development Inc.[7]

And technology is not only making it possible for humans to live in the undersea depths; it is also enabling them to harvest the seas to unprecedented levels. In 1983, the oceans of the world yielded 76.8 million tons of fish. By the year 2000, the amount harvested could possibly grow to around 100 million tons, which will fall short of projected demand. A number of fish species are already in jeopardy, causing a growing tendency to fish for secondary species.[8] There is mounting alarm that ocean fish stocks will be rapidly depleted and this vital part of our ecosystem could be placed at risk for all of us.

In addition, because of the cost of the sophisticated technology, poorer nations will undoubtedly have a harder time competing in the race to harvest the seas. Instead, they will probably attempt to supply their protein needs through aquaculture in bays and estuaries as well as in ponds. Aquaculture now provides only about 10 percent of world fishery products. A five to tenfold increase is predicted by the year 2000.[9] At present we see a wide range of projects from the "simple carp ponds of China and India, to more sophisticated shrimp production facilities of Panama and Venezuela."[10]

But more than fish will be garnered from the deep. In coming decades, we will see a growing emphasis on mining the huge deposits of copper, nickel, zinc, cobalt, and other minerals that lie under the ocean floor. The mining of the ocean floor presents another risk of damaging the ecology, as well as the threat of international conflict over mineral rights. Over ten years ago the International Law of the Sea Conference mandated that the resources of oceans beyond continental boundaries be considered the common property of humankind. This was done so that the more powerful technologically advanced nations wouldn't dominate this area of frontiering. Regrettably, the United States was one of the few nations who refused to sign the Law of the Sea Conference Treaty. The United States military also views major areas of the ocean floor as its private preserve and is not interested in welcoming others into that domain.[11]

Increased pollution is perhaps the most threatening by-product of our expanding use of the oceans. We have only begun to leave our technological trash in space, but we have for centuries allowed the sewage of our industrial society to pour into the oceans.

Our wanton use of the oceans as garbage dumps is seriously threatening the very life of the oceans. Battelle Research scientists recently discovered very high levels of lead, copper, and organic contaminants in the microlayer—the upper fifty micrometers of surface—of bays, inlets, and rivers. "Traditional plankton sampling for water pollution often overlooks the high densities of fish and shell fish eggs and

larvae concentrated on or near the water surface," explains John T. Hardy of Battelle. The water surface in the bays and estuaries of the world's oceans is a primary reproductive site for sea life. If we destroy this reproductive site through increasing pollution, we are placing the life of our oceans and therefore our lives at peril.[12] This is true not only because we depend on the oceans for food, but also because of the important role they play in our global ecology.

Again, it is difficult to find any Christian organizations that have developed an agenda for the responsible stewardship of the seas. Central to this discussion is the question of how we will use increasingly sophisticated technology to harvest, mine, and militarize the world's vulnerable oceans.

Welcoming the Machine into the Frozen Frontier

"Only one continent in the world has never felt the bite of a miner's shovel. But its days of untouched soil may be numbered. After six years of arduous negotiations, thirty-three nations have hammered out an 'historic' agreement to allow mining on the frozen continent of Antarctica."[13] We are on the threshold of welcoming the machine into the last unspoiled corner of the terrestrial garden. Untold billions of dollars of mineral wealth are reported trapped beneath Antarctica's frozen terrain, and new technologies will place these resources within reach of the nations that can afford the high-tech equipment.

Environmentalists warn that the Antarctic ecology is unusually delicate: an oil spill in this region could linger a hundred years. They point out that with vicious storms and icebergs the size of small countries, disasters are inevitable. And they conclude that the potential financial benefits are not worth the risk of polluting this fragile and unique ecosystem.[14]

The Greenpeace organization has been circulating petitions in thirty-eight countries and securing millions of signatures among those who would favor making Antarctica into a world park. If this were done, the continent would be set aside for scientific study and selective visitation for the benefit of humankind.[15]

As this book went to press, I heard a report on National Public Radio that as a result of Greenpeace's activism and the advocacy of other groups, a new treaty is set to be signed that will forbid all mining in Antarctica for fifty years. The United States is the only nation that appears reluctant to sign the treaty. Therefore, the future of Antarctica is still in question.

We will, in the twenty-first century, make major advances in the conquest of our physical environment. We will likely witness the colonization of space, the mining of the oceans, and perhaps the development of Antarctica. Since we first welcomed the machine, the garden has never been the same. What will be the costs of these new advancements, and how will they shape our common future?

WELCOMING THE MACHINE INTO HUMAN COMMUNITY

Since we first welcomed the machine into the world, that world has been forever changed in ways we couldn't have imagined. In this century we have invited the machine into human community as well. We in industrial societies have become chronically dependent on telephones, automobiles, planes, radios, television, and computers to expedite our communication and travel. And most of us have assumed we could enjoy the utilitarian benefits of these new technologies without experiencing any undesirable consequences.

Reflect for a minute how fundamentally these technologies have altered family life, neighborhoods, and how we relate to one another. The telephone, for example, enables us not only to "reach out and touch" those we love but also to avoid those we would rather not face. Sociologists tell us that the introduction of the automobile into American life played a major role in liberating teenagers from parental influence and creating an adolescent subculture. Of course, television has, over the past forty years, radically changed how families relate to one another. And computers have totally altered how people relate to one another in the workplace.

For some of the lonely and alienated in our midst, television, radio, and personal computers have become surrogate intimates. Others are already imagining a future in which we will consciously create machines to become simulated intimates. We will intentionally create machines to become a real part of our human communities. Otto Nelson, who works at a think tank called Anticipatory Sciences, and Arthur Harkins, a cultural anthropologist, look forward to a future in which we design robots with the expressed purpose of meeting our needs for closeness. "There are a lot of areas about robotics that people avoid talking about," Nelson says. "A robot as a companion. A robot as a best friend. A robot as a lover."[16] Nelson and Harkins see such relationships as an inevitable consequence of our evolving relationship to technology.

Woody Allen does a monologue in which he parodies our growing intimacy with our technology. He relates how one evening he called a meeting of all his appliances in the living room. He arranged his toaster, TV set, stereo, and iron in a semicircle and warned that if they messed around with him anymore, he would take decisive action. The TV set ignored his threat and developed a chronic flutter the next night. And in rage, Woody Allen drove his foot through the screen. He reports that it made him feel very manly. But the next day, as he was riding an elevator up to his dentist's office, the car stopped between floors. And a voice asked ominously, "Are you the guy who killed his television set?"

I suspect many of us can relate to the growing discomfort of awakening to a world in which our technologies are no longer just appliances, but are increasingly an integral part of our lives and communities. And that brings us back to the future. For we are at the threshold of an explosion of new technologies whose novelty and promised benefits are certain to be almost irresistible. Technology promises to link us to persons and information from all over the world more efficiently than we ever dreamed of. But before we succumb to the novelty of these new technologies, we must ask how they are likely further to alter the human community in the coming decades.

Waking Up to a Global Nervous System

Much has been written about our transition into a new information age. Not only are we approaching a future in which we will have unprecedented access to information. The technologies which make that access possible have been changing as well.

In less than two hundred years, we have gone from the most primitive telegraph communications to satellites girdling the globe. In the process, as someone has written, "for better or worse we have woven ourselves into a global electronic nervous system from which we will never be able to extricate ourselves." Our vast network of electronic systems is binding us ever more tightly together. These systems affect every area of our planetary life—including economics, politics, and religion.

In the nineties the wiring of our global village will become a trillion-dollar enterprise. National boundaries are already giving way to a transnational electronic society. We are witnessing nothing less than the globalization of planetary society through this vast electronic network. How is our being linked to this vast electronic nervous system likely to further alter our human community as we enter a new century?

Of course, this global neural network will dramatically increase our ability to share research internationally as well as to carry out conferences electronically. The United Methodist Church is one of the first denominations in the United States to make use of teleconferencing by satellite.[17]

As we enter the twenty-first century, we are likely to see not only a dramatic increase in use of electronic communications such as "E mail" and facsimile machines, but also an explosion of new technologies and combinations of existing technologies. Stewart Brand, in his book, *The Media Lab,* points out, for example, that as different media become digitalized, they become translatable into each other and thus capable of escaping their traditional means of transmission.

> A movie, a phone call, letter or magazine article may be sent digitally via phone line, coaxial cable, fiber optic cable, microwave, satellite, the broadcast air, or a physical storage medium such as a tape or disk. If that's not revolution enough, with digitalization the content becomes totally plastic— any message, sound or image may be edited from anything into anything else.[18]

For the creative arts, the phenomenon of digitalization clearly opens a whole new imaginative field of interaction and invention. Holography and other technologies also promise to create "total experience chambers" in which we can simulate three-dimensional reality through holographic projection. The implications of such chambers for education are enormous. We will be able to set participants down in the middle of the Battle of the Bulge, take them into stellar space or on a guided tour inside of molecular structures. But the possible abuse of this technology for those creating violent and pornographic "experiences" is also vast.

Obviously, these new technologies and the larger global network hold the promise of increased understanding with those all over the world. But in spite of such evident benefits, the development of a global information network is not without drawbacks. First, we are likely to see a growing polarization between the information rich and the information poor. Even now, information that many Two-Thirds-World countries need to operate their governments and economies is available only in the computers of more powerful nations. As access to information becomes increasingly crucial to development, certain nations will almost certainly find themselves in positions of information power.

Increased dependence on a global electronic network also raises questions of invasion of privacy, distortion of information, and abuse of power. For example, the manipulation of images and information made possible by the digitalization of media also provides a powerful tool for the political and economic manipulation of people. High-tech devices can already be used to edit images and information used in the media. The digitalization of media means that individuals can be inserted or removed from photographic and video images, and "simulated" events that are indistinguishable from the "real thing" can be manufactured at will. As we become increasingly dependent on electronic communication, therefore, the accuracy of what is communicated—and who is communicating it—will become an important question to be addressed.

Finally, the weaving of the global electronic network is already altering the nature of human community—making it both more international and more impersonal. If we aren't clear regarding how we want to incorporate these new technologies into our human communities, we may wind up with communities very different from those we might choose.

Waking Up to the "Electronic Cottage"

The electronic nervous system that will tie the world community closer together in coming decades will hook our homes into the global network as well. The highly connected "electronic cottages" predicted in Alvin Toffler's classic, *The Third Wave,*[19] are closer than ever to becoming reality.

For many, this trend to "hook up" our homes to the global network will mean living in fully automated homes. Every aspect of life in these "intelligent" houses will be controlled from a central computer. Computers will run the environmental systems and the security systems—and will even fix breakfast in the morning.

Tomorrow's homes will even be decorated electronically—the president of a West Coast computer firm has already adorned his walls with electronic copies of master works digitalized from originals in leading museums.

A neural connection to the larger planetary nervous system will not only transform our homes into electronically controlled environments; it will also no doubt give individuals an incredible window on the world. In the near future, many Americans will trade in their old color TV sets for home entertainment and information systems that will include a wall of high definition, interactive television. Through this interactive system we will be able to secure virtually unlimited entertainment, information, and shopping without ever leaving our homes.

But as we will see later, such convenience can carry hidden costs—including serious encroachment on privacy. And given television's tendency to foster passivity and threaten the communal quality of family life, it seems reasonable to speculate that more sophisticated systems could create a huge population of terminal sofa slugs and entertainment junkies.

The ability to hook up the home to the worldwide network is already changing the way many people make a living. Use of computers and communications technology is making it possible for more people to work at home, either as independent contractors or as employees who telecommute. For some families this option could mean more family time. It could help solve the day-care problem for some single parents and two-income families and could provide increased employment opportunities for the disabled. Telecommuting offers many people, especially professionals, the freedom to set their own hours and work in a more comfortable environment.

But the trend toward telecommuting could bring serious problems as well. Individuals who telecommute may feel isolated, cut off from the interaction of the workplace. Others may experience growing domestic conflict from being with their families twenty-four hours a day. In addition, as benefits packages for in-house employees become more expensive to provide, the trend may well be toward independent contractors who are paid only according to the volume they produce. This suggests that home offices could become modern electronic versions of the "sweatshops" of earlier days. In these electronic sweatshops, individuals could be coerced to make a living doing piecework without benefit of sick time, vacations, or other benefits most employees have come to expect.

Waking Up to Electronic Lifestyles

By the end of the century, amazing new technologies will increasingly wire us, as individuals, into the global nervous system. The laptop computers and electronic organizers now proliferating in the business world are the vanguard in a trend toward miniaturized devices that will link individuals with the rest of the world. Within the very near future, many of us will carry a hand-held, voice-responsive computer/telephone that connects us with an array of global data banks and, of course, persons all over the world. There are already reports of attorneys from New York vacationing on the beaches of Maui with cellular phones affixed to their heads. Can you imagine what it will be like when we are all carrying our computer phones with us or perhaps even have them surgically implanted in our heads?

In addition to a hand-held computer phone, the citizen of Century Twenty-One will probably have a "smart" card, which will look like an ordinary credit card but will contain a microchip to store information. The smart card will serve as a debit card, a credit card, an automatic teller card, a library card, and a security card. It could contain all health records, financial records, and other personal data you would want to have at your fingertips. But it is not difficult to imagine how such a card could be used to control individual access and monitor individual interaction in tomorrow's society. There are serious dystopian possibilities.

Not only will our future contain smart houses, smart telephones and computers, and smart cards; we will drive smart automobiles, too. We may well see cars that contain miniature offices, complete with laptop computers, fax machines, and even small microwaves for a quick snack.[20] Engineers are also designing smart freeways that will rely on computers to move cars more quickly and more safely along major conduits.

Waking Up to Terminal Gridlock

Even before we were knit together in this global electronic nervous system, our continent was transected by ribbons of asphalt, rails of steel, and plumes of jet exhaust. However, as we are becoming part of a sophisticated international electronic network, our domestic network of interstate highways, rail lines, and air corridors is in danger of serious deterioration.

In the first place, we haven't adequately maintained existing highways, bridges, and rail corridors. As a consequence, they will probably continue to deteriorate, increasing the likelihood of accidents and major spills of toxic substances. And even if these ground transportation systems were in good shape, they are inadequate to bear the growth projected for our cities. Gridlock—constant, bumper-to-bumper traffic—will likely become a permanent part of all of our futures.

With the growing problems of gridlock and the escalating costs of highway construction, communities like Los Angeles are introducing light rail transportation systems. But we are a decade behind the new megalift trains being developed in Germany and Japan—trains that ride on magnetic waves at speeds up to three hundred miles per hour. We desperately need to expand our mass transit capability in the next two decades, introducing megalift trains in our most heavily traveled corridors to reduce massive congestion.

Not only are our ground systems overloaded; so, increasingly, are our air systems. Rapid growth in commuting by air is already taxing the capabilities of many of our airports and air controllers, reducing our safety. Unless investment in upgrading ground and air transportation systems increases significantly, current systems will probably be inadequate to meet the escalating transportation demands of the coming century. And failure to properly maintain this important element in our national infrastructure could have a profound long-term impact on the United States economy. Clearly, our emerging communications technologies and our deteriorating transportation infrastructure will continue to alter the character and quality of human community.

WELCOMING THE MACHINE INTO THE CREATION OF LIFE AND THE REDESIGN OF THE HUMAN SPECIES

We have come a long way since the first steamboats churned through our rivers and the first steam locomotives breached our pastoral landscapes. And belatedly, we have discovered the high price we have had to pay for technological progress. Today, satellites crowd the sky and personal computers populate our homes. And not only have we welcomed the machine into our natural environments and human communities; we have invited it into the inmost levels of our beings— into our bodies and minds and the very fabric of life itself. How is this growing intimacy with technology likely to alter our definition of life in general and human life in particular?

Waking Up to the Redesign of Life

In *The Mustard Seed Conspiracy,* published in 1981, I reported on a 1980 Supreme Court ruling that new forms of life created in the laboratory could be patented. I stated that this ruling, in the eyes of many, would be a harbinger of a whole new age:

> Developers of these new life forms promise they will gobble up oil spills, clean up toxic waste sites, duplicate photosynthesis, enable plants to fix nitrogen, create inexpensive chemicals, produce synthetic proteins, and manufacture antibiotics. "Theoretically, any process occurring in nature can be harnessed for man's use," reports Irving Johnson, President of Research for Eli Lilly.[21]

Since those forecasts were made, we have indeed seen the emergence of a new genetic age. In the years following that landmark Supreme Court decision, the patent office has been flooded with eight thousand patents for new life forms, twenty-one of them for genetically engineered animals.[22]

Designer genes are big business. Since the early seventies some six hundred biotechnological companies have been started. Most are in the United States, but Japan, Brazil, and a number of other countries are "jumping into designer genes," too. The top twenty biological drug firms were predicted to see sales increase fivefold from 1988 to 1990, reaching more than $2.5 billion. United States sales of biotechnology-related agricultural products will exceed $100 billion by the turn of the century, according to *The Economist.*[23]

We could see a genetic lift-off in the nineties that parallels the emergence of the transistor and the microchip in the seventies and eighties. And as with other frontiering ventures, one of the major motivations for genetic engineering will be economic. There are tremendous fortunes to be made in biotechnology.

Of course, scientists working in these fields are also motivated by genuine impulses to improve further human understanding and improve the human condition. Not only are scientists laboring to create more effective drugs through genetic engineering; they also want to correct inherited genetic disorders such as cystic fibrosis, Down's Syndrome, and Parkinson's disease. The *New York Times* recently heralded an important advance: "Scientists have cured cystic fibrosis cells in the laboratory." But gene therapy based on the result is still years away.[24]

However, in spite of the promised benefits of this amazing new technology, the risks are also great. Chief among them, of course, is the risk that new life forms released into the environment could have deadly side-effects. In the sixties, the film *The Andromeda Strain* chronicled such a frightening possibility of a "killer virus" released. Now, with development of new genetic strains, such a scenario is actually possible.

Regulations have been established for releasing new life forms into the environment to minimize risks. But recently, Gary Strobel, a microbiologist at Montana State University, grew tired of waiting for approval for a genetic experiment and expressed his "civil disobedience" by releasing a newly created organism without approval.

Fortunately, Strobel's actions do not seem to have been harmful. But all it would take is one slip—an accidental or deliberate release of a hostile organism into our environment—to wreak widespread havoc. And we don't even know what levels of risk we are dealing with—we don't have enough information to do a risk analysis.[25]

As we have crossed the final frontier into the mystery of life itself, our concept of the possible is changing rapidly. Suddenly we discover we have in our hands the power to alter conditions that have caused other generations to live in silent terror. We see on the horizon the possibility of being more than we are, of improving the quality of and perhaps extending the length of human life. But who will have access to this new Promethean power, and whose values will determine how it will be used? Tragically, the average citizen has little input regarding the oversight or direction of genetic research and application. The public generally and the church specifically need to participate in the steering of this new technology for the sake of our common future.

Waking Up to the Building of a Better Baby

"Will my baby be all right?" The question is as old as parenting. A decade ago, mothers and fathers had to wait for such answers until their child was born. Today, through the process of amniocentesis—withdrawing and testing a small sample of amniotic fluid— they can know within weeks of conception whether their child will suffer from any of two hundred genetic diseases. None of these diseases is yet curable. There are effective treatments for only a few."[26]

But amniocentesis not only provides the means to answer parental concern; it also significantly increases parental control over the kind of offspring they bring into the world. Obviously, discovering that a fetus is not perfect puts the parents under tremendous pressure. There is growing emphasis in our society on raising perfect children, and abortion is increasingly being seen as a legitimate "therapeutic" option for even minimal defects.

Amniocentesis can be used to reveal not only certain facts about the health of the unborn, but also the fetus's sex. And in the future we will increasingly see couples have abortions by "whimsy" to bear the child of the gender they choose. And this could well give expression to a strong antifeminist bias in society. This has already begun a demographic revolution in China, where efforts to limit family size are also creating a lopsided, male-dominated society.

Amniocentesis and other early diagnostic devices are just the first wave of a trend toward using technology to ensure healthier or more desirable offspring. Increasingly, we will have the technical means to actually "build a better baby"— using genetic engineering to "control people's initial genetic design and constitution." Joseph Fletcher, an ethical relativist, views such intervention as a means

> to start people off healthy and free of disease through the practice of medicine preconceptively. It is a matter of directed and rational mutations, over against the accidental mutations now going on blindly in nature. It aims to control people's initial genetic design and constitution.[27]

We aren't able to do genetic surgery (actually altering genetic structures through surgery) yet, but it will almost certainly be part of our future. It is difficult to imagine that, given this capability, there will not be those who want to use that level of knowledge to propagate "superior" offspring. This means that in the twenty-first century we will probably hear increasing advocacy not only for correcting genetic defects, but also for creating "designer fetuses" in order to improve society.

> Eugenics [the science of improving the qualities of the human race] has traditionally concerned itself with creating or maintaining a superior human race, mostly by encouraging some to breed, others not to. But the new eugenics has a different twist: ensuring that one's own offspring will be superior. "There's now a powerful movement in science to make the perfect human being," says Daniel Callahan, Director of the Hastings Center.[28]

The first major step to building a better baby was recently taken by the United States Senate. It approved a three-billion-dollar project recommended by the National Academy of Science to map every single one of the one hundred thousand human genes. The intention is to detail the entire human genetic code in order to create new weapons against genetic defects. But as genetic activist Jeremy Rifkin points out, genetic mapping carries with it some serious risks:

> Over the next several decades, genetic screening of individuals will become a commonplace occurrence. Knowledge of an individual's genetic make-up may be used both by government institutions and the private sector as a new tool of discrimination. According to a recent Office of Technology Assessment (OTA) study, many American corporations expressed an interest in the genetic screening of workers in order to match genetic predispositions with the "appropriate" work environments.
> Educators are concerned that school systems might require mandatory genetic screening of students to track developmental disabilities at the genetic level. The right of genetic privacy will emerge as a central political issue in the years ahead as new gene screening techniques become more accurate, detailed and widely available.[29]

Rifkin goes on to recommend that a permanent congressional board and citizen's committee be established to provide oversight to ensure that this information will not be misused. Certainly the Christian community should be active participants in this discussion. And fortunately, the National Council of Churches has taken leadership in addressing these important issues.

Waking Up to a Reproductive Revolution

Genetic research, of course, does not confine itself to building a better baby. In fact, science is moving at an alarming rate toward technological control of the entire human reproductive process. Earl Joseph, a staff futurist at UNIVAC, looks forward to a day when we can replicate human organs from a single cell. Once you can grow an organ, the "cloning" or replication of a complete human organism is a possibility.[30]

As I write, growing a new person from a single cell is still in the relatively distant future. But another alternative to traditional human reproduction is being done with cattle and so is technically feasible for humans. An ovum would be fertilized in vitro and have its nucleus replaced with the nucleus from a nonreproductive or body cell from another person. The "renucleated" ovum would then be implanted in the original womb or in the womb of a surrogate:

> The child produced in this way has all his genetic inheritance solely from the body cell—that is, he will have only the genotype of the person whose body cell was used, invariably including the same sex. The new individual has one parent only, not two and . . . is that parent's identical twin.[31]

This research suggests not only the probability of continued controversy over human surrogate mothers, but the very real possibility of bringing infants to term in a totally artificial womb. When that technology comes on line, not only will childless couples likely avail themselves of it, but some professional women will likely opt for this less "inconvenient" way to give birth. And I would imagine there are those in the gay movement who would look forward to "bearing" children through the new reproductive technology as well.

While we haven't fully learned yet how to alter genetic structures or clone new offspring, we are already manipulating the genetic future of the unborn. We are well on the way to a new eugenic future of building a better baby through genetic selection.

Afton Blake, a psychologist living on the East Coast, decided it was time for her to have a child. As a single woman, her options were limited. She decided on artificial insemination and went "shopping for daddy" at a local sperm bank. Her first choice was the sperm of a Nobel Prize winner, but the sperm turned out to be dead. Disappointed, she poured over a catalog from the Repository for Germinal Choice. Blake finally selected a donor—a blond-haired, white computer scientist who is an accomplished classical musician as well—but, of course, she never met the man. She didn't have to meet Mr. Right. All she had to do was buy his genes.[32] And even though she and her son are outwardly indistinguishable from millions of other single-parent families, they are a part of a growing wave of genetic choice.

Waking Up to the Terminating of Life

Indications are that modern science will increasingly force us to discuss ethical issues regarding not only the beginning of human life and its design, but also its termination. Our sophisticated health-care technology has, in recent years, enabled us to keep alive those who in other days would have died. For many who are able to remain vital and active, this ability to prolong life has been a blessing. But for many who are comatose and brain dead—and especially for those who love them—this technology has been a curse.

The Supreme Court ruled in the late eighties that persons must specify in their wills that they do not want life-sustaining technology if they become comatose through accident or illness. Of course, voices are being raised to liberalize this ruling.[33] In fact, I wouldn't be surprised if the "right to die" surpasses abortion as the major prolife issue of the nineties. In particular, active euthanasia, "mercy killing," or "assisted suicide" will be the focus of debate. And it will be very difficult to find consensus on the troubling ethical issues this topic will raise, even among people of faith.

There are many who favor passive euthanasia—choosing not to have extraordinary life-saving technology used in cases of long-term coma or acquiring a terminal illness. But the voices advocating active euthanasia—removing life-saving technology after it has been applied or assisting a person to die—are already being heard with growing frequency in the nineties.

Of course, the euthanasia movement has been born out of a sincere desire for death with dignity. People don't want themselves or their loved ones to suffer undue pain or have physical life sustained when mental activity has ceased. In fact, there are committed Christians who argue passionately for the legalization of active euthanasia. Harriet Goetz, for instance, who is a nurse and a Christian, writes out of years of seeing the terminally ill suffer:

> Mercy killing is certainly killing. But which word do we emphasize? The "mercy" or the "killing?" There's no way to make it sound acceptable. Killing sounds wrong and violent. "Assist death" or "stop life" sounds better, but euphemisms are dishonest evasions; the issue is killing. Why is it so difficult to bring oneself to kill a person? Often it isn't that we want a person to live longer in a state of suffering; it's just that we don't want to be the one to end it. Yet why do we want to keep a person alive who has no hope of recovery, who is in dreadful agony and is begging for death?[34]

One can certainly understand Goetz's concern for those who are suffering. But there are major complications in legalizing active euthanasia. There is evidence, for example, that "mercy killing" of elderly people is taking place increasingly in Europe without the elders' knowledge or consent. A recent poll in Holland, for instance, showed that

> 77 percent of respondents expressed "understanding" for those who, out of mercy, kill their parents without their consent. So ominous has the situation become that some elderly nursing home patients are afraid to drink their orange juice for fear it may contain a lethal substance.[35]

It seems logical to assume that if active euthanasia is legalized in this country, if the cost of senior care dramatically escalates, and if the incidence of elder abuse continues to grow, we will see many give their failing parents an early send-off without the knowledge or consent of those parents. The same question could be raised about the retarded or severely handicapped. With growing economic pressures, especially escalating health care costs, and the general graying of the population, Christians need to draw on biblical principles to be prepared to help form public opinion as to the care of the elderly, respecting every person's interest in death with dignity. Christians also will want to shield the elderly and infirm from arbitrary or selfish decisions that would do them harm. (The hospice movement represents one very compassionate response to these concerns.) In the area of death, as with that of procreation, the fundamental questions remain: Whose responsibility is it to control issues of life, death, and procreation? And whose values will be used in these critical decisions? A 1991 Supreme Court decision essentially shifted the issue back to the states to resolve.

Waking Up to the Augmentation of the Human Species

Not only is there growing concern to gain greater control over human reproduction and issues of life and death. In the twenty-first century, even those of us who have not been "improved" at the beginning of our lives through genetic engineering, will increasingly look to science and technology to make us all we can be—to heal us, to replace defective parts, and to augment our strength and intelligence.

Already, for those who can afford it, hearts, kidneys, lungs, livers, corneas, and skin are all replaceable through transplant surgery. No one has yet transplanted any human limbs from one body to another, but this will likely happen in the very near future.[36]

And transplants, of course, are not the only way to replace defective organs and limbs. A whole range of mechanical organs and electronic implants are increasingly available, and a new generation of bionics promises to make us even more than we can be now. The present capability of steroids to increase body strength (even with all the deadly side effects) points to the future development of more powerful drugs that enhance or extend life and increase physical prowess.

Not only are we intent on repairing our bodies and augmenting our physical prowess through technology; we want to enlarge our mental powers as well. Brain mapping, pharmaceutical research, and behavioral conditioning all have the potential to significantly strengthen human intellectual capacity as well as to treat mental disorders.

As with the other areas of advancing technology, however, the push to be more than we can be through science and technology has its down side. The question of transplants, for instance, raises the same important questions of who can afford them and who will receive them.

Even more problematical is the question of who the donors should be. As affluent citizens from Western nations demand more and more replacement parts, increasingly they are looking beyond their own borders. Once again, the world's poor are being given the opportunity to make life a little more complete for the world's wealthy, and this trend seems likely to increase. India is a major donor nation. "If this business is allowed to continue, most of India's poor will be minus a kidney by 2000," says Dr. K. M. Chugh of the Kidney Foundation of India, who is waging an active campaign against the trade."[37] Although this is obviously an exaggeration, the problem *is* real—and growing.

In response to this growing commerce in organs, twenty-one European nations recently agreed to ban companies from profiteering in human body parts. They have agreed to draw up guidelines to protect the donors and their families from economic exploitation. And they insist that living donors should receive compensation for financial loss caused by the removal of organs, and that use of living donors should be restricted to donation of replaceable body substances such as skin and bone marrow. But even this level of transaction between poor donors and rich benefactors raises serious ethical questions for the future.[38]

Perhaps one of the most controversial areas of employing technology to make us all that we can be is the use of fetal tissue. Transplanting fetal tissue from an aborted fetus into the brain of a person suffering from Parkinson's disease shows promise of restoring some neurological performance; other benefits may eventually surface as well. Predictably, antiabortionists are fervently opposed to such research, and even many prochoice advocates are concerned with potential abuses. In speaking to such issues, the National Institutes of Health make it clear that

> informed consent for research must be obtained subsequent to consent for abortion, there can be no variation in abortion procedures to facilitate research. "Donations" to designated beneficiaries must be prohibited, as must conception and abortion in anticipation of "donation."[39]

Even with these guidelines, the use of fetal tissue in research will probably continue to be a stormy issue in the nineties. A story in early 1991 created wide interest. A California couple decided to conceive a baby in hopes of providing a bone marrow transplant for their teenaged daughter. Such a story obviously raises serious ethical questions about conceiving babies to provide biological resources for others.

The quest to become all we can be through technology raises many other questions. As we begin to manipulate our own genetic design, augment our capabilities through science and technology, and keep our bodies running by replacing defective parts with implants and appliances, how will our view of human nature change? How will this growing human control of our own destiny and intimacy with technology alter the human future? These are not questions that are easily answered. But they are questions that the Christian community must address before we unquestioningly embrace these new technologies.

Waking Up to Smart Machines
That Expand the Reach of the Human Species

The push to become more than we can be through science and technology is not limited to altering the human body, of course. In the nineties we are also embarking on a historic course to expand our cerebral and physical powers through artificial intelligence (popularly abbreviated A.I.) and robotics. "The second industrial revolution, the one that is now in progress, is based on machines that extend, multiply, and leverage our abilities," declares Raymond Kurzweil, an A.I. entrepreneur.[40]

The movement to create artificial intelligence is an intentional effort to take charge of human "evolution" and through computer science to expand our intellectual prowess. A.I seeks to replicates human intellectual processes and then to expand those processes significantly beyond the capacity of the human mind. Like all new technologies, this one comes promising to be our servant. But like other efforts to augment human potential through technology, A.I. also raises serious questions for the human future.[41]

A.I. devices are now capable, for example, of recognizing continuous speech with a high level of accuracy and therefore operating computers on voice commands.[42] They can scan printed documents or even handwriting and "read" the text aloud using voice synthesizers. They can orchestrate or arrange simple tunes in the "style" of various composers. A.I. has already been useful in the development of devices to aid the handicapped; for instance, it has enabled the development of "reading machines" for the blind, "smart" artificial limbs, and communication devices for people with cerebral palsy. But the business community and Pentagon are in the forefront of the race to utilize the Promethean power of A.I. In the world of business, for example, A.I. systems are being used to assess both short- and long-term market trends. A.I. is presently only a small fraction of the $250 billion computer industry, but it is in the fast lane and is expected to enjoy a high growth curve during the nineties.[43]

Such plans and potential developments raise—or should raise—questions. How comfortable do we feel, for instance, turning more and more of the responsibility for military decision making over to "intelligent systems" in view of the number of reported computer errors at North American Air Defense headquarters over the last two decades?[44] Perhaps more important, to what extent will we turn over vital areas of human decision making to intelligent machines—taking an intellectual back seat to our technologies.

In the twenty-first century, a growing share of medical diagnostic work will most likely be done by A.I., as will a growing portion of architectural design work.

And higher levels of management in business, government, and the military will probably turn the operation of increasingly complex systems over to A.I. Even as factories once dramatically reduced the need for skilled craftspersons, A.I. is likely to downgrade the skills presently needed in many areas of employment. At the same time, there are likely to be growing levels of technological control and influence by those who run and program the A.I. systems.

Closely related to the development of new "smart" systems is the emergence of new "strong" systems. Science and technology are providing not only a way to expand our intellectual power through A.I., but also to increase our power through robotics. Unquestionably, the Japanese are far ahead in this race, but the United States and the Soviet Union are making a concerted effort to catch up.

As we see a marriage between intelligent systems and robots we will see the growth of factories that will virtually run themselves. NASA is already looking into the possibility of self-replicating factories in space.[45] Of course, such technologies are still in the distant future, but the ground is being prepared for them.

Robotics have long played a key role in space exploration and may be used in place of astronauts for probes into deep space since robots aren't troubled by the human problem of aging. Back on earth, robots hold tremendous promise for the disabled. On voice command, "Egbert" is programmed to turn on the TV, dial the telephone, adjust the bed, and open the drapes; Egbert even talks back in a human voice. A more advanced voice-activated model can actually open the microwave, take out dinner, and retrieve books from the shelves. For quadriplegics needing twenty-four-hour care, Egbert could be a godsend.

Not every disabled person, of course, can afford a $47,000 Egbert or some of the other new high-tech innovations for those who need extra help. But a whole generation of low-tech, less expensive adaptive appliances are also being designed. Recently the Museum of Modern Art in New York City held a show of the new adaptive technologies called "Designs for Independent Living."[46]

Robots come in all sizes. Researchers at Bell Laboratories have actually designed a motor that generates a half-pound of force but weighs in at only .013 ounce. This promises to be the engine for a whole generation of microrobots, which will be used primarily in medicine. And these developments may well pave the way for "nanocomputers" small enough to be released into the blood stream to repair damaged cells or attack malignant ones. Such technology probably won't be a part of the nineties, but it will be a part of the twenty-first century.[47]

Initially, robots were designed to reduce human labor and reduce workplace danger—for example, to handle nuclear and toxic wastes. But they will also displace many semi-skilled workers on one end of the continuum while creating only a few highly skilled jobs on the other end. In other words, expanded use of robots is likely to contribute to growing unemployment by replacing much of the unskilled and semiskilled work force. Of course, this will hit those on the bottom of the rung the hardest.

Waking Up to the Ultimate Arrogance—
Technological Immortality

As we increasingly blur the lines between humanity and our technologies, some scientists are beginning to imagine whole new combinations and even to look toward actually overcoming death. For example, Hans Moravec, the senior research scientist at Carnegie Mellon University's autonomous mobile robot laboratory, looks forward to a day in which a person can be wheeled into an operating room, anesthetized, and have his or her skull opened for a very unusual operation. Everything in the brain will then be directly "downloaded" to a large computer and the resulting data placed in a robotic body.

> As the centuries passed, you could dedicate part of your endless time to searching out the very finest chassis builders and downloading your computerized self into the very latest in biological or mechanical artificial bodies.[48]

Of course, this dystopian dream is not within human reach today. But it is within human aspiration. And the principalities and powers work through our fallen aspirations even to the point of ultimate arrogance—attempting to achieve immortality through science and technology.

As we have seen, our expansive technologies, while providing many benefits, have not only taken a very high toll on the created order, but are also altering the human community. In the future, they will increasingly move toward manipulating life itself.

We invited the machine first into the garden, then into our communities, and now increasingly into our own bodies and minds. Now we are awakening to the specter of the intimate machine. Technology is no longer just a part of our landscape and our human communities; it is part of our very lives. Now we must try to anticipate how this development might affect our future. While fully recognizing the possible benefits of coming breakthroughs, we must make decisions not only about how they will be applied, but about how intimate we want our involvement with the machine to be as technological breakthroughs continue.

THE INTIMATE MACHINE: AN AGENDA FOR RESPONSE

As we stand at the threshold of a new technological lift-off, an array of unprecedented challenges confronts us. We all have a responsibility to anticipate and to respond to these new technological and ethical challenges. But we also need to discuss what kind of a future we want and what role technology will play in that future. Here is a summary of the challenges we have discussed in this chapter— challenges that are likely to confront both the church and society in coming decades:

- influencing public policy regarding the exploration and development of space, the oceans, and Antarctica,

- anticipating the likely long-term consequences of becoming ever more closely linked to a global electronic nervous system,

- assessing the possible positive and negative use of the digitalization of media, the total-experience capabilities of holography, and similar technologies,

- anticipating how "electronic cottage" technologies are likely to alter family life,

- identifying the possible positive and negative consequences of a growing number of persons telecommuting to work,

- insisting that citizen oversight boards (with Christian representation) be created to provide input on ethical issues from genetics and eugenics to reproductive sciences and euthanasia,

- providing regular forums within the church in which persons can understand and discuss these issues in a biblical context,

- assessing the potential positive and negative consequences of our growing reliance on artificial intelligence and robotics,

- developing a science policy task force comprised of Christian ethicists, theologians, and lay leaders to propose guidelines for the development and application of these new technologies,

- anticipating how our growing intimacy with our technologies is likely to fundamentally alter our human communities, the nature of human life, and the essence of life itself,

- imagining and inventing new technologies that are motivated not by a vision of dominance and power, but by one of servanthood and restoration,

- examining more critically the visions and values that drive modern science and technology in order to more clearly understand the future to which they are taking us.

THE INTIMATE MACHINE: SIGNS OF HOPE

As we enter a future of new technologies and largely unanticipated consequences, there are of course some signs that technology can be used in positive ways without usurping human initiative, weakening human community, or undermining human values.

One of the most hopeful examples is the promotion of small-scale or "appropriate" technologies in both Western and Two-Thirds-World countries. These include the alternative solar, wind, and geothermal technologies that we discussed in the previous chapter. But appropriate technologies also include pedal-driven flour mills, solar food dryers, and alternate means of cooking food to reduce firewood consumption. For example, a group of Kenyans in one village have designed an improved model of the traditional Jiko stove that uses half as much fuel as the traditional model. For the average Nairobi family, which spends about $8.25 a month on charcoal, the new stove will pay for itself in two months.[49]

Another hopeful development is research being done to protect seed stock for the future. Our growing reliance on hybrid seed has, as the climate changes, made us vulnerable. Approximately 75 percent of the native seeds and crop varieties in the Western hemisphere has been lost since the days of Columbus, and more species are at risk. The new scientific hybrids are proving more vulnerable in extreme heat. If the "heat trap" effect does indeed begin to warm up the planet, we could all become acutely aware of our vulnerability.[50]

In response to this growing vulnerability, the National Seed Storage Laboratory in Fort Collins, Colorado, is trying to develop a new technology to preserve seeds for future generations. Findings thus far indicate that freezing seeds at extremely low temperatures—minus 196 degrees Fahrenheit—provides the best promise for long-term preservation.[51]

Technology is even being put to use to fight the negative results of other technology. Despite resistance by the auto industry, for example, the city of Los Angeles is considering a bold new antipollution program that over the next two decades would require all vehicles to convert to the "clean" fuel methanol, which packs more power and is only half as polluting. The plan calls for all bus fleets to convert by 1991, all taxis and rental cars by 1993, and all private vehicles by 2009.[52] The state of California has recently mandated that cars be designed to burn alternative fuels and that auto emissions must be significantly reduced by the end of the century. California is also encouraging the development of electrical cars.

Technology is also being put to direct use in the service of the gospel. Computerized Bible study aids abound, and each year they become more sophisticated. For example, Word Publishing has just released The Word Advanced Study System with Graphics, which can simultaneously display Greek and Hebrew texts along with other study helps such as *Strong's Concordance.*

Jay Parish, a geophysicist, has started a new organization called "Information Transfer." Parish is encouraging the larger ecumenical church to consider placing its own satellite in space to provide an independent perspective on what is happening in terms of global disarmament and governmental and corporate treatment of the environment. Such a satellite could thus be used to more responsibly steward the development of the earth. The creative use of satellite technology could thus provide an important new tool in working for "peace, justice, and integrity of creation."

THE INTIMATE MACHINE:
WAKING UP TO OUR CHRISTIAN RESPONSIBILITY

In spite of the incredible rate of technological change, there has been surprisingly little discussion in the church about our growing intimacy with our technology. Ecumenical churches have, of course, periodically held symposia on science and religion. They have frequently expressed concerns regarding the negative consequences of technology on the environment. They have been particularly outspoken regarding the use of science and technology to develop weapons of mass destruction. Catholic ethicists, in particular, have been in the forefront of examining the ethical issues our technology is raising for society. But rarely have I found a serious ecumenical critique of the assumptions on which modern science and technology are premised or a discussion of the ways in which technology might shape our future.

I suspect the reason for this oversight is that mainline intellectual thought, like that of science and technology, is deeply rooted in the values and viewpoint of the Enlightenment. In fact, it seems like most mainline Christians tend unquestioningly to accept not only the role of science and technology, but also the assumptions on which they are premised. Mainliners particularly seem to give unquestioned approval to using empiricism and rationalism as the primary windows on the larger world, just like those in the scientific community. Of course, Catholic moral theology raises important questions about technology. But most Catholics seem to embrace modernization and all that goes with it just like mainline Protestants.

Conservative Christians, on the other hand, seldom seem to raise questions regarding any of the consequences of science and technology, with the possible exception of a "right to life" area such as fetal research. There are, of course, able ethicists at evangelical seminaries from Gordon Conwell to Asbury. But conservative Christians on the whole seem to have embraced Western science and technology even more uncritically than their mainline counterparts.

For instance, the late Francis Schaeffer, an influential evangelical author, wrote glowingly of the rise of modern science, viewing the rise of science and technology as a by-product of the Reformation and Western Christian culture. As a consequence, Schaeffer and many other evangelical leaders have seldom questioned the assumptions on which technology is premised nor anticipated its negative societal consequences. They tend to view technology in largely utilitarian terms, simply asking how it can be used to improve our lives or extend the gospel to remote regions.

In fact, I've found that people in all branches of the church, as well as those outside it, tend to view our technologies in basically utilitarian terms. We tend to see them as so many value-free tools we use to better our lives and society. I was amazed to find in speaking to Christians who are scientists and students at Carnegie Mellon University that most of them believe the new robotic technologies they are constructing are inherently value neutral. They stated that the only place they believed values came in is at the point of how the technologies are to be applied. And they insist that they have very little influence on how the robotics they design are used in society.

All cultures, of course, have their tools and technologies. But contrary to popular opinion, I would argue that none of our technologies is value free; rather, they reflect the values of the cultures that spawned them. Certainly the technologies of Native Americans, Polynesians, and the Shakers all strongly reflect the values of those cultures. For example, the Shakers' high value of simplicity is reflected in every aspect of their lives, from the design of their furniture to the tools they use to make their furniture and their homes. And that is true of Western technologies born of the Enlightenment, as well.

I am not suggesting for a moment that we join the Luddites and destroy modern technology or the Amish and try to avoid it. But I am urging that, like the Polynesians and the Shakers, we design technologies based on a different values paradigm than that associated with modernization and the Western dream.

Since we first tasted the fruit in the Garden, humankind has been driven by a desire to know as God, to be powerful as God is powerful. Nowhere is this quest for knowledge as power more evident than in the Western Dream and the emergence of Western science and technology. What characterizes our technology is not only the dream it aspires to but the power it is obsessed with.

The Western Dream is premised on some very clear values assumptions:

- defining the "real" world and the better future in largely economic and materialistic terms,

- selecting empiricism and rationalism as the twin windows through which we know and understand that "real" world,

- creating an increasingly technological society in which systematization, conformity and—above all—efficiency are seen as the most important societal values,

- emphasizing consumerism as a primary human value while significantly diminishing spiritual, relational, and creational values,

- supporting unequivocally our commitment to technological determinism— that is, what can be done through science and technology must be done.

Our Christian responsibility, therefore, must begin by recognizing that there is no such thing as value-free technology. I join Theodore Roszak in acknowledging that our technology and the values within it pervade every aspect of modern culture and human life. These pervasive, relatively invisible values systems are likely doing more to shape society than even the technologies they generate.

At the center of these values is the unrelenting quest for power that pervades every aspect of Western life. And as we have seen, our lust for power and technological mastery is not limited to the natural world. We are also seeking greater control over the human species and indeed over the essence of life itself, until our intimacy with our technology blurs all historic distinctions.

A notable group of authors has argued that our technological culture in its quest for power is actually out of our control and is taking us to a future we would never have chosen—a future that denies the inherent mystery of our world and the essential spirituality of our lives. These authors include Theodore Roszak, Lewis Mumford, and Jacques Ellul.

Ellul, in his seminal work, *The Technological Society,* argues that as our society has become increasingly technological, humankind has lost control. Something has emerged he calls "technique." The term refers not just to the machines or to the technology itself, but to "the totality of methods rationally arrived at and having absolute efficiency in every field of human activity."[53]

Ellul argues that "technique" has become a largely autonomous force that is increasingly shaping both the character and direction of the larger society. He predicts, "When technique enters into every area of life, including the human, it ceases to be external to man and becomes his very substance. It is no longer face to face with man but is integrated with him, and it progressively absorbs him."[54] Not only are we facing a growing intimacy with our technology that will cause us to redefine what it means to be human. In addition, Ellul argues, the values of the machine are gradually absorbing us, becoming an inherent part of who we are, threatening both our spirituality and our humanity.

However, Ellul does not feel that this progressive absorption of humanity into a technological culture is inevitable. In fact, he asserts, "If an increasing number of people become fully aware of the threat that the technological world poses to man's spiritual life, and if they determine to assert their freedom by upsetting the course of this evolution, my forecast will be invalidated."[55]

In light of Ellul's insights, it isn't enough simply to anticipate the positive and negative consequences of emerging technologies, as important as that is. And it isn't even enough to anticipate the new ethical issues these technologies will raise, important as those are. We must also evaluate the fundamental values on which our technological society is based. We must determine if those values are indeed absorbing us into a technological intimacy that will alter our humanity and undermine our spirituality. If we find, with Jacques Ellul, that the problem is pervasive, we must take strong initiative to unmask the powers and recover a new vision for the human future . . . a vision that will set us free to imagine new technologies born of a very different dream.

Questions for Discussion

1. What early efforts did America make to manage the first technologies that came to its shores?
2. What are three final "frontiers" our technologies will help us conquer as we enter a new century?
3. What are some of the new electronic technologies that are a part of the global "nervous system"? What are the potential benefits and drawbacks of using these technologies?
4. What technologies are increasingly becoming more intimate parts of our lives? What are the potential benefits and drawbacks of developments in these areas?
5. What are some signs of hope in the development and use of our technologies in the future?
6. What are the values underlying Western technology?
7. What seems to be the single major driving force behind our expansive Western technology?
8. Where do we begin to unmask the powers operating through Western technology?
9. How can we as the people of God begin the social management of our technology?
10. What are some ways we as Christians can bring our influence to bear on the broad range of ethical issues that will fill tomorrow's society?

4

Waking Up to
an Economic Tsunami

Abraham sat motionless on a small mound looking out at the waves. "Gone," he murmured, almost inaudibly. "All of them—gone."

Abraham and his wife and three children and one cow had always lived in Andhra Pradesh—as had their parents before them. Everyone who lived in this small beach community on India's east coast were "tribals." Tribals are completely outside of the traditional caste system, and as a consequence are seen as lower than even the untouchables.

The fifty million tribals who inhabited India at this time didn't even enjoy the protection of the law since they were legally not considered human beings. It was not uncommon for them to be exploited, even brutalized, by those who had higher station and more power within society.

Abraham and his family, like virtually everyone else in his village, worked on a huge agricultural estate owned by a high-caste landlord. The landlord allowed these landless tribals to farm his land in exchange for giving him back 75 percent of what they produced on his land. Because the farmers were unable even to provide basic subsistence for their families on this very minimal level of income, they became hopelessly indebted to the landlord—essentially slaves to land they farmed and to the landowner who leased it to them.

Yesterday, Abraham was working inland on the farm. And while he was gone, tragedy struck. A giant tsunami—a tidal wave—had swept away all he knew—wife, children, cow, house, the whole village. The small mound where he was sitting was all he had left. Abraham sat there in stunned isolation as the darkness enveloped him.

We live in a world buffeted by massive waves of changes. Some people of the world are lifted by these waves; others are dashed by them. Invariably, however, those at the margins of society, like Abraham and his fellow villagers, are the ones most vulnerable to the tidal forces of change.

As we approach the twenty-first century, which economies will be lifted by the waves of change? Which will be trapped in the doldrums? And which are likely to be violently hammered by the oncoming waves? Will the United States continue to ride the crest of the big one, or will its preeminent position be challenged? Most important, how will the coming waves of economic change affect the people with whom we share the planet—especially those who, like Abraham, live at the economic margins?

The purpose of this chapter is to outline some of the most compelling waves of economic change that are likely to confront us globally and nationally as we approach the twenty-first century. This chapter won't attempt to address the future of the corporation or provide forecasts for those looking for promising economic investments—other books address those interests. Instead, I will focus primarily on how the waves of economic change will affect society, particularly those who live at the periphery. I will attempt to explore the economic future "as if people mattered."[1] And I will, in the conclusion, summarize the challenges facing us, identify some signs of hope, and also struggle to understand something of our biblical responsibility in a very uncertain economic future.

Waking up to the Coming Waves of Economic Change

Looking toward the distant horizon, we can see the waves coming. What are some of the likely changes that will accompany the waves? One of the most dramatic areas of economic change evident as I write, in 1991, is the worldwide eclipse of centrally planned economies. The dramatic changes in the Soviet Union and Eastern Europe have raised a host of new challenges for Western economies. Former members of the Communist bloc are struggling to turn toward some version of a free-market economy, and privatization has become the watchword of the early nineties.

In the decade of the eighties, we witnessed yet another remarkable wave of change. National economies from all over the world became electronically linked in a single global economic system. National economic boundaries have almost totally dissolved as we have all become connected to this dimension of the global nervous system. As a result of this remarkable change, worldwide economic transactions now occur at incredible speed, and a new transnational global economy is emerging.

Not only are our national economies becoming linked into a single global economic order. That global economic order is also becoming the conduit through which our regional cultures are becoming homogenized into a single, transnational consumer culture. Those who are orchestrating the creation of this planetary consumer society are intent on persuading all of us to alter out values and our preferences so we will all drink the same soda, watch the same videos, and become addicted to the same consumer impulses.

Someone has written that the economic aspirations of the American Dream have become the dream of an entire planet. Regrettably, that seems to be true. Modernization is replacing traditional cultures at an alarming rate. Only two years ago, for instance, a remote African village had no electricity. Today, it has not only electricity, but also a village TV and VCR. Instead of families' spending their evenings together with their children, they spend every evening at village video parties watching Chuck Norris and Sylvester Stallone videos. You can imagine how these developments are beginning to change both family life and village culture.

Daniel Boorstin describes what is being created as a global "consumption community" held together by a bond that transcends tradition, race, and geography—the bond of universal consumerism. "The challenge of the Global Shopping Center, as the world managers see it, is to retail old needs to new customers and to create new needs for old customers."[2]

Unfortunately, the effect of such global consumerism will be the growing devastation of traditional cultures and destabilization of these societies. Often these displaced cultures are not only more stable, communal, and spiritual; many of them reflect values more congruent with biblical values than the values of modernization that are replacing them. We will all be poorer for the loss of these richly variegated cultures.

In addition to the electronic linking of national economies and the homogenization of cultures, we are also seeing increased regional competition within this global economic order. National industrialized economies seem to be joining regional economic coalitions. Not only do they hope to gain access to huge internal markets within their coalitions; they also look to their coalitions to give them an edge in an increasingly competitive international marketplace.

Essentially, we are witnessing the emergence of three major economic regions:

- the Asian region,

- the European region, and

- the American region.

These three regions appear to be lining up for a three-way race that will determine which is economically dominant as we enter a new century. (Of course, with growing economic power comes growing political power as well.)

It will be particularly important to anticipate the likely impact of this three-way competition on those who are essentially excluded from the race. At this point, no Two-Thirds-World or Eastern-European countries are a part of any of these coalitions. These countries could be the big losers as regional economic competition heats up.

THE ASIAN REGION:
RIDING AN ECONOMIC TSUNAMI INTO THE TWENTY-FIRST CENTURY

The Asian region appears to have caught the crest of a huge tsunami and is intent on riding it confidently into the twenty-first century. The Asian region, which includes countries such as Japan, Korea, China, Singapore, Hong Kong, and Taiwan, has been experiencing the highest level of economic growth of the three major regions, ranging from 4 to 10 percent growth annually . . . though this growth slowed a bit as we entered 1991.

Business Week exults,

After decades of looking to America for economic growth, the nations of East Asia are undergoing a tidal change. Their economic focus is shifting toward Japan. This is letting Japan build a new power base that helps integrate Asian countries into its economic and political agenda. Today, the region's economy is the fastest growing on earth. Its industries spew forth cars, computers, microchips, and toys for the world. Not counting Japan, growth rates average eight percent. Per capita income has risen dramatically.[3]

Someone has written, "The Cold War is over, and Japan has won." And even with the graying of Japanese society, the Asian region is looking forward to a future of continuing high growth.

Japan's "new power base" is no accident, but the result of a deliberate set of policies. Japan is the largest donor of development aid in the world, but very little of it goes to the impoverished people of Africa and Latin America. Instead, fully three quarters is invested in helping Asian countries develop their economies.[4] In addition, Japan has built plants all over Asia, expanding not only its markets, but also its power and influence. Recently Japan has also begun to extend development aid to Eastern-European countries, no doubt anticipating a potential new market there.

Japan has also worked hard to establish beachheads for its economic expansion in the other two regions—Europe and North America. In 1986, Japan invested $27 billion in plants, equipment, and property in the United States, employing some 250 thousand Americans. And those working for Japan, Inc. could grow to 840 thousand in the nineties.[5]

Predictably, the change in the economic balance of power has led to powerful protectionist sentiments in the United States and we are seeing an increased incidence of "Asian bashing." "Buy American" campaigns, proposed trade restrictions, and aggressive world marketing campaigns are all attempts to respond to the growing economic influence of Japan and her neighbors on the United States economy.

Regrettably, some of the products being pushed most aggressively by American corporations and the United States government to increase exports to Asia are products of addiction: alcohol and tobacco. Consumption of cigarettes is growing at 5.5 percent a year in Asia. Phillip Morris envisions a sales increase of up to 35 percent by 1999.[6] However, there is a growing protest in Asia regarding the human consequences of this kind of an American marketing strategy.

If Japan and the newly industrialized economies of Asia continue to ride the crest of this huge economic wave into the twenty-first century, they will obviously become not only one of the most affluent regions of the world, but increasingly one of the most powerful politically. One question is: How will they use this growing power in an increasingly uncertain future?

EUROPEAN COMMUNITY 1992: WAITING FOR THE BIG ONE

Europeans have no desire to be left behind in the backwaters of 2- to 3-percent annual economic growth. They have watched with envy as their Asian competitors ride their tsunami into the future. And twelve countries in Western Europe have responded with a Herculean effort to bring their economies together. By 1992, they intend to create a single economic entity which has been called European Community 1992 or E.C. 92. These plans, if they succeed, will result in a single Western European market of 320 million people. Tariffs and economic restrictions will be removed within this new economic community, giving all participants access to a huge new internal European market. It is predicted that a reunified Germany will be the economic powerhouse of this confederation, representing fully one-third of the community's economic productivity, though it will probably take the Germans the better part of the decade to turn the economy of their eastern half around.

Plans for E.C. 92 have revitalized the European business climate. An extended period of European pessimism is giving way to a buoyant new optimism. Some Europeans are predicting economic growth in Western Europe could range from 4 to 7 percent. But I don't think these upbeat forecasters have fully anticipated the high short-term costs that many in Europe will be asked to pay to standardize everything from currencies to electrical outlets. While the benefits of E.C. 92 are potentially very great, the process of getting the system underway could cause the nineties to be a decade of sacrifice for many in Western Europe. Already there are signs that some nations—with Britain at the forefront—are beginning to resist a complete economic union.

Outside observers' reactions to E.C. 92 plans are mixed. Some worry that E.C. 92 could lead to protectionism, a sort of "fortress Europe." Those fears, however, seem to be diminishing. Increasingly, outsiders are looking on E.C. 92 as an economic opportunity.

Not surprisingly, the non-European nation in best position to benefit from this European lift-off is Japan. Already, Japan, Inc. controls 36 percent of London's international banking, and Japanese auto producers in Europe are gearing up for a new, more open market. United States corporations are also expanding investments in Western Europe in an effort to catch a ride on the promised wave of prosperity.[7] And E.C. 92 has gained the full attention of Eastern European nations, who are struggling frantically to avoid being dashed on the rocks by the changing economic order. They are eager to become a part of this European economic lift-off, too.

As I write, the centrally planned economies of Eastern Europe are in shambles. In fact, one of the obvious motivations behind the impressive democratic reforms going on in the former Warsaw Pact countries is the realization they must radically restructure their economies if they are to survive.[8] Many seem to be particularly attracted to the Swedish version of a free-market economy because they feel the Swedes have been successful in developing a free market with a "human face"—a high level of concern for human needs and social benefits.

Revamping the economies of Eastern Europe will be no small task and may take an entire decade. Poland, however, is trying to do it in one wrenching transition—and at this writing, the Poles seem to have the best chance of success. Hungary and Czechoslovakia's chances at making the transition also seem reasonably good. But the nineties don't look particularly promising for the other Eastern European countries. If they fail in their bid to become free-market economies, the result could be growing economic and political destabilization, civil conflict, and floods of people immigrating to areas where the economies are healthier. This could have a very negative impact on Western Europe.

Even if economic prosperity does blossom in parts of Eastern Europe, such prosperity may not be good news from a religious point of view. Under the repression of Marxist states, a smoldering spirituality slowly grew to a flame. And God moved through both Protestant and Catholic churches to bring renewal even in the face of persecution. As Eastern Europeans join those of us in the West in bending a knee to modernization and the great consumer society, there is danger that secularism could snuff out this vital spirituality and this beginning renewal.

Waking Up to a Struggling Perestroika

In the Soviet Union, as I write, the economic news is far from positive. Even though Mikhail Gorbachev's policy of openness is directly responsible for the beginnings of economic and political reform in Eastern Europe, economic reform is not nearly as promising in the Soviet Union as it is in Poland, Hungary, and Czechoslovakia.

Since Gorbachev first announced his policy of perestroika, the Soviet economy has progressively worsened. Not only are there steadily diminishing supplies of consumer items in the stores; there are now reported bread shortages and widespread citizen unrest are causes for concern. The Soviet economy seems to be literally coming apart at the seams before anything has been constructed to replace it. A joke overheard in Leningrad: "The stagnation period took us to the edge of the precipice. Now we are ready to step forward."[9]

In 1990, progressive leaders concerned about the growing public cynicism and unrest formulated a bold "five-hundred-day plan" to enable the Soviet economy to change over to a free market economy.[10] But not only has Gorbachev refused to bite the bullet and inaugurate this radical plan; he has apparently given in to some of the most conservative elements in the Soviet Union in order to survive.

Gorbachev's failure of nerve and the renaissance of Soviet conservatism has significantly increased the likelihood that the Soviet Union will be unable either to develop a free-market economy or to bolster its sagging centrally planned economy. However, Gorbachev is looking to the West for a massive bailout that could still result in major economic reform in the nineties. And Boris Yeltsin's decisive victory in the 1991 Russian presidential election provides guarded hope that the reform process might still go forward. Without wholesale reform, the Soviet future will almost certainly be disastrous.

In light of the 1991 war in the Middle East, United States oil companies are still looking longingly to the vast and largely undeveloped oil resources in Siberia. Other corporations are eager to develop the huge internal markets in the USSR. But with the growing influence of the KGB and the military, the Soviet economic future still doesn't look terribly promising—again, unless major reform takes place.

As in parts of Eastern Europe, Soviet society is likely to face growing destabilization and, to preserve order, an increasingly active role of the military. In addition, the brightest and best of Soviet society are likely to immigrate to countries that provide greater economic opportunity.This, too, seems likely to add to the growing destabilization. And an unstable USSR is a threat to everyone.

A number of Western economists, including John Kenneth Galbraith, anticipated the Soviet economic crisis:

> In the vast Soviet organization are many people . . . in positions of comfort and security as well as power, who find things eminently satisfactory as they are, and who rejoice in the power they now exercise, the privileges they now enjoy. On such persons and their initiative rests in no small part the responsibility for change. Thus a formidable contradiction: change must come in some measure from those who least want change.[11]

And Paul Kennedy's monumental book, *The Rise and Fall of Great Powers,* may indeed have been prophetic. Looking backwards over five hundred years of the rise and fall of major world powers, Kennedy made a forecast for the future. He stated that spending too large a share of a nation's total income on arms would imperil that nation's economy and ultimately result in declining political power.

Kennedy's reluctant forecast was that both the Soviet and American economies are in serious trouble, partly because they both have invested too large a share of their national wealth in the arms race. "Great powers in relative decline instinctively respond by spending more on 'security,' and thereby divert potential resources from investment and compound the long-term dilemma," Kennedy explained.[12]

Of course, the Soviets' primary problem is the failure of their centrally planned economy. But their economic woes have certainly been compounded by the enormous amounts they have invested in the arms race. And the United States economy has also been seriously strained by the massive weapons expenditures of the eighties. Some economists credit these expenditures for our high borrowing and present economic distress.

THE AMERICAS: STUCK IN THE DOLDRUMS

While the Asian region has been experiencing economic growth at 4 to 10 percent a year and the European region aspires to grow at 4 to 7 percent, the Americas, including the United States, Canada, and Mexico, seem to be stuck in the economic doldrums. As I am completing this chapter, Canada and the United States are both in recession, experiencing economic growth at about 1 percent.

The United States has spent so many years riding the crest of the post-World-War-II boom that I really think we assumed we were destined to ride the crest of the wave forever. But while the United States is still the most productive economy in the world, it is slowly losing its grip on first place. The United States has slipped from producing nearly 50 percent of the world's goods and services after the Second World War to producing only about 20 percent today.

As the eighties ended, the United States had fallen from being a leading creditor nation to being the world's leading debtor nation. On top of that, we are chronically in trouble with our balance of trade. The Savings and Loan debacle has proved to be far more serious than we were led to believe, and now our banks and insurance companies are in serious trouble also. Savings are down. Unemployment and welfare applications are significantly up. The dollar has plummeted. And we are still grappling with inflation. The administration and Congress struggle to reduce our huge deficit, and the success of their efforts is far from evident.

Canada not only shares our tendencies for very slow growth; its national debt is higher than ours per capita. And the Mexican economy is chronically in trouble. It is hoped, however, that new agreements among Canada, the United States, and Mexico will serve as a foundation for a new economic coalition to strengthen the North American Region.

It should be remembered that the United States's economic slide cannot help but impact its political strength. Former Secretaries of State Henry Kissinger and Cyrus Vance both point out that

> economic strength is . . . central to the way America is perceived by friends and potential adversaries. United States political leadership in the world cannot be sustained if confidence in the American economy continues to be undermined by substantial trade and budget deficits.[13]

The decline in the United States's economic leadership, therefore, raises several questions that the United States's historic victory in the Persian Gulf should not be allowed to eclipse. As the economies of our planet undergo major change, what is the future of the American economy? Are our days as leader of the pack behind us, or will we see a major recovery before the end of the decade? Will the United States, Canada, and Mexico find a way to challenge the remarkable economic growth in Asia and the pending lift-off in Europe? And what is our responsibility as a nation to the desperately poor with whom we share the planet, both overseas and at home?

Waking Up to Living Off Our Kids' Inheritance

The United States is facing an unprecedented federal deficit of almost three trillion dollars. This figure, combined with personal corporate debt, means that Americans are in hock to the tune of over nine trillion dollars. That is almost four times our national indebtedness in the mid-seventies. It represents thirty-five thousand dollars' worth of debt for every man, woman, and child in the United States.[14] And much of the federal borrowing was done to enhance an unprecedented military buildup in the eighties.

Lester Brown convincingly argues that we are borrowing from the future environmentally as well as economically. The high level of affluence we still enjoy is coming in part from the increasing degradation of our land, air, and water. This means that to get a true picture of our economic status, we need to include the depreciation of natural capital, including nonrenewable resources as well as renewable resources such as forests.[15]

In many ways, as the bumper sticker says, we really are "living off our kids' inheritance"; we have borrowed from the future to finance the present. In retrospect, the prosperity of the eighties didn't come principally from our productivity, but from our borrowing. We can no longer borrow from the future to finance the present. Our days of nonstop binging on borrowed money are behind us.

In an effort to manage our federal deficit, a new method of ordering the federal budget has also been introduced. The budget has been broken into three major categories: domestic, foreign aid, and military. Each category will now be handled independently of the other two. This means, of course, that cuts in one area—such as military spending—could not be used to offset overruns in domestic programs. The essential result of this restructuring is the shifting of significant budget power from Congress to the administration.[16] Before, Congress was able to shift available money around as needed; now, the administration sets the parameters and Congress has less flexibility in shifting money around.

As we enter 1991, we are facing other serious economic problems. Of particular concern to many is the growing instability of the banks and insurance companies, not only in the United States, but throughout the world. *The Economist* predicts that the United States government could wind up owning "1,700 bust banks, accounting for more than half the American banking industry's assets."[17]

In light of America's serious level of indebtedness, our trade shortfall, the decline in economic growth, and growing unemployment, a few economic forecasters are predicting a major economic depression for the United States. One of the most prominent is Ravi Batra, who wrote the bestselling book, *Surviving the Great Depression of 1990*. But admittedly, economic doomsayers such as Batra represent only a minority viewpoint.

A few, like corporate futurist Marvin Cetron, remain bullishly optimistic about America's economic future. Cetron, for example, predicts nothing less than an "American renaissance" in the nineties. He asserts, with very little supporting evidence, that the United States will solve its many economic and social problems and enter a new era of affluence. "By 2000," he gushes, "there will be no mistaking the trend toward a more comfortable, more equal America."[18] And a few economists are speculating that "kicking the Vietnam syndrome" in the Gulf War will somehow introduce a new era of high economic growth.

Most economists, however, take a more moderate position. They feel there is little likelihood of a thirties-style depression, because the circumstances are different today and because the United States has more economic safeguards than in the twenties.

As I write, there seems to be a widespread consensus among economists that we will likely emerge from the present recession by the end of 1991. But there is little consensus as to the rate at which the economy is likely to recover. Economic consultant firm DRI McGraw predicts the United States economy will come bounding back at a rate of "more than 5 percent by year end, running well into 1992."[19] But other economists point to a high unemployment rate and sagging consumer confidence and predict a much slower rate of recovery.

Over the longer term, a number of questions are being raised regarding the ability of the United States economy to achieve and maintain a high level of economic growth. Undeniably, the United States has tremendous economic capacity. But the economic challenges we face are formidable.

We are only beginning, for example, to learn of the hidden price tag for the formation of the Persian Gulf coalition in 1990—not to mention the cost of the war itself. The price of the Savings and Loan bail-out of the early nineties continues to swell. It looks as if the federal government will either have to shore up or buy out some of our leading banks and insurance companies. And we haven't begun to spend the billions of dollars necessary to clean up our toxic waste sites or nuclear storage areas. Add these problems to our escalating battle with inflation, our chronic trade shortfall, our huge national debt, our eroding industrial base, our deteriorating transportation systems, and our struggling educational system, and it is difficult to imagine how the United States can lead the economic pack in the increasingly competitive nineties. In fact, in the three-way race into the new century, there is every possibility that the Americas could come in dead last.

Waking up to the Erosion of the Middle Class

Since the beginning of the eighties, we have been at work fashioning a new American economic order. We have been creating a society in which the economic status of the middle class is changing rapidly. While some have joined the increasingly more affluent upper 20 percent of American society, many others are reluctantly migrating to the bottom 20 percent. In other words, we are headed toward becoming a more polarized, more class-oriented society, with a small segment that is becoming much more wealthy and a growing number that are joining the lower class.[20] As a result, we are witnessing the steady erosion of the middle class.

The pursuit of the American Dream requires at least two full-time incomes. Fewer and fewer middle-class families can achieve all their economic goals and afford to have one spouse stay home with the kids, too. As a result, a growing number of women have been entering the work force. That trend is certain to continue through the nineties, creating a growing need for quality child care. This need is felt by middle-income families, but it is even more of a problem for low-income families.

A growing share of the middle class can no longer afford either to buy or rent a house. They are joining a new population called "the hidden homeless," living with family and friends because they no longer can afford their own housing. As we approach the new century, I think we are likely to see more of these "hidden homeless" as we witness the steady erosion of the middle class.

Not only are young people having to spend more of their time and money trying to secure housing; they are having to spend more for education, too, particularly those who seek a college education in private institutions. Their costs have gone up much faster than the rate of inflation. For example, a parent laid out only sixteen hundred dollars (unadjusted for inflation) for a private college education in 1960. In 1986, that same education cost ten thousand dollars per year.[21]

And the cost of health care is going up for everyone. Since 1969, health-care costs have risen more rapidly than anything else on the Consumer Price Index, escalating between 9 to 13 percent per year. In 1985, we spent a whopping $425 billion for health care, compared to $289 billion for defense in 1986.[22] The *World*

Almanac predicts that by the end of by the year 2000 our national health-care bill will come to an unbelievable $1,529.3 billion.

Thirty-four million Americans have no health insurance at all. And since growing numbers of American businesses are cutting back in providing health insurance, that number is almost certain to grow. In our increasingly market-oriented health care system, many will have no access to health care at all because they cannot afford it. As a result, we will see part of our health care system providing a level of care no better than that of the Two-Thirds World for some, while extravagant amounts are spent to keep the wealthy healthy. In light of this possibility, there is growing advocacy for some kind of federal health-care program or federal health insurance.

Another result of costly health care is that many of us will take more responsibility for our own health and well-being. We will all be encouraged to take greater preventive action through diet, exercise, and stress management. And we will also learn to take more responsibility for treating minor maladies.

Finally, the high cost of health care will mean that the church and private sector must create new health initiatives for those excluded from the market-driven system. Justice demands we find ways to provide a decent level of health care for all citizens. Christian Community Health Fellowship is providing vital leadership in providing accessible health care for the poor. Such organizations will need our support in the nineties.[23]

We are likely to see a growing number of the middle class, particularly those who are younger, lose economic ground. They are likely to have increasing difficulty gaining economic access to housing, health care and postsecondary education. But while some are losing ground, others have been gaining. The eighties were in many ways a decade of unbridled bingeing and unprincipled extravagance. *Forbes* and *Fortune* magazines both celebrated the growing circle of wealth and affluence.

Waking Up to the Idolatry of Affluence

The United States leads all other nations in spawning the most billionaires. At least 47 Americans have a net worth of over a billion dollars.[24] During the last twenty years, the number of millionaires worldwide has increased more than sixfold—including 1.3 million Americans. In 1962, the richest 1 percent of Americans owned 31.8 percent of the national wealth. Two decades later, that group gained control of 34.4 percent of American wealth, and the percentage is still rising.[25] Of course, growing economic power brings with it greater political power as well. That's the "other" golden rule—"he who has the gold rules."

But even those of us without "the gold" seem to be obsessed with it. In the eighties, we lived in a society that worshiped money and wealth. And as a consequence we celebrated, envied, and did homage to the "rich and famous" in our midst:

Open the scarlet covers of the Saks Fifth Avenue Christmas catalog. For starters look at what Santa offers today's young family, from Dad's $1,650 ostrich-skin briefcase and Mom's $39,500 fur coat to Junior's $4,000 15-mph miniature Mercedes, driven by a 5-year-old Donald Trump look-alike in pleated evening shirt, studs and red suspenders. Take a stroll along Manhattan's Madison Avenue and gape at the Arabian Nights' Bazaar of shop windows, where money translates life's commonest objects into rarities rich and strange. Behold embroidery-encrusted sheets, or sumptuous lace underwear and pick up five matched crocodile suitcases for $75,000.

Statistics tell the same glitzy story as the evidence of your senses. Luxury car imports more than doubled between 1982 and 1986. An overwhelming 93 percent of recently surveyed teenage girls deemed shopping their favorite past time, way ahead of sixth-rated dating.[26]

In a real sense, money did indeed become the sex of the eighties, and as a society we were doing everything we could to help the young catch the fever. In 1987, for example, *Newsweek* reported on a summer camp held for the children of the aspiring and covetous at a posh resort in Florida. The campers played games like "Money Management Mania," learning how to be the Lee Iacoccas and perhaps the Ivan Boeskys of the twenty-first century.[27]

We have largely succeeded in our efforts to teach the American young— Christian and non-Christian alike—what is most important. In 1967, 80 percent of college freshmen reported on a survey that their major reason for going to college was to develop a meaningful philosophy of life. By 1986, freshmen reported the number-one reason was to be well-off financially.[28] (In more recent studies, there are some indications that entering college freshmen are becoming more concerned about issues like the environment.)

As we entered the nineties, however, and tough times loomed, even the yuppies began to turn their backs on upscale lifestyles. Simplicity and frugality suddenly became "in." Many Americans began to tighten their belts, seeking ways to do more with less. At the same time, however, those on the top were doing everything they could to secure their position so they wouldn't have to scrimp.

Economist Robert Reich asserts, in fact, that the "fortunate fifth" are in the process of seceding from the larger society. Not only do they gather in transnational resorts exclusively for the very affluent; increasingly, they are using their wealth to create their own separate society . . . including luxury recreation centers and health clubs, private schools, and independent security systems. Reich reports that much of their charitable giving—funding the fine arts, private hospitals, and elite univer- sities—benefits not the poor but themselves. In creating their enclaves of affluence, they are turning their backs on their responsibility to work with the rest of us for the common good.[29]

There is little evidence, however, that greed and the desire for more is limited to the rich; it affects our entire society. And in spite of our sudden return to frugality there is still a lingering hope that we can strike it rich. Gambling is on the rise across the country. Sixty-eight percent of the American people live in states that have legalized gambling. By the turn of the century, more revenues will be generated in state lotteries than the combined take of Las Vegas and Atlantic City. Of course lotteries help support schools and other social programs for which we are unwilling to pay taxes, but they do so by fostering a major social addiction which seduces our poorest citizens. Gambling as taxation is one of the most regressive forms of revenue production in our society.

While gambling addiction soars in the United States and families are compromised, the church in many states is strangely silent about the growth in gambling and its high human costs. In the nineties, we are likely to see a dramatic increase in legalized gambling as well as its hidden costs.

What we are witnessing is the emergence of a two-tiered American society. Both tiers are growing. But the bottom tier is growing most rapidly, and our society is becoming increasingly more polarized and potentially very volatile.

Waking Up to a Widening Gap between Rich and Poor

"While the seventies were the 'Decade of Me,' the eighties are likely to be the 'Decade of Us and Them,'"[30] I predicted in 1980. Regrettably we did, in the eighties, see increased polarization between rich and poor. In the nineties, I believe we will see growing polarization not only between rich and poor, but between elders and youngers as well.

Twenty years ago, one third of all seniors lived below the poverty line. But demographics have significantly changed over the last two decades, and so has the face of poverty. Today, those over fifty are among the most affluent members of society. They are the ones who buy the "Love Boat" cruises and do much of the luxury spending. Furthermore, they are determined to protect their privileged status. They are politically organized, and they vote.

The new poor of the nineties are young mothers and children—tens of thousands of them who are flooding the homeless shelters of America. Children make up the most rapidly growing population in the shelters. They aren't politically organized. They don't vote. And frankly, unless someone intervenes, their future doesn't look very promising.

The number of children living in poverty has grown from three million in 1968 to fourteen million today. One child in five born in the United States is born into poverty. And half those children are black.

But let's go beyond the statistics and meet just one example of this growing wave of the impoverished mothers and kids. Terry is twenty-eight. She has three kids. After she graduated from high school in Flushing, New York, she worked eight years as a lab assistant. Then her life started going downhill. The family was burned out of their home. She lived with her sister's family for two years. Then she moved in illegally with her cousin Wanda and her four children in a room that is barely nine by twelve. There are nine people in one tiny room with no hot plate and no food in the small refrigerator. Terry is panicked. She not only is having difficulty finding housing for her family; she is in a financial crisis as well. She is not on Medicaid. She has been removed from Aid to Families with Dependent Children and is now in the process of reapplying. The reason for her panic is that she is due to give birth to her fourth child, Christmas is approaching, and she insists, "If I can't be placed before the baby is born, the hospital won't let me take the baby. They don't let you take a newborn if you haven't got a home."[31]

Waking Up to Economic White Water for the American Poor

The upshot of all this human struggle is that as we move into the final decade of the twentieth century we are likely to see not only an increasingly polarized society, but a poorer one as well. The simple reality is that the bountiful economic showers of the Reagan years didn't trickle down to everyone. Instead, they drenched some, often at the expense of others. For those at the bottom of the economic heap, they didn't even moisten the soil.

In the South, rural blacks increasingly are being forced by economic necessity to sell the only stake they have against the future—their land—and migrate into the overcrowded cities. Native Americans, easily the poorest people in our midst, are living in communities often reminiscent of Two-Thirds-World villages. Estimates of homeless people in our cities are ranging as high as three to four million and growing. One congressional study predicts that we could see the number of homeless people increase to 19 million by 2003.[32] One reason for this is that the administration is selling off public housing to the people who live in it. The problem is the government isn't replacing it. As a result, there is likely to be a serious shortfall in the availability of public housing for the next generation of the poor.

There is every possibility that, in this decade, the economies of cities like Philadelphia and New York could collapse under the growing weight of providing for their swelling ranks of poor and homeless people. Such cities could quickly become desperate concentrations of poverty and misery, lacking even essential services.

Many have observed that we are in danger of creating a permanent underclass in the United States—an entire generation of young people who will live and die without ever holding a job. And this is not because they are lazy or shiftless. They simply can't read and write (23 million Americans are illiterate); they have no job skills. And there is no place in America tomorrow for young people like this— except perhaps in the ranks of drug dealers, who promise opportunity and prosperity to young people who can see no other option.

But the growing ranks of the poor aren't all young, poor, black, and urban. David T. Ellwood helps us in his book, *Poor Support*, to identify another major group—the working poor. Among these are two-parent families who barely manage to survive on their combined income. They typically receive no government benefits. Over a third have no health insurance. And they typically live one paycheck away from disaster.

Over half of the poor children in America live in two-parent families. During good times, this population is able to survive and sustain a basic existence. They are hard-working and industrious, but with limited education and job skills, and they often wind up working minimum-wage jobs. If the economy stagnates or declines, these families are the first to join the ranks of the unemployed and, increasingly, the ranks of the homeless.[33]

A growing number of single-parent families also make up the ranks of the working poor. Many women, especially, who lose their spouse through separation, divorce, or death suddenly find they have slipped out of the middle class. Working for minimal salaries and paying child care keeps them at a bare subsistence level. Often they don't even receive promised child support from absent fathers. The resulting "feminization" of poverty will be a growing problem through the nineties.

If present economic trends simply continue without interruption, we are almost sure to see a continued erosion of the middle class and a swelling of the ranks of the impoverished. A permanently polarized, two-tiered society may well characterize America's tomorrow. I will be very surprised if this polarization doesn't spill over in violence—and I doubt it will be limited to the inner cities this time.

Ellwood recommends five reforms to address the mounting needs of the American poor more effectively:

- provide a basic level of health insurance for all citizens,

- arrange for an adequate salary (so people aren't chronically trapped in poverty) by expanding earned income tax credit, raising minimum wage, and making child-care credit refundable,

- adopt a uniform child-support assurance system using the social security network to ensure that all absent parents are located,

- convert welfare into a transitional system to enable single parents and two-parent families to get education or whatever will help them return to self-reliance,

- provide minimum-wage jobs for people who have exhausted their transitional support.[34]

In the wake of the 1991 victory in the Middle East, the Bush administration has an unprecedented opportunity to launch a new domestic initiative and address the urgent and growing needs of the poor and dispossessed. If the administration attacked the problems of our cities with the same vigor with which it prosecuted the war, we might witness a rebirth of hope in America's desperate urban wastelands.

It is essential that we recognize that the coming waves of economic change will not only batter the poor this time. There is white water ahead for all of us. As the three-way regional competition between the Asian, European, and American regions heats up, all of our lives will be changed. And you can be certain that if North America comes in a very slow third, we will all have to adjust our economic expectations downward.

For many of us in the middle class, a downscaling of the economy could be a blessing in disguise. We might choose to aspire to some goals that have less to do with acquisition and more to do with celebrating relationships and spirituality. We might find some ways, in community with others, to do more with less and start to become more sensitive to other people's needs, particularly the poor, the homeless, and the children.

But further downscaling the United States economy will not be good news for those on the bottom rung. In a faltering economy, they are likely to be pushed even further under, and our society will be under greater indictment for failing to recognize their plight. Stepped-up competition among the regions of the world could render their situation almost impossible.

THE TWO-THIRDS WORLD: STUCK IN THE BACKWATERS

Of course, those who are likely to be hurt most by the three-way regional competition are not those of us who happen to live in Canada and the United States—even the American poor. The people who will be affected most will likely be those who aren't even a part of this three-way race—those living in the Two-Thirds World.

> The new reality of the 1980s and 1990s is that our spectacular consumer party is over! For the past two hundred years, most of those in the West have been enjoying the party, and we in the United States have had the very best of it. But the new reality is a future in which over half the people on this planet will never get to come to the Western party.[35]

Tragically, this forecast, which I made in 1980, is coming true. Growing numbers in the Two-Thirds World don't even have the essentials of life. And as the competition grows between the Asian, European, and American regions, many poorer nations will have difficulty breaking in. Of course, there will be markets for their natural resources. But they are likely to have difficulty gaining access to these huge regional markets for their manufactured goods. In any case, the poorer nations are not playing on a level playing field with their rich neigbors, and this inequity will continue to call their future into question as international economic competition continues to heat up.

Perhaps it would help to look back for a moment to understand why some regions have greater economic leverage. And then we will look forward to examine why population growth could undermine future economic growth in these countries.

At the beginning of the twentieth century, world population was only 1.6 billion, and the gross world product was approximately $640 billion. By mid-century, global population had grown to 2.5 billion, and the gross world product to roughly $3 trillion. Then, between 1950 and 1986, population doubled to 5 billion and per-capita income doubled as well. The gross world product swelled dramatically to over $13 trillion.[36]

The sheer economic power of this unprecedented growth has captured the attention of nations all over the world. Many of us in Western nations have directly benefited from this unparalleled period of economic lift-off, and we are now using the ground we gained to participate in the three-way race for economic supremacy.

Unfortunately, however, the benefits of this growth have not been universal. While most industrialized countries have successfully caught the waves of economic growth, many nations in the Two-Thirds World seem to be stuck in the backwaters.

It is true that Two-Thirds-World countries as a whole have seen gradual improvement in life expectancy, literacy, and other indicators. Still, however, they lag far behind the industrialized nations, and the distance in between seems to be growing. For a number of reasons, the economic future for many in these regions is far from bright.

Waking Up to Standing Room Only in Our Global Village

One of the major reasons Two-Thirds-World countries are caught in the economic backwaters is, of course, rapid population growth. This century has seen an unprecedented population explosion that is concentrated in the poorest regions of the planet.

By the year 2000, we will share our planet with over 6 billion people. By 2030, world population is projected to reach 7 billion. We added ninety million people to our high-rise village last year. And 92 percent of that growth is taking place in poorer nations, where population growth ranges from 2.2 percent to over 4 percent a year.

By 2025, predicts the World Bank, India's population will double to 1.365 billion, surpassing China as the world's most populous country. During the same period, Mexico's population is projected to nearly double, approaching 141 million.[37] Nations on the African continent are also expected to experience unprecedented levels of population growth. Kenya, for example, is growing at the rate of 3.9 percent a year.

On the basis of this rate of growth, it isn't difficult to predict who will make up the majority of the population in the Two-Thirds World as we enter the twenty-first century: children and mothers with young children. Already, over 50 percent of the population in Nigeria today is under fifteen years of age.

Another important demographic forecast is identifying where population growth is likely to be concentrated. As growing numbers of people despair of making a living in rural areas and flood into the cities, we may face nothing less than an urban apocalypse in the twenty-first century.

Demographic forecasters have predicted that by the year 2000 over 75 percent of the people living in Latin America will live in cities.[38] Cities will contain almost 80 percent of the citizens of East Asia. Even in Africa, the numbers will surpass 40 percent. Mexico City will be the largest city in the world, containing almost 30 million people by the year 2000. São Paulo will have 25 million and Calcutta, 19 million.

The reason I used the term "urban apocalypse" is that these burgeoning Two-Thirds-World cities simply don't have the infrastructures necessary to sustain this level of population growth. They don't have the sanitation, community health, or food delivery systems to begin to support this level of growth. Lima, Peru, is on the verge of collapse today and is suffering a cholera epidemic as I write. Other cities are not far behind.

Reducing the human cost of this urban apocalypse will require much more than simple relief measures. It must involve land reform and community development in the rural areas and the creation of whole new approaches to urban agriculture, sanitation systems, and economic cooperatives. Unfortunately, I have found virtually no Christian organizations who are preparing to meet this growing urban challenge. Churches and relief and development agencies need to begin mobilizing resources today in partnership with churches and governments in these Two-Thirds-World cities to create new strategies for the exploding cities of the coming decades.

Waking Up to a Bleak Future in the Backwaters

While uncontrolled population growth is a problem throughout the Two-Thirds World, Asia, Latin America, and Africa are all struggling with poverty and economic marginalization in different ways. While some nations in Asia—notably Japan, Korea, Singapore, Hong Kong, China, Taiwan, and Thailand—will be a part of the Asian lift-off, others—such as Nepal and Bangladesh—face the possibility of total economic and environmental collapse in the nineties. And within those nations that are prospering, the gap between those who are catching the waves of economic growth and those who are left behind is widening. The people of Andhra Pradesh, whose story I told at the beginning of the chapter, are representative of 180 million landless poor who live in Asia. Their numbers are the largest on the planet and growing.

Latin America lost a decade to their debt crisis, and there is every indication that it may well lose another decade. This means a tremendous reverse cash flow to Western banks—cash that is desperately needed to initiate economic growth among the marginalized in these countries. The economic futures of Haiti, El Salvador, Nicaragua, and Bolivia are particularly bleak. And the economies of Brazil and Argentina are also under incredible stress.

But by far the continent at greatest risk is Africa. As I write, African nations are simply not growing enough food or generating enough economic growth to address the basic needs of their exploding populations. The Horn of Africa is experiencing a monumental human crisis which is being seriously underreported by the Western press. We are likely to see major food crises throughout much of Africa by the end of the century. And as I will discuss later, the devastation of a continent-wide AIDS pandemic will cause enormous human suffering, and destruction of family units.

What is happening in Africa is happening throughout the Two-Thirds World. In some thirty-four nations, population growth is outstripping economic growth and food production. Many other nations are struggling simply to remain even.

What will happen in nations whose population continues to grow in excess of 3 percent a year while economic and agricultural growth is significantly lower? It probably means that the gap between rich and poor will widen into a chasm as we enter the twenty-first century. In fact, the United Nations Food and Agricultural Organization has predicted that between thirty-six and sixty-four countries are likely to experience "critical food problems by the year 2000."[39]

Waking Up to the Victims of the Backwaters

Within the poor nations of Asia, Latin America, and Africa, who are likely to be at greatest risk as we journey together toward the next century? James Grant, Executive Director of the United Nations International Children's Emergency Fund (UNICEF), answers by citing current trends that are likely to continue: "For one-sixth of mankind, the march of human progress has become a retreat." He goes on to say that, "by far, the heaviest consequences are being borne by children."[40] I have seen the children struggle for survival on the garbage dumps of Manila and in the slums of Calcutta—millions of children have little hope for the future.

In some Asian and African countries, children are intentionally crippled to make them more effective beggars. The Norwegian government reports that more than a million children a year all over the world are coerced into prostitution, pornography, or other forms of sexual exploitation. The Quakers report that two hundred thousand children have been conscripted into the armies of the Two-Thirds World.[41]

And millions of children all over the world work in virtual slavery in sweat-shops that would be appalling to Charles Dickens. They are often separated from their families and forced to work long hours producing rugs, textiles, and electronics for Western markets."[42]

On 28–29 September 1990, representatives of seventy nations meeting in New York at a United Nations summit on the plight of the world's children approved a declaration and set goals for the caring for children in the nineties. The World Bank pledged to increase lending to $509 million a year for health care and educational aid for children.[43]

But children are not the only ones at risk in the economic backwaters. Women are particularly vulnerable in communities of poverty. Women tend to bear a disproportionate burden in economically depressed areas. Bearing children, always a risky venture, is particularly dangerous in the Two-Thirds World, where poor nutrition and inadequate medical care contribute to a high mortality rate for both mothers and infants. Women, often discriminated against in Western nations, are even more oppressed economically in many of the poorer countries.

And women in the Two-Thirds World are also at increased risk from family violence. In Nepal, female babies often die of neglect because families prefer sons. In India, young brides are sometimes murdered by their husbands to secure their dowries. And as in industrialized nations, battering is common in many countries. Fifty percent of women in Thailand say they are beaten regularly by their husbands. In the *barrios* of Ecuador, 80 percent of women report they are abused.[44] Of course, the abuse of women and children is not simply a by-product of economic conditions; it is also a result of cultural factors . . . in all nations. But it is safe to assume that the pressures of living in poverty make abusive situations more likely to erupt.

Women and children, though larger in numbers, are not the only vulnerable groups in poor countries. Few Two-Thirds-World countries have any kind of "safety" net for the disabled and the elderly. If the family doesn't provide for their needs, their survival is their business alone. Anyone without family, therefore, is extremely vulnerable. So is anyone without land. In agrarian societies, the landless are at the mercy of those who possess land and power.

Refugees are at risk in any society, but especially so in the economic backwaters. More than thirteen million refugees are struggling for survival in the world today—fleeing from the conflict in the Middle East, famine in East Africa, or political oppression in Central America. As environmental systems increasingly break down civil strife continues, and as death squads remain active, it seems likely that the number of these refugees will increase in the nineties.

Beyond the issues of the impoverished, the exploited, and the landless in the nineties, we seem to be on the threshold of a new international disaster: a global AIDS epidemic. The total reported cases of AIDS internationally in July of 1989 was 167,373 cases—and the actual figure may be closer to a half million. It is predicted that by 1992 there will be at least 250,000 cases in sub-Saharan Africa alone. But those numbers represent sketchy and incomplete reports. Concern is growing that the African AIDS pandemic may be much worse than anyone now says. In some parts of Uganda, for instance, it is reported that one pregnant mother in four tests positive for the HIV virus. And it is unlikely that either public or private health care resources in Africa will be adequate to deal with this growing human tragedy.[45] By the end of the century, millions of children in Africa may be orphaned by this epidemic. In addition, we are seeing AIDS spread rapidly to Two-Thirds-World societies, such as Thailand and Brazil, that have widespread prostitution.

For those who have missed the rising tide of economic opportunity, the future is not promising. Already, more than one billion people with whom we share this planet live in a condition called "absolute poverty." Absolute poverty isn't quite starvation, but it isn't really subsistence, either. It means earning $370 dollars per person per year.

According to the World Health Organization, about 1.3 billion persons, more than 20 percent of the world's population, are seriously ill or malnourished. Access to clean water, immunization, and adequate nutrition could drastically change these statistics in the future.[46]

> Every three days the same number of people die of starvation as were killed by the Hiroshima atomic bomb. Approximately 40,000 children die each day from starvation. Fifteen million people are dying each year from starvation, malnutrition and hunger-related diseases. The numbers are staggering, incomprehensible.[47]

Our God is being crucified all over again in the suffering of the vulnerable ones. And as their suffering increases in the nineties, people of faith must significantly increase our compassionate response to the growing numbers of poor. We must mobilize a whole new movement of compassion and empowerment in partnership with our sisters and brothers in the Two-Thirds World.

David Korten, in his book on empowering the poor, reminds us that

> being among the world's privileged, you and I have a special obligation to think and act as a global citizen, to be a steward of whatever power we hold, to contribute to the transforming forces that are reshaping the world. The future of human society, of our children, depends on each of us.[48]

WAVES OF ECONOMIC CHANGE: AN AGENDA FOR RESPONSE

As the waves of economic change engulf the planet, the church is going to be confronted by a broad range of new challenges. Both in the Two-Thirds World and in the United States, the ranks of the impoverished are growing. If we fail to anticipate these new areas of human need and to respond compassionately, literally millions will lose their lives. Millions of others will lose their opportunity for a decent existence in tomorrow's world.

Outlined below is a summary of some of the economic challenges we have discussed in this chapter:

- anticipating the destabilization of families, communities, and entire societies when traditional cultures give way to modernization,

- questioning how the Asian and European regions might use their anticipated increase in affluence in response to escalating human and environmental needs,

- anticipating how these two regional coalitions will also use their growing political power to shape our common future,

- advocating that the United States reduce its export of unsafe or addictive products to other countries,

- encouraging economic growth in Eastern Europe and the Soviet Union in a way that doesn't smother the emerging spiritual renewal,

- calling all nations, but particularly the superpowers, to dramatically decrease their investment in military expenditures,

- preparing all Americans and particularly the young within our religious communities to downscale their economic expectations for the future and find other aspirations to which we can all give our lives,

- lobbying the United States government to get its economic house in order in a way that minimizes the impact on the poor overseas and at home,

- insisting, if a peace dividend does emerge by the end of the decade, that it be used to address the growing human and environmental needs in our midst,

- designing a strategy involving churches, the private sector, and the governments to empower the poorest members of our society economically,

- promoting sustainable agricultural and economic growth in the Two-Thirds World so that people are less vulnerable to the waves of economic change,

- advocating an open trade policy in which small nations have as much opportunity as those in regional coalitions to participate in international trade,

- promoting land reform, village level development, and urban empowerment to give hope for their rural communities while helping create the necessary infrastructure in Two-Thirds-World cities,

- creating programs that are particularly designed to empower the most vulnerable members of our global society—children, women, refugees; the aged, the disabled, and the landless.

WAVES OF ECONOMIC CHANGE: SIGNS OF HOPE

In spite of the escalating economic challenges that are likely to confront us in the nineties and beyond, God has not abandoned those in need. God is working through Christians all over the world to offer signs of hope.

Bread for the World has been particularly successful in lobbying the United States government to achieve structural change. In 1983, for example, it successfully lobbied to include a land-for-food provision in a piece of legislation offering aid and trade incentives to Caribbean-basin countries. "This provision set safeguards against removing land from the production of food for local consumption and turning such land into export crop production."[49]

HEED Bangladesh, a Christian relief and development agency, enabled Kamalganj, a beautiful rural area, to change from a net rice importing area to a net rice exporting area over approximately ten years, using loans to small farmers. As a result, the people who live in this region of Bangladesh have achieved "sustained livelihood security" and are much less vulnerable to changes in the international marketplace than they were before.

Another sign of hope that God is giving birth to something new is the rise of spontaneous Christian support groups called base communities. In Latin America and Asia, we are seeing both the church and the larger society being transformed from the bottom up through these communities of the poor that are both Protestant and Catholic. People come together in these small groups to study the Bible and pray in order to change their lives and their villages.

Base communities have been particularly fruitful in Brazil. "Alone, life is hard, but in a group, things begin to get easier," explained a member of a base community in a Rio de Janeiro slum, or *favela*. Slum mothers in São Paulo spoke similarly of how the base community was a rock of unity in the midst of hunger, sickness, and frequent repression by the police and military.

Though small, the base community groups in Brazil are spreading to the next street or village, crisscrossing the country in eighty thousand communities. In a country in which the poor have never had a voice, the growth in a relative short time of a movement with more than four million poor Brazilians is politically and socially significant.

For most poor people, the communities offer the first genuine experience of democracy at the local level. "'Fundamental in this experience,' said Frei Betto, a base community member, 'is liberty to think, to speak, to discuss, to decide, and to create.'"[50] And this new experience of democracy includes a growing sense of economic democracy; through cooperative action, the poor have a growing sense of control of their own economic future.

Similar cooperative action has been taken in the United States through organizations like community land trusts, which seek to preserve both farmland and housing for the poor. The community land trust offers the benefits of home ownership, security, fair equity, and a legacy for descendants "within a context which practically articulates the principle that land and housing should be treated as a covenant from one generation to the next, rather than as a commodity."[51]

Eastern College in St. Davids, Pennsylvania, is the first school in the United States to offer an M.B.A. to train students to be entrepreneurs among the marginalized. Graduates are working overseas and in the United States to enable those at the margins of society to become economically self-reliant.

WAVES OF ECONOMIC CHANGE: WAKING UP TO OUR CHRISTIAN RESPONSIBILITY

We are receiving a wake-up call from the twenty-first century. We are being awakened to a world in which centrally planned economies are in eclipse, in which national economies are being globalized. We are awakening to a future in which the gap between rich and poor is continuing to widen.

How can we as Christians live responsibly in such a world? How can we address the growing needs of the poor? Where will we find a vision that will enable us to live and respond with integrity as we seek to steward our lives and institutions in a new, more unequal future?

There are probably few topics which invite greater division between mainline and conservative Christians than the topic of economics. Both groups are concerned for the needs of others, but they have vastly different notions of how to address those needs.

Mainline Christians typically take the position that political and economic structures need to be changed to operate more justly in behalf of the poor. Recent statements expressing this viewpoint include The United Church of Christ's (FCC) 1987 study paper, "Christian Faith and Economic Life"; the United Methodists' 1988 Resolution on Economic Justice; the Episcopal Urban Bishops' Coalition's 1987 Study Guide, "Economic Justice and Christian Conscience"; the Presbyterian Church's (USA) 1984 statement, "Christian Faith and Economic Justice"; and the Catholic bishops' pastoral letter of 1988, entitled, "Pastoral Letter on Catholic Social Teaching and the U.S. Economy." Of all these statements, the Catholic pastoral letter was most widely publicized and therefore provoked the greatest amount of discussion.

In contrast, conservative Christians have invested little energy developing denominational statements reflecting their positions on economic issues. However, there is no shortage of books and articles authored by conservatives on economic issues, from George F. Gilder's *Wealth and Poverty* to Michael Novak's *The American Vision: An Essay on the Future of Democratic Capitalism.*

It is important to recognize that not all conservative Christians share a conservative economic ideology, which generally involves giving the marketplace the maximum amount of freedom to operate without governmental interference. For example, in 1987 a group of evangelical economists, theologians, and social ethicists met in Oxford, England. They represented a broad spectrum of economic views. Together they hammered out "The Oxford Declaration on Christian Faith and Economics."[52] This statement attempts to build bridges between economic views that are often seriously polarized and to find a biblical viewpoint that brings Christians together.

Mainliners and conservatives find some of their greatest conflict regarding what causes economic inequities between rich and poor and how those inequities should best be remedied. Conservatives, for example, tend to dismiss out of hand any suggestion that the prosperity of the wealthy has anything to do with the impoverishment of those who are poorer. They tend to blame the poor for their condition, insisting that their poverty is largely a by-product of local corruption, cultural conditions, and a failure to develop an effective free market economy.

One example of this perspective is reflected in the conservative Catholic lay response to the Catholic bishops' pastoral letter:

> We reject as empirically unfounded the proposition that the wealth of some causes the poverty of others. We reject the proposition that the poverty of poor nations is caused by the wealth of richer nations.[53]

Several years ago, commentator Paul Harvey presented this viewpoint even more starkly. Backward nations, he said, could solve their problems if they would "stop producing more babies and start producing more food."[54]

Ecumenical groups, on the other hand, don't blame the poor for their condition. In fact, they seldom mention how the local conditions in the communities of the poor contribute to their impoverishment. Instead, they focus their attention almost exclusively on external economic and political structures. In other words, they tend to blame the wealthier nations and corporations for the condition of the world's poor.

It is utter nonsense, in my opinion, for conservatives to contend that, in an interdependent and interconnected world, there is no relationship between the plight of the poor and the prosperity of wealthier nations. Ron Sider documents the fact that from colonial times to present, the entire international trade structure has been designed to benefit wealthier nations, often at the expense of poorer nations.[55]

But greed is not the exclusive province of wealthy capitalist nations and corporations, as some ecumenical material would seem to imply. Greed is also very much alive, well, and at work both within Two-Thirds-World governments and even the local communities in which the poor struggle for existence. During the seven years I worked with projects in Haiti I saw a number of examples. Sometimes Haitian farmers would not save back enough rice from their harvests to feed their families for a full year. When they ran out of rice two-thirds of the way through the year, they would discover the reality of local greed. Typically, during this kind of food crisis, local merchants would raise the price of their rice fourfold, causing many families to sell not only their livestock but some of their children into servitude, simply to survive.

There is also a great gulf fixed between mainliners and conservatives on how to ameliorate the poverty of the marginalized. Ecumenical Christians lean toward "statist" solutions that place primary emphasis on government redistribution of resources. The Episcopalians insist, for instance: "Government at all levels must be challenged once again to play a responsible role in correcting the inequities in the economic crisis."[56]

While the state must certainly continue to play a major role in addressing the needs of those at the margins, times are changing. There is a growing question of how much the state can or should do. It seems clear that the church and the private sector are going to have to do more. And yet I have found that many mainline churches that speak out the most about social justice and the poor often invest the least money and time in directly addressing these issues. Their level of investment calls into question how serious they are about the poor and issues of justice.

It is not only time for mainline churches to look at their own giving patterns and direct involvement in working with the poor; it is also time for them to look at the potential of the market for empowerment. There is tremendous promise in small economic initiatives to empower the poor both overseas and at home.

Conservatives usually look to the marketplace rather than to the state. Michael Novak argues that the marketplace is like a lottery in which everyone has an opportunity to play. "The system doesn't guarantee success," Novak explains, but "it does guarantee opportunity. It multiplies occasions for luck and good fortune."[57] Mark the Match Boy, a creation of novelist Horatio Alger, was of the same opinion as Novak. His idea of what it takes to succeed was "a little luck and a little pluck."[58]

But neither Novak nor Alger nor many other conservatives recognize the reality that many simply don't have a genuine opportunity to participate in this game. The world's poor will need a lot more than "luck and pluck" to have a chance to succeed in the worldwide economic lottery—because the playing field simply isn't level.

While the poor can successfully participate in local economic initiatives, ecumenical Christians are correct in insisting structures must be changed if the poor are to successfully participate in larger economic arenas. We must all bring pressure to bear to enable the market to operate more justly. If we are to have any hope of addressing tomorrow's escalating waves of human need, ecumenical and conservative Christians must resolve their differences and find ways to work together. We will need to develop a collaborative initiative that creatively brings together Christians, the government, the private sector, and the communities of the poor, empowering those at margins fully to participate in life as the Creator intended.

If ecumenical and conservative Christians are to work together, we must begin by developing a common vision but not the common vision they already seem to share—the Western Dream. Many conservative Christians, out of their conservative economic ideology, enthusiastically embrace the essentially economic aspirations of that Dream. Many ecumenical Christians uncritically embrace the Western Dream as well; the only difference is that they want to build an escalator into the Dream so the poor can get a little taste of the "good life" as well.

Certainly, as more and more people turn to a free-market economy, the Western Dream is gaining favor all over the world. In fact, Francis Fukuyama has written a very controversial essay that suggests that this worldwide turn toward a market-oriented economic system may indeed mark "the end of history"[59]—that when all nations adopt a full-market economy we will have arrived at the ultimate destination history intended.

Fukuyama's essay highlights my fundamental problem with the Western Dream. Is our ultimate human destiny nothing more than the international embrace of free-market economics? Are we really content to view the better future, as the Western Dream does, in largely economic and materialistic terms? Aren't the vision and the values of the Western Dream part of the driving force that is placing our common future at risk?

Isn't our environment imperiled because of our unquestioned commitment to a vision of conquest and consumerism? Isn't our humanity and spirituality imperiled by our unexamined devotion to a vision of scientific and technological progress? Aren't the lives of our young imperiled because we have sold them the wrong dream—a dream of acquisition, consumption, and status? And aren't the world's poor imperiled by our unashamed pursuit of a dream that requires such an enormous share of the earth's bounty?

I believe the hardest work Christians have to do in the economic arena is to struggle toward a new vision—an alternative vision that transcends the acquisitive, materialistic, and reductionist impulses of the Western Dream. That new vision will not find its origin in an economic ideology of either the right or the left, but in the God who created all things—and wants us to be collaborators in making all things new, including economic conditions of all peoples.

Douglas Meek in his provocative work, *God the Economist,* asserts that "God does not appear in the modern market. For many economists this is as it should be." He goes on to ask, "Is God absent from the modern economy? One could hardly claim that God is absent from the social order that surrounds and shores up the market economy."[60]

This absence of God from our economic conversations is at the root of our inability to reach consensus on important economic issues. We tend to think about economics as divorced from both God and God's intentions for the human future. As a consequence, we find ourselves limited to either the economics of the right or the left.

As soon as we bring God into the equation, everything begins to change. The Scripture presents an economic premise that is Good News to neither the capitalist, the liberal, nor the Marxist: "The earth is the Lord's and the fullness thereof." If we accept that premise, then our economics can ignore neither God's role nor God's purposes. If we believe that God is actively involved in all arenas of life, including the economic, then we can no longer leave economic issues exclusively to the marketplace or to the state.

In that first covenant community, God's purposes weren't seen as just spiritual and relational, but as economic, too. The people of God were expected to "manifest a special concern for the most vulnerable members of the community: widows, orphans, the poor and strangers in the land."[61]

In the nineties, we must unmask the powers and expose the outrageous physical suffering they cause for millions all over the earth. And we must return to Scripture, not to develop a new economic theory, but to hear God's call to us. It is a call to follow a new vision—and radically to alter the present systems so that they conform more fully to God's purposes both for creation and for those "most vulnerable members."

Questions for Discussion

1. In what major ways are national economies being globalized as we approach the twenty-first century?
2. What are likely to be the three major economic regions as we conclude the century, and which are likely to experience the greatest growth?
3. What is the probable economic future of the Asian region?
4. What is the probable economic future of the European region?

5. What is the probable economic future of the Soviet Union?
6. What is the probable economic future of the Americas?
7. What will be the impact of a chronically stagnant or recessive economy on the young in the United States? On the middle class? On the poor?
8. What is likely to be the future of economic growth among the poorer nations in Asia, Latin America, and Africa?
9. What kind of economic growth do we need to see in the Two-Thirds World?
10. What is our biblical responsibility as the people of God to address the urgent global economic challenges in our own lives, congregations, and Christian organizations?

5

Waking Up to a Changing Parade of Power

As the two black limousines cruised quietly down California Street on a sunny San Francisco afternoon, I stood in stunned silence. Flags flew from their fenders, motorcycle police provided escort, people stopped to stare. In the front limo rode President Harry S. Truman, apparently oblivious to the stir his arrival was causing. Behind him, in another car, Soviet Foreign Minister Vyacheslav Molotov sat very erect, his eyes straight ahead. And several car lengths to their rear, but gradually gaining on them, stretched other limos containing other foreign dignitaries. I watched in awe as the multipower parade wound slowly toward the Fairmont Hotel.

It was June, 1945. President Truman, Foreign Minister Molotov, and dozens of leaders from other countries were meeting in an attempt to create an international peace forum.

The Allied invasion of Normandy had recently ended the war with Germany, and the war with Japan was rapidly drawing to a conclusion. World peace was in the air; you could almost reach out and touch it. Never again did people want to see the earth girdled by an international conflagration. As a consequence, the world's leaders were highly motivated to find nonlethal ways to resolve future international conflicts. And as you know, that gathering in San Francisco was successful. It culminated in the historic signing of the United Nations Charter on 26 June 1945, creating a new forum for the resolution of international disputes.

As an eight-year-old living only a block away from this historic happening, I would walk up Nob Hill to watch the parade every afternoon after I completed my paper route. But one afternoon I varied my routine. Instead of racing up to California Street to watch the dignitaries come and go, I went exploring on the roof of the apartment house where I had delivered my last copies of the *San Francisco News*.

To my amazement, I found two-dozen soldiers bivouacked on the roof with tents, supplies, and machine guns. Apparently, because we were still at war with Japan, San Francisco was an armed camp. I was told that every five-story building on Nob Hill had a contingent of soldiers secretly stationed there. And every building sixteen stories or higher actually had antiaircraft guns. After my discovery, I changed my routine, heading up to the rooftops daily to exchange my extra newspapers for candy bars before scaling Nob Hill to watch the parade.

Looking back on that experience, I see it as something of a metaphor for our world today. While earnestly desiring and struggling toward peace, we still find ourselves preparing and arming for war. In this in-between time, peace doesn't come very easily. And the global parade itself is rapidly changing, as even a glance at the headlines tells us.

Nearly a half-century after the founding of the United Nations, we find ourselves at another historic watershed. The lines drawn exactically after World War II to divide East from West have been suddenly erased. Walls have been torn down and military checkpoints destroyed. Germany is reunited. Even as I write, major new negotiations are beginning between Arabs and Jews. Despite ongoing threats, something new is being born that hates walls, despises oppression, and opposes war. New songs of freedom are being sung not only in the streets of Bucharest and Warsaw, but in Soweto and Port-au-Prince. And God is in these songs of freedom, giving birth to something new. We need to pray that these new movements of freedom will not be aborted.

Listen to Javier Perez de Cuellar, Secretary-General of the United Nations, speaking in 1989. "The last three years have witnessed almost unimaginable changes, the prospects of realizing the vision expressed in the charter of the United Nations seem better than at any time since the organization was founded."[1] And every indication signals that the United Nations is likely to play a more significant role in the search for peace in the future than it has in its first fifty years.

In this chapter we will seek to anticipate how the political parade is changing and where it is likely to take us as we enter the twenty-first century. We will briefly review the rise of the state in the twentieth century and the struggle for human rights before going on to discuss the dramatic changes in the international power parade. Then we will explore how the political parade in our own country is likely to change as we journey through the nineties. We will look at some signs of hope. And we will discuss what our Christian responsibility is to respond to both the political opportunities and the political challenges that are likely to fill our common future.

WAKING UP TO A MULTIPOWER PARADE

Looking Backward on the Passing Parade

Zbigniew Brzezinski calls the twentieth century "the century of the State." He asserts that during this time "the State, by harnessing political power and by employing the newly available tools of social engineering made possible by the onset of industrialism . . . became the central focus of social life, of social obedience, and of personal loyalty."[2]

Brzezinski holds that the marriage of human rationality and emerging technological power to political ideology spawned the duel totalitarian offspring of fascism and communism:

> Philosophically, Lenin and Hitler were both advocates of ideologies that called for social engineering on a vast scale, that abrogated to themselves the role of arbiters of truth, and that subordinated society to an ideological morality, one based on class warfare and the other on racial supremacy, and that justified any action that advanced their chosen historical missions.[3]

And, of course, Marxism was in part a reaction to yet another type of modern state—the capitalist state. The emerging blend of industrialization, capitalism, and the power of a technocratic elite caused severe economic disparities and social dislocations in nineteenth-century Europe. And the economic disparities created by the "class oriented" capitalist system were a primary reason Karl Marx's theories gained a philosophical toehold. Brzezinski explains,

> Marxist theory seemed to provide the key to understanding human history, an analytical tool for assessing the dynamics of social and political change, a sophisticated interpretation of economic life, and a set of insights into social motivation. At the same time, the emphasis was placed on political action to promote a redemptive "revolution," and on all-embracing state control to achieve a rationally planned just society.[4]

The twentieth century has indeed been "the century of the State" in many ways. In the thirties and forties, the combination of German and Italian fascism, and Japanese nationalism threatened to dominate the world. Fortunately, it was defeated. In addition, for most of the century, a huge percentage of the world's population lived under the totalitarian rule of Marxist regimes in the USSR and China. But now Marxist regimes all over the world are in eclipse. Even those such as Cuba, North Korea, and China, haven't succumbed to the pressure to join the parade toward democratic reform, are finding the costs of isolation are growing. And despite the fact that conservative forces are taking back some power in the Soviet Union, they are unlikely to silence the cry for democratization.

In these countries, God is stirring something within the human spirit that will no longer endure subjugation to any state—Marxist, fascist, or capitalist. People are insisting that they be granted freedom, basic human rights, and the opportunity to have a voice in the political organizations that shape their lives. As we will show, the singular power of the state will in the future be under assault by those inside forces who want to share power and outside forces who want to influence power.

Welcoming the Worldwide Parade
for Human Rights and Political Freedom

"As the twentieth century comes to an end, a movement for the renewal of democracy is gaining strength around the globe," declares Richard J. Barnet, a policy analyst in Washington, D.C.

> Local experiments in grassroots democracy are emerging in the Philippines, Brazil, and other Two-Thirds-World countries where the state is unable or unwilling to provide services or help create economic conditions that will enable their people to meet basic needs. From South Korea and Chile to Poland and South Africa, people are demanding a voice in their own lives, including the political right to participate in public decisions and a freedom from state abuse of their basic human rights.[5]

Even as refugees return to a devastated Kuwait, they are returning with a call for democratic reforms.

What does it mean to live without such rights—to live at the whim of the state? What does it mean to be arrested by your government and held without due process? What does it mean to be in detention awaiting interrogation, torture, and possibly death? Winnie Mandela answers these questions out of her own experience in a South African prison:

> It means being held in a single cell with the light bulb burning twenty-four hours a day so that I lost track of all time and was unable to tell whether it was night or day. . . . The frightful emptiness of those hours of solitude is unbearable. Your company is your solitude, your blanket, your mat, your sanitary bucket, your mug and yourself. . . . All of this is preparation for the inevitable HELL—interrogation. It is meant to crush your individuality

entirely, to change you into a docile being from whom no resistance can arise. . . . There have been alleged suicides in detention; you keep asking yourself whether you will leave the cell alive.[6]

From Guatemala to Beijing, thousands of prisoners have *not* left their cells alive. Tens of thousands have disappeared. Millions have been tortured or killed by their governments. The principalities and powers have in this century worked relentlessly through the state to crush the human spirit. Today, hopefully, the totalitarian regimes are beginning to lose their grip.

The founding of the United Nations in 1945 represented one of the first major challenges to "the century of the State." In 1948, the United Nations published the first Universal Declaration of Human Rights, which challenged the unqualified right of the state to abridge the essential human rights of its citizens.

In the intervening years since the U.N. was established, a score of human-rights organizations have arisen—including the effective Amnesty International and Americas Watch. Such organizations have had considerable success using the pressure of international opinion to persuade governments to stop the kidnapping, torture, and murder of their citizens. And the Carter administration made the concern for human rights a centerpiece of American foreign policy in the seventies.

Granted, the abuse of human rights on the part of the state continues in many parts of the world. Since 1980, the U.N. working group on enforced disappearances has investigated more than fifteen thousand cases in forty different countries. In 1989 we experienced afresh the callous brutality of the Marxist state in China as it massacred protesters at Tienanmen Square and relentlessly suppressed the cries of its people for political freedom and human rights. Salvadoran death squads, with the complicity of the military and the government, have killed seventy-two thousand of their own people—including Archbishop Romero, four women from a religious order, and six Jesuit priests, along with the housekeeper and her daughter. At this point, no one has been brought to justice for these atrocities. Particularly troubling is the ongoing United States support of this regime and its military, many of whom were trained in the United States.

Until recently, despite the efforts of individuals and organizations, the war for human rights didn't seem to be going very well. But somehow the winds of change blowing over the last few years seem to be influencing regimes of both the right and left to slowly move toward the rule of law and the guarantee of basic human rights of all their citizens.

Frank Laubach, in his classic work, *The World Is Learning Compassion,*[7] argues convincingly that this growing concern for the rights and dignity of the individual wasn't born in New York, Bonn, or Tokyo; it had its origin in a small Palestinian village called Bethlehem. He reasons that the impulse to protect and promote human rights comes directly from a Judeo-Christian affirmation of the inherent value and dignity of the individual. Of course, people from many socioreligious backgrounds have embraced a concern for human rights out of their own values, but I still believe Laubach's analysis is accurate. And I believe that the church must remain alert to the fact that protecting the rights of all people is inherent in our religious commitment. In the nineties, we must find creative new ways to collaborate with all that God is doing to defeat the powers and ensure the human rights and dignity of all people.

Making Way for a Multipower Parade

As we race toward a new century, not only is there a growing demand for citizens to have a greater voice in their governments and a greater freedom from human-rights violations; there is also a growing realization that nations besides the United States and Soviet Union are likely to play a greater role in shaping our global future. As World War II ended, these two superpowers emerged as the two obvious leaders in the planetary parade. But the abrupt end of the Cold War at the close of the eighties signaled the beginning of a fundamental realignment in global power. And the changing balance of economic leadership makes a major realignment of power almost inevitable.

In an increasingly interdependent world, change in any sector has significant impact on all other sectors. Over time, for example, the critical economic decline in the Soviet Union will erode its political influence in the international arena. The United States's slide from its preeminent economic position will affect our country's political power as well. Over the long term, I believe our obvious military supremacy will not be enough to halt this slide.

Robert Keohane, in his seminal work *After Hegemony*, points out that, since World War II, the United States has been the center of a vast economic hegemony that has largely dictated the terms of economic relationships among Western nations. But that picture is changing rapidly, and the change has political implications as well. Keohane writes,

> The United States is less willing than formerly to define its interests in terms complementary to those in Europe and Japan. The Europeans, in particular, are less inclined to defer to American initiatives, nor do they believe so strongly that they must do so in order to obtain essential military protection from the Soviet Union. Thus the subjective elements of American hegemony have been eroded as much as the tangible power resources upon which the hegemonic system rests. But neither the Europeans nor the Japanese are likely to have the capacity to become hegemonic powers themselves in the foreseeable future.[8]

Since neither Japan nor Europe is likely to fill the hegemonic vacuum soon, Keohane predicts we will enter a period of growing economic and political destabilization until a new alternative arrangement is found.[9]

If Keohane is correct, what are some of the implications of the erosion of United States hegemony for the global political future? The clearest possibility is that the international scene will no longer be dominated by only two super-powers.

For decades the American-Soviet contest has dominated the international conversations. But as the Soviet economy faces possible chaos and the American economy struggles with chronic slow growth, other nations with economies on the upswing seem to be vying for superpower status.

By the end of the century, therefore, we are likely to see not only the regionalization of our global economy, but a rapid movement from a bipolar to a multipolar world. As we enter the twenty-first century, the parade of superpowers will probably include not only the United States and the Soviet Union (if it doesn't totally self-destruct), but also Japan, Germany, and even the new European Community. And in the wings will be still others that aspire to superpower status, including the People's Republic of China.

How will the geopolitical balance of power change if the two nations who lost World War II become superpowers? As the United States and the Soviets continue to scale down their nuclear stockpile, what is the possibility we could move into a period of sustained global peace? Indeed, as pressure grows for totalitarian regimes of both right and left to move toward the rule of law, will we see a new international order emerge in the nineties?

Joseph S. Nye argues in his book, *Bound to Lead: The Changing Nature of American Power*,[10] that the influence of the United States in the world is not in decline. But with all due respect, how can we enter a multipower world, in which there are more key players, without seeing the influence of both the Soviet Union and the United States diminish somewhat? And how can the United States hope to maintain the same level of political influence when it is evident we are losing our dominant economic position in the world? Can we really count on our unquestioned military superiority to replace the steady erosion of our economic preeminence?

David Abshire, president of the Center for Strategic International Studies, points out that times are changing and that our approach to the use of power must change as well. "The nature of American global economic leadership in the nineties will necessitate a different approach. As our relative power position declines, persuasion, coalition building, and the art of the 'indirect approach' become increasingly important."[11] And the Soviets are also rapidly learning to use greater diplomatic initiatives to achieve their foreign policy goals.

The new reality of a multipower world may also force the United States to think twice about violating international law. No longer will we be able to mine the harbors of nations like Nicaragua or invade nations like Panama in violation of not only international law, but also international treaties. We will be pressured to work at solving international problems multilaterally instead of unilaterally.

The increasing interdependence of our world means that all participants will need to become more internationally informed and also more sensitive to the culture and concerns of other peoples. This could be a particular problem not only for American leadership, but for the American populace. My travels to other industrialized nations have convinced me that American citizens are less informed on international issues than virtually any other people I have visited. And quite frankly, the level of international illiteracy seems to be getting worse, particularly among the young in the United States. If this condition isn't remedied, I can see only increasing problems for the Americans required to be team players in a game they don't understand. And our national leadership will become even more successful in manipulating the opinions of the uninformed.

In light of this prevailing provincialism, the church, which is an international movement, will have yet another new assignment in the nineties. The church will have the responsibility to enable its members—Americans in particular—to become world Christians, developing a global perspective not only on the emerging religious issues, but also on the political, cultural, and economic concerns that will fill tomorrow's world.

The Changing Parade in the Soviet Union and Europe

Ironically, while the Soviet Union is slowly losing ground politically and Marxist ideology is losing influence all over the world, Mikhail Gorbachev is still recognized by many as one of the most influential political leaders of this era. "Mikhail Gorbachev is what Sidney Hook called an 'event-making man': a man whose actions transform the historical context in which he acts."[12]

Increasingly, however, it appears that Gorbachev has lost control both of the reforms he inaugurated and of the nation he rules. In early 1991, Gorbachev's future seems very uncertain and the future of the Soviet people is also in question.

Nevertheless, it is doubtful that anyone, including Gorbachev or even the Soviet military, will be able to stop the process of reformation taking place in Eastern Europe, the momentum of expanding treaties in arms control, and the new-era openness in the Soviet Union. Allen Lynch, a scholar in Soviet studies at Columbia University, argues that the reforms have gone too far to ever return to a neo-Stalinist political order. However, he predicts that without the requisite economic power, the USSR will be unable to sustain its political preeminence. Lynch concludes that "preoccupation with what Russians call the 'international relations' within the Soviet Union itself, practically assures the marginalization of Soviet Russia in global affairs. This is as true for any future Soviet or Russian leadership as it is for Gorbachev today."[13]

Vitaly Korotich, editor of a liberal Soviet weekly, forecasts that a number of Soviet republics are likely to secede and then be reintegrated in a new political coalition. He speculates that these republics could even become a part of a new integrated Europe.[14]

But conservative Soviet leaders, the military, and the KGB have shown they will resort to whatever action is necessary to maintain the integrity of the Soviet Union and their own power. (Part of their motivation, no doubt, is the realization that the Balkanization of the Soviet Union would mean the eclipse of the Soviet Union as a superpower.) The struggle toward national self-determination within the Soviet Union, therefore, is likely to be prolonged and possibly bloody. If the Soviet Union is fragmented, there would be immediate international concern about who is in control of their widely dispersed nuclear arsenal.

Such ongoing Soviet unrest could mean a period of growing destabilization, ethnic unrest, and bloodshed in the republics. It is also likely to have a destabilizing impact on Western Europe in particular and international politics in general.

Two primary scenarios have been proposed for the future of Eastern Europe. The first is a "common European home" . . . the vision of a united Europe that includes the Eastern-European countries. This is the optimistic scenario in which all the nations of Eastern Europe successfully adopt democratic governments, negotiate the transition to free-market economies, and begin working cooperatively with Western-European neighbors for common European goals and possible participation in both a new European economic and political order.

A number of leaders have had such a vision for a united Europe. Even before the destruction of the Berlin Wall, Pope John Paul II advocated "a European future and echoed [former French president Charles] de Gaulle's 'Atlantic to the Urals' call and prefigured Gorbachev's 'common European home.'"[15]

And one cannot listen to the inspiring words of Czech president Vaclav Havel without believing that God is indeed at work within history and that this growing advocacy of democratic government and human rights can touch not only the nations of Eastern Europe, but all nations:

> In less than 15 years, this simple concept of human rights came close to accomplishing what the theories of "containment," "deterrence," and "mutual assured destruction" could not. Let us note that unlike these concepts, backed by the most impressive collection of hardware that man has ever assembled, this was a concept purely spiritual. These changes and steps towards integration in the West now offer Europe a chance to become whole after 40 years of dual existence (or non-existence). And for the first time in its history, the old continent has a chance to do so not through war, but through a consensus of its nations and people. Such chances do not occur twice.[16]

Not everyone shares Havel's unifying vision, however. The second scenario that is proposed for Eastern Europe is not one of consensus and cooperation, but rather one of conflict and destabilization. Several historians have called up memories of Europe before World War I, a time of ethnic unrest and civil strife. They argue that, without the restraints of totalitarian governments, old ethnic and national divisions may be renewed.

Frankly, I believe the pessimistic scenario seems more probable. A number of the nations involved are fighting an uphill battle to turn their economies around or to develop truly democratic forms of government. If these nations are not effectively brought into the new economic community of Western Europe, you can be sure this failure will provoke growing unrest, ethnic conflict, anti-Semitism, and civil conflict—and perhaps even war. Growing nationalism is likely to spawn the kind of destabilizing fragmentation that took place in Yugoslavia in the summer of 1991. The nineties is likely to be a stormy decade for the USSR and for Eastern Europe.

One of the major keys to the future of both the Soviet Union and Eastern Europe is the future of the reunified German state. To the extent that Germany grows in economic and political power, it will have the ability to draw others into its orb of progress, growth, and influence. But right now, even Germany is finding the challenge of rehabilitating its eastern addition more difficult than it anticipated.

Of course, with the end of the Warsaw Pact and the cessation of Soviet expansionism throughout the world, many "client states" are scrambling to find alternative sources of military and economic aid. Leftist regimes from North Korea to Cuba are attempting to assess the implications of the Soviet reforms for their own futures.

The implications for Cuba are abundantly clear. It can no longer count on $15 million a day from the Soviet Union to sustain its bankrupt economy. Like it or not, Fidel Castro and the leadership of Cuba will be forced in the nineties to initiate major economic reforms and perhaps democratic reforms as well.

WAKING UP TO OPPORTUNITIES FOR PEACEMAKING AND DISARMAMENT

Opportunities for Peace in the Middle East

The events in the Persian Gulf War during 1990 and 1991 took many people by surprise. No sooner had we begun celebrating the end of the Cold War and looking forward to a new era of peace than we found ourselves plunged into the largest military campaign since World War II.

It will be left to historians to debate whether this massive military action was really necessary to force Iraq to withdraw from Kuwait—the stated objective for the United States's involvement. As the war progressed, however, a second major objective became clear: to neutralize Iraqi president Saddam Hussein's considerable war-making capability. And this raises a number of questions that cast the war in a very different light.

For instance, how did Iraq develop this enormous capacity for military aggression? Why did it take governments who eventually formed the international coalition against Saddam so long to recognize this growing regional threat? Who helped Saddam create this huge war machine? And why were we so concerned for the future of the small monarchy of Kuwait in the first place?

Part of our concern was obviously motivated by our growing dependency on oil imported from the Middle East and by our total failure during the eighties to develop any kind of a national energy policy to reduce our dependence on foreign oil. In 1980, I wrote in the *Mustard Seed Conspiracy*:

> Amory Lovins, in his article, "Energy Strategy: The Road Not Taken?" and the Harvard Energy Study both maintain the United States could learn to live "within our energy income" if we mounted a serious national program of conservation (our cheapest energy source) and the creative use of energy alternatives. Such action not only would improve our economic situation and reduce our political vulnerability; it would also mean more energy at lower prices for other planetary inhabitants—particularly the poor. And it would greatly reduce the chance of young Americans' being sent to war to maintain our energy-extravagant lifestyles. Unfortunately, our national energy policy seems to be moving in the opposite direction.[17]

Regrettably, this forecast was accurate. Young Americans were sent to war, along with thousands of young Brits, French, Saudi Arabians, Kuwaitis, Syrians, Egyptians—and tens of thousands of young Iraqis.

Not only was this war precipitated in part because we lacked a national energy policy (and the one proposed by Mr. Bush after the war still lacks any mention of energy conservation and development of alternative forms of energy). It also came about because we lacked a coherent foreign policy in the Middle East for almost a decade. In the absence of such a policy, we repeatedly found ourselves reacting situationally. For example, during the war between Iran and Iraq in the eighties, we first aligned ourselves with Saddam Hussein against Iran and supplied him with arms. Then, in the series of negotiations that resulted in the "Irangate" debacle, we traded arms for hostages—thus arming the Iranians as well.

It's becoming clearer that the major reason we went to war had little to do with Kuwait and everything to do with destroying Iraq's enormous war machine, which we helped create. Virtually everyone in the coalition who had a hand in destroying Saddam's war machine also had a hand in creating it. The USSR provided Baghdad with 47 percent of its military supplies. France supplied $6.7 billion worth of war materiel. West Germany not only provided $860 million worth of arms, but West German businesses helped the Iraqis build their infamous chemical warfare plants. (Since the Gulf War, Germany has been struggling to make amends to Israel, because the memories of German gas chambers are still so vivid for Jewish people.) Italy and Britain supplied $520 million, while the United States provided military supplies worth $360 million. And much of the money for these purchases came from the nations of OPEC . . . specifically Kuwait and Saudi Arabia.[18]

One of the lessons from this war, therefore, is that the militarization of the Middle East is not likely to bring stability to the region. Some imaginative new diplomatic initiatives and a gradual demilitarization of the region will be required to defuse this powder keg.

Of course the big losers in our assisting Saddam to create this huge military capability were the people of the region . . . particularly those living in Kuwait and Iraq. We still have no idea of the full extent of Iraqi casualties—they have been estimated at a hundred thousand or more.

As a Christian, I am frankly appalled at how readily most Americans celebrate our remarkably low casualties and seem largely indifferent to the enormous human loss suffered by Arab peoples in this war. I am equally appalled at the total failure of the United States government to anticipate the devastating consequences of the war, particularly for Kurdish peoples.

I know of a few churches, mostly affiliated with the National Council of Churches, who have contacted Iraqi churches (approximately 10 percent of the Iraqi people are Christians)—reaching out in a spirit of reconciliation, asking for forgiveness, and working for healing in the midst of devastation. But the majority of American churches seem relatively unconcerned with the pain of their Arab sisters and brothers. I encourage Christians in North America and Western Europe to make a special effort, in the aftermath of this devastating war, to reach out to Arab people both abroad and in our own countries and to begin the process of reconciliation and the restoration of their homelands.

Americans also seem largely oblivious to the extent to which the enormous devastation of Arab populations and Arab lands has affected Arab attitudes toward the West. My travels in the Middle East and my listening to conversations with Arab peoples convince me that the Gulf War has fueled deep animosities among many Arabs and has renewed ancient resentments of "Western interests." I am afraid these animosities will simmer for decades, bringing about a permanent Arab-Western schism, if we fail to respond to the aspirations of Arab peoples.

What else can we expect from this region in coming decades? We will likely see a growing struggle in the Middle East between those who want to replace Arab monarchies and dictatorships with democracies and those who want to create Islamic states. I suspect those preferring the Islamic option are likely to gain the upper hand. At any rate, change is definitely on the way for the entire region.

The major positive consequence of the Gulf War has been to set up a historic opportunity for lasting peace between the Arab nations and Israel. If the United States pursues this unique opportunity for Middle East peace with the same vigor with which it prosecuted the war, there is a possibility of success.

Any successful accord will, of course, require that Arab nations recognize Israel's right to exist. But it will also require Israel to exchange land for peace and to allow the institution of some kind of Palestinian homeland. Since Israel occupied the West Bank and the Gaza Strip, it has systematically confiscated huge parcels of land that belonged to Palestinian peoples. There will never be peace in the region until Israel acts justly and relinquishes land to a people it has systematically dispossessed.

Achieving peace in the Middle East could bring a welcome period of stability not only to the region, but to the entire world. But failure to conclude a successful Middle East accord between Israel and its Arab neighbors could significantly increase international destabilization and the danger of a conflagration that threatens everyone's future. The people of this region could enter a new century held hostage to the same old fears and animosities—and the danger of conflict would grow.

Muslims, Jews, and Christians are children of the same parents, Abraham and Sarah. We are people of the same book—the Old Testament—and our faiths intersect in the same city—Jerusalem. We need to join hands in praying for the peace of Jerusalem and indeed of the entire region.

Opportunities for Peace in South Africa

South Africa is in the throes of a very traumatic birth process. What isn't clear is what type of nation is being born. Demographic change will most likely play a decisive role in South Africa's future, because the black majority is growing much more rapidly than the ruling white minority. So will the actual events that surround the restructuring of South Africa. Will we see the emergence of a new government in which blacks and whites truly share power—or something less? Will the new government be delivered peacefully, as Namibia was, or will it be a violent birth?

There are no guarantees that the new South Africa can be born without further bloodshed. Killings in the townships during 1990 and 1991 were seen by many as a deliberate effort to interrupt the process of peaceful change. And yet the government took decisive action during those years to dismantle apartheid.

With the release of black leader Nelson Mandela in 1990, South African president F. W. de Klerk took an important first step to end apartheid and create a new South Africa in which all peoples have a voice in their government. Then, on 1 February 1991, President de Klerk took further decisive action

> to smash the legal bedrock of apartheid by announcing he would scrap the remaining laws on which South Africa's ideology of racial discrimination has long rested. In a major speech opening the 1991 session of the Parliament, Mr. de Klerk said legislation would soon be introduced to repeal the land acts of 1913 and 1936, which reserved most of the country's land for a white minority, the Groups Areas Act of 1966, and the Black Communities Act of 1984, which entrenched the separate status of black townships.[19]

As this book went to press, the last of this legislation was being dismantled.

As we in the United States know all too well, political freedom is only the first step to full equality. Is it possible that South African blacks could be granted political equality but continue to be victimized by whites as second-class citizens in the economic arena?

In any case, it seems clear that a new South Africa will be born before we cross the threshold into a new century. And Bishop Desmond Tutu, a consistent voice for both justice and reconciliation, calls all the people of South Africa to be fully involved in this historic birth process:

> White South Africa, please know that you are deluding yourselves, or you are allowing yourselves to be deluded, if you think the present ordering of society can continue. Blacks will be free no matter what you do or don't do. That is not the question. Don't let the when and how be in doubt. Don't delay our freedom, which is your freedom as well, for freedom is indivisible. Let it be now, let it be reasonably peaceful. I call on all Whites to join the liberation struggle on God's side for justice, peace, righteousness, love, joy, laughter, compassion, caring and reconciliation.[20]

Opportunities for Peace in Central America and Worldwide

As I write, the peoples of Central America have suffered from decades of repression, violence, and civil war. And there is little sign that these conditions will change in the near future. The ruling oligarchies in Guatemala, Honduras, and El Salvador seem willing to go to any length to protect their power. In El Salvador, for example, high-intensity conflict, death-squad activity, and the persecution of church workers continues to be a tragic reality for many citizens.

And yet there are some signs of hope as well. Nicaragua, as a direct result of the influence of the Arias Peace Plan drawn up in 1988, is becoming a democratic nation. And since the ending of the Cold War, the strategic significance of many South and Central American nations has diminished. Because these countries have lost their strategic importance, we can expect them to receive much less military aid, and there will be growing pressure for them to resolve their conflicts through negotiation.

The question for the nations in Central America is whether they will be able to achieve peace with justice. Will leadership be able not only to end the civil strife, but actually to share land and power with the poor? There will be no permanent peace in any region of the world that doesn't resolve the issue of social justice.

Beyond Central America, South Africa, and the Middle East, there are also significant opportunities for peacemaking between India and Pakistan, North and South Korea, and warring factions throughout the African continent. We in the church have a responsibility to anticipate these new opportunities and strategically work with others to see both peace and justice brought to all the world's peoples. And as peacemakers, we also have a responsibility to anticipate what is happening in the development of new weapons systems and work to see swords actually transformed into plowshares.

Opportunities in Weapons Reductions

By the end of the century we will likely see major disarmament between the Soviet Union and the United States—reductions of conventional forces in Europe, as well as land-based and strategic missiles. Together, the two superpowers are beginning, thank God, to creep back from the brink of madness. The church must wholeheartedly work at all levels to expedite this peace race.

And yet several developments emerged in the early nineties, that threatened the cause of peacemaking. One is the growing power among conservative or reactionary elements in the Soviet Union, which could undermine disarmament efforts. But another, perhaps more dangerous, threat was the success of the Gulf War. By refusing to vigorously search for a nonlethal way to resolve the crisis with Iraq, President Bush and the international coalition selected the war option. And since the military initiative was so remarkably successful in its prosecution, I am afraid the high-tech military option will seem much more attractive in the future.

It is particularly important to note this setback in light of the increasingly higher stakes posed by the development of new and deadlier weapons. We must maintain acute awareness that even with proposed disarmament, the world remains a hostage to nuclear weapons. In addition, research and development of chemical and biological weapons is dramatically increasing. And it doesn't take much imagination to see that use of certain genetically engineered biological agents (for instance, a virus for which there are no vaccines) could imperil the entire planet.

In 1972, the United States and 110 other nations signed the Biological and Toxic Weapons Convention Treaty banning the creation, production, stockpiling, and use of biological weapons. But there is no way to ensure that nations are abiding by the terms of this treaty.

Even while talking about peace and reducing weapons stockpiles, then, both the United States and the Soviet Union are continuing to research and develop more sophisticated and destructive nuclear and chemical weapons. Equally disturbing is the proliferation of these highly developed weapons systems in smaller, sometimes politically unstable, countries. It is predicted that some thirty nations will have nuclear weapons by the year 2000. And a number of these countries are also developing missile technology in order to have a means to deliver these weapons.

Some experts feel, in fact, that nuclear weapons are more likely to be used in a regional conflict between smaller nations than in an international conflagration between superpowers since the Cold War has ended. Yet another sobering—and entirely plausible—possibility is that terrorist groups could gain access to some of these weapons and use them to hold entire cities, or even countries, hostage.

In light of these facts, it is difficult to understand the almost total failure of the world community, the United States government, and the church loudly to condemn Iraq's widespread use of chemical weapons during its war with Iran, which took place over much of the eighties. Our silence sent the wrong message. Since the end of the Gulf War, however, there is renewed interest in reducing the production and distribution of these weapons of mass destruction.

If we don't stop proliferation of chemical, biological, and nuclear weapons, there is growing danger that they will be used. And one has only to look back over the last forty years to learn who is usually victimized most by sophisticated weapons. It isn't usually those in industrialized nations.

Senator Mark Hatfield points out that since World War II there have been over 140 wars, and all but one of these conflicts occurred in the Two-Thirds World. Most of these fights, then, were proxy superpower wars—a kind of substitute for World War III. In other words, we in the United States were able to avoid international conflicts that endangered our lives and families by supporting wars in poorer regions that placed other people's lives and families at risk.[21]

Now that the Cold War has ended, proxy wars are likely to become largely nonexistent. As Two-Thirds-World countries lose their strategic significance, they will likely see a cutback not only in military, but also in humanitarian aid. Tomorrow's wars will likely be waged in those parts of the world experiencing the greatest destabilization—as an expression of that instability, rather than to pursue territorial expansion.

There is some good news on the peace front, however. Michael Renner, a senior researcher at World Watch Institute, reports that worldwide military spending probably peaked in 1986 at $921 billion and has slowly been declining since then. Renner insists that lethal conflict is becoming an ineffective strategy in achieving political goals. In this century, aggressors have won four out of ten wars. In the eighties they won only one out of ten.[22]

But the brutality of war will not come to an end easily. The principalities and powers have too much to lose. Ending conflict and violence will require that people of faith wage aggressive peace in collaboration with what God is doing throughout the world. We must anticipate new areas of opportunities for peacemaking and, with others from many nations, create strategies not only to protect the rights of individuals, but to actually see global demilitarization.

WAKING UP TO A POWER SHIFT

The twentieth century has indeed been "the century of the State." But as we stand at the threshold of a new century, the role and influence of the state are changing. In the twenty-first century, we are likely to see some dramatic changes in the number of power players and the new ways power is used. These changes are likely to diminish both the importance and the power of the state.

For the first time since the United Nations was founded in 1945, there is a real possibility of the creation of a new international order—a community of nations who work in concert both to preserve the peace and to promote the rule of law. But the establishment of such an international community will require that each nation relinquish some of its sovereign power. Cooperative international policy making for the care of the environment and the promotion of economic growth will also require some relinquishment of national power. New international organizations are already operating for these purposes.

At the same time that sovereign states are relinquishing some of their power in order to participate in new international organizations, they are also feeling growing pressure to share power with those at the grassroots within their nations. Alvin Toffler, in his 1990 book, *Power Shift*, illustrates how our global electronic nervous system has unwittingly contributed to empowering those at the grassroots in nations all over the world:

> When Armenians are attacked by Azeris in Baku, Armenians in Los Angeles know it instantly and begin mobilizing political action. When Jesuits are murdered by a death squad in El Salvador, the entire world knows it. When a trade unionist is jailed in South Africa, the word gets out. The new global media are in business to make a profit. But they are inadvertently raising the cross-national political action by a dazzling diversity of activist groups.[23]

This growing international pressure to share power is both diminishing the power of the state and altering the way it is used.

Perhaps the greatest force changing the character of the state today is the marketplace. Increasingly, the agenda of the marketplace seems to be driving the agenda of the state. From the Soviet Union and Eastern Europe to Japan to European Community 92, political identities are being modified in the effort to maximize economic growth. One of the primary motivations in the fashioning of a new international order is to create a stable global environment that will enhance economic commerce.

Add to this market-driven environment a whole range of new participants on the world scene. For example, transnational corporations wanting to capitalize on the new economic opportunities are becoming increasingly active in the political arenas of a number of different nations. These corporations often develop their own "foreign policy" premised not on the constitutions of the nations that spawned them, but on the bottom line of the board that runs them.

We have begun discovering that transnational investors are also seeking to shape the political character of the nations in which they invest their resources. Not only is this altering the nations in which they make campaign contributions and otherwise seek to influence policy; it is blurring the lines between the economic and the political. Interlocking economic interests necessarily create interlocking political interests and over time could even make it difficult to determine where the lines are drawn between the economic and the political.

The twenty-first century, therefore, is not likely to be "the century of the State." What we are likely to see is a more complex array of international, national, and regional—political, economic, ethnic, and sometimes religious—organizations vying for power and the control of people's lives.

WAKING UP TO A CHANGING PARADE IN THE UNITED STATES

A Crisis of Leadership

Ironically, while a strong surge toward democratization is raising the tide of hope all over the planet, the world's leading democracy seems to be at a loss to address its own urgent and worsening domestic issues. People in blighted cities, for example, have little influence on public policy, and our leaders seem unable or unwilling to act. The administration provides rhetoric and the democratically controlled Congress makes promises. But no one seems willing to provide moral leadership in addressing the growing human crisis in our nation.

Some blame a congressional system that ensures members of Congress lifetime tenure. More than 98 percent of incumbents won reelection to the House of Representatives in 1988.[24] And part of what ensures a system of lifetime tenure is special-interest campaign funding:

> The number of political action committees grew from 608 in 1974 to 4,268 in 1988. Their giving rose from $73.9 million to $448.4 million over that time. More than 90 percent has been contributed to incumbents in both parties.[25]

Members of Congress have staunchly resisted all efforts at campaign reform to change this system. As a result, we tend to wind up with "the best Congress money can buy." As a result, the interests of the powerful, not the needs of the marginal, shape much of the United States's domestic policy.

Other people blame a "rudderless" presidency for the crisis. President Bush seems to prefer to focus his attention on global diplomacy, leaving domestic issues to others. In light of his extremely high popularity rating after the Persian Gulf victory, Bush has an unprecedented opportunity during the rest of his tenure in the White House to develop bipartisan legislation that addresses the escalating domestic needs of our nation and to secure strong congressional support for it.

From homelessness and poverty to health care and education, our society desperately needs some thoughtful, long-term initiatives that involve not only government, but the private sector and the church. When called upon to make decisions in the coming decade, will our leaders be willing to pursue policies with long-term benefits instead of settling for short-term fixes? Will they provide moral leadership that will enable us to enter a new century as a people who compassionately care for our own? I think there is reason to question whether they will be up to the challenges of tomorrow's world.

In 1980, in *The Mustard Seed Conspiracy*, I predicted that the United States was entering a period of "limping liberalism and galloping conservatism."[26] And the eighties were indeed a time when liberalism was in eclipse and conservatives took over the parade. But who is going to take leadership of the parade as we travel toward a new century?

One of the major causes of our crisis of leadership is that neither Democrats nor Republicans, liberals nor conservatives, are able to offer a compelling new political vision for the American future. Meg Greenfield of *Newsweek* points out that we who live in the United States have

> defined ourselves as a contrast to the East. They were tyranny, we were freedom; they were command economy, we were market; they were godless, we were sympathetic to and protective of religion; they were predatory, we were peaceful; they were aggression, we were defense.[27]

Since the Cold War abruptly ended, however, no one has come forward with a compelling new vision for the United States or its role in a changing world. Frankly, I am very dubious as to whether Republicans or Democrats, conservatives or liberals, will be able to offer us a vision that will enable us effectively to engage the escalating challenges of tomorrow's world.

Can't we find a dream for our nation beyond a preoccupation with economic growth, technological progress, and military prowess? Can't we find a dream that will enable us to reach beyond ourselves? Can't Americans of all political stripes find a dream that transcends both partisanship and narrow national self-interest? For a brief moment, Dr. Martin Luther King called us all to a stirring national vision that emphasized themes of reconciliation, community, and dignity instead of consumerism, individualism, and militarism. Aren't there leaders who can again call us to the best that is within us . . . to a new American dream?

With the end of the Cold War, the conservatives have lost their enemy. Somewhere in the eighties, the liberals seem to have misplaced their mission. I am not at all sure we should look to the ideologies of the right or the left to articulate a new American vision. Couldn't the larger religious community in the United States host a national forum to enable us to discover a new national vision that calls us beyond ourselves as we enter a new century?

As I write, in the aftermath of the Persian Gulf war, we are looking toward another round of presidential elections. And many analysts believe the results of the 1992 election were settled in the deserts of Kuwait. Very few Democrats appear to have any interest in running against a very popular Republican incumbent.

And yet Kevin Phillips, who predicted the GOP's post-1968 dominance of the presidency, thinks that dominance might be coming to an end. Writing before the Gulf War, he predicted that the Republicans will lose the White House before the year 2000.[28] Changing demographics and changing issues could favor the Democrats in 1996, although the Republicans tend to be tenacious and don't easily relinquish power.

Not only could national issues begin to favor the Democrats; we may also see growing Democratic influence at state and local levels. This will especially be true in regions with growing minority representation. And in the nineties we will see growing numbers of minorities and women moving into political leadership.

In the nineties, we also are likely to see a growing emphasis on state, regional, and local politics. This will be due in part to the growing complexity of urban, suburban, and regional issues, which will call for a new regional planning capability. But in all candor, the changing emphasis is also due to a shifting of responsibility from the federal to the local level.

In many ways, the vows of the Reagan-Bush White House not to institute new taxes were kept by simply moving the burden of providing government services back to state and local municipalities. Those local entities are now having to raise the taxes that the federal government spared us. Mr. Bush was right when he ran for the presidency in 1980—Reagan's economic proposals really were "voodoo economics." But now, Bush is offering a new version of this return to local control. He wants to return more services to state and local governments with some initial funding but no promises of long-term funding.

Changing the Direction of the United States Military Parade

Since the end of World War II, the United States has seen a steady buildup in military expenditures, from $77.8 billion in 1948 (figured in 1990 dollars) to a high of $319.3 billion in 1987. As a consequence, our entire society has been transformed into a warfare state, with a huge share of our total national resources devoted to the military.[29] The most difficult challenge in the nineties, therefore, will be to change the direction of this parade and turn it in the direction of peace. This will be particularly difficult in light of the military's remarkable performance in the Persian Gulf. But there is still the possibility we could see both significant cutbacks and the long-awaited peace dividend.

Changes must indeed be made—in the interest of the United States economy as well as that of world peace. And we cannot be satisfied with modest cuts of military personnel and a slight scaling back in research on major weapons projects. Many of these expensive projects are threatening our economic security while not assuring our military security.

It is becoming increasingly clear that the day of Soviet expansionism is over. We simply do not need expensive new weapon systems to protect ourselves from

Soviet attack. Jack Beatty argues convincingly as editor of *The Atlantic Monthly* for a broad range of cuts in expensive military projects while maintaining a high level of national security. He recommends that we immediately cut back all development of the Stealth, Trident I, Trident II, and SDI (Star Wars) projects, as well as reducing our involvement in NATO and the numbers of our troops in Korea. He also recommends that military retirement benefits be cut back by half until retirees reach their sixty-second birthday. This, he says, could result in savings of hundreds of billions over the next ten years.

Beatty predicts that

> each $50 billion reduction in the deficit would produce a one point drop in the real interest rates. It would also lower the trade deficit by $25 to $30 billion, because we would not have to borrow so much foreign capital to finance the budget deficit. Moreover, a $50 billion cut in the budget would by lowering interest rates, increase investment by $15 billion to $20 billion. That new investment would fuel economic growth, which in turn would lower the pay out for unemployment compensation, welfare.[30]

Changing the direction of this parade is not going to be easy. We must begin now developing strategies to move from a wartime to a peacetime economy without putting thousands of people out of work or closing down entire towns that are dependent on military complexes for business.

Washington is the first state in the nation to pass a bill to help facilitate such a transition. House Bill 2706 shifts the state economy from the prospects of war to the prospects of peace by establishing a program within the Department of Community Development to help communities and businesses dependent on military spending to convert and diversify their lines of production. The bill brings together representatives from business, labor, military and community organizations on an advisory board to oversee the program. This effort began more than two years ago when a coalition of peace, labor and church groups persuaded the state legislature to fund a study on our defense dependency. A peace organization called Sane-Freeze has helped provide leadership. And hopefully, other states and the federal government will emulate this model.[31]

Courts and Prisons—Shifting the Parade into Reverse

While much of our nation seems to be slowly shifting into a more moderate political direction, the Supreme Court is shifting to the right. Ronald Reagan's Supreme Court appointments clearly leaned the court in a more conservative direction, and Bush is likely to continue replacing aging liberal jurists with constitutional conservatives. His appointment of David Souter in 1990 certainly fits this description.

Even as the Warren Court shaped American life with its liberal rulings years after the Democrats left office, we can expect the more conservative rulings of

Reagan/Bush nominees to shape our future for at least the next ten to fifteen years. In fact, their rulings could do more for the conservative cause than all the conservative legislation passed in the eighties.

In light of a series of court decisions in the late eighties limiting the protection of civil rights under federal law, a number of civil-rights organizations are up in arms. If this trend continues, we could, before the end of the nineties, see a series of civil-rights protests explicitly directed at the Supreme Court and the administration.

The initial issues to watch for in the nineties are abortion, "right to die" issues, civil rights, child abuse, privacy issues, capital punishment, church-state relationships, and issues relating to the arrest and prosecution of those indicted for criminal activity.

We could also see a growing advocacy for children's rights. Rulings in the late eighties that young women who are minors can get abortions without their parent's approval are representative of a societal trend that could result in the liberation of the young from parental control. We could see children's rights being elevated above those of parents.

Abortion is probably the most divisive issue in society and the church today. Political liberals and many ecumenical Christians argue passionately that a woman should have complete control of her own reproductive life. Religious conservatives argue just as passionately that not one, but two, persons must be considered. They argue that the rights of the unborn infant must be protected even if those rights conflict with the privacy rights of the mother.

There are no easy answers on this or a number of issues facing the court. Liberals want to protect the rights of the poor to have "safe" and inexpensive abortions. Conservatives want to save the lives of some 1.5 million infants that are aborted every year in the United States.

James Skillen, writing for the Association for Public Justice, articulates a reasoned and conservative position on abortion that I find persuasive:

> We believe that human life ought to be protected by public law from the time of conception. This we hold not only out of respect for the unborn who may one day be born but also for the public legal definition of the responsibility and meaning of sexual partnership. Public legal protection of human life should be oriented toward the whole context of life-generating and life-sustaining institutions and relationships, thus covering all human life from conception until death.[32]

Organizations like JustLife, sponsored by Catholics and Protestants, argue convincingly for a consistent life ethic which recognizes that abortion, world hunger, and the nuclear arms race are all prolife issues. As image bearers of God living in communities of faith devoted to life, somehow Christians of both liberal and conservative persuasion need to struggle to find a consistent life ethic. We must protect the innocent lives of the unborn while being concerned for the rights of the mothers, too. We must create loving homes for the unwanted unborn. We must adopt lifestyles and government policies to fight hunger and disease that are killing millions of the poor with whom we share the planet. And we must work to eliminate chemical, biological, and nuclear weapons that threaten the future, as well as work to restore God's good Creation.

Essentially, the Supreme Court's 1989 decision in *Webster* v. *Reproductive Services* shifted the battlefield on abortion from the federal government to the states. At this point it appears that twenty-two states will vote to restrict abortion and thirteen will maintain their present laws that permit abortion. The remaining states are likely in the nineties to become battle zones between prochoice and prolife forces.[33] And at this point, prochoice forces seem to be gaining the edge.

But the struggle over abortion may be academic. The recent invention of the so-called "abortion pill" may take the issue out of the court and state legislatures altogether. Roussel Uclaf, a French pharmaceutical company, is already marketing a drug in France called Mifepristone. A similar drug is being marketed in Holland. Taken early in the pregnancy it will cause an abortion. Obviously, it would be extremely difficult to prohibit use of such a product. But it is difficult to imagine that this drug won't be available in the United States in the near future.

Let's look beyond abortion to state-church issues. Several years ago, Congress passed the Equal Access Act, which requires state-run colleges to allow religious groups to meet on campus. Recently, the Court has ruled that religious groups have a right to meet on public high school campuses too. On this and other matters, the present court is likely to be more sympathetic to religious groups than previous courts were.

But while religious organizations can look forward to an era of more favorable treatment by the Supreme Court, they are likely to come under increasing scrutiny by the legal system in terms of enforcement of existing laws and reduced protection from lawsuit and liability.

For example, the Civil Rights Restoration Act of 1987 affirmed Congress's view that an organization that receives federal funding must not discriminate according to gender or race. In the nineties, this law is likely to be enforced more strongly against Christian organizations who practice discrimination in hiring employees or accepting students. (It is unfortunate that government coercion is required to force some Christian organizations to do what biblical ethics should already require of them.)

Dennis R. Kasper, an attorney in southern California who lectures on church-state relations, reports a rapidly increasing incidence of wrongful termination suits between churches and their employees. He reports there is also a dramatic increase in liability suits toward churches and religious organizations. Day-care centers, drug and alcoholic rehabilitation programs, and even counseling centers located in churches will be more vulnerable to lawsuits in the future, and church-run programs will consequently find it more difficult and expensive to obtain liability insurance.

There is likely to be much more government regulation regarding fund raising, employment, and ministry activities, as well as a growing number of court cases involving misuse of funds, sexual misconduct by religious professionals, and sexual abuse of children. Nondenominational churches without formal membership policies may have difficulty legally enforcing church discipline on their "members," since the government only tends to recognize the more traditional model. Issues of privacy and professional morality will increasingly come under greater legal scrutiny.[34]

Taxation of religious organizations will almost certainly be an important church-state issue in this decade. Widely publicized cases of tax fraud on the part of religious organizations—for example, the case of Jim and Tammy Bakker—seem to have heightened public sentiment against tax protection traditionally enjoyed by churches. Reportedly, the IRS has conducted twenty-five high-profile audits of American TV ministries. Hopefully, its findings will not lead to any more religious scandals. Even if they don't, however, the tax-exempt status of many Christian organizations may come into question in the future.

Beyond the issues of state and church relations, in coming decades we will see significant changes in the field of criminal justice. There is likely to be a dramatic increase in white collar, computer, and environmental crimes. But the tendency has been to let the rich and powerful off easy, whether they are involved in illegal insider trading or misappropriation of funds through illegal computer entry. But with the Savings and Loan scandals of 1989 and 1990, public sentiment is beginning to change toward the more affluent criminals in our midst.

We have often strongly insisted on full punishment for the poor who commit crime. Perhaps it's because street crime engenders more personal fear in the United States. The FBI reports that recent levels of violent crime have sharply risen, with a 41-percent increase in aggravated assaults since 1980. Robberies have risen by 16 percent, forcible rapes by 7 percent, and homicide by 13 percent since 1985. The use of firearms in assaults increased by 8 percent.[35]

With the growing use of assault weapons in crimes, America's law enforcement professionals have become united against the National Rifle Association in working to pass legislation for a basic level of gun control comparable to that in most industrial nations. As I write in 1991, the "Brady bill" for handgun control has received widespread congressional support and will face a tougher battle in the Senate.

The reason for taking on the powerful gun lobby is that violence in our cities is out of control. "Our homicide rate is going through the roof," says Ronald Castille, a district attorney in Philadelphia. The changes in homicide rates from the first six months of 1989 to the first six months of 1990 illustrate why law enforcement officers are alarmed. Homicide was up 19 percent in Philadelphia, 14 percent in Chicago, 12 percent in Houston, 8 percent in Los Angeles, and a whopping 45 percent in New York City.[36]

And there is every indication that levels of violent crime will continue to rise, possibly causing the "Lebanonization" of sectors of major American cities. A great deal of this violence, of course, is related to the growing nationwide network of gangs and the growing traffic in illegal drugs. But there is also an alarming increase in "wilding"—random violence that is totally unrelated to any other crime.

The typical response to the rise of street crime in the eighties has been to emphasize—as President Bush's proposed legislation does—"getting tough." Unfortunately, little emphasis has been placed on providing resources to house those sentenced under new, "tougher" laws—much less trying to find ways to effectively rehabilitate and restore criminals to society once they have been punished. As a consequence, recidivism rates are up and prisons are bursting at the seams. It's absolutely insane to spend more money on law enforcement, pass laws for longer sentences, and then fail to allocate money necessary to house and rehabilitate men and women who break the laws. But that's exactly what we are doing. The criminal justice system in many states is already in chaos. In the nineties, in some regions, it could totally collapse if we don't find some resources and innovative alternatives.

In 1978, the population of state and federal prisons was 284,000. More arrests and tougher sentencing swelled the inmate population to 627,000 in 1988—and it could top the one million mark by the year 2000. Overcrowding has helped turned prisons into very dangerous places—plagued by growing violence, group intimidation, drugs, AIDS, and sexual assault.

Problems of overcrowding in prisons may stimulate development of a number of alternatives to public incarceration in the coming decade. For example, a growing number of offenders will probably be sent to privately operated prisons where they will work to learn a trade and help defray the high costs of their care. And a growing number of nonviolent criminals will be kept under electronic supervision in their own homes, wearing electronic ankle bracelets that notify authorities if they leave a designated location.

The future demands not only that we create alternatives to overcrowded prisons. We must also develop alternatives to a criminal justice system that is no longer adequate for the times and alternatives to urban communities that no longer nurture human life.

Clearly, the political parade is changing in the United States in every area, from our national politics to our local law enforcement systems. But Stanley Hoffman insists,

> if U.S. statesmen do not address the domestic issues that deeply worry the people but that, in the absence of leadership, leave it adrift, America's ability to affect world affairs positively will decline further, and we will find ourselves on a road comparable to the one on which the Soviet Union is now skidding.[37]

In other words, Hoffman argues, America's ability to play a leadership role in an increasingly multipolar world will be determined not only by our military successes and economic viability, but our ability and willingness to address a broad spectrum of growing domestic ills effectively.

But there is also another very important issue, one that is just below the level of visibility, that will decisively shape our common future. That issue is how political power is used within a democracy. There are some disquieting trends in this area that could even call the future of our democracy into question. They include:

(1) *A power elite and an alienated majority.* "One Person, One Vote" is a fundamental tenet of our democratic system. But that adage belies the fact that increasingly, in our system, some people are much more equal than others. As in other nations, the United States has a ruling elite that exerts much greater political influence than its numbers would suggest. I am talking not only of specific interest groups, but interlocking networks of power.

G. William Domhoff, in his important work, *Who Rules America Now?* persuasively argues that an affluent elite exerts inordinate influence on the direction of our nation. Domhoff points out that this relatively small group is overrepresented on interlocking corporate and foundation boards and also plays significant roles in government. He concludes,

> There continues to be a small upper class whose members own 20 to 25 percent of all privately held wealth and 45 to 50 percent of all privately held corporate stock. They sit in seats of formal power from the corporate community to the federal government, and they win much more often than they lose on issues ranging from the nature of the tax structure to the stifling of reform in such vital areas as consumer protection, environmental protection, and labor law.[38]

As we illustrated in chapter 4, the numbers of the wealthy and those joining these elite circles of power and influence seem to be growing. It is reasonable to assume therefore that the political influence of the average citizen is diminishing as the numbers and influence of the wealthy grow. According to Louis Harris, that is exactly how most citizens feel. He reports that Americans are feeling increasingly more powerless, more alienated from their government. And he states that this sense of powerlessness stems from a widespread feeling that "there are two tiers of justice, one for those who are insiders in power in Washington, Wall Street, corporate America and major institutions across the nation, and another for ordinary citizens."[39]

A more recent survey by the Times-Mirror poll reports that Americans express even greater alienation toward their government and politics today than they did three years ago, and virtually all of the increase has been among people from families earning less than $50,000 a year.[40]

This growing socioeconomic split within our country threatens to undermine the entire political system. "The public in unprecedented numbers associates Republicans with wealth and greed, Democrats with fecklessness and incompetence. This cynicism," said the study, "threatens to subvert traditional partisan politics or block the effective resolution of social and economic issues."[41]

(2) *Manipulation and censorship of media.* Both those on the political right and on the political left have long complained about slanted news reports. For example, I was in Washington D.C. in April, 1990 during the historic Right to Life march on the White House. The press reported that approximately two hundred thousand people had participated in the march. I checked the estimate with those who routinely do crowd estimates for protests in the nation's capitol. They insisted that the press had seriously underreported attendance in this prolife march and that the actual numbers were closer to a half-million people.

But the issue we are facing here is much more serious than simply accuracy in reporting. Those in positions of power, both Democrats and Republicans, have taken deliberate action to censor and falsify information and to manipulate public opinion.

We know, for instance, that a Democratic President, Lyndon Johnson, used the deception of the Gulf of Tonkin incident to commit American ground troops to the war in Vietnam. The American public was also fed falsified information about enemy body counts during that war to secure our ongoing support.

And Republican President Ronald Reagan instituted a deliberate policy of press censorship regarding the Contra war in Nicaragua during the eighties. Otto Reich was hired as director of a State Department "A" team whose task was to control what the American public was told about the war in Nicaragua. Reich's team reported having successfully "killed purportedly erroneous news stories." And when an occasional story aired that did not conform with administration view, "Reich often met personally with editors and reporters to press for more sympathetic coverage."[42]

As a result of the success of Mr. Reich and the "A" team, Americans repeatedly heard detailed descriptions of Sandinista abuse of the Miskito Indians. However, while we heard the term "Contra abuse," news stories rarely described in detail what the Contra abuses were.

A reading of European newspapers or human-rights reports during that period would have exposed us to the wholesale brutality of the Contras toward civilians on a scale far beyond anything carried out by the Sandinistas. Contras attacked, tortured, raped, and murdered thousands of civilians. They burned fields and blew up health clinics—all as a way of bringing pressure on the Sandinista government.

If a single European was killed in Lebanon during this time, we would read about it in all our newspapers. And yet the Contras (using American-supplied arms) killed European doctors and raped European nurses without a single mention I could find in the United States press. You can write the Americas

Watch organization for the details of Contra abuses toward both civilians and European volunteers.[43]

And, in the aftermath of the Persian Gulf war, one has to ask why we've been spared any significant coverage of the human cost of that war. I have yet to find, for example, a single organization that has done photodocumentation of the some one hundred thousand Iraqis who were reportedly killed in the bunkers and battlefields of Kuwait. I suspect the government feels it would be in our own best interest not to be exposed to the brutal human cost of this "Super Bowl of all Wars."

I predict that the falsifying and censorship of information by those in power will continue, breeding greater public cynicism and alienation. At the same time, sadly, it will probably condition many Americans simply to accept a carefully filtered view of our world.

(3) *Surveillance and the invasion of privacy.* I am very concerned that we are rapidly moving into a period of high surveillance that could erode our freedom and compromise our privacy. In the seventies, we were flooded with unsettling revelations regarding the Federal Bureau of Investigation's systematic—and illegal—invasion of the privacy of United States citizens.[44]

> Starting in 1981, despite the FBI guidelines forbidding investigations of purely political action, at least 52 of the FBI's 59 field offices have been involved in investigating (spying upon) individuals and groups that opposed U.S. policies in Central America. There is little indication that any of these investigations had even the remotest connection to suspected criminal violations.[45]

One of the most troubling of recent government surveillance activities is the FBI's recent covert activities within churches. Even those religious leaders who don't support the Sanctuary Movement (churches providing sanctuary to "illegal" Central American refugees) expressed alarm that the government took the unprecedented action of secretly infiltrating church meetings. Never before, to my knowledge, has the United States government infiltrated church groups to tape meetings, do surveillance, and collect information regarding political dissent.

But it's not just dissidents and churches that are under surveillance. The average American already has information about his or her private life stored in eighteen federal computers, sixteen state and local computers, and twenty-five private-sector computers. Every time we place our name in a phone book, apply for a driver's license, buy a house, have a baby, or shop with plastic, we feed this system, which has an insatiable appetite for information about us.

Increasingly, the workplace is coming under high-tech surveillance. The Congressional Office of Technology Assessment has published a report on increased electronic monitoring of workers that in some cases turns offices into "electronic sweatshops." It is estimated that between four to six million clerical employees are currently being monitored by such methods as eavesdropping on telephone conversations, counting "keystrokes," and checking "idle time" at work stations.[46]

The evolution of interactive entertainment systems brings with it yet another opportunity for surveillance. Already, we are being invited to shop, vote on critical issues, and participate in interactive TV programs. But the hitch is that those who run the system are able to monitor everything that we do with that system—what we purchase, what products we prefer, what our political leanings are—and design "narrowcast" commercials to appeal to those preferences. They thus have much greater ability to manipulate not only our consumer choice but our political opinions.

I am convinced that the greatest threat to our freedom in the nineties will not come from those who attempt to invade our shores or abridge our Constitution. Instead, it will come from those who become increasingly more sophisticated in manipulating our values, opinions, and worldviews. One of the urgent tasks of the church in the nineties, therefore, will be to unmask the powers—determine the extent to which the interlocking networks of interests seek to alter our values and viewpoints to suit their agendas and alter our collective future to conform to their vision of a better future. Instead, all Americans must join hands to work for a new national vision that promotes the common good and calls us beyond narrow national self-interest.

A CHANGING POLITICAL PARADE: AN AGENDA FOR RESPONSE

As the political parade changes, the church and society will be confronted by a broad spectrum of new political challenges. People called to work for peace, justice, and reconciliation will enter a future filled with opportunity. But if we fail to anticipate these new opportunities and provide strong leadership to help guide the parade in new directions, all the newborn signs of hope could be lost. Opportunities to make a difference include:

- supporting the growing advocacy for human rights and the rule of law,

- anticipating the long-term consequences of the ending of the Cold War and movement toward a multipolar world,

- anticipating the long-term consequences of political reform in the Soviet Union and Eastern Europe as the new Western-European coalition is launched,

- advocating and working for a just and lasting peace among all who dwell in the Middle East,

- taking new initiatives to work for peace with justice in South Africa, Central America, India/Pakistan, North/South Korea, and strife-torn areas on the African continent,

- lobbying for disarmament, not only of the United States and the Soviet Union, but of the whole planet—including an immediate global moratorium on research and development of chemical, biological, and space-based weapons systems,

- developing comprehensive strategies of movement toward a peacetime economy,

- anticipating the changing nature of global political power, the diminishing influence of the state, and the implications of these developments for human society,

- laboring to enable the United States to find a new vision for a rapidly changing future that emphasizes becoming a nation for others and finding leaders who can effectively work for this vision,

- repudiating party lines of right and left and calling Christians to become more involved in politics at the federal, state, and local level, seeking biblical responses to the complicated challenges of tomorrow's world,

- anticipating the potential impact of court decisions on the larger society and the church,

- creating a forum in which both ecumenical and evangelical Christians can prayerfully explore together their biblical position on the abortion issue and a consistent life ethic,

- supporting reform of our entire criminal justice system to ensure that it operates fairly, promotes rehabilitation, and deals directly with the socioeconomic causes of crime,

- researching the extent to which an economic elite exerts political power in American society and shapes our common future,

- anticipating the long-term implications of the growing alienation of the American people from their government,

- monitoring the censorship, falsification, and manipulation of the news and lobbying for a more open press and a more responsible use of communications technology,

- advocating policies for the greater protection of privacy in our lives, congregations, and society, and

- creating an international Christian forum where Christians from all over the world can struggle together in community to find biblical responses to the growing issues of our time and bring their positions back to their respective nation states for action.

A CHANGING POLITICAL PARADE: SIGNS OF HOPE

We are living in a world in which the multipower parade is changing. In many ways, however, the tide of hope seems to be rising. Let's look at a few signs of hope.

Former President Jimmy Carter has a remarkable second career. In a world that is struggling toward peaceful resolution of conflict and adoption of democratic principles, President Carter is playing a front-line role. You may have read, for example, about his providing oversight of elections in Panama and Nicaragua. President Carter is also frequently being called upon to serve as a peacemaker between contending factions in both civil and international conflict.[47] In addition to working for conflict resolution throughout the world, the Carter Center also sponsors Global 2000, Inc., which targets Two-Thirds-World disease and agricultural problems. Zbigniew Brzezinski once said President Carter's stand on human rights during his presidency was one of the major factors contributing to an end of the Cold War. Now, through the programs of the Carter Center, human rights progress is an ongoing concern.[48]

Panna Maria is a small Texas community that has been struggling with a very large problem—a uranium mine on the outskirts of town run by the Chevron and Dupont corporations. Townspeople have been concerned about radiation's reaching the ground water supply and being released into the air from the mining operation. But they have felt impotent to resolve the matter because they couldn't get those running the mine to listen to their concerns.

The Interfaith Council for Corporate Responsibility,[49] which is connected with a religious order, heard of the problem and began working with the towns-people. Members of the order visited Panna Maria. They heard the people's health complaints and saw firsthand the tailings pond where the mining by-products ended up and the place where the uranium ore was loaded on the train. They concluded the townspeople had legitimate concerns.

This religious order was a shareholder in both Dupont and Chevron. Its members wrote the corporate leadership regarding the problem, but received a response informing them that there was no problem. Then the religious community sponsored a shareholder's initiative. Because of this action, the corporations have agreed to clean up the tailings pond, review loading procedures, and begin to monitor the health of the people in Panna Maria. We as Christians have the opportunity to see structures change, by the power of God's kingdom, as well as to help those victimized by the structures.

In 1987, Jubilee Partners,[50] a Christian community based in Comer, Georgia, that helps resettle Central American refugees, became aware of the tremendous need for prosthetic care for Nicaraguan civilians who had encountered Contra mines:

> There are thousands of amputees in Nicaragua, largely as a result of attacks on civilians by the Contra rebels. . . . Most of the amputees are young people, women, and children. Funds are scarce. Doctors and nurses have to work without enough equipment. . . .[51]

In response to this need, Jubilee Partners started a new ministry called "Walk in Peace." Amancio Sanchez, a Pentecostal minister, and his sister-in-law, Carmen, were fitted with new legs after their truck hit a Contra mine. They are beginning their lives over again. Even though the war is over, there are two to three thousand amputees who need prosthetics, and Jubilee Partners' work goes on. In addition, it recently raised two hundred thousand dollars for vaccination campaigns and medical assistance because the promised United States aid after the 1990 Nicaraguan election was never forthcoming.

In the United States, there's a growing consensus that simply building more prisons will not solve the crime and prison crisis we are heading for in the nineties. Chuck Colson, chairman of the board of Prison Fellowship, has stated,

> The truth is new prison construction can never catch up; California's Corrections Commissioner announced recently that when the $1.2 billion dollars worth of new prisons is completed, there will still be a 10,000-cell shortage. Prisons are like parking lots—once built, they get filled up.[52]

But Prison Fellowship is working to help solve some of these problems through programs of reconciliation. For example, it has recently worked with the Florida state legislature to develop an alternative track for nonviolent prisoners that emphasizes restitution and reentry into society instead of incarceration and punitive treatment. Using an expanded program of probation and early release for nonviolent offenders, the prison population has stabilized: "Wholesale construction has been averted, overcrowding eased and the crime rate declined 6.9 percent."[53]

Colson's prison work, along with that done by Quakers and Mennonites and other Christians, fundamentally calls into question many of the assumptions on which the modern criminal justice system is based. For example, instead of accepting the adversarial approach of the present system as a given, the Mennonites invented a new alternative premised on reconciliation instead of alienation. Believing that the Scriptures call us to be reconciled even with our enemies, they created the Victim Offender Reconciliation Program—VORP for short. It brings together those who are victims of crime with those who committed the crime. Often restitution is made, victims and offenders are reconciled, and, in some cases, friendships are born.

A CHANGING POLITICAL PARADE: WAKING UP TO OUR CHRISTIAN RESPONSIBILITY

As the seventies ended, the most politically influential religious voices came from ecumenical churches located on Riverside Drive in New York City, from the National Council of Churches, and from various ecumenical lobbying groups on Capitol Hill. The advocacy generally came from a more liberal political perspective, and ecumenicals were leading the parade.

At the same time, Billy Graham, Wheaton College, and *Christianity Today* were in the forefront of the evangelical parade. They were very cautious in speaking out on political issues and, when they did speak out, they tended to reflect a more conservative political viewpoint. On the fringes of evangelical Christianity were groups such as Sojourners and Evangelicals for Social Action, who tended to disavow both liberal and conservative agendas.

Out of nowhere in the late seventies, the religious right emerged and took over the evangelical parade—Jerry Falwell, Tim LaHaye, and Pat Robertson became the new parade masters. And the religious right stole a march on ecumenical political influence as well. And, of course, this movement took a very conservative stance on both foreign and domestic issues. It dominated the discussion of our Christian responsibility in the public square throughout the eighties.

As I write, however, we seem to be embarking on a new era. Ronald Reagan is back on the ranch. The Moral Majority has quietly folded its tents and slipped away. Falwell has gone back to preaching at Liberty Baptist, and Pat Robertson has his old job back on *The 700 Club* TV show.

But it would be a mistake to assume that the influence of the religious right is behind us. Pat Robertson, for example, is still working behind the scenes to garner influence in the Republican Party. In addition, a new group who call themselves "reconstructionists" have emerged within the evangelical community. Though small in number, they are very vocal. And like Muslim extremists, they want to take power and create a new theocracy ruled by the "men of God." They want to see the creation of a Levitical theocracy, linked with a libertarian economic system in which democracy is replaced by a ruling male elite.

The Institute for Religion and Democracy, a more sophisticated organization, has developed a very serious program of advocacy for a neoconservative agenda. And members of this organization have taken it as their particular mission to attack those in the more liberal mainline churches with whom they disagree. Their leading spokespersons are Richard Neuhaus and Michael Novak.

In light of these developments, a primary question facing the church is: Who will lead the parade in the coming decade? To answer it, I believe we must all go back and examine our own shortcomings—whether we think of ourselves as mainliners or evangelicals.

In the past, for example, many mainliners have tended to embrace the liberal political agenda uncritically. In foreign policy, they have been much more critical of regimes of the right than of regimes of the left—even when leftist regimes clearly violated human rights. They were extremely reluctant to criticize, for example, the Soviet invasion of Afghanistan, and they remained largely silent regarding the brutality and repression of Marxist governments in Eastern Europe.

The mainline church's position regarding the oppression in Romania before the overthrow of the Ceausescu regime in 1989 has particularly been called into question. Emilio Castro, the General Secretary of the World Council of Churches, admitted in early 1990, "I think we didn't speak strongly enough. That is clear. That is the price we thought we needed to pay in order to help the human rights situation inside Romania." (Romanian Orthodox leaders threatened to pull out of the World Council of Churches if it spoke out against human rights abuses in Ceausescu's Romania.)[54]

Conservative Christians, on the other hand, have tended to embrace the political agenda of the right uncritically—in the process turning a blind eye toward human rights abuses and covert United States intervention in other countries. Because of their overarching fear of an eminent global takeover by the Soviets, those on the right seemed to feel that almost any "patriotic" behavior could be justified. That included a United States government official's (Colonel Oliver North) running drugs with the help of a Central American dictator (Panama's Manuel Noriega) to provide arms for antigovernment guerrillas in Nicaragua.[55] And thus far I have not seen any letters from those on the religious right expressing regret for their silence regarding such activities.

As I reflect on the political polarization of ecumenical and conservative Christians in the eighties, I find one striking area of convergence: Both liberal and conservative Christians are strongly committed to statism. This commitment to the power of the state takes a different form for each camp, however.

Meeting with the executive leadership of a major Protestant denomination in 1984, I urged the church to expand significantly its local congregational response to the needs of homeless families as we approached a new decade. I immediately was taken to task by one of the executives. "It is not the church, but the state, that must expand its services to those in need!" He insisted, "We must put pressure on President Reagan to expand state services to the poor again."

Quite apart from his illusory expectations that Mr. Reagan could be persuaded to reverse his domestic policy, that church leader's words reflected a larger issue. Many ecumenical Christians, like liberal Democrats, have come to depend almost exclusively on the state to address the urgent human needs in our society. They have come to see the welfare state as the primary vehicle for social amelioration. And undeniably, the government will continue to play an important role in the future for those in need. But as mentioned earlier, I believe "the century of the State" is behind us; political power is likely to be much more diffuse in the future. And with escalating human needs in tomorrow's world, it will quickly become evident that the state simply can't do it alone. Nor should it!

Before the Social Security Act of 1935, the care of those in need was primarily the responsibility of family, community, and church. Increasing government provision helped many people, but often in a way that undermined informal care structures and the sense of responsibility felt by individuals, families, and communities to care for others. In coming decades, I believe, we must find ways to reactivate these primary circles of human response. And we will also need to fashion new coalitions of government, the private sector, the church, and neighborhood networks to help empower those who struggle on the fringes of society—providing them with opportunity and means to help themselves rather than simply doling out enough charity to enable them to subsist and keeping them dependent.

Conservatives, of course, don't look for the state to do more to help those in need. Their statism takes a different form—an unexamined allegiance to the American nation. Some conservatives even assume that the interests of the church and the larger Christian community are subordinate to the interests of the state.

From the founding of the United States there has been a chronic tendency to confuse the symbols and agenda of the American nation with those of the Christian church. This has led many conservative Christians to challenge believers, out of religious commitment, to promote national agendas of the American state.

For example, Richard Neuhaus, in his brilliant book, *The Naked Public Square*,[56] argues convincingly that Christians dare not leave the public arena devoid of their presence and advocacy. He is right, of course. He insists we must speak out with a strong sense of ideals. I fully agree. But then he tells us the ideals we need to promote are not the ideals of the transnational kingdom of God, but the ideals of the American nation state.

In 1986, the National Association of Evangelicals published "Guidelines for Peace, Freedom and Security Studies." This entire document is premised on the unspoken assumption that we as Christians have a fundamental Christian responsibility to protect the national security of the state. I find the implications of this position immensely disturbing. For while such an expectation could certainly be claimed as an integral part of *citizenship*, it is not an expectation of biblical *discipleship*. Without any scriptural justification, however, the NAE blends the two together—in the process subordinating the church to the state and its agendas.

John Richard Burkholder accurately observes, "For the NAE, the U.S. Nation State appears to be the primary frame of reference; the U.S. national agenda seems to be accepted without question, and the concern is simply how the church can contribute to it."[57]

Those of us who follow God are called to a vision and a system of values that transcend the vision and values of the state. We are a part of a new transnational order that is destined by God to be a part of a new transnational future.

In 1988, I was asked to participate at a Seattle Pacific University panel on "Faith and Foreign Policy." In my brief presentation, I argued that our first loyalty as Christians was not to a nation state, but to our God, and to that international community of people who swear allegiance to God.

Robert Pickus, the founder of the World Without War Council and a somewhat less than objective moderator, challenged my comments. He said, "I understand for you Christians your first loyalty is to God, but your second loyalty isn't to the church; it's to the nation." He then gave me an opportunity to retract my assertion.

I responded, "Not only won't I retract; I will add that, for Christians, giving loyalty to a nation state before our loyalty to God and the people of God is idolatrous."

As Christians, we are part of an international movement that must, by its very existence and call, transcend all our other loyalties to our various nation states. In other words, I believe we need to create an international forum through which Christians all over the world can come together and struggle to formulate biblical responses to some of the emerging political issues that trouble our world. Our stance on political issues as citizens of a particular nation must be informed by our prior commitment to God's transnational kingdom and the consensus we reach in the forum of the international church. Central to such a conversation would be the affirmation of a biblical vision that transcends the self-interested agendas of our nations and offers all people a transcendent hope.

And then, when we begin to work in our respective nations, we must assess what visions and values underlie the existing systems and seek to influence those systems in a way that brings them somewhat closer to the biblical vision.

Glenn Tinder, in a very provocative *Atlantic Monthly* article, asks "Can we be good without God? Can we affirm the dignity and equality of individual persons—values we ordinarily regard as secular—without giving them transcendent backing?"[58] Of course, the values underlying our entire Western democratic system, the values that affirm the dignity and equality of the individual, are rooted in our Judeo-Christian heritage. But as we have seen, there seems to be a steady erosion of those values in all areas, including the political.

In this area, especially, we must remember once again that we wrestle not against flesh and blood, but against principalities and powers that are committed to working not for the dignity and equality of individuals within a nation, but for the self-interested agendas of a few. As Christians we must seek to unmask the powers of the ruling elites and expose their agendas of power and control.

But we must also remember we are not to play by their rules. It is not our role as Christians to grasp power. Rather, we are called, in both our words and actions, to try to prophesy against the misuse of power as suffering servants. Even as Christ was asked to lay down his life for a new order, we may be asked to lay down ours. If we look closely at the story of God, we will see that again and again, God influences human events from the underside of history, through the insignificant and unsuspecting . . . the broken and the disenfranchised.

A mother of an infant born in a Palestinian village many years ago reminds us of God's intention to turn the world right-side up:

> And his mercy is on those who fear him
>   from generation to generation,
> He has shown strength with his arm,
>   he has scattered the proud in the imagination of their hearts,
> he has put down the mighty from their thrones,
>   and exalted those of low degree;
> he has filled the hungry with good things,
>   and the rich he has sent empty away.
>
> (Luke 1:50–53, RSV)

Questions for Discussion

1. How have the hopeful events in the Soviet Union, Eastern Europe, and South Africa affected the international struggle for human rights?
2. As we move from a bipolar to a multipolar world, who are likely to be some of the new superpowers?
3. What do you believe will be the political future of the Soviet Union and Eastern Europe?
4. What are some opportunities for peacemaking in the nineties and the threats to it?
5. What are some political forces at work in the world that could diminish the power of the nation state as we enter the twenty-first century?

6. What are the implications of a growing alienation of the citizens in the United States from their government?

7. Given our changing demographics and the changing political issues, how are politics likely to change in the United States in the nineties?

8. Politically, what will be required to bring a halt to major military projects, make the transition to a nonmilitary economy, and steward whatever is left of the peace dividend creatively?

9. What are likely to be the issues facing our legal system in the nineties? How do you think we should seek to influence the legal system?

10. What are some possible threats to freedom in the United States, and how should the people of God seek to address the emerging national and global issues in the nineties?

6

Waking Up to a Demographic Revolution

Cold, biting winds whipped Rea's slender legs as she reluctantly made her way back home to the housing project. It was a cold, gray January morning in Seattle, and the Park Lake Apartments almost seemed part of the ominous dark clouds surrounding them.

Rea quietly opened the door to her family's apartment and took off her shoes. She was immediately greeted by the strong aromas of garlic and fish sauce. On the wall, encircled by a string of small, flickering Christmas-tree lights, a dozen photos of Rea's Cambodian relatives, living and dead, stared at her. The TV was playing in one corner of the living room, but no one was watching it. And from the kitchen came the sound of an intense discussion.

Rea took a deep breath and walked into the kitchen, where her parents, sisters, and grandparents sat at the breakfast table. She greeted them in English, and the room fell into a hushed silence; all you could hear was the television humming in the other room.

Suddenly her stepfather jumped to his feet and began berating her in Cambodian. He called her a harlot and asked why she had brought such shame on her family—a fifteen-year-old staying all night with her boyfriend.

Before she could reply, her stepfather, working up to a full rage, ordered her out of the house and told her never to return. As tears brimmed in Rea's eyes, her mother, Sonni, came to her rescue. Putting an arm around Rea's shoulders, she declared that no one was going to kick her daughter out of her home.

Infuriated at this challenge to his authority, Rea's stepfather began banging the table and shouting, "Out, out, out!" in English. Sonni's elderly parents joined the fray, and sided against their own daughter, shrilly lecturing Sonni to obey her husband and kick Rea out. In their view, a young woman should never be out unchaperoned with a young man, and Rea's staying out all night had shamed the entire family.

Sonni sent Rea, in tears, to the room she shared with her sisters. Then, while her other daughters watched in silence, Sonni began to do wholesale battle with both her husband and her parents. They scolded Sonni, reminding her that ever since Rea had gotten an after-school job and her own spending money she had been defying family rules and ignoring her Cambodian culture. "All she wants is to hang around her American friends," her grandfather shouted. "If she wants to live like the immoral Americans, let her go live with them. She has no place here."

Caught between two cultures and two generations, Sonni lowered her voice and tried to reason with her parents and her husband, promising to see that Rea changed her ways. But they would have none of it. Her husband stormed out of the apartment. And her parents went off to their room, waving away her words with their hands, locking themselves away from everything they detested in the corrupt American culture. Sighing and shaking her head, Sonni turned and headed toward the girls' room to reason with Rea.

This story of clashing cultures and warring generations could be told a thousand times over in the United States today. As America becomes ethnically more diverse and as new generations emerge into adulthood, we are likely to see increasing conflict both within and between cultures.

In this chapter, therefore, we will explore two distinct demographic trends:

(1) *Ethnic revolution.* The United States is being transformed from a "melting pot" to a very rich ethnic stew in which the accent is on diversity, not homogeneity. In this chapter we will briefly explore what it will be like to live in a much more cross-cultural, ethnically rich America.

(2) *The generational revolution.* The combined forces of the graying of America and the growing disaffection of the American young could turn our demographic apple cart upside down and decisively change the character of our culture.

Each generation dives into the historical stream at a different juncture. And for some reason, we are always surprised at how different each generation is from its predecessor. This has always been true, of course, but I believe the increasing tempo of change will exacerbate problems between generations.

In this chapter, we will attempt to anticipate where the generational revolution is likely to take us. To do this we will particularly focus our attention on three generations: (1) a group I call the "Boosters," born between 1927 and 1945; (2) the often-discussed "Baby Boomers," born between 1946 and 1964; and (3) the generation sometimes called the "Baby Busters," born between 1965 and 1983.

Regrettably, space doesn't allow me to include the far ends of the generational continuum. But I believe this overview of the three major generational groupings will give us some idea where the generational revolution is likely to take us as we enter a new century and how the church needs to engage this revolution.

Having explored the generational dynamics of the coming decades, I will look at some signs of hope for reconciliation among cultural and generational groups. And then I will explore what our Christian responsibility should be as the ethnic stew becomes richer and the generational revolution reorders our society in the coming decades.

WAKING UP TO AN ETHNIC REVOLUTION

In a number of ways, the twenty-first century has already arrived—at least in demographic terms. The United States labor force of the next century is already born—although not all are in the United States yet. Next century's first high-school students (as well as its first dropouts) are already in grade school; the elderly of the twenty-first century are already well down paths that will determine their financial and health-care needs for old age.[1] And a much more racially diverse society has been born.

At the turn of the last century, ethnic minorities constituted only about 13 percent of the United States population. But higher fertility levels and immigration are changing those percentages significantly.[2] Another important factor is immigration. Total immigration to the United States was assessed at approximately six hundred thousand per year in 1988, and this rate was expected to decrease only slightly, to five hundred thousand a year, in the coming decade.[3] As a result of this influx of immigrants, the United States, despite a low overall birthrate, is expected to experience continued demographic growth in the future. The population of the United States at the turn of the last century was only 76.3 million. In 1989 it stood at 245 million. It is projected to climb to 268.2 million by the beginning of the twenty-first century.[4] And the majority of those coming in to swell the United States population will be of nonwhite, non-European background.

Between 1931 and 1960, 79 percent of immigrants to the United States came from Europe and Canada. Between 1983 and 1988, 40 percent came from Asia and 38 percent from Latin America[5]—and that trend seems likely to continue through the nineties. Today one American in four defines himself or herself as Hispanic or nonwhite. By the year 2000, one child in three will be from a Hispanic or nonwhite background.

By 2020, the number of United States residents who are Hispanic or nonwhite will have more than doubled, to nearly 115 million, while the white population will not have increased at all. And by 2056, the "average U.S. resident will trace his or her descent to Africa, Asia, the Hispanic world, the Pacific Islands, Arabia—almost anywhere but white Europe."[6]

In a real way, this demographic revolution reflects a larger global change. As we reach the midpoint of the twenty-first century, people from European background will have proportionately decreased in numbers, too. And with their decreasing numbers will come declining influence. Those from non-European background will lead our global society into the twenty-first century.

How will this demographic shift affect American life and culture? And how will those of white European background, the cultural majority of the United States since its beginning, respond to these changes? Will whites be able to anticipate how the demographic shift will enrich our society, or will they feel threatened and retreat into culturally isolated enclaves? The answers to these questions will have a profound effect on the future shape of American society.

Between 1980 and 1988, Hispanics experienced a 34 percent increase in population. They expect to grow from 8 percent of the United States's population in 1988 to 10 percent by the turn of the century. It is important to remember, however, that the term *Hispanic* encompasses a broad collection of nationalities, races, and cultures, including Mexicans, Puerto Ricans, Cubans, Central Americans, and South Americans—the common bond being the Spanish language. Because of their national diversities, Hispanic political viewpoints are much less homogeneous than those of the African-American community.[7]

In the past few decades we have seen a growing Hispanic influence in the political arena, music, cinema, and the arts, and this trend is likely to continue into the nineties. Presently Congress has ten Hispanic Members; that number can be expected to grow with growing numbers of Hispanic voters. And of course, Hispanic culture has long been established as part of everyday life in the American Southwest, which was first settled by Spanish-speaking people.

However, there is another side to the story of Hispanic influence. Although many cities have successful Hispanic business communities, Hispanics as a whole tend to wind up with the low-paid, entry-level jobs—partly because of a language barrier, and partly because of limited education. Only 26.4 percent of Hispanics finish high school. As a consequence, median income for a Hispanic family is only $20,306 compared to $30,850 for the general population.[8]

Overall, the demographic picture of African Americans is similar to that of Hispanics: a growing population and a significant cultural influence, but a shrinking slice of the American pie. By the year 2010, for example, the nation's African-American population is projected to increase from twelve million in 1980 to thirty-nine million.[9] However, while median income for the United States in 1987 was $30,850 for the general population and $20,300 for Hispanic families, it was only $18,000 for blacks.[10]

Even more ominous is the fact that blacks are losing ground economically. Reportedly, the income of black males under thirty who are starting families is half the income they earned in 1970, and their unemployment rate is about two-and-one-half times that of whites.[11] Young black males are a particularly endangered species. Having limited access to both education and jobs, large numbers are being drawn into the violent drug culture of our cities. And they are being killed or imprisoned at an unprecedented rate.

One reason African Americans, like Hispanics, are falling behind is the shrinking of educational opportunities. While the number of black young people who graduated from high school increased from 67.5 percent in 1976 to 76.4 percent in 1986, African-American enrollment in our nation's colleges slipped from 33 percent to 28 percent over the same period. This decline was caused in part because of spiraling costs and shrinking sources of financial help. From 1976 to 1986, for instance, average tuition costs nearly doubled, while financial aid failed even to keep pace with inflation.[12]

This decline is especially unfortunate in light of the rich contributions those from African-American backgrounds have made to the culture. During the early struggle for black empowerment, leaders such as Frederick Douglas and W. E. B. DuBois helped shape a nation. Contemporary American history has been profoundly influenced by leaders such as Dr. Martin Luther King, Jr., Malcolm X, Barbara Jordan, and Jesse Jackson. It is hard to find an area of American life that hasn't been enriched by the African American contribution. In particular, both the fine arts and American popular culture owe a profound debt to men and women such as Marian Anderson, Langston Hughes, Gwendolyn Brooks, and Alvin Ailey—not to mention the gospel, jazz, and blues artists whose contributions underlie much of American popular music today.

But many other peoples in addition to Hispanic and African-American citizens enrich the "American stew." Asians are by far the most rapidly growing segment, settling primarily along the Western seaboard. They currently represent 10 percent of all minorities. Asians have a history of strong family structures that often emphasize societal advancement through education. Many Asian Americans make tremendous economic sacrifices to enable their young people to pursue postsecondary education. As a consequence, they have a higher rate of educational completion than other minority groups. Not surprisingly, therefore, the typical Asian family (with the exception of those from Southeast Asia) earns incomes at or above the national norm.[13] The Asian contribution pervades all modern society in literature, religion, and the arts, as well as philosophy and commerce.

Unfortunately, the prospects for the Native-American future are not as bright. Although Native Americans are virtually invisible in most demographic charts, their contribution to American culture belies their numbers—from their arts and environmental sensitivity to their spirituality and their influence on American governance. (The governing principles of the Iroquois nations were a primary source in drawing up the founding principles of the United States Government.)

Despite their many contributions, Native Americans are having increasing difficulty holding their own in contemporary America. Their numbers are not growing. And they are by far the poorest residents of this continent. Their average annual family income is only $13,676.[14]

Recently, Native Americans from all over the United States organized to protect themselves legally against further efforts by public and private interests to compromise treaty agreements with the government. They realize that such compromise of existing treaties will have a further devastating impact on the struggling economic situations of native peoples.

Against the backdrop of this growing ethnic pluralism, we need to say a word about the future. Part of the dynamism that is uniquely American has come from the constant infusion of new peoples and new cultures. As the United States begins its downward slide from its preeminent position in the world, it will need the energy and imagination of all those who share this land. In fact, our only hope of continuing our economic growth as we enter the twenty-first century lies in employing a much greater percentage of Hispanics, African Americans, Asians, and Native Americans in the work force than we are doing today.[15]

This means, of course, that minorities will need equal access to education and the opportunity to participate in all sectors of the economy. And unfortunately, as we have seen, the trend is toward less opportunity, not more. As Jim Wallis of *Sojourners* magazine explains, we are presently creating a two-tiered economy:

> one a highly lucrative level of technicians and professionals who operate the system, and the other an impoverished sector of unemployed and underemployed, and unskilled labor from which the work of servicing the system can be done.[16]

Thus an entire segment of our society is increasingly being relegated to a second-class economic status.

In 1981, in *The Mustard Seed Conspiracy,* I wrote that

> riding on the coattails of the new conservative movement, although repudiated by most conservative leaders, are the most reactionary movements in American society. The "new" Ku Klux Klan has set out to achieve an image of social respectability as it expands its blatantly racist activities across the United States.[17]

But when I made this prediction, I had no idea how deep were the streams of ignorance and bigotry or how long they would last. Tragically, this growing racism hasn't peaked yet, and I believe it threatens the future of all Americans.

Of course, racial discrimination exists in virtually all societies. But Jim Wallis insists that what we are contending with in the United States is a systemic racism, which "has to do with the power to dominate and enforce oppression" and which "is in white hands."[18] From the rise of Aryan supremacist groups in Idaho and skinhead beatings on the West Coast to victimization of minority students on campuses across this country and brutal racial killings on the East Coast, ignorance, racial hatred, and violence are becoming epidemic. Unless leadership in the church and the society takes decisive initiative to reverse this trend, we are likely to see intensified racial polarization and violence.

Some in the black community see the racism, drugs, violence, and AIDS as a conspiracy against African Americans. And many Black Muslims want to have a separate black nation. Muslim leader Louis Farakhan is promoting a comprehensive agenda to empower the black male, remove drugs from the black community, and deal with out-of-wedlock pregnancy. Farakhan is a bright, charismatic leader with the potential to become the most influential African-American leader of the nineties. If he or another leader like him gains access to nationwide media, the number of his followers is likely to increase quickly—with converts even coming from African-American Christian churches. And it should be noted this movement also has a militant edge.

Increasingly, tensions seem to be growing between various minority groups as well as between whites and blacks. Some experts, for instance, have worried that the growing Hispanic presence might heighten competition with the African-American community for shrinking government funds. A few even point to the Miami riots between blacks and Hispanics in the mid-eighties as forerunners of what we could see increasingly in the nineties between various ethnic and cultural groups. And the trouble is not just between blacks and Hispanics. In some areas there is growing tension between Asians and African Americans, who resent the financial inroads Asians have made in black communities.

Jim Wallis reminds us,

> Put simply, racism negates the reason for which Christ died—the reconciling work of the cross. It denies the purpose of the church: to bring together in Christ, those who have been divided from one another.[19]

But tragically, the church has usually failed in this part of its vocation. In the sixties, some mainline churches joined hands with black churches to struggle for racial justice and civil rights. In those days, even an occasional evangelical leader spoke out. But today it is unusual to hear white Christians of any stripe speak out against the growing racism that threatens the very fabric of our society. And eleven o'clock on Sunday morning is still the most segregated hour in American life.

We are headed into a future in which we have the opportunity to be enriched by the many and expanding ethnic cultures that comprise our country. But before we can receive each other's gifts, we must repent and be reconciled to one another across racial and cultural barriers. And the people of God also have the opportunity to provide leadership in responding to the unbelievable challenges that will be introduced by another area of demographic change—the generational revolution.

WAKING UP TO THE GENERATIONAL REVOLUTION

As we mentioned, we will review three generations: the Boosters, the Baby Boomers, and the new Baby Busters as a way to try and understand where the generational revolution could take us in the twenty-first century.

Boosters: The Stabilizing Edge

In a sense, the Boosters are the stabilizing edge of the generational wave of the nineties. As we will see, they tend to be most supportive of American culture, institutions, and values. But they are also the smallest of the three groupings. Born from 1927 to 1945, this generation is only forty-nine million strong. And, of course, it is not only the front edge of these three generational groups; it is also the graying edge. But the Boomers are rapidly catching up.

The reason I call the generation born between 1927 and 1945 "Boosters" is that these people played a major role in building the infrastructure of the United States and promoting the economic boom that followed World War II. Most Boosters remember the war. Older Boosters remember the Great Depression as well. More particularly, Boosters remember that their generation was instrumental in overcoming the Depression and defeating fascism and totalitarianism. They remember the tremendous sense of national unity and exhilaration that accompanied those two victories.

Not surprisingly, these memories of overcoming hard times and helping win a war have given this generation a bedrock confidence in the United States and its future. Boosters also have shared memories of Hula Hoops and of Les Brown and "his Band of Renown." They invited the first TV sets into their living rooms. Then they listened as the ads exulted, "Dare to dream . . . dare to cut yourself a slice of heaven. Some day you will have it . . . the storybook house, the crackling fire . . ."[20]

The Boosters not only bought the storybook (single-family, detached, suburban) house; they filled it with children. By the end of 1946, the Boosters had produced "a record number of births for the United States—3.4 million."[21] And by the time this population boom had ended in 1964, the Boosters had given birth to almost 77 million children.

Obviously, the American Dream was working very well for them. No wonder most Boosters gave their unqualified support to American institutions and values. More surprising, even many blacks and Japanese who had experienced discrimination, internment, and violence during their growing-up years were still boosters of the American Dream.

The Booster generation is still the leading edge of American nationalism and patriotism. Both Democratic and Republican Boosters tended to support Ronald Reagan—partly, I suspect, because he stirred memories of a day when the world seemed simpler and the United States was its unquestioned leader.

Vance Packard disturbed the ease of this generation with books like *The Organization Man* and *The Status Seekers.* He was one of the earliest to question the values underlying the American Dream. In particular, he questioned the unexamined pursuit of money, power, and status, and he asked if the good life was really synonymous with consumerism, accumulation, and status.

His writings provoked discussion, but little serious change—even for Christians. Most Americans seemed to accept the pursuit of the American Dream and conformity to the values that went with it as almost obligatory aspects of citizenship. Even religious institutions seemed more interested in promoting traditional values of sexual morality and family life than in questioning the values underlying American culture. Boosters still show the greatest concern for "preserving traditional American values."

According to pollster George Gallup, not only did expectations for this generation include conformity to American cultural values, but attending church was also "the thing to do." Religious interest reached new heights in the fifties, with 49 percent of Americans reporting that they attended church or synagogue regularly. "In 1952, 75 percent of Americans said, 'religion was very important in their lives.'" Since that time, church attendance has been steadily declining.[22]

Boosters: Catching the Big One

Economically speaking, the Boosters caught the big one. As the war ended, the American economy began to experience an unparalleled period of economic growth. Many of this generation caught the wave that is still giving most of them a remarkable economic lift. Regrettably, many African Americans, Native Americans, Hispanics, and some rural whites never caught the big one; in their graying years, they are struggling for survival. On the whole, however, Boosters settled the suburbs, sent many of their young to college and trade schools, and are looking forward to a relatively comfortable retirement. Not that they found it easy; on the contrary, many members of this generation made major sacrifices for economic security. It wasn't unusual for them to work for decades at jobs they disliked to provide for their families and for a secure retirement.

More and more, the American Dream looked like a split-level in Southern California. In the fifties, you could purchase a three-bedroom house with a swimming pool located an hour from the surf, mountains, and desert—all on a single salary.

Not only were you treated to great weather, superb highways, and reportedly the best schooling in the country, but the part of society that didn't work well for all its citizens—the society of crowded ghettos and impoverished barrios—was out of sight and out of mind. Until the civil rights movement, many white Boosters didn't even realize it existed.

By the end of the eighties, however, the California dream was rapidly becoming the American nightmare. The gridlock was becoming impossible, the air unbreathable, the housing unaffordable, and life in the California suburbs seemed increasingly undesirable. While people were still moving to the Golden State, there was also a swell of migration from California to Oregon, Washington, and Idaho.[23]

I suspect this growing disillusionment with California may in fact be part of a larger disillusionment with the American Dream itself. While the Boosters have clearly benefited from the economic lift-off, that lift-off has come at a very high price. Fully 89 percent of American adults—158 million—report that they are chronically stressed out. Sixty-four million report they suffer regularly from stress and are doing absolutely nothing about it. Louis Harris notes that stress appears to be part of the price paid for being affluent and successful. Close to twice as many high-income as low-income people report suffering from such tensions.[24] And many of these are people from the Booster generation.

In spite of the hidden price tag of affluent living, Boosters celebrate the fact that they have the highest per-capita income and by far the highest discretionary income of the three groups.[25] And as a consequence, they are the ones who are giving the most to support the church and religious organizations.

> Today, members of the 50+ population: own 77 percent of all the financial assets in America, own 80 percent of all the money in U.S. Savings and Loan institutions, purchase 43 percent of all new domestic cars and 48 percent of all luxury cars, spend more money on travel and recreation than any other age group, purchase 80 percent of all luxury travel, spend more on health and personal care products than any other age group, account for a whopping 40 percent of total consumer demand.[26]

This is the generation that has bought most fully into the American Dream. Boosters are the pacesetters of the kind of extravagant, luxurious living that is fundamentally out of touch with the kind of world we live in. This is the generation who has defined what the good life in America looks like—and increasingly its dream is being called into question.

Boosters: The Graying Edge

The Booster generation is the leading edge of the graying of America. "Over the past 40 years, the size of the older population has increased dramatically. In 1950, only 12 million Americans were age 65 or older. Today the number is close to 30 million." And as the Boomers begin to retire, the numbers of seniors will jump to sixty-five million by 2030. It is especially important to note that those age eighty-five and older represent the fastest-growing segment of the American population.[27] As people live longer, we will have a demographically significant category of the *very* elderly.

But the graying of America implies more than a simple increase in the number of the elderly. It also means that the median age in the United States is steadily increasing. The number of younger people is declining in direct proportion to the number of seniors. And the bottom line of this trend is that fewer and fewer young people are available to support the growing number of retirees.[28]

Many nations in Western Europe are already beginning to experience stress from their growing senior populations. In fact, Switzerland has been called "the nursing home of Europe" because such a large percentage of its population is moving into retirement age. Japan is facing a similar crisis. The United States, however, will likely not experience its own crisis for another twenty years or so, when the huge numbers of Baby Boomers begin to retire.

Retirement lifestyles of the Boosters vary from maintaining their own homes, long since paid for, to entering generationally (and often racially) segregated retirement facilities, to hitting the open road in their RVs. In coming years, growing numbers may return to the labor force because of growing demands of the marketplace.[29]

In the meantime, a growing number of "long lived humans" are not content to accept stereotypical expectations of what people are supposed to do with their so-called retirement years. A growing number are starting whole new vocations in international or domestic service. For example, retired business people across the country are providing advice and support to new businesses through Senior Corps of Retired Executives (SCORE). And not a few seniors are returning to school to finish degrees—and this trend is redefining the whole idea of "college student." At age seventy-five, for instance, Olga Skala went through the graduation ceremony together with her forty-five-year-old nephew, Gary Nielak.[30] And Elder Hostel education programs for travel and education are springing up literally all over the world.

Boosters: The Escalating Cost of Senior Care

At the beginning of the nineties, many of the Booster generation are already retired, and many more are approaching retirement age. With longer life expectancy, however, members of this generation can look forward to many more postretirement years than could their parents and grandparents. As such, they are the front edge of a major demographic trend—the graying of America. Many of the issues now emerging for the Booster generation will become major issues as the huge population swell of the Baby Boomers moves toward retirement.

As the Boosters and then the Baby Boomers move into their senior years, they are going to place unprecedented demands on both our health-care systems and our family-care structures. The high cost of senior care could not only deplete the resources of the seniors, but also could place heavy financial and emotional burdens on their grown children. As people live longer, many in the next generation—particularly women—will have responsibility for extended parental care:

> Another demographic trend promises even heavier burdens for the children of aged parents. Because family sizes have been shrinking, there are fewer potential care givers, making it ever more likely that a woman will end up caring for more than one elderly relative.[31]

And increasingly, in four-generation families, women could wind up caring for both their parents and grandparents and raising their children . . . all at the same time.

You can be sure that the growing population of seniors will be lobbying for long-term care insurance to cover the costs of their long-term care. "More and more experts say, planning ahead for the possible expense of chronic care will have to be a customary rite of aging."[32]

For the time being, however, the graying Booster generation is well set up to take care of itself. Although there are many exceptions, especially in the Hispanic, African-American, and Native-American communities, the Booster generation of seniors has the financial and political clout to lobby for its own interests.

In fact, no other generational group is as well organized politically as the older-American lobby. Senior advocacy groups include: (1) the Gray Panthers, a fiercely activist organization with seventy-four thousand members; (2) the National Council of Senior Citizens (NCSC), with four and a half million members in four thousand local chapters; (3) the American Association of Retired Persons (AARP), whose membership has skyrocketed to over thirty million members. The AARP has twenty full-time lobbyists working in Washington and another twenty advising volunteer lobbyists at the state level.

The primary question, in the face of this growing senior influence, is how that influence will be used to shape our common future?[33] Will seniors lobby not only for those in the white middle class, but also for those from lower socioeconomic backgrounds? Will they focus only on their own generational needs, or will they lobby for needs of impoverished children as well? The growing tension between old and young in areas with large retirement communities points to an important fact: Unless the powerful senior group can muster the compassion and courage to look beyond its own interests, the generations are likely to become more and more polarized.

The graying of America represents a rapidly expanding economic market as well as a swelling political power. A magazine called *50 Plus* has exploded from fewer than two hundred thousand subscribers in 1981 to five hundred thousand in

1987. Industry insiders predict that every major magazine-publishing company will soon have a special publication geared to a middle-aged or older audience.

For the next two decades, the Boosters will continue to be the stabilizing edge of society. They represent the new volunteer corps for the nineties. And the church needs to tap in to this resource to address other areas of growing human need. But as this generation begins to decline, the costs of its members' care will soar and their giving to established religious and charitable organizations will probably decrease considerably. The church must find creative new ways to use this generation's considerable gifts and available time to address the urgent issues of tomorrow's world while the Boosters are still with us.

Boomers: The Influential Bulge

One of the greatest impacts the Boosters will have on the future is their production of the next generation—the seventy-seven million people born between 1946 and 1964 and commonly known as Baby Boomers. Boomers comprise the largest single generation in the history of the United States; that's why some demographers have characterized them with the somewhat inelegant imagery of "a pig passing through a python." Because of their sheer numbers, the Boomers will have much more impact on the immediate American future than any other generation:

> The Baby Boomers packed the maternity wards as infants, the classrooms as children, and the campuses and employment lines, and mortgage markets as young adults.
> To the extent [that they] think alike, they define the contemporary culture. To the extent they buy alike, they shape the economy. To the extent they are both preceded and followed by much smaller generations, they stand out in sharp contrast to those around them.[34]

Although many Baby Boomers share a common set of memories—"the bomb," Vietnam, the civil rights movement, rock music—they are far from monolithic in their attitudes and opinions. Some fought in Vietnam, for example, while others protested it. Some became the newly rich of Wall Street. And others "dropped out" of the "establishment." Still others found themselves hopelessly locked into the dismal American underclass. Some stuck to their parents' religion; some left traditional Christian faith but found their way back through the Jesus movement. Some turned to Eastern religion for spiritual fulfillment. Some celebrated the music of the Beatles and the Beach Boys; others danced to disco.

Some demographers and economists divide the Boomer generation into those born before the late fifties and those born later. These experts accurately point out that older and younger Boomers encountered different times growing up. But they still seem to share many common characteristics.

Yet in spite of the differences, many demographers argue that there are clearly discernible similarities in the drives, the values, and the politics of this population. Despite the protestations of some young people in the sixties, this generation as a whole, like their parents before them, craves the material benefits of the American Dream. Unlike many of their parents, however, they are unwilling to spend a lifetime working at a job they hate to provide economic security for their families and for their future. Boomers want it all—not just economic affluence, but personal fulfillment as well.

In fact, Daniel Yankelovich in his classic, *New Rules,* argues that the Boomer generation values personal fulfillment most of all, even more than economic accumulation, and that this change of values has fundamentally altered the way Boomers approach life in general. Yankelovich states,

> The ethics of the search for self-fulfillment discard many of the traditional rules of personal conduct. They permit more secular freedom, for example, and they put less emphasis on sacrifice "for its own sake." In their extreme form, the new rules place the old ones on their heads, and in place of the old self-denial ethic, we find people who refuse to deny themselves anything— not out of bottomless appetite, but on the strange moral principle, "I have a duty to myself."[35]

That "strange moral principle" has molded the Boomers' attitudes on everything from personal morality to psychotherapy. For example, a *Washington Post/ABC News* poll found that Baby Boomers were twice as likely as those of the previous generation to approve of men and women living together without benefit of marriage.[36] In other words, the criteria for social conduct shifted for the Boomers from accepted social norms to "what's best for me in my life now." And of course those changing norms have begun to change the social behavior of an entire generation and indeed our larger society.

Never has a generation believed so strongly that their first duty is to themselves:

> It is an understanding of life generally hostile to older ideas of moral order. Its center is the autonomous individual, presumed able to choose the roles he will play and the commitments he will make, not on the basis of higher truths but according to the criterion of life-effectiveness as the individual judges it.[37]

As Robert Bellah and his colleagues point out in their bestseller, *Habits of the Heart,* Americans from the very first have tended to value autonomy and individualism over community and tradition—what Bellah calls "utilitarian individualism." But the individualism of the Boomer generation has a fundamentally different character. Boomers, more than any previous generation, believe that individuals are totally responsible for their own lives and thus should be free to live in any way they choose.

That premise, which Bellah and his coauthors call "expressive individualism," has already altered American morality, religion, and politics, and this trend will undoubtedly continue to shape our culture and society as we cross the threshold into a new century.

Because of this ethic, Baby Boomers tend to be more tolerant of divergent moral practices and less likely to sacrifice themselves for family, friends, or society than the Booster generation. It is reasonable to assume that tendency affects even those Boomers who are moving into church leadership positions—that they may be less concerned about issues of personal morality and less willing to sacrifice themselves for the sake of others or some sense of a greater good. (This will likely be less true of some ethnic groups who emphasize greater family loyalty.)

This will likely mean, for example, that there will be a growing tolerance of homosexual relationships both by those outside and within the church. There will be a welcome decline in homophobia, and the civil rights of gays will likely be more consistently upheld. But a growing area of polarization in the nineties will develop between those who want to ordain "practicing" homosexuals and those who, out of traditional views of Christian chastity, are strongly opposed. This issue may become one of the most divisive issues in the church—particularly between more liberal and more conservative believers.

For many Boomers, the high valuing of autonomy translates into a political eclecticism that eschews traditional political labels of liberal and conservative. As a group, Boomers tend to be relatively liberal on issues of personal choice, including reproductive rights for women. They also tend to support civil rights and to be concerned about the environment. On the other hand, however, they favor capital punishment and conservative fiscal policies. That explains in part how this population as a whole could support Gary Hart in the 1984 presidential election and then turn around and vote for Reagan in 1988 without missing a beat.[38]

Despite their ethical relativism, however, the Boomer generation possesses an undeniable inherent idealism. While their elders overcame the Great Depression and won World War II, Boomers helped secure the victories of the civil rights movement. They also marched to get the United States out of Vietnam and worked to secure passage of our first environmental legislation—all before most of them even entered the labor force. Boomers have been in the forefront of the passage of new federal legislation that provides public access and provision for the transportation needs of disabled Americans. And Boomers were in the forefront of political initiatives to secure equal rights for women and promote a nationwide feminist agenda.

That idealism means there is a potential for this generation to take on leadership in solving some of the emerging social issues of the nineties. And as James Engel and Jerry Jones point out, that is true in the church as well. In fact, the future responsiveness of the church to the issues outlined in this book will be determined in large measure by its effectiveness in bringing the Boomers back into the active life of the church. But that will require more conservative churches to wake up to their responsibility to work for social justice and societal change as well as spiritual transformation.[39] And it will require ecumenical churches to rediscover evangelism in order to bring the Boomers back into the fold.

Boomers: Redefining the Family

The "expressive individualism" of the Baby Boom generation affects not only its members' political views, but their approach to marriage and the family. Many Boomers, when making decisions about marriage and family, have made those decisions according to "what is best for me."

What will be the consequences for the larger society of a generation who rewrites the rules on marriage and the family around the autonomous concern "of what most fully meets my needs"? What will be the impact on the children and aging parents they care for and the men and women they relate to? How will sex roles be affected?

In the seventies and eighties, we saw growing tolerance toward those who chose to stay or become single— and the ranks of singles grew. Society also evidenced a growing understanding for those who chose to remain childless. In 1957, 54 percent of those who were under thirty regarded having children as a purely positive experience; by 1976, that percentage had fallen to 32 percent. And by 1976, 70 percent of the Boomers (compared to only 42 percent of the previous generation) reported neutral attitudes toward couples who opted out of parenthood.[40]

Boomers have moved steadily away from traditional definitions of family and traditional living arrangements. Whereas in 1960, married couples (with or without children) comprised 75 percent of all households. By 1980, this proportion fell to 60 percent, and by the year 2000 that number is expected to decline to 53 percent. While nonfamily households constituted 15 percent of all household units in 1960, by the year 2000 that percentage will almost double.[41]

One surprising new demographic trend, however, is that the Boomers seem to be producing their own baby boom. Births in 1990 were predicted to surpass the estimated 4.02 million in 1989. "It does appear to be a real upswing in U.S. fertility," states Carl Hanks of the Population Reference Bureau.[42]

Demographers predict that while nine of every ten Baby Boomers will marry at least once, one in five Boomers will divorce twice. And the children of these divorces will rarely see their biological fathers. Fully one third of the children of Boomers will live with stepparents,[43] in "blended families," with their own particular set of challenges.

Boomers have diverged from the traditional methods of supporting their households, too. Today, only one family in ten fits the model of the family in which only the father works outside the home. In the typical Boomer family, both husband and wife have outside jobs. According to the 1991 *World Almanac,* by the year 1989, more than fifty-three million women over age sixteen—many with preschool children—had joined the labor market. Nearly six million households are headed by single parents, and the percentage of single-parent homes is especially large in the African-American community.

As a result of these kinds of demographic changes, we seem to be headed for a fundamental redefinition of the family. The Census Bureau currently defines the family as "two or more persons related by birth, marriage or adoption who reside in the same household."[44] In the future, however, there will be increasing pressure to redefine families as "a group of people who love and care for each other." And vying for the title of "family" will be a number of living arrangements: single-parent households (including those of women who had children through artificial insemination), heterosexual and homosexual couples living together without marriage (some with children), and Christians living in family-like residential communities.[45]

However we define family, most churches I work with are targeting virtually all their ministries to the intact nuclear family. It is the unusual church that has made any effort to address the special needs of single parent and stepparent families, recognize the reality of "alternate living arrangements," or minister to those living together cooperatively.

Despite efforts to redefine and rediscover family, however, the expressive individualism of the Boomer generation seems to be resulting in a general deficit in the quality of family nurture and care. Boomers who are intently involved in the pursuit of careers and personal fulfillment simply don't have time or energy left to spend in taking care of one another. As Arlie Hochschild asserts in her controversial book, *The Second Shift,* "Husbands, wives, children are not getting enough family life. Nobody is. People are hurting—both in the suburbs and the inner city."[46]

Violence toward women is becoming epidemic in many communities. But children are being hurt, too. And the problem is not just one of insufficient nurturing. Children today are increasingly being raised in fragmented, addictive, and abusive homes. Violence appears to be a growing part of family life. And this is not only true of those in "traditional families." It is also happening in single-parent families, blended families, and gay and lesbian relationships.[47]

The problem is that Boomers want it both ways. They want the freedom for both spouses to pursue their careers and have family life, too. They want all the luxuries two incomes can provide, and they want to be good parents, too. But they are increasingly being faced with the hard truth that something has to go. They can't be engaged in the unqualified pursuit of individual fulfillment and create a strong, nurturing family environment at the same time.

This doesn't mean, of course, that all Boomers are uniformly selfish and uncaring. And of course, for the working poor and many ethnic minorities, two incomes are essential for survival. But other Boomers are beginning to seriously reexamine their priorities. They are beginning to look at other options so they have more time with their families.

During the twentieth century, we have witnessed the corrosive impact of expressive individualism in the demise of nurturing nuclear families, close extended families, and cohesive supporting communities. As we approach a new century, our growing preoccupation with autonomy and expressive individualism threatens the very fabric of the American family and, with it, the American future as well. Therefore, the church has as a special mission the creation of small groups that call Christians back to accountable community, that provide loving support structures for all kinds of families and for those living outside of families.

Boomers: Chasing the Big One

Members of the Baby Boom generation, particularly the middle-class segment of that generation, were programmed by their parents to expect to have everything the Boosters had economically and a little bit more. A few Boomers have realized that expectation. Most haven't. Many more, especially younger Boomers, never will. But most of this generation is still chasing after the material success the previous generation enjoyed. Despite a temporary wave of antimaterialism in the sixties, the Boomers are far from immune to the American Dream. In spite of the current emphasis on frugality, Boomers haven't given up on attaining the American Dream.

Of course, at the center of the American Dream is the promise of home ownership (again, for the middle class). But for the younger Boomers, that promise is increasingly difficult to obtain. While the Boosters could typically purchase the split-level on a single income, the Boomers need at least two incomes. And a growing share of younger Boomers and Busters may never own a home.

In 1975, the average price of a new home was $44,600, with an average mortgage rate of 8.75 and a down payment of approximately $8,920—that translated into a monthly payment of $280.69. An income of $13,473 or more a year would qualify a person to purchase this typical home. A scant six years later, the average housing price had more than doubled—to $94,100—with a mortgage rate of 14.1 percent and monthly payments of $897.93! This would require an income of $43,101—roughly three times higher than what was needed in 1975.

All of this means that home ownership will become a more difficult challenge, particularly for younger Boomers and the Baby Bust generation. And those who do manage to buy will find that the house takes up a much larger portion of their income. This situation has placed increasing pressure on both husbands and wives to work—and often, work longer hours—to meet income requirements.

But even those Boomers who don't buy a home are finding that the cost of housing takes up a bigger and bigger chunk of their income. And for those on the lower end of the income scale, the picture is especially bleak. In New York, for instance,

The sharp escalation in costs throughout the region has had a disproportionate impact on the poor, many of whom are Black and Hispanic and has severely limited their mobility. The conversion of many rental apartment buildings to co-ops and condos has diminished significantly the number of available rentals in the city and the suburbs.[48]

Over a half-million low-income housing units are lost every year to condo conversions, demolition, abandonment, and arson. During the eighties the rental rates climbed to the point that more than six million households now pay over half of their income on rent. And thousands of those struggling to survive in homeless shelters are Baby Boomers.

The combination of dramatic economic changes and deliberate federal cutbacks has made housing one of the major human crises in America. And unfortunately, there is no sign the problem will go away. In the coming decades, the area of housing for the poor and the young will need to be a top priority for the church.

But in spite of the fact that home ownership and affluent lifestyles are increasingly difficult for Boomers to attain, there is no evidence that they will give up trying to attain it. More likely, Boomers will continue working two jobs and extra hours if necessary to continue their pursuit of the big one.

As a consequence, they are likely to have less leisure time. And this will be especially troubling for them, because they were raised to expect not only more material goods than their parents had, but more leisure time as well. But they are discovering, along with the rest of the nation, that the promise of ever-increasing leisure time isn't coming true. Pollster Louis Harris reports, in fact, that the number of leisure hours for the average American declined from 26.2 hours a week in 1973 to 17.2 hours in 1985.

In order to get the most out of their limited time, Boomers are cutting back on their sleep, spending less time in church, and turning to catalogs and cable TV to do their shopping. They are insisting that fast food isn't fast enough. And they are increasingly taking advantage of any product that promises to help them overcome their time crunch. It has even been predicted that in the immediate future we will see the emergence of "time stores" that specialize in "selling time-saving goods and services."[49]

The growing time pressure not only could be debilitating in terms of mental health and corrosive to relationships, it could seriously erode the spirituality of an entire generation. The Boomers are the first "wired in" generation, continually tied to their portable stereos, cellular phones, miniature TVs—and chronically unable to "turn it off" for times of renewal and relaxation.

Boomers: The "Youth Generation" Grows Older

By 2020, most Baby Boomers will be retired. Between now and then, they are going to be grappling with the reality of growing older. Remember, this is the "youth generation." As no generation before them, they love their youth, vigor, and vitality. And I believe they will resolutely refuse to age graciously. They will enter their senior years thrashing and kicking—and fighting the aging process with every tool they can find:

> For five years after its appearance in 1982, Jane Fonda's Workout videotape outsold every other non-theatrical videotape. Sales of home gym equipment rose from $75 million in 1982 to over $1 billion in 1985. In the past ten years, 29 percent of all smokers have quit, and the proportion of Americans who exercise is two-and-a-half times that of the early 1960s. The dollar value of membership in health clubs spiraled from $227 million in 1972 to over $8 billion by 1984. The Boomers would prefer to grow old youthfully.[50]

As the Boomers age, therefore, they can be expected to create a growing demand for a broad range of products and services that promise to slow the aging process—from plastic surgery to nutritional regimes. And Boomers are likely to become increasingly dependent on everything high-tech magic can offer—from body parts to bionics—to sustain life and youthfulness.

Recently the *New England Journal of Medicine* reported on an experimental six-month regime, using a synthetic hormone, that had been tested with twelve male seniors. Reportedly it reversed the aging process ten to twenty years in terms of skin, muscles, and bone deterioration. While scientists insist that such a hormone regime isn't an anti-aging panacea, I predict many Boomers will manage to come up with the $14,000 it will take annually to purchase such a therapy to sustain their youthfulness.[51]

The aging of the Baby Boomers will be a major new social movement well into the first half of the next century. Imagine nearly seventy-seven million Americans all hitting their senior years together! The Population Reference Bureau has predicted that seniors will outnumber teenagers more than two to one by 2025. By 2050, it is likely that one American in four will be over sixty-five.[52]

This enormous demographic shift will have far-reaching social, political, and economic consequences for all Americans during the twenty-first century. Clearly, the voting patterns are likely to lean toward meeting the concerns of this emerging senior population. Hospitals, nursing homes, and retirement programs will be strained to care for growing numbers of older Americans. And the swelling senior population is likely to drive up insurance, retirement, and health care costs for the entire population. And the succeeding generation, many coming from fragmented Boomer homes, may well rebel against the higher taxes they will have to pay for the care of a population they feel often checked out on them.

I suspect the Boomers will not be as content as their parents were to retire in ghettos for the elderly. Instead, I believe, they will opt for cross-generational theme communities—communities held together by a common interest in the arts, outdoor activities, or meditation. That, of course, will depend on whether they can afford such options. For numbers of Baby Boomers who fail to achieve the American Dream, trying to achieve the financial security they need for retirement may very well become a nightmare. Churches, therefore, will be called upon to gear up their health-care and retirement facilities to cope with this challenge, while continuing their outreach to other generations.

Because of the medical advances of the last half a century, the Boomers are likely to live longer than the preceding generations. And this life extension is likely to be both a blessing and a curse. Along with increased opportunities for enjoyment and service will come a need for an increased economic base to support additional nonproductive years. There will also be an increased risk of long-term disability in later years, and an increased need for long-term care and catastrophic health insurance.

Matthew Greenwald points out that most long-term care of the elderly is presently done by families and particularly the daughters and daughters-in-law. But most Boomers cannot count on that level of family care. First of all, many Boomers have chosen not to have children or have become separated from their children by divorce. And even those who do raise families may not be able to count on those children to care for them in later years, because of a growing erosion of both discretionary time and money. Therefore, government, corporate, and church resources may be stretched to the limit to meet the expanding needs of the aging Boomers.[53]

One way or another, the Baby Bust generation will wind up with the major part of the gargantuan responsibility of caring for the aging Baby Boomer generation. A few will directly care for aging parents. But all will share an increased tax load to provide essential government services for graying Boomers. When you add growing secularization and alienation between persons to this rapidly increasing economic burden, you end up with an increased likelihood of both elder abuse and support of active euthanasia for the elderly.

For better or worse, the Baby Boomers are the wave of the future. By virtue of their enormous size they will continue to play a dominant role in shaping the American future for everyone—for the Boosters who precede them and especially for the Busters who follow them.

Busters: An Uncertain Future

While the Boosters are the stabilizing edge of the generational revolution and the Boomers are the influential bulge, those in the Baby Bust generation are harbingers of our very uncertain future. This generation is already beginning to have a telling influence on our common future, and that influence will expand into the middle of the next century.

The Baby Bust generation, comprised of those born between 1965 and 1983, numbers only sixty-six million—fully ten million less than the Baby Boom generation. These young people, raised in increasingly destabilized Boomer homes, already show signs of having difficulty in engaging the world of which they are a part.

One can't fully generalize the characteristics to an entire generation, of course. I frequently encounter Busters on campuses and in churches around the country who are bright, capable, and committed to making a difference in their world. However, I am afraid they are at variance with many of the trends I will outline in this section. I can only hope they will have an influence disproportionate to their numbers.

We need to understand that the Busters are hitting the historical stream at a very difficult time. And previous generations need to learn to see the world through their eyes.

The Baby Busters are the first generation in modern American history that have no memories of any major dislocations (until the Gulf War). They don't remember the Great Depression, World War II, or the Korean Conflict. And most of them have few firsthand recollections of Vietnam, the civil rights movement, the student protests of the sixties, or the Watergate scandal of the seventies. As a consequence, unlike the other two generational groupings, Busters have little personal experience in overcoming societal challenges or slaying dragons.

Perhaps the new environmental movement will be the cause that helps shape the Busters' character. But it could be difficult for many of them to rise to the challenge, for Busters are both the most indulged and the most neglected generation to cross the American stage. Many have been raised in affluent suburban cocoons in which they have their own private phones, stereos, TVs, VCRs, and automobiles. A number of these young people have never had to work for anything. And they expect their lives to continue very much as they are now.

At the same time, the number of young people growing up in poverty has dramatically increased, partly because of the rapid growth in the number of single-parent homes. For example, in California the number of children living in poverty doubled from 1969 to 1987—to 1.78 million. And the picture is the same nation-wide. An alarming report released by Columbia University in April 1990 reports that "nearly one in every four children under six years of age in the nation is poor."[54] As already mentioned, the new poor of the nineties will be children. And a disproportionate percentage of these kids will be Hispanic, Native American, and African American. Many of these Busters are growing up in neighborhoods in which drive-by shootings and other forms of violence are routine.

As the Boomers were growing up, the United States was unquestionably still a child-oriented society. The situation has radically changed for the Buster generation. Fewer people are choosing to have children, society is aging, and families are falling apart. As a consequence, there is a declining number of adults who have an investment in children and are therefore inclined to support child-oriented programs, including public education. And not only are we becoming a less child-oriented society; we are also a society which increasingly neglects and abuses its young.

We have already described the growing fragmentation of the American family and the increase in family violence. (Tragically, this happens even in Christian homes.) Such troubled families are now filling the streets of our cities with a new generation of homeless youth—kids who have either run away or were pushed out of impossible family situations.

> The preliminary results of the Federal Government's first effort to count them has found that there are about 500,000 of these runaways and "throwaways" yearly under the age of 18. They are adding to a growing horde of homeless youths and creating a rising financial burden for the nation.[55]

Marie and her brother, Matt, are runaways who live on the streets of Portland, Oregon. Matt has tried to protect and support his sister so she wouldn't have to turn to prostitution to survive.

> She says that she has only had a few "dates" when she really needed money. He has also pleaded with friends not to give her drugs with mixed success. But Matt's support has come at a high cost to both of them. She has always felt guilty that he was turning tricks to help her. And on her 16th birthday, he told her he had contracted AIDS.[56]

Marie and Matt are representative of millions of Busters who are likely to flood the streets of American cities in the nineties.

A major reasons kids leave home is the sexual abuse they experience at home. The Baby Bust generation has grown up during a period in which sexual exploitation and sexual abuse have risen at a staggering rate—and many of them have been the victims. Dr. Robert Geffner of the University of Texas's Family Violence Research and Treatment Program reports that one in four girls will be sexually abused within families by the time they are eighteen; with boys the chances are one in eight. Geffner states that sexual abuse, especially within families, will be the crime of the 1990s.[57] Of course, we know that those who are abused often become abusers, so the contagion is likely to continue spreading.

Many who have been sexually abused are drawn into lives of prostitution and pornography. Pornography is an eight-billion-dollar industry in the United States and growing. Because pornographic films and publications exploit women and children, often brutally, mainline Protestant groups are beginning to join with Catholics and conservative Protestants to oppose this demonic activity. And recently Congress passed legislation that makes it illegal to traffic in child pornography.

The Busters are not only being raised in increasingly fragmented, abusive homes, but addictive ones as well. According to Louis Harris, fully 32 percent of our nation's homes include someone with a serious drinking problem. And 30 percent report that their lives have "been affected in a major way by someone who drinks too much."[58] Thirty-seven percent of people under thirty—Baby Busters— admit that their families have drinking problems.

The Busters themselves are experiencing the problems of addiction at epidemic levels. Eighteen- to twenty-year-olds report the highest incidence of trouble with alcohol—44 percent. While alcohol use in our society as a whole seems to be slowly declining, it will still bedevil the future of many from the Baby Bust generation.[59] And the same is true of drug abuse. Although drug use seems to be declining overall, the use of crack cocaine and other drugs is spiraling among many of the young in the inner cities. We have seen a dramatic increase in the numbers of "crack babies"—infants born to crack users. Most of these children, who are born addicted, who often suffer from mental retardation or neurological damage, and whose parents are unable or unwilling to care for them, face a bleak future indeed.

Busters: A Purposeless Generation?

As the Baby Busters are thrust into society from increasingly fragmented, abusive, and addictive homes, how is their background likely to impact their ability to engage the world? How will it alter their sense of self-esteem? How will it influence the formation of their value systems? And how will it alter their ability to nurture the next generation?

Steve Hayner, President of Inter-Varsity Christian Fellowship, suggests one consequence. He says he has not seen a generation of college students less able to focus outwardly on the needs of others. And he blames that situation on the fact that such large numbers of Busters come from dysfunctional homes. These kids are still struggling to get their own lives together; they have little energy left to reach out to others. There is serious question, therefore, as to how successful Busters will be in marriage and parenting. But many of them are determined to do a better job with their kids than their parents did.

Another deeply troubling trend is the high suicide rate among the Buster generation. Suicides among those who are under twenty-five have tripled in the past three decades. Some of the affluent young are taking their lives because of heavy pressure put upon them to achieve. Other young people, wandering the streets of our cities, take their lives out of despair. In any case, the high suicide rate among the Busters is a clear indication that the nurturing environment of the American young is in serious trouble.

Like previous generations, the Baby Busters have been fully indoctrinated in the values of the American culture, but they are giving the culture their own twist. While many Busters disavow the crass materialism of the yuppies, they are still acquisitive. And they place high value on the expressive individualism and autonomy of the Boomers. It is not clear whether they will be as concerned for self-fulfillment as the Boomer generation. However, more than any previous generation, the

Busters have been seduced by the sirens of instant gratification. Unlike preceding generations, they seem to have little capacity for deferred gratification.

Recently the Josephson Institute on Ethics released a report on the "Ethics of American Youth." This report, which was drawn from dozens of studies as well as original research, described the members of the "twenty-something" generation as "I-Deserve-Its" or "IDIs." Their "IDI-ology" is exceptionally dangerous and self-centered; they are preoccupied with personal needs, wants, don't-wants, and rights. The IDI worldview results in a greater willingness to abandon traditional ethical restraints in the pursuit of success, comfort, or personal goals.[60]

When it comes to politics, Busters tilt more to the right than the Baby Boomers, but their political views tend to be a much more visceral, less informed conservatism. Like the Boomers, however, they reflect a growing concern for the environment. They tend to be more liberal on the issue of gender equality than many of those who are older. And yet fewer and fewer of them ever express their political views at the ballot box.

A political cause that may well catch on with the Boosters is that of children's rights. In light of the growing number of abusive homes these kids come from, they may well support legislation to grant young people the right to direct the course of their own lives at an earlier age.

In terms of religion, George Gallup reports that those under thirty are less interested in religious matters than those over thirty. And "while 50 percent of those over thirty say they attended church or synagogue in the past seven days, only 28 percent of those under thirty report doing so."[61] In both Canada and the United States there is a steady decline in church attendance by those under thirty. The fact that many are not gaining a firm ethical foundation in their homes or churches indicates that a growing number of the young are having to develop their own ethical and moral system as they go.

The Baby Buster generation is getting married later but becoming sexually active much earlier than previous generations.[62] And this is true for Christians as well as non-Christians! According to *Christianity Today,* 65 percent of churched young people have had some kind of sexual experience by age eighteen, and 43 percent have had intercourse.[63]

Since the Busters become sexually active earlier and are active longer before they marry than older generations, they are more at risk from sexually transmitted diseases. Even the specter of the AIDS epidemic hasn't altered the sexual practices of the Buster generation. But many of the young are being rudely awakened from their casual sexual practices by a sudden and dramatic increase in other sexually transmitted diseases.

Approximately two million new cases of gonorrhea occur annually, one fourth of them among teenagers. Thirty million Americans are reported to have the painful and incurable disease of herpes. The incidence of genital warts has jumped seven-fold since 1966 and may be linked to cervical cancer. Finally, the number of babies born with congenital syphilis increased from 150 in 1983 to nearly 700 in 1988.[64]

As I write, three thousand people a month come down with Acquired Immune Deficiency Syndrome in the United States. By the year 2000, one million Americans who currently test positive for the HIV virus will be sick with the disease; we will almost certainly run out of public health money in many of our cities to care for AIDS victims. The number of heterosexuals contracting AIDS is dramatically rising, and Busters are ripe targets for this devastating disease. Dr. Gary Nuble of the Federal Centers of Disease Control estimates that at least 20 percent of today's AIDS victims were likely infected as teenagers.[65]

But disease is not the only potential consequence of changing sexual mores in the Booster generation. We can expect sexual promiscuity among the young to have a devastating long-term impact on family formation, with continued redefinition of family values and responsibilities.

One of the reasons these young people are sexually active and so materialistic is that many are extremely insecure and suffer from very low self-esteem. While some affluent Boomers are raising highly indulged children who come to see themselves as "too precious children," even these kids tend to feel they are worth very little. As a consequence, these kids fail to apply themselves in school, have problems in the workplace, and are less successful in forming and sustaining long-term caring relationships. The contemporary American church rarely reaches out to young people beyond its doors to draw them into a loving, affirming community. In the nineties, this must change.

Epidemic insecurity and low self-esteem among the Busters may also be behind another disturbing characteristic of this generation—their seeming reluctance to grow up:

> Something happened on the way to the twenty-first century: American youth, in a sharp reversal of historical trends, are taking longer to grow up. As the twentieth century winds down, more young Americans are enrolled in college, but fewer are graduating. They are taking longer to get their degrees. They take longer to establish careers, too, and longer yet to marry. Many, unable or unwilling to pay for housing, return to the nest, or are slow to leave it. They postpone choices and spurn long-term commitments. Life's on Hold; Adulthood Can Wait.[66]

This generation as a group also seems to be becoming more nihilistic and purposeless than either of the previous generations. You can hear the nihilism in much of their music. Although some Busters will listen to a sampling of popular music, as a group, they are very heavy for heavy metal. And rap is the fastest growing musical form for this generation. Not only do these last two forms often reflect a nihilistic outlook, many songs openly express violent attitudes toward women, animosity toward religion, and hostility toward certain racial and ethnic groups. The music of groups such as King Diamond and Slayer contains undisguised satanic images. And tragically, some of these young people are drawn into Satanism and the occult through this music.

Some analysts report that the violence and nihilism that are dominant in Buster-oriented entertainment are contributing to an insensitivity to human suffering. Others report that many of this tribe are so involved in music, film, MTV, video games, and other forms of electronic entertainment that they seem totally disengaged from the issues of the larger world. And Baby Busters may well be the leading edge of a new postmodern world that repudiates traditional values and welcomes a more chaotic, anarchic future.

Busters: A Closed Generation on the Open Market

The Population Reference Bureau tells us that in spite of all the difficulties facing the Busters, they are going to be in high demand in the workplace.

> As the Baby Bust generation enters the work force, there will be fewer younger adults to fill entry level positions and an increase in the average age of workers. What concerns the business community is the growing mismatch that seems to be developing between workers' skills and job requirements. Results from recent surveys suggest that many of our current workers and the young students lack not only basic skills in reading, writing and arithmetic, but also the ability to perform higher order tasks such as conceptual and problem solving. Workforce readiness, more than actual size of the future labor force, will be the most troubling issue of the twenty-first century.[67]

A shortage of skilled and educated employees means that in the future employers will have to pay entry-level workers more and spend more to train them as well.

> Shortages of qualified workers may coexist with a surplus of unqualified job seekers, especially among minorities who have not fared well educationally. There is growing awareness that when today's first-graders reach adulthood they will compete within a global labor market and will need intellectual skills and levels of education and literacy never demanded of their predecessors.[68]

This growing demand for a well-educated work force to compete in an increasingly international marketplace will place increasing demand on schools in the United States, and the business community is likely to become more directly involved in school reform.

Already, concern about losing business to foreign companies with better-educated employees and dismay at the crippled pace of educational reform has caused a number of corporations to become directly involved in the reform process.[69] Companies have started adopting schools and developing comprehensive learning materials for schools. However, this may not be an unmixed blessing.

Corporate learning materials tend to emphasize utilitarian, materialistic, conforming values instead of enabling the learner to evaluate his or her culture and learn how to anticipate societal change.

Many in the Baby Bust generation don't seem to be highly interested in learning as such, although they are very interested in acquiring any training that increases their employability and income level. In working with college students all over the country, I have found that this generation reads much less than any generation I have worked with. My experience confirms the assertions of Alan Bloom, who in *The Closing of the American Mind* indicts

> American students of the current generation for many things: A lack of understanding of the perennial ideas of Western civilization, an absence of a coherent intellectual outlook on the world, an addiction to novelties in cultural life, a hypersensitivity to mind-numbing modern music, the pursuit of sex as a kind of organized sport, a glorification of freedom and an openness of mind whose consequences in fact close the students' mind to moral, metaphysical and religious truths which constitute the true legacy of liberal civilization."[70]

Perhaps one of the most disconcerting characteristics of the Busters is their apparent lack of appreciation for the larger world of which they are a part. As that world is becoming increasingly more transnational, the Baby Bust generation seems to be much less internationally aware than either of the two generations that have preceded it.

In mid-1988, the National Geographic Society released a sobering report on "the dismal state of Americans' knowledge about the globe." The survey compared geographical literacy of United States citizens with that of our neighbors in Canada and Mexico and in other industrialized countries. Even though overall the United States came in sixth, ahead of the United Kingdom, Italy, and Mexico, in the eighteen-to-twenty-four-year age bracket, the United States came in dead last.[71]

In other words, the Busters don't know where in the world they are, and there is growing concern that they may not care. In 1988, when a group of North Carolina college students were surveyed on their knowledge of geography, the results were disastrous. Some located Africa in North America, the USSR adjoining Panama, and the "state" of Atlanta next to North Carolina.[72]

The culturally disadvantaged of the nineties may well be the middle-class white young raised in United States suburbs—those Baby Busters who speak only one language, have had no cross-cultural experiences, read no more than is required, and have little or no sense of geography. How will these young people begin to compete with their European or Asian counterparts, who often speak three to five languages fluently, read widely, and have grown up with broad cross-cultural experiences? In particular, how will the out-of-touch American young be able to participate in and provide leadership for the cross-cultural work of the church in the twenty-first century?

The Baby Bust generation is only one to three decades away from taking over leadership of both society and church. And I am convinced that the number-one crisis of this emerging generation will be a crisis of values. In view of the values previous generations have inculcated in the Busters and the ways they have been nurtured and educated, how effectively will they function as leaders of tomorrow's society? Will they be able to learn from the many shortcomings of the Boosters and the Boomers and chart their own unique course into a new century—creatively and compassionately engaging the mounting challenges of a brave new world?

THE DEMOGRAPHIC REVOLUTION: AN AGENDA FOR RESPONSE

In this chapter, we have looked at ways in which demographic changes are likely to alter the landscape of tomorrow's society. The ethnic pluralization of America will enrich and energize society, but it will also challenge society and the church to come to grips with the growing contagion of racism. Tomorrow's society will be altered by the generational revolution. All three generations bring both gifts and problems to our common future. One of the most urgent challenges for the church and the society in the nineties, then, is to anticipate how the values of all three generations are likely to alter our common future. As the melting pot is transformed into a rich ethnic stew and as the generational revolution changes the face of America, the church and society will need to tackle these challenges:

- advocating racial justice and economic opportunity for all people in the United States,

- creating new ways for different ethnic groups to share their many gifts in a way that enriches our society in the future,

- anticipating the consequences of losing the Boosters' presence and leadership in American society,

- anticipating the consequences of losing the Boosters' personal and economic support of the American church,

- anticipating the consequences of the graying of America on both the society and the church,

- analyzing how the Boomers' expressive individualism is likely to continue shaping the character of America's society, family, and church,

- creating new forms of outreach, worship, and nurture to reach the Boomers and draw them into the vital life of the church,

- creating small-group networks within the church that provide support structures for divorced, single-parent, blended, and nuclear families and also provide accountability for all believers,

- advocating public policy that strengthens the fiber of family life in the United States,

- designing creative community housing alternatives to enable younger Boomers and Busters to reduce their shelter costs so they have more time and money for service and nurture,

- creating new models for extensive marriage preparation, training in parenting skills, and community-support structures to increase the nurturing quality of new families,

- designing alternative Christian environments for the care and nurture of the growing numbers of unwanted, addicted, and abused young people,

- advocating new public-policy initiatives that significantly reduce the availability of pornographic materials in our society,

- designing new programs in the arts to reach children on the streets who are particularly at risk and to draw them into loving Christian communities,

- anticipating how ably the younger Boomers and the Baby Busters are likely to support the ongoing work and mission of the church, given the changing values and reduced discretionary income of this population,

- training Busters to become world Christians and provide leadership for the church of the twenty-first century,

- anticipating the consequences of the growing secularization of each succeeding generation on America's religious future, and

- designing a churchwide program to anticipate the demographic changes in the United States and to create imaginative new ways to respond to these changes.

THE DEMOGRAPHIC REVOLUTION: SIGNS OF HOPE

As we face historic demographic changes in the future, there are signs of hope. The ethnic pluralization of America promises to enrich our society. And there are those who are continuing the battle against racism and economic oppression and for reconciliation and empowerment of the poor.

For instance, Native Americans, who are among the poorest people in United States society, are finding some creative ways to empower their own people. For example, the Ojibwa in Minnesota have started marketing wild rice. The Oglalla Sioux reservation in South Dakota has opened a women's shelter and a center to build low-cost, energy-efficient housing. And the Navajo produced and sold $230 thousand worth of produce using drip irrigation last year.[73]

There are also those who are beginning to address the distinct problems the generation revolution brings with it. A Presbyterian Church in the Alaska

Northwest Synod, for instance, has become increasingly concerned about the rising cost of child care for single-parent families on limited income. Out of that concern they have started a low-cost child-care program for this population. And the major way they reduce the costs is to use qualified seniors, most of whom volunteer their time.

Although the incidence of abuse and family violence seems to be increasing, fortunately the number of resources aimed at helping victims of abuse is also growing. Dr. Sandra Meyer, for instance, has drawn on her experiences as an abused child to minister to other children of abuse. In her early life Dr. Meyer, like many victims, struggled with a sense of worthlessness, but over time—with help— she learned to stop intertwining experiences from her abusive past with her identity. And she has now started a unique program called "Bridge for the Children" to help others with the same struggle. Dr. Meyer explains, "We teach the children how to change the conclusions they drew about themselves because of what happened to them. We do not change what happened to them."[74]

Several Christian groups have been successful in reaching out to young people through the arts. A group in Seattle, for example, involved some young people who had been caught up in prostitution, organizing them instead to put on the musical *Man of La Mancha.* By the time they had put on their last performance those young people discovered they had more to offer than their bodies, and some have gotten off the streets.

Seven Christian women—all younger Boomers and members of the Baby Bust generation—are bridging social and generational gaps in Washington, D.C. These professional women, all of whom work on "the Hill," have joined together to form the Esther House, a cooperative Christian household in a transitional neighborhood. They have chosen to live together to reflect something of the values of God's kingdom and to reduce their living costs so that they have more to share with those in need. One way they share is to open their home on Tuesday evenings for a neighborhood story hour. Increasingly, mothers as well as children are coming to share in the stories, the warmth, and the festivity of Esther House.

THE DEMOGRAPHIC REVOLUTION: WAKING UP TO OUR CHRISTIAN RESPONSIBILITY

At this point, neither ecumenical nor evangelical Christian groups seem fully aware of nor responsive to the challenges represented by the demographic revolution discussed in this chapter. Ecumenical Christians are generally aware of the increasing ethnic character of the American stew, and they are on record as opposing racism. And the National Council of Churches has begun providing leadership in this area again. Conservative white Protestants in general seem out of touch with the larger ethnic communities and with the African-American, Hispanic, and Asian churches. And they have expressed little concern, publicly or privately, regarding the growing racism in our society; it is not an issue that seems to touch their lives.

Neither mainline nor evangelical Christians seem to be significantly aware of the generational revolution or the ways in which it is likely to shape our future. More specifically, there seems to be very little awareness or critique of the pervasive and growing secularism that is intertwined with the demographic revolution.

Richard Niebuhr began a dialogue on that subject in 1951 with his classic, *Christ and Culture*.[75] This watershed book helped us explore a range of options which include seeing "Christ against culture" or "Christ transforming culture." However, its most important contribution was to remind us that the values of Christ and the kingdom are not the same as the values of modern culture.

Building on this foundation, ecumenicals led the conversation on the nature of secularism and its influence on society during the fifties and early sixties. During this period, however, many leading ecumenicals seemed more and more to embrace modern culture and modern values as normative. In the process, they lost much of their ability to appraise and criticize that culture.

When the religious right took over the political parade in the late seventies, it also took over leadership in defining the nature of the secular. Francis Schaeffer gave us the term. Tim LaHaye provided the definition. "Secular humanism" became the normative description of secularism in the eighties. Schaeffer traced the origins of "secular humanism" to the Renaissance emphasis on "man as the measure of all things."

Tim LaHaye dedicated his book, *The Battle for the Mind*,[76] to Francis Schaeffer. Then, in this bestseller, he took Schaeffer's term "secular humanism" and defined it as a global conspiracy run by a small handful of men who had signed something called the "Humanist Manifesto." LaHaye alleged, without a shred of supporting evidence, that this small group has somehow taken over all elementary and secondary education in the United States, all commercial TV and radio, and, of course, all liberal organizations and labor unions. LaHaye argued that this conspiracy has a single purpose—to create a one-world, communistic, atheistic society which teaches evolution in all the schools. *The Battle for the Mind* became the apologetic of the religious right in the eighties and explains in part the fear that still motivates much of this movement today.

The problem, as we approach a new century, is that "secular humanism" is still the operative term for the growing secularism of our society. And I believe the term is totally inaccurate and inadequate—both historically and biblically.

First, as we will explore later, the secularism that bedevils our age comes much more profoundly from the Enlightenment than from the Renaissance.

Second, Scripture doesn't call us to return to traditional American values, as the majority of those who war against secular humanism do. We are called, in Jesus Christ, to conform our values to those of the kingdom of God, not to the values of the recent American past.

Third, the popular understanding of "secular humanism" is totally inadequate to come to grips with the values changes that are a part of the ongoing generational revolution. As popularly understood by conservative Christians, secular humanists are those people who support abortion, gay rights, and other items of the liberal political agenda. Conservative Christians, not finding themselves on that list, tend to assume they are pure as the driven snow. And of course, nothing could be further from the truth.

We have *all* been co-opted by modern culture more than we realize. And neither mainline nor conservative church groups have offered a viable critique of modern culture that enables the church to understand its captivity or compels it to find its liberation.

Conservatives tend to be singularly concerned with issues of personal morality. They want to return to the moral values and the emphasis on chastity and family life that the Boosters grew up with. And they want to make those values normative for an entire society. On the whole, they pay little attention to issues of social and structural morality.

Mainline Christians, on the other hand, have little desire to turn the clock back to the thirties, forties, or fifties. And the values with which they are principally concerned are not those involving personal morality. When it comes to issues of personal morality, ecumenicals tend to place a very high value on autonomy and stress that sexual preference, sexual conduct, and family life are very much a private affair. As a consequence, there is often little sermonizing or literature in mainline churches on issues of personal morality. The personal value that is esteemed above all others is *tolerance* for differences in belief and behavior.

Instead of focusing on personal morality, mainliners tend to devote their attention to issues of societal and structural morality—they are intent on changing structures that oppress and brutalize people. Whereas conservatives find evil and sin almost exclusively in the fabric of people's personal lives and social relationships, mainliners find it principally within the structures and institutions of the larger society. They strongly advocate that governments, corporations, and communities conform to their standards of moral behavior by correcting unjust hiring practices, ending racism, and acting more justly toward the poor.

Who is right? I believe that both camps are!

Conservatives are right in asserting that we face a serious moral crisis in the Western world—one in which all moral values are up for grabs. If this trend isn't checked, we are almost certain to inherit a society of increasing family breakdown, sexual promiscuity, and moral chaos. Those of us in all traditions need to call people compellingly not to return to "traditional American values," but to recover the biblical values of living life with integrity and maintaining relationships with fidelity and love. We need to help people, particularly the young, to reorder their sexual and reproductive lives in the context of strong families and stable support communities. We need to teach that chastity is not a four-letter word. And as a part of this emphasis on recovering a biblical emphasis on morality, we must insist on much more emphasis on extensive preparation for marriage and parenting. We must create much more substantial networks of support for family maintenance and nurture of the young, paying particular attention to providing support for single-parent and blended families. And we must help families find ways to reduce their living costs so that they have more time to spend with their kids and to address the needs of others.

But mainliners are right, too. Immorality isn't just a personal affair; it entrenches itself in societal and institutional structures. One cannot read the Old Testament without clearly understanding that God judged the children of Israel just as forcefully for their institutional oppression of the poor as for their personal sexual immorality. And structural evil threatens the future of society every bit as much as personal evil. Churches of all traditions must join in speaking out against the growing epidemic of racism in our country, the economic injustice of our society, and the degradation of our environment. And we must devote ourselves to action as well—working within the political and economic structures of our nation to end systemic injustice and promote justice, peace, and restoration of the created order. We must unmask the principalities and powers of darkness and call both individuals and institutions to live under the reign of God.

But while both mainliners and conservatives are right in their emphases, both seem unaware of the value of the other side. And both seem blind to a larger threat—the encroaching seduction of the vision and values of modern culture and the Western Dream.

The Western Dream, with its inherently acquisitive impulses and autonomous values, is embraced as an unquestioned given by *both* mainline and evangelical Christians. As we will see in chapters to come, the materialistic, individualistic, self-seeking values of this Dream pose the greatest threat to both personal and structural morality . . . as well as to the larger purposes of God.

The only way we will be able to address the mounting challenges of the demographic revolution is to be set free from our captivity to this alien dream. And the only way this can happen is for us as a church to become captured by the Wild Hope of God's vision for the future.

Christians of all traditions celebrate the newly found freedom of many in Eastern Europe. But in the United States there is growing evidence that we have not only taken our freedom for granted, but have also trivialized it.

Aleksandr Solzhenitsyn, in an address at Harvard University, charged:

Two hundred or even fifty years ago, it would have seemed quite impossible, in America, that an individual be granted freedom with no purpose, simply for the satisfaction of his whims. . . . Man's sense of responsibility to God has grown dimmer and dimmer. All the celebrated technological achievements of progress, including the conquest of outer space, do not redeem the twentieth century's moral poverty, which no one could have imagined even as late as the nineteenth century.[77]

In other words, political and economic freedom is not enough. For many, including Christians, freedom is little more than an opportunity to satisfy our personal whims. The Creator God calls us to turn our backs on the seductions of our consumer culture and the values it espouses—to reach out for a new dream and a reawakened morality to engage the host of new ethical issues that await us in the twenty-first century.

Questions for Discussion

1. How is the racial composition of United States society likely to change as we enter the twenty-first century?
2. How can the church work not only to bring reconciliation between different ethnic groups, but to encourage them to share their gifts in creating a new future?
3. What have been the primary contributions of the Booster generation?
4. How is the graying of the Boosters and Boomers likely to change the future in the United States?
5. What have been the primary contributions of the Baby Boomers?
6. How is the nature of the family likely to change in the United States in the nineties?
7. What can be done to enable the Baby Bust generation to make a positive contribution to our common future?
8. How are the values of American society likely to continue changing in response to the changing values of each generation?
9. How is religious involvement likely to change in the future in response to the religious involvement of these three generations?
10. What are specific ways the church could seek both to increase the involvement of each generation and to enable it to embrace biblical values in place of its secular values?

7

Waking Up to a Church Out of the Running

Sarah sighed as she hung up the phone. There was no change in Natalie's condition—not that she had expected any. When her daughter was put in that institution years before, the doctors had made it clear that Natalie's schizophrenia wasn't likely to improve. But they had said Sarah could visit any time she liked. The only problem was she had no way to get to the institution.

Sarah is sixty-seven. Thirty-four-year-old Natalie is her only child—her only living relative. But the problem is that Sarah lives many miles away from the hospital where Natalie is cared for. She has no car, no friends who can take her, and meager resources. And there is no public transportation in Buffalo, New York, where she lives. Sarah can't manage to see her daughter even once a year. That's why Sarah was so elated when the woman at Concerned Ecumenical Ministries promised to help. She told Sarah that someone would drive her to visit Natalie twice a year—once at Christmas time and once during the summer.

Sarah represents the human side of a problem I predicted for a group of American Baptist executives in 1984. "How do you plan to respond to the escalating challenges of tomorrow's world?" I asked these Christian leaders at a futures seminar I conducted.

They responded immediately: "We plan to expand our international and domestic mission in the future."

"Have you looked at your own internal demographics?" I asked, and they shook their heads. So I shared some statistics with them, including the fact that the projected median age for American Baptists in 1992 will be nearly sixty years. Then I asked, "What implications will this rapid graying of the American Baptist Convention (ABC) likely have in terms of your future resource base?"

Nodding heads indicated that these denominational leaders understood my point. For the first time, many of them realized they might not be able to expand their missions thrust if they didn't reverse the demographic direction of their denomination. They were on the way toward becoming an aging and declining church.

In the intervening years, regrettably, they haven't taken effective action to counteract these trends. And as we turn the corner into the nineties, giving for that denomination, while still rising a bit in some regions, is not keeping pace with inflation. As a consequence, a number of ABC regional offices are already experiencing the severe shock waves of reduced giving. Tragically, so are the people they are called to serve.

For example, reduced giving forced the Buffalo Regional Office of the ABC to drastically cut back its support of urban ministries in the community at a time when that support needed to be increased significantly. Last year, for example, it was forced to reduce its support for Concerned Ecumenical Ministries. CEM, in turn, had to make cutbacks in its senior-citizen programs in the Buffalo area— including a program that organizes volunteers to check on seniors living alone, visit them, and offer rides in a community that has no public transportation. And one of the first casualties of those cuts was the volunteer coordinator who was arranging transportation for Sarah. As a direct result of the cutbacks, Sarah was informed that her twice-a-year trip to see Natalie in the hospital had been canceled.

In this chapter I will argue that what happened in Buffalo, New York, is only the tip of the iceberg. Unless the church takes a serious look at its own changing demographics, changing giving patterns, and changing values, we could see a wholesale decline in support for both domestic and international mission over the next three decades. And the human and environmental costs could be staggering.

In the first six chapters I have attempted to outline some of the overwhelming environmental, technological, economic, political, and societal challenges that are likely to confront the church as we enter the twenty-first century. And the ringing message of these chapters is that business as usual won't cut it. Simply doing a little more of what we are already doing will not begin to respond to tomorrow's challenges. We must dramatically increase our investment of both time and money if we are to begin to engage the escalating needs and challenges which will flood our common future. In many cases we will need to double and even quadruple our efforts.

Now it's time for the hard question: *How likely is the church, given its changing values, priorities, and demographic profile, to respond to these mounting challenges in coming decades?* Will we be able to increase our response significantly? Will we even be able to sustain our existing effort? Or will we be forced to cut back our investment in mission? That's the focus of this chapter—to assess the probable capacity of the church—particularly the church in North America—to respond to the mounting challenges we have outlined.

This chapter, of necessity, is premised on the assumption that current trends will continue. But obviously, there is no way to anticipate where the Spirit of God might choose to renew the church. If the Western church were to undergo major renewal, my analysis would no longer be valid—and I would rejoice at the alteration of these forecasts.

I will focus much of my assessment in this chapter on the changing demographic and giving patterns of the present church and how those might alter our ability to respond to tomorrow's challenges. I do this with full realization that it takes very few resources to manifest something of God's realm incarnationally in community with other sisters and brothers. But seeing God's love extended into a rapidly changing world *does* take resources. It takes time, energy, money, and devotion to God's purposes. Remember, next to the kingdom of God, the subject Jesus spoke about most was our stewardship of resources.

Finally, this brief assessment is offered not as a definitive analysis, but as a beginning conversation. As such, it can't help but be speculative in character. But I know of no one who has attempted to answer the questions raised in this chapter. I hope my struggling beginning will motivate others to do a more thorough, in-depth analysis of this important topic in order that we can more responsibly, strategically, and compassionately address the challenges of the twenty-first century.

Let me most emphatically add that, while the conclusions of this chapter aren't terribly optimistic, there are many churches in North America and throughout the world that run counter to the prevailing trends. My prayer is that their numbers will flourish. We need to be assured, regardless of whether we are successful or not, that God's kingdom will most certainly come.

Let's begin, then, by briefly examining something of the changing religious ferment in our world. First we will examine the projected growth of other major world religions in relationship to Christianity. Then, against this backdrop, we will assess the anticipated responsiveness of Christianity in general—and the North-American church in particular—in addressing the growing challenges of our uncertain future.

WAKING UP TO COMPETING WORLD RELIGIONS

Ours is a world in which many different religions and ideologies are competing for the hearts and minds of people. In the eighties, to the surprise and dismay of many, religious fundamentalism enjoyed a worldwide resurgence. This revival of fundamentalism has heightened a spirit of contention in some places and led to armed conflict in others.

Witness, for example, the simmering animosities between Sikhs, Hindus, and Muslims on the Indian subcontinent. In Lebanon those of Muslim and Christian traditions have been at war for years. (Thankfully, that conflict seems to be coming to a conclusion.) Of course, the ancient animosities between Catholics and Protestants tear away at the very fiber of life in Northern Ireland.

Eric Hoffer, in his classic work, *True Believers*,[1] argues that while the various religions are certainly different, the characteristics of religious fundamentalists aren't. Whatever our religious orientations, as human beings we are all driven by the same fears and desires. And those on the rabid edge of any group, whether it is militant Shiites in Iran or militant Aryan supremacists in the United States, have more in common than they might realize. "For a long time," Martin Marty observes, "scholars and historians thought of fundamentalism 'as neanderthal as a fossil.' What we're learning is it's extremely dynamic."[2] And I believe the dynamism is often driven much more by the fears of some external threat, real or imagined, than by deeply held beliefs.

But the recent upsurge of fundamentalism is less significant than the changing demographics of world religions. Let me outline some demographic projections that help clarify tomorrow's religious picture:

There are some 908 million Muslims in the world today. And Islam is growing at about 2.7 percent a year, which means there will be roughly 1.2 billion Muslims by the year 2000.

Hindus comprise 690 million of the planetary population, and their growth rate is a bit slower at 2.3 percent a year. By the turn of the century, their ranks will expand to 859 million.

Presently, there are 320 million Buddhists. Their growth rate is only 1.7 percent, which means that by the year 2000 their number can be projected to reach 359 million. And a growing number of adherents are to be found in Western countries.

Jews number only 19 million persons at present. At their 1.1 percent growth rate, they will likely reach 20 million by the end of the decade. Obviously, since their rate of growth isn't keeping pace with global population growth, they will make up a smaller percentage of the world's people. And in the United States, intermarriage is further diminishing the ranks. But there's also a countertrend. A growing number of young Jews are returning to an Orthodox faith and a traditional Jewish lifestyle. This means that in the future we could see a growth in Judaism in the United States.[3]

Orthodox, Catholic, and Protestant Christians comprise some 1.7 billion adherents at this time. Christianity is growing at about 2.1 percent a year. This means that by the year 2000, Christians will constitute roughly 1.9 billion people, or roughly 31 percent of the planet's population—down from 33 percent of planetary population in 1989. That means that if present trends continue, the actual number of Christians will increase, but Christians will constitute a smaller percentage of the world's population.[4]

More optimistic forecasts regarding growth in the Christian population are available. Nevertheless, given present growth rates and the rate of secularization, I believe Christians will do well to hold our own as we enter a new century. Although more short-term missionaries are going out, more "unreached people groups" are being reached, and the Scriptures are being translated into more new languages and dialects, population growth seems to be outstripping the church's efforts to complete its task in world evangelization.[5]

But the major religions of the world are not the only "faiths" competing in the world. Paul G. Hiebert insists, in fact, that the ideology of modernization or "modernity"—the unquestioning belief in science, technology, and "progress"—is

> one of the greatest missionary movements of our age. Schools have appeared in the remotest villages, and children around the world are learning science, mathematics and history divorced from a faith in God. Universities, hospitals and research labs have become the status symbols of nationhood.[6]

And unless we in the church seriously assess the extent to which we have been co-opted by this alien ideology, modernization may well beat the competition.

Almost inevitably, as we will see, the ideology of modernization precipitates increasing secularization and disbelief. The number of persons claiming no religion at all is projected to rise from a few million worldwide in 1900 to a billion by the year 2000.[7]

Advancing secularization, however, does not mean that the major world religions are retreating. In fact, all world religions are becoming increasingly international in their outreach. As their demographics show, Islam, Hinduism, and Buddhism are all on the rise, and their growth will have an impact on all our futures on all continents.

Islam, for example, is no longer exclusively a faith with regional boundaries. Mosques can be found in every major part of the Western world. The challenge this poses is that Islam, unlike Christianity, is essentially theocratic; its basic tenets are specifically and inseparably linked to commitment to the Islamic state. Therefore, Muslims tend to want not only freedom to worship according to their beliefs, but the conformity of the larger legal, political, and institutional order to their religious teachings as well.

Africa today is witnessing a major contest between Islam and Christianity, with both movements growing very rapidly. Ironically, the Muslims have borrowed many of their strategies from Christian missionaries. And Christians have much to learn from Muslims in terms of their devotion and acculturation of faith.

Although Hinduism and Buddhism have been expanding into the West for a number of years, their influence has been particularly evident since the sixties. In recent years, both religions have taken on a newly evangelistic stance. A whole series of Hindu gurus, from Maharishi Mahesh Yogi of Transcendental Meditation to Swami Prabhupada of the Hare Krishnas, have established themselves in Europe and the United States. And a large facility called the International Buddhist Progress Society was recently constructed in Los Angeles with the simple purpose of reaching the West with the message of the Buddha.

Unlike the Muslims, these Eastern religious leaders haven't sought to establish a new theocratic order. Rather, they try to win converts to their particular brand of spirituality within the context of the existing social and political culture. On the whole, they have been quite successful.

The New Age movement has been particularly effective in borrowing from both Hindu and Buddhist philosophies, packaging them with a little self-improvement psychology, and marketing the product to an entire generation. The Baby Boomers have been especially responsive to this popularized version of Hindu and Buddhist philosophy and religion.

The competition between religious groups and the growing influence of world religions outside their traditional spheres will present an important challenge to the church in the nineties: How can we work for understanding and cooperation with those of different religious viewpoints while faithfully carrying out our mission in the world? Striking such a balance is not an easy challenge, and few Christian groups seem to manage it well. Instead, most tilt one way or another.

Ecumenical Christians, for example, generally provide leadership in interfaith dialogues, yet they sometimes tend to be uneasy about stating the claims of their own faith. Evangelicals, on the other hand, give high priority to world evangelization, but many appear reluctant to participate in serious interfaith dialogues with Jews, Muslims, Buddhists, and Hindus.

Frankly, I am convinced that both groups are missing an important opportunity. Evangelicals, for instance, in shying away from open dialogue with those of other faiths, are denying themselves an important chance to grow in understanding of other religious traditions. In addition, they are missing a valuable opportunity to share the faith they hold so dear.

E. Stanley Jones, a Methodist missionary to India and an evangelical, is proof of the fact that interfaith dialogue and evangelization are not mutually exclusive. Throughout his missionary career, he listened carefully to his Hindu, Sikh, and Muslim friends and learned from them. Then he challenged them to consider the unique character and claims of Jesus Christ. Mahatma Gandhi was one of his closest friends. The two talked often together of Jesus and his teachings. And though Gandhi never embraced Christianity, he was profoundly affected by the person of Jesus and his teachings.

If evangelical Christians have missed opportunities and contributed to misunderstandings by remaining wary of interfaith dialogue, I believe many ecumenical Christians are in danger of minimizing the distinctiveness of their own faith. Harvey Cox points this out even while bewailing an overall decline in interfaith dialogue. He expresses dismay that when such dialogue takes place, many of his fellow ecumenicals tend to "play down the Jesus factor—surprisingly—[when it] is just that figure that the non-Christian participants often seem most eager to discuss."[8] Sometimes those of us who are Christians—especially those in the mainline churches—fail to recognize what an appealing and attractive figure Jesus is to people of other faith traditions and how interested they are in talking about him in open dialogue.

I am also finding a growing number of mainline Protestants and Catholics who, in their quest for a greater openness, uncritically embrace aspects of other faiths—failing to recognize that Islam, Hinduism, Buddhism, and Christianity are based on radically different world views and fundamentally different assumptions about the nature of reality. At the very center of our Christian faith is the belief that Jesus Christ is uniquely the full disclosure of the Creator God, extended in love to all the peoples of the world. And I believe that exchanging a weakened Christology for improved interfaith dialogue is a dangerous mistake. The way to improve dialogue is not to relinquish what we hold as essential, but to be more tolerant of one another's differences.

Such tolerance begins, of course, with calling for an end of religious persecution toward those of other faiths. Historically, Christians have been guilty of brutal atrocities toward Jews, Muslims, and sometimes other Christians. In parts of Europe, Latin America, and the United States, people of other faiths still suffer discrimination and sometimes persecution from Christians.

But Christians are not the only ones given to intolerance. In the various Islamic republics of the Middle East, practicing any faith other than Islam is illegal, and citizens who are identified as Christians in these countries are at serious risk. Numbers have been imprisoned, and some have lost their lives for converting from Islam to other faiths. Nepal, which is the only Hindu kingdom in the world, had more than two hundred Christians in its prisons until recently when, under international pressure, the king of Nepal released them.

One of the most urgent topics for interfaith discussions, therefore, should be the ending of religious persecution and imprisonment of people for practicing their religious faith. Interfaith forums ought to commit themselves to working for the release of any people who are imprisoned for their religious practices. Not only can we learn from one another in interfaith dialogues. Together, we can also work for the promotion of basic religious freedom in every continent and nation.

WAKING UP TO A DIVIDED CHURCH IN A NEEDY WORLD

Against this backdrop of growing global competition for the hearts, minds, and loyalties of people, Christians are seriously divided regarding what they believe the mission of the church is.

Many evangelicals see the mission of the church almost exclusively in terms of verbal proclamation of the gospel, church planting, and discipling. As a direct result of a narrow view of redemptive theology, evangelicals tend to see God's activity as limited to the spiritual and relational areas. Fortunately, their practice is often better than their theology, and many do work with the poor, the homeless, and the abused.

In contrast, many ecumenicals see the mission of the church largely in terms of working for economic, political, and societal change. They tend to have a broader view of redemptive theology that includes economic, political, and creational realms. But sometimes mainliners, particularly mainline Protestants, tend to neglect the more spiritual aspects of the faith. Some operate on what I call "commitment by assumption." They seem to assume that just hanging around a church means that a person has somehow committed his or her life to God. Some mainline Protestants would do well to consider the model of Catholics in Belgium and parts of the United States, who re-evangelize their own members and call them to clearly commit their lives to God, not simply to support the institutional church.

In any case, given these very different views of mission, it shouldn't be surprising to anyone that evangelicals and mainliners have vastly different levels of optimism about the ability of the church to carry out its mission in a changing world.

For example, the evangelicals who are advocates of the A.D. 2000 movement are confident that we can see the completion of the church's mission by the year 2000. "Like a worldwide symphony orchestra conducted by God, the A.D. 2000 movement is seeking to fulfill the Great Commission by the end of the century," explained Thomas Wang, speaking at the Lausanne II conference in Manila in 1989.[9] While the enthusiasm of the A.D. 2000 movement for world evangelization is most welcome, its understanding of the Christian mission is troubling.

In my opinion, the reason this small handful of evangelical leaders is so confident is that they have whittled the vast mission of the church into one small, relatively manageable task, virtually ignoring many of the challenges that will flood tomorrow's world. Instead of concerning themselves with the unprecedented threats to the global environment and the widening gap between the planetary rich and poor, for example, they have fixed their attention almost exclusively on "unreached people groups."

The A.D. 2000 people estimate that there are some twelve thousand "ethno-linguistic groups" who have never heard the gospel. They have reduced their mission, therefore, to the narrow task of attempting to plant "a church for every people by the year 2000."[10] In other words, if they can successfully plant a token worshiping community in each of the "unreached people groups" by the year 2000, they will have, in their minds, completed the Great Commission. With that task completed, they can sit back and wait for Christ to return.

In all fairness, a number of evangelicals, including many in attendance at Lausanne II, see the mission of the church in much broader terms that include concern for economic justice and social action. Nevertheless, in my experience, many evangelicals tend to limit their view of the church's mission to evangelism, church planting, and discipling.

Ecumenicals, on the other hand, tend to circumscribe the mission of the church to addressing the urgent economic and political needs that fill our world. At an ecumenical conference on world mission I attended recently, many participants wouldn't even include a traditional concept of evangelism as a part of their view of mission. When they used the term *evangelization,* they redefined the term to mean standing in solidarity with the poor, not sharing the claims of Jesus Christ. Their view of mission therefore focuses largely on working for social justice and world peace. And because this task is simply not manageable, they are not nearly so optimistic that they can see their mission completed by the end of the century.

For some on the ecumenical side of the street, the mission of the church is simply defined as working for "humanization" of the larger society. Their normative vision is to see people act more humanely toward one another. While one can hardly argue with the worthiness of that vision, one has to ask—is that all there is? Is the church—or even God—essential to the attainment of such a vision?

In spite of the evident division between ecumenical and evangelical views of the mission of the church, there are some welcome signs of convergence. At the World Council of Churches Conference on Mission and Evangelism held in San Antonio, Texas in May of 1989, persons with "evangelical concerns" proposed a joint conference. They proposed "that the next world conference of the Lausanne movement be planned to take place with the next World Council [of Churches] Conference on Mission and Evangelism, that they be held simultaneously on the same site and share a number of sessions."[11] James Scherer, a Lutheran missiologist, reminds us that both the Roman Catholics and the Orthodox communities should be included in any such conference on the mission of the church in the twenty-first century.[12]

Of course, there are a number of ecumenical Christians who are committed to world evangelization and a number of evangelical Christians who are working for peace and justice. A joint conference would not only bring those who are in essential agreement together; it would enable those from both camps to begin talking to one another and learning from one another in a true spirit of ecumenicity. Quite frankly, I don't believe we can begin to address the escalating challenges of the twenty-first century unless we learn to listen to one another, pray together, and labor side by side to see God's reign established on earth.[13]

WAKING UP TO A WORLDWIDE CHRISTIAN SHORTFALL

Even though clearly there is no consensus among ecumenical and evangelical Christians as to the church's mission, for the purpose of this assessment let's assume that our mission is both word and deed. We will assume God has called the church to both the proclamation of the gospel and the demonstration of that gospel in working for justice and peace.

Lesslie Newbigin, a British missionary and author, argues persuasively that the mission of the church indeed involves both word and deed and that one cannot establish a priority:

> The Word is essential, because the name of Jesus can't be replaced by anything else. But the deed is equally essential because the Gospel is the good news of the active presence of the reign of God, and because this presence is to be made manifest in a world that has fallen under usurped dominion of the evil one."[14]

In the following section, having defined the mission of the church as concerned for both word and deed, both proclamation and demonstration, we will briefly assess how ably the church in Latin America, Africa, Asia, Europe, Australia, and New Zealand will be likely to respond to the challenges of the future. Then we will turn our attention to the church in North America and assess its capacity for response.

One of the most encouraging trends in the international church today is that leadership is slowly shifting to the Southern Hemisphere. As we approach the twenty-first century, we will see more and more initiative coming not from Western mission agencies, but from churches in the Two-Thirds World. The day of American missions imperialism is over, and a new day has dawned.

In 1972, statistics indicated there were only twenty-four hundred non-Western cross-cultural missionaries worldwide. By 1982, the number nearly quadrupled to twelve thousand. According to Larry Pate's 1990 book *From Every Nation,* the number jumped to thirty-six thousand by the end of the eighties.[15] And Paul Hiebert predicts, "By the end of the century the number of missionaries sent by Two-Thirds-World churches will probably equal or exceed those sent by the West."[16] And it should be noted that by the year 2000 over half of the Christians in the world will live in Two-Thirds-World countries. It is time for us to receive not only leadership from the "Third" church, but instruction and renewal as well.

(It should be clear that when we talk about missionaries in this chapter we are not describing the traditional stereotype of the itinerant Western evangelist serving about in a foreign country. We are talking about Christians from all over the world who have professional training in economic empowerment, agriculture, village-level development, community health, nonformal education, and church planting and who are committed to sharing their expertise—as well as the gospel—with communities in need.)

The speed of this transition to true partnership in mission, however, will be largely determined by the ability of Two-Thirds-World churches to become more self-reliant economically in their operation and missions efforts. Let's very briefly look at the likely ability of these churches to secure the resources they need to continue expanding their global mission efforts as well as to respond to needs within their own regions.

A Church in Conflict in Latin America

By the end of the century, nearly half of the nearly one billion Catholics in the world "will live between Tiajuana [Mexico] and Tierra Del Fuego, at the tip of the continent [of South America]."[17] While Latin America is predominantly Catholic, however, Catholics in that region are far from united.

Only about 10 percent of Latin American Catholics participate in the Mass, for example. And Catholics in many Latin American countries since Vatican II have become highly politicized. Base communities have grown, and liberation theology has flourished. Some elements of the church in Latin America have embraced Marxism and have advocated armed struggle against the oligarchies of power and wealth.

In recent years, the Vatican has shifted its strategy from a frontal assault on Marxist influences in the church to an emphasis on the appointment of more conservative bishops. For example, Pope John Paul has appointed more than a third of the bishops in Chile. With that strategy, and with recent changes in the Soviet Union and Eastern Europe, Marxist influence seems to be waning in Latin America.

Democratization of parts of the region has relieved some of the economic and social pressures that originally led to the Marxist influence in Latin America. But vast inequities between rich and poor still exist. The continuing injustices, along with a severe shortage of priests, means the lay leadership base communities will probably continue to grow in numbers and influence in the coming decades.[18]

Although the Catholic church has clearly been dominant in Latin America, evangelical and Pentecostal movements have enjoyed remarkable growth in recent years. Reportedly, four hundred Latin Americans convert to a more conservative Protestant faith every hour. Fully one-eighth of the population has converted from Catholicism to conservative Protestantism. And by the year 2000 the percentage could approach one quarter. This rapid growth clearly presents a challenge to the historic hegemony of Catholicism in the region—as the archbishop of El Salvador recently warned, "The springtime of the sects . . . could also be the winter of the Catholic church."[19]

There is evidence, moreover, that conservative faith is meeting significant human needs among the marginalized in Latin America. Even *Christianity in Crisis* admits that Pentecostalism in Bolivia has helped the poor. It has provided them with an accessible faith where they can be set free from spiritual forces that victimize them and, in community with others, take charge of their own lives and faith. People have been liberated from alcohol and drug addiction. Domestic violence has been curtailed, and believers have reported physical healings.[20]

Unfortunately, this particular brand of conservative faith has too often been exploited by evangelists from the United States who call Latin Americans to commit their lives not only to God, but to a United States right-wing political ideology as well. And regrettably, they have been very successful. As both evangelicals and base communities continue to grow, we are likely to see more polarization, politically as well as theologically, between Catholic and Protestant believers. Therefore, there is little reason to hope that these two very different Christian traditions will be able to cooperate in the foreseeable future to address the many urgent needs that will fill their countries—much less reach out to the church in other regions.

The Latin American debt crisis, which threatens to be protracted, is another factor limiting the ability of Latin American churches to meet the needs of their own people and reach out in mission together. This regionwide problem is likely to increase the human-need factor among the poor in that region while continuing to curtail the incomes of those who support the church. As a consequence, both Catholics and Protestants will probably have little more money to invest in the advance of God's kingdom in the nineties than they had in the eighties—in Latin America or overseas. Countries like Argentina and Brazil will no doubt continue to provide a growing number of missionary candidates to work in partnership with churches in other countries. But they are unlikely to secure a significant increase in international mission funding from their own adherents.

A Church in a Pressure Cooker in Africa

On the African continent, the church is growing rapidly, even in the face of rapid Muslim expansion. There is vitality, growth, and renewal among Christians of many persuasions. Pentecostals and various indigenous African sects are experiencing rapid growth, often accompanied by supernatural healing and spiritual deliverance.

But how can even a rapidly growing church begin to respond to the gargantuan challenges facing the African continent in coming decades? Hunger, famine, environmental breakdown, an AIDS epidemic, mounting violence and bloodshed—all threaten this continent. As Olusegon Obasanto, a former head of state in Nigeria, declared, "The bold fact of Africa is a continent in dereliction and decay. We are moving backwards while the rest of the world is forging ahead."[21]

One reason the African church will have trouble making a significant impact on these issues is that it will likely be compromised by the same economic trauma that threatens the entire continent. Rapid population growth is birthing a society of children hard-pressed to find employment or even to sustain existence. In many African countries, population growth will continue throughout the nineties to outstrip both economic growth and food production. By the end of the century, we could well see environmental breakdown, an AIDS holocaust, and the death of millions.

In the nineties, Africans will be faced with unprecedented political, economic, agricultural, and societal challenges. The church will be hard pressed simply to enable people in its congregations to keep their heads above water. It is likely to have a surplus of workers but inadequate resources to train and support them. And it almost certainly will have little money to share in the work of the kingdom in other parts of the world.

A Church Torn by Wealth and Poverty in Asia

Asia is looking forward to catching the front edge of the wave of economic growth in the coming decade. And as the Asian economy is lifted, the economy of the church in those regions of growth is likely to be lifted as well. The question is: How will the relatively small Christian community in Asia use its additional resources in light of pending world challenges?

Ephorus Soritua Nababan of Indonesia's Protestant Christian Batah Church is alarmed about the possible consequences of an economic lift-off in Indonesia on his church. Already concerned about economic disparity within churches in his country, he wants to see economic growth include a structure for more equitable sharing.

At the Lutheran World Federation held in 1989, Nababan wondered aloud whether Indonesian churches can avoid the consequences of modernization and industrialization that have radically impacted the church in Europe. He pointed out that since 1970, 3.1 million people have left the church in West Germany. Not wanting his church in Indonesia to lose significant numbers to secularization as has happened in Europe, he has been searching for other models.

The Korean experience has caught his attention. "The South Korean churches have had a remarkably successful growth since they entered their industrialization era. The church in South Korea now represents almost 25 percent of the population, and is not shrinking or left behind," he adds.[22]

But some Korean leaders are less confident their model has escaped the influence of modernization and secularization, even though they haven't yet seen a drop in numbers. Son Bong-Ho, professor of philosophy at Seoul National University, admits, "[Korean] theology is very this-worldly. We look for blessing of this world. Very few can resist the temptation to teach health and wealth."[23] Essentially, the church in Korea appears to be supporting not only the forces for industrialization and modernization, but also the dream behind the lift-off, the dream of ever-increasing economic affluence.

Only time will tell how the church in Indonesia and Korea, as well as other upwardly mobile Asian countries such as Taiwan, Singapore, and China, will be affected by rapid modernization and growing economic prosperity. One Chinese

Christian leader told me he believed the greatest threat to the church in China was not Marxist repression, but Western modernization.

Even if Asian Christians somehow avoid getting caught up in the Western Dream, their total numbers are so small against the vast backdrop of Asia's burgeoning population that they could easily use all of their expanding resources attempting to evangelize Asia and still never make a significant dent. There is a growing international missions awareness in Asian countries from Korea to India, and we may reasonably anticipate that growing numbers of personnel and some economic resources will come from this region of the world as we approach a new century. But in the face of the global challenges that lie ahead, this expansion in Asian personnel and resources will likely have modest international impact— although it is still very welcome.

A Declining Church in Europe

It is not surprising that Christian leaders in Asia should look to the Western-European model of modernization with apprehension. But it is unlikely that most of them are aware of the level of attrition that the European church is likely to experience as a consequence of modernization and secularization as we enter the twenty-first century.

Western Europe is graying even more rapidly than the United States. This will mean rapidly escalating health-care and retirement costs and an increasing tax burden on a shrinking working population. Even if E.C. 92 achieves 4 to 7 percent annual economic growth, the dramatic increase in the senior population will put a strain on the entire economy. In addition, the high levels of economic growth will act like a magnet to draw floods of immigrants from the Soviet Union and Eastern Europe into the West.

Obviously, a rapidly graying population is going to have an impact on the demography of the Western-European church as well. A rather grim forecast called the "2036 Report," published by the Evangelical Church in Germany, predicts that the church will lose at least half of its membership between 1980 and 2030. This prediction is based in part on lower fertility rates and in part on the fact that many German young people feel the church has nothing to offer them. One Lutheran church leader from Germany summarized: "Last generation we lost the working class. This generation we are losing our young people."

Some European Christian leaders have told me what is happening in Germany is taking place throughout Western Europe. Between now and the year 2030, we can expect a startling decrease in the membership of traditional churches all over Western Europe. This will mean a devastating loss of witness for the gospel not only in Europe itself, but throughout our entire global community. Obviously, at a time when the church needs to increase its investment of personnel and resources dramatically, this part of the church will have significantly less to invest, not more. Its dwindling resources are likely to be consumed in caring for a huge aging population, trying to preserve its historic sanctuaries, and maintaining a remnant bureaucracy.

Of course, in addition to the traditional churches in Western Europe, there is a broad range of what the British call "nonconforming" churches. These include house fellowships and charismatic assemblies such as the Alban Works in Basel, Switzerland, and Ichthus Fellowship in London. Like conservative Protestant groups all over the world, these fellowships are generally growing, not declining. And many, like the two mentioned above, give very high priority to mission both in Europe and throughout the world.

These more evangelically and charismatically oriented churches have, in the last ten years, brought a genuine sense of renewal to the Christian community in Great Britain. But there has been no comparable renewal on the continent as yet; even though there are many small flickers of renewal in Holland, Germany, Spain, and Switzerland. Overall, these evangelical and charismatic assemblies are vital and growing but remain relatively small in numbers and influence.

Even if E.C. 92 achieves its optimistic economic growth projections, that achievement will probably only augment the growing secularization in "post-Christian" Europe. It will mean that Christians, while declining in numbers, may experience a modest increase in income. But whether European Christians can be effectively challenged to give an increasing share of their income and their lives and resources to the work of God's kingdom is another question.

In contrast to the general picture of church decline and decay in Western Europe, parts of Eastern Europe and the Soviet Union show signs of stirring renewal—a renewal that perhaps could ignite something dormant in the Western church. As the Republic of Germany has reunited, for instance, the German church is giving important signals of reunification as well. In March of 1990, the two regional synods of the Evangelical church of Berlin-Brandenburg held their first meeting in thirty years.[24]

When the Orthodox Church celebrated its millennium in the Soviet Union near the end of the eighties, many of the West got a glimpse into one of the most ancient expressions of this Christian tradition. Reports from the USSR that monasteries are being rebuilt and churches reopened give some guarded hope that the Orthodox faith might be allowed to expand its spiritual influence in Soviet society and throughout Eastern Europe.

We will undoubtedly also see a growth in conservative Protestantism in Eastern Europe and in the Soviet Union as well. Peter Kusmik, a Pentecostal, has started a new seminary in Yugoslavia to train leaders to meet the needs of all Eastern Bloc churches that aren't Orthodox or Catholic. Denver Theological Seminary has recently planted a Seminary for Evangelical Protestants in the Soviet Union.

However, while welcoming these signs of positive relationships between the churches of East and West, we need to pray that an "American invasion" doesn't corrupt the emerging spirituality in the Soviet Union and Eastern Europe. We really don't need to see the worst aspects of the American religious culture transplanted into this vulnerable new setting.

In light of the crippled Eastern European economies, however, neither the Roman Catholic, Orthodox, nor evangelical traditions in Eastern Europe and the Soviet Union will likely be able to invest much money or personnel in the work of the church beyond their own region. As these societies join the march toward modernization and the Western dream, this smoldering spirituality could be extinguished and this promising renewal quenched by the headlong rush to a Western consumer society.

A Struggling Church Down Under

The nations of the Southern Pacific seem to be a mixed story. Both Australia and New Zealand are essentially affluent Western countries, though the New Zealand economy is in a bit of a hard place at the present moment. Many of the other islands of the South Pacific are more Polynesian in their culture, but are fully engaged with Western modernization as well. There are a number of strong, growing, vital churches in both Australia and New Zealand, but reportedly that isn't the whole story.

"New gods have arisen in the South Pacific to displace the God of Abraham, Isaac and Jacob; a consumer's society set its heart on the pursuit of mammon," asserts Brian Carrell, a church leader from down under.[25] Reportedly, secularization is particularly evident in Australian culture, even though a strong Christian presence remains. As we have found elsewhere, the evangelical and charismatic churches seem to be growing more rapidly than traditional churches. But like their counterparts in the United States, as Mr. Carrell points out, they apparently tend to embrace the culture of consumerism more or less uncritically.

Historically, this part of the world has been very generous in sharing its daughters and sons in Christian mission. It has also been generous with its financial resources. The question is: Will the church down under be able to increase its investment in mission significantly in response to the growing challenges? Frankly, given the reported growing materialism of the culture, I don't think it is reasonable to expect the church in the South Pacific to do much more than it is doing now. But I hope to be proven wrong.

WAKING UP TO A CO-OPTED CHURCH IN NORTH AMERICA

The Pluralization and Privatization of Religion in North America

The religious character of North America is changing dramatically. As we enter the twenty-first century, the character of religion in Canada and the United

States will be vastly different from what it was as we entered the twentieth century. At that point of transition, traditional mainline denominations were the most prominent features on the religious landscape. In the last three decades of the twentieth century, we have seen the rapid pluralization and privatization of religion in North America. As we will see, these changes are likely to have a telling impact on the future mission of historic Christian churches in North America.

Historian Will Durant predicted in the early fifties that the final major confrontation in Western history would not be between democracy and communism, but between Christian and Eastern worldviews.[26] And as I have already mentioned, in recent decades we have seen a growing influence of Eastern religions in North America. This incursion comes not just through the New Age movement, but increasingly through Eastern influence in mainline Protestant and Catholic churches.

But Eastern religions won't be the only influence on the changing face of North American religion. Interest in the occult, various forms of animism, and even Satanism will probably continue to rise as well. And although Christian groups across the country—particularly charismatics and Pentecostals—are organizing "spiritual warfare" to challenge the powers represented by these new religious trends, I am concerned that these groups haven't done their homework. Churches in the nineties will undoubtedly need to confront potentially destructive spiritual powers. But practices based on their own speculations could become more aberrant than the forces they oppose. I urge the leaders of these groups, therefore, to work with their theologians to develop a solid biblical statement as a premise for this ongoing confrontation.

Beyond the growing influence of Eastern religions and the occult, we are likely to continue to see a growth in cults and similar movements. Cults range from Scientology and the Children of God (now in eclipse) to the Unification Church, which has expanded beyond being a religious cult to becoming a prosperous economic enterprise and a formidable right-wing lobbying organization.

One of the most rapidly growing American religious groups in the eighties was the Reorganized Church of the Latter Day Saints—the Mormons. The LDS had 5.2 million members in the United States and 7.9 million in their international church in 1990—and they are growing at a rate of 4 percent a year. It is projected that their United States membership will increase to 7.7 million and their international to 11.7 million by the year 2000. Their effective use of media, combined with their aggressive style of personal witness, will make them a force to be reckoned with in the twenty-first century.

"Twelve Step" spirituality—the basic program behind Alcoholics Anonymous, Overeaters Anonymous, and similar organizations—is yet another growing area of spirituality disassociated from any religious institution. These programs have helped thousands of addicts, and many who go through these programs do develop a strong personal faith. But the "Higher Power" advocated is not necessarily the God of the Judeo-Christian tradition. And because Twelve-Step programs are usually divorced from any religious structure, they do little to connect these people to a historic faith.

One of the most popular religious emphases today is the secular mythology of Joseph Campbell. Though Campbell died in the eighties, his views and persona are kept very much alive through videotapes and books. Don Latin, Religion Editor for the *San Francisco Chronicle*, writes, "For Americans alienated by Christian fundamentalism, Roman Catholic dogma or the soft under-belly of 'New Age' psycho-babble, Campbell's ideas swept across the religious landscape like a fresh invigorating breeze."[27]

Campbell's teachings essentially offers a religion separated from a personal God and from religious structures, freed from any sense of divine intention, to serve the spiritual needs of an increasingly secularly oriented society. Campbell called people back to the reality that we live in a world filled with mystery. In his recorded messages and writtings, he compellingly outlines his brand of cosmological understanding, inviting people to explore a broad range of religious mythologies. Then he tries to show people "how to live a human life under any circumstances." And he encourages his followers, very much in the spirit of autonomy, fully to experience being alive—"to follow your own bliss."[28]

Campbell's and other forms of "create your own mythology" are tailor-made to appeal to the Baby Boom generation, with its emphasis on personal autonomy, mythology, and self-fulfillment. What we are seeing is a growing religious eclecticism in which growing numbers are autonomously making up their own religion as they go. They may combine the teachings of Unity with a little motivational psychology and Canaanite fertility deities, supplemented by a generous array of New Age crystals.

This entire trend represents a widespread, rapidly growing hunger for a vital spirituality. If the church fails to respond to this hunger, non-Christian movements will, and many individuals will create their own autonomous spirituality.

The trend toward privatized, noninstitutional religion may well have serious social consequences. Peter Berger states that such "do it yourself" spirituality, "however real it may be to the person who adopts it, cannot any longer fulfill the classical task of religion, that of constructing a common world within which all of social life receives ultimate meaning binding on everybody."[29]

In addition, as Wade Clark Roof and William McKinney convincingly argue in their important book *American Mainline Religion,* the combination of the growing secularization of society and the growing privatization of faith may well result in a lessening of "a religiously grounded moral basis for society."[30] In other words, as America becomes more secular in its character and more pluralistic in its religious expressions, it is also likely to become more ambivalent regarding the commonly accepted moral norms that undergird our society and institutions. This growing ambivalence could place American moral culture in serious question.

Not surprisingly, these same trends of religious pluralization and privatization are also increasingly at work within historic Christianity itself. And we can expect the growing shift toward greater personal and congregational autonomy and growing pluralism of religious beliefs and practices to have a significant impact on the church's future. As society cuts loose from its moral moorings, the increasingly secularized church is likely to be less able to provide moral leadership and will expect less moral accountability.

Another outgrowth of increased autonomy and pluralism in the church is an increased blurring of boundaries between different traditions and denominations. Robert Wuthnow, in his important work, *The Restructuring of American Religion*,[31] indicates that confessional differences between denominations began to break down in the sixties. Now, for growing segments of the American population, being born a Baptist or a Methodist doesn't mean you will die one. Increasingly, church selection is seen less as a birthright and more as a matter of personal choice, the criterion often being "what meets my needs."

And with the growing emphasis on autonomously deciding what best meets my needs, the doctrinal differences between various traditions or denominations are becoming largely irrelevant to the rank and file. Somehow seminaries haven't gotten the word yet. Many are still struggling with the intricacies of the Heidelberg Confession when they should be equipping tomorrow's pastors to share the central teachings of Christian faith compellingly .

As autonomy gains even greater preeminence over any sense of community, Christians in some communities are beginning to change churches as readily and as often as they change supermarkets. And as people "shop around more," the churches which draw the most people are those that present the most dazzling array of consumer options. As a result, tomorrow's church may well be patterned less after a religious fortress (protecting faith) or a mission station (sharing faith) and more after a shopping mall (marketing faith)—providing a broad range of consumer options from which religious consumers can choose.

Such a trend will likely have a number of repercussions for tomorrow's church. First, traditional churches will lose adherents to churches that are more sensitive to the consumer desires and demands of their patrons. According to current trends, that means that mainline denominations and traditional congregations will likely decline more rapidly while conservative churches, which tend to be more "consumer oriented," will continue to grow. It also means that both mainline and conservative churches will feel the pinch to spend more resources on marketing and public relations and to create more educational, social, and recreational activities than their smaller competitors. Some of today's megachurches—such as the gigantic Willow Creek congregation in South Barrington, Illinois—are reportedly reaching numbers of unchurched peoples. But many others spend vast amounts on buildings, parking lots, and programs to evangelize principally suburban communities—and, I suspect, to persuade people to switch from "less interesting" smaller congregations. While megachurches will continue to grow in size and numbers in decades to come, I hope we will also see a growing number of "alternative congregations" that use fewer resources and do more outreach. If we are indeed trying to reach all the people, it should be patently evident that only the most affluent in our midst can really afford to build and staff megachurches.

The growth of megachurches is not the only current trend likely to continue in the nineties. Mainline Protestant churches are experiencing a dramatic and welcome increase in the number of women being ordained for ministry. Between 1977 and 1986, there has been an astounding 98 percent increase in the ordination of women for ministry in mainline churches.[32] The total enrollment of seminaries affiliated with the association of theological schools is fifty-six thousand students. Women make up one-third of the enrollment.[33]

Much more effort, therefore, must be put into opening opportunities for women in both pastoral and professional positions in tomorrow's church. Conservatives need to wake up to the reality that, if we have any hope of addressing tomorrow's issues, we will need the gifts of the entire church—women as well as men. That means conservatives need to struggle with their unquestioned commitment to male-dominated hierarchical structures and rediscover through Scripture the fact that God has always used both men and women in positions of leadership to advance the kingdom.

The Roman Catholic church is experiencing a serious attrition in clergy and in candidates for the orders, and there is little evidence of a reversal in that trend. Due to the Catholic church's refusal to ordain women or to waive the celibacy requirement, it is predicted fewer than seventeen thousand priests will be available to serve a projected seventy-five million people by the year 2005. Not only is the Catholic church having a difficult time recruiting new candidates for the priesthood; it is having trouble keeping the ones it has. For example, the Archdiocese of Chicago, the nation's largest jurisdiction, loses one priest every eighteen days.[34]

We will continue to see a renaissance of lay leadership by both women and men in local Catholic parishes. But as the religious orders decline, the church as a whole will be poorer for the loss of those who devote their entire lives to prayer and service. But perhaps the enthusiastic renewal of interest in spirituality by the laity will help offset this loss.

It seems evident that the Vatican is slowly taking back some of the ground given away to the laity under Vatican II. This is likely to mean increasing tension with the American Catholic church, whose growing lay leadership tends to be more independent in its own ideas than clerical leadership might be. This tension is unlikely to be resolved in the foreseeable future.

A Crisis of Vision and a Crisis of Leadership

I believe the number-one crisis facing the church in North America is a crisis of vision—or, more accurately, the absence of a truly biblical vision. This crisis affects all segments of the church—mainline and evangelical alike.

Regrettably, millions of conservative Christians in the eighties seemed to relinquish their responsibility to read the newspaper and the Bible for themselves; they simply played "Follow the leader." As Christian literacy continues to decline in the nineties, I fear this mindless following of concerned but often ill-informed leaders on the religious right will not only continue, but will grow among conservative Christians.

In the eighties, the National Conference of Catholic Bishops provided another kind of leadership that challenged peoples of all faiths to find an authentic biblical response to the urgent issues of our society. Their pastoral letters on everything from the economy to peacemaking stirred an important national conversation among Catholics and Protestants.

As we approach a new century, however, there appears to be a vacuum in Christian leadership. Catholics, mainline Protestants and more moderate evangelicals seem to have no shortage of button-down bureaucrats and retiring intellectuals. But I see few strong leaders calling us to a vision that has the power to motivate us and that equips us to engage the challenges of a new century.

An Increasingly Visible Ethnic Church

As our society becomes much more pluralistic and cross-cultural, so will the church. Black, Hispanic, Asian, and Native American congregations that have been almost invisible to many white Christians will in the nineties begin to move into view and into leadership. In the Christian media, we will begin to hear from a much broader range of ethnic groups. And you can be sure that those we hear from will reflect a broader range of social and political religious viewpoints than those that have dominated Christian publishing, radio, and television in the past. Leaders in ethnic churches have helped me prepare this section, which briefly examines some of the characteristics and trends in African-American, Hispanic, Asian, and Native American churches as we journey toward a new century.

The African-American church encompasses such major denominations as Catholic, Presbyterian, and American Baptist (over 30 percent of American Baptist congregations are black, Hispanic, or Asian), as well as traditionally black denominations, such as the African Methodist Episcopal.

Typically, black churches follow one of four main traditions:

- Baptist (the largest group),
- Pentecostal (in which the Church of God in Christ is the fastest growing),
- Methodism (three different branches), and
- a charismatic church that has emerged out of the black Pentecostal tradition.

Many of these black churches are independent and are deeply rooted in the African-American culture. They make major contributions not only to the black community, but to the larger society. However, some black congregations have felt the impact of the white prosperity gospel. Churches like the Crenshaw Centers and Faith Dome in Los Angeles attract eight to ten thousand adherents every week to learn how to live a more prosperous life.

I am told that there tends to be a socioeconomic split among black churches between the "mass" church, which serves blue collar and non-employed constituents, and a "class" church, which serves a community of college graduates, professionals, and entrepreneurs. In addition, there is sometimes tension between black Christians in the inner cities and those who have escaped to the suburbs. Although many of those who have left drive back in for church, I am told that others have less commitment to those left behind in the city and their needs. Others in the suburbs, however, maintain a very high commitment to the communities from which they came.

The African-American church will, in the future, continue to provide vital leadership for the larger society in general and in the civil rights struggle in paticular. Concord Baptist in Dallas, for example, is one of a number of churches that has started a mentoring program to empower black males. Its congregation reflects a growing concern for peace and justice issues as well.

Elward Ellis, president of a black organization called Destiny, reports a global awakening in the African-American church. "No longer do we derive our reality from dining at the European table. We are awakening to our own unique identity as a people," Ellis explains. "And out of our struggle, we are discovering that we can identify with the pathos and pain that people of color are experiencing all over the world. We will, in the future, see a dramatic increase in the mission of the African-American church, not only to the urgent needs of the inner city, but to the growing challenges in Africa, Latin America, and the Caribbean."

The large majority of people from Hispanic backgrounds in the United States are Catholic. But conservative Protestantism is growing among Hispanics in the United States, just as it is in Latin America. Pentecostal and Baptist churches enjoy the fastest rates of growth, with Pentecostals in the lead. Many of these Hispanic Protestant congregations are vital and exciting. Young people are converted from lives of drug addiction, the sick are often healed, and their services are exuberant.

I am told that most of these Pentecostal and Baptist churches are essentially rural congregations planted in urban areas. (Like blacks, many Hispanic members have migrated out of the city, but commute back in to go to church.) They are usually neither bicultural nor bilingual. As a consequence, younger Hispanics who are bicultural and bilingual find they no longer fit the more rigid churches in which they were raised. Some of them drift to Anglo churches, only to find they don't fit there, either.

Fortunately, a growing number of multiethnic churches are beginning to emerge that not only meet the needs of young bilingual Hispanics, but address urgent urban needs as well. Glad Tidings Church in the Bronx is an example of such a multiethnic congregation. Its music has a definite African-American flavor; its pastor is Hispanic; its congregation is multicultural. And Glad Tidings carries out a vital ministry among its urban neighbors. This type of multiethnic church may well be the wave of the future, providing leadership for a new century.

Not surprisingly, Hispanic Catholics tend to dislike the proselytizing of the Pentecostals and Baptists. And many are working to offer a vital ministry in order to keep their congregations. Even though the number of priests is dwindling, virtually all priests in Hispanic areas are fluent in Spanish. There are Catholic churches in many cities that not only have Spanish language services, but that conduct classes for Hispanics in marriage enrichment. And these churches work in a broad range of urban programs, from drug rehabilitation to housing programs. Tomorrow's urban leadership may well come from these socially active Catholic congregations.

However, Manny Ortiz, a professor at Westminster Seminary, expresses dismay at the growing brown and black flight from the inner cities. Many who are leaving are the educated professionals. Ortiz questions what impact this growing exodus will have on the leadership of tomorrow's urban churches.

Asian churches are essentially divided between established churches that have been here for at least three generations and immigrant churches. The established churches are comprised of Japanese, Chinese, Korean, and Filipino congregations.

Japanese churches, like Hispanic ones, tend to be divided between those who are bilingual and bicultural and those who hold to the "old ways." Unlike Hispanic churches, however, they often have two-language services. Chinese churches are divided between Chinese who have been raised in the United States and those who have recently immigrated from Hong Kong, China, and Taiwan. Korean churches are usually Presbyterian congregations comprised of small business owners. Filipinos worship in both Catholic and Protestant congregations.

The more recent immigrant churches are comprised of Vietnamese, Mien, Hmong, Laotian, and Cambodian congregations. They often lack a trained leadership and, like the conservative Hispanic churches, tend to be legalistic and rigid. Also like the Hispanic congregations, they are likely to have difficulty keeping their young people as these youth become bilingual and bicultural.

Both the established Asian churches and the immigrant congregations are having trouble retaining their members. Established churches are losing many of their young people to the aspirations of an upscale professional culture. Immigrant churches are experiencing a growing generational gap between the immigrant generation and their young. Again, the question we are faced with is: Who will provide leadership for these churches in the future?

Native Americans were evangelized by mainline religious groups during the Settlement Period. However, those efforts were seen by many Native Americans as simply another tool to extend white domination over native peoples. Today, a small remnant of Native Americans still identify with mainline Protestant churches. A scattering of Alaskan natives, for instance, are members of the Presbyterian church, and a few from other tribes belong to the Catholic church, particularly in the Southwest.

But by far the largest Christian grouping among Indian peoples is the Native American Church of North America. This group has received a great deal of attention because of its use of peyote (a cactus containing a hallucinogen) in worship services. In the Northwest, a number of native people are involved in a very ecstatic Shaker faith. As in many other ethnic groups, Pentecostalism is also growing among Native Americans, in part because Pentecostals take the supernatural realm seriously, as do many Indian peoples.

But Native American spirituality is also attracting renewed interest as Indians return to more traditional ways. Remarkably, this interest isn't restricted to native peoples. Mainline Christians are also showing an interest in Native American spirituality. Roy Wilson, a Native American who is a Methodist minister and who speaks at a large number of mainline churches, reinterprets Native American spirituality in the context of traditional Christian beliefs and spirituality. And the response is reportedly quite enthusiastic. Such a trend would certainly add to the eclectic blending we discussed earlier.

There is an emerging separatist movement among a growing number of ethnic groups. In December 1990, for example, Pew Foundation brought together Hispanic church leaders from all over the United States to discuss the future of the Hispanic church. One of the major outcomes of the gathering was the discussion of the possibility of creating their own seminaries and support institutions instead of being chronically dependent on the Anglo church. African-American church leaders are also talking about starting their own seminaries and support institutions.

It is possible that such a separatist movement among various ethnic churches could not only lead to a better job of educating their own leaders, but could provide a prophetic witness back to the larger white church—sparking renewal and the new cooperative mission we all seek. Perhaps we could eventually see the creation of a new consortium of ethnic churches, Catholics, mainliners, evangelicals, and nontraditionalists working together to address the challenges of a new century.

Mainline Decline and Conservative Captivity

As we approach the twenty-first century, then, we will see a proliferation of religious options both beyond and within the church. Conversions to secularism will increase, but growing numbers will create their own eclectic religious forms. Meanwhile, traditional and conservative churches will try, with varying degrees of success, to preserve their identities and meet the challenges of a changing world.

For mainline churches, the biggest challenge will be the graying of their congregations and decline in their numbers. Mainline denominations have declined steadily in the last half of the twentieth century. And according to analyst Reginald W. Bibby, Canadian churches are at the vanguard of this trend. Bibby reports that in 1946 two out of three Canadians would typically be found in mainline churches on Sunday morning. Today, he observes,

> that 1946 scene looks increasingly old-fashioned. My parents have been among those astonished to find that, just forty years later, a typical Sunday finds only one in three adults making their way to the nation's places of worship. Two-thirds to one-third in forty years![35]

According to Bibby, Canada is following close on the heels of Western Europe's post-Christian society, and secularization has become the rule rather than the exception. Most Canadians still identify themselves with a major denomination, Bibby declares, but

> religion has also ceased to be life-informing at the level of the average Canadian. People hold some beliefs and pray at least once in awhile. They occasionally find themselves at a wedding, perhaps a funeral and maybe a christening. But for most Canadians, religious commitment is a former acquaintance rather than a current companion.[36]

The same general pattern seems to be taking place in the United States, although not quite as rapidly. And several factors contribute to this decline. To begin with, mainliners aren't having as many children as their conservative counterparts, and their congregations are graying more rapidly. They are losing their young in greater numbers. And they are gaining fewer members through "church switching," which historically has been a primary source of new members.[37]

Lyle E. Schaller, an author and consultant in parish life, provides one example of what this decline looks like for Lutherans:

> During the 1970's the ELCA's [Evangelical Lutheran Church of America's] three predecessor churches lost more than 100,000 members of this generation through death. During the 1980's another 200,000 plus died. Actuarial tables suggest that at least 425,000 of the survivors of this loyal church-going generation of the ELCA Lutherans will die during the 1990's. When combined with other losses, this means ELCA will have to receive at least 3.2 million new members during the 1990's to remain on a plateau in size.[38]

But it is very unlikely the Lutherans will achieve anything like this level of growth . . . in part because they aren't retaining enough of their own young.

Mainline churches are particularly vulnerable to the rising tide of secularism in North America. In fact, Roof and McKinney assert that

> liberal Protestantism's real competition is not the conservatives they have spurned but the secularists they have spawned. Liberal churches have trouble stopping the secular drift of their own members, particularly those younger members who would otherwise be supplying the liberal Protestants of the future.[39]

The extent of mainline troubles can be seen in the recent fortunes of the National Council of Churches, which represents some forty million members in a broad spectrum of some thirty-two mainline denominations. Reportedly, the NCC budget has remained at about $13 million a year since 1975, which represents a real reduction of 53 percent in income. As a consequence, the National Council is in a state of disarray. Already, it has had to make major cutbacks in staff and services, and its situation shows no sign of improving.[40]

Stanley Hauerwas and William Willimon characterize mainline Protestantism as an aging dowager who is totally oblivious to world changes or its own failing condition:

> Mainline American Protestantism, as is often the case, plodded wearily along as if nothing had changed. Like an aging dowager, living in a decaying mansion on the edge of town, bankrupt and penniless, house decaying around her but acting as if her family still controlled the city, our theologians and church leaders continued to think and act as if we were in charge, as if the old arrangements were still valid.[41]

I am frankly dismayed at how many of the denominational executives I talk to seem indifferent to the graying and declining of mainline churches. I frequently ask, "Who do you expect to take over the work for peace, justice, and the integrity of creation as the mainline church is marginalized?" "Are you really expecting the growing number of independent fundamentalist churches to take over your mission in these critically important areas?" And few of those I ask are able to give me satisfactory answers.

While no one is predicting a 50 percent attrition in membership by 2030, as was forecast for the German church, most analysts expect mainline decline in North America to continue. Roof and McKinney predict, "The churches of the Protestant establishment, long in a state of relative decline, will continue to lose ground both in numbers and in social power and influence."[42]

Of course in light of the challenges we are facing in the coming decades, we can ill afford to lose the influence of any segment of the church. But mainline decline is particularly regrettable because mainline Protestants, along with

Mennonites and Catholics, appear most likely to engage tomorrow's urgent issues.

For many years, Mennonites have quietly worked with those in need all over the world, maintaining their witness for peace and justice often at a very high price. While Mennonites haven't yet joined the mainline decline, their membership is static and their membership is graying. And not even Mennonites are immune to encroaching secularization. There are signs that they are beginning to relinquish their historical concerns for peace, justice, and social responsibility to embrace a more popular and privatized brand of Christianity and a more comfortable way of life. Unless present trends change, they are likely to be less, not more, responsive to the challenges of the twenty-first century.

At present, Catholics are speaking out with clarity and conviction regarding the important issues of our time. And Roman Catholics constitute the largest single block in American religious life, comprising 25 percent of the religious community in America. After Vatican II, they moved rapidly into the mainstream of American life and experienced all the attendant benefits and dangers of that new status—most notably, acceptance by society and conformity to culture.

During the same period that mainline Protestantism has been declining, Catholicism has experienced modest growth. Some attribute the continued growth to rapid expansion of America's Hispanic community, along with continuing migration from Latin America.

But while membership hasn't dropped as it has for mainline Protestants, Catholics are experiencing real decline in church participation. While 74 percent of Catholics attended the Mass in 1958, only 51 percent attended in 1982. "Declines in mass attendance were most pronounced for young, upwardly mobile Catholics."[43] (Again, the young are most vulnerable to the secularizing values of American culture.) As we will show later, Catholic giving has also declined.

Reduced church involvement on the part of Catholics cannot help but negatively affect the Catholic church's ability to engage the issues of tomorrow. Members who are simply names in a book will not be available with their lives and resources to participate fully in the vital life and mission of the church.

All over the world, as we have seen, conservative Protestant churches are enjoying a general pattern of growth. That is certainly true in Canada and the United States as well.

Among those denominations that are still growing one finds Seventh-Day Adventists, the Church of the Nazarene, the Salvation Army, and the Assemblies of God, plus a broad spectrum of smaller Pentecostal and Holiness denominations. In addition, a growing number of independent fundamentalist and Pentecostal churches are springing up.

The Southern Baptists, while a mainline denomination, tend to be theologically conservative and are still experiencing slow but steady growth. But with the conservative takeover of the Southern Baptist Convention, there are growing signs that more moderate congregations could secede from the denomination. This would likely reduce the Southern Baptists' numbers and influence in American society.

Some of the most rapid growth is taking place in the independent charismatic network. Church growth specialist Peter Wagner estimates that this sector could experience 100 to 200 percent growth by the year 2000. A number of these groups, such as Vineyard Fellowship, are becoming de facto new denominations.

A number of noncharismatic churches are also experiencing high growth. Many of these are independent fundamentalist churches. A Church of Christ in Boston, however, has grown to over four thousand members. These Christians are committed not to use their money for buildings, so they worship in the Boston Commons. And contrary to the "homogeneous principle," this church attracts people from many different races and cultures.

A group of Baby Busters in Southern California have planted their own church. They call their church "New Song," and they worship to heavy metal music. They tell visitors, "If the volume is too loud, you are too old." Planting such new types of churches may well be necessary to attract the young and those on the margins back to the fold.

Conservative congregations tend to keep a much larger percentage of their young than mainliners—plus they have higher fertility rates. And this is only one of many reasons that conservative churches are growing.

Roof and McKinney believe that another reason for the strong growth trend among the conservatives is a popular turn toward experiential religion. I suspect this growth also reflects a profound human need. Conservatives stress the possibility of a personal encounter with the living God. Of course this same possibility is present in Catholic spirituality and other sources, but conservatives place it within the reach of all peoples.[44] And for many that encounter is life transforming.

Unfortunately, this vital encounter is often co-opted by right-wing or nationalistic political agendas. Or it is frequently twisted into a self-centered faith, oriented only around meeting the individual's needs and desires.

A number of conservative Christians, because of the pervasive influence of autonomous American values, have succumbed to what I call "the evangelical distortion"—the tendency to place the individual, rather than God, at the center of the gospel. From this viewpoint, instead of Christians' being co-conspirators in God's agenda of redeeming the world, God becomes a co-conspirator in their agenda of getting what they want out of life. God is there to help them get ahead in their careers, acquire their house in the suburbs, improve their relationships, and "color them beautiful."

While conservative Christians are growing in numbers, therefore, I don't believe they are always growing in their commitment to God and God's mission in the world. To the contrary, many conservatives are finding all kinds of ways to use their faith to sanction their own private pursuit of prosperity, position, and power. For this reason, although conservatives still talk a great deal about mission, I fear they may be even less available than they were in the seventies and eighties to commit their lives and resources in response to the compelling challenges of the nineties and beyond.

Remember, what we are up against in the nineties is not just changing demographics, but the pervasive and growing influence of secular visions and values. Secularization is increasingly drawing mainliners and Catholics—especially the young—away from church involvement. And although conservatives have found ways to hold and gain new members, my experience shows me that they are far from immune to secularization. The vital interests of many conservative young people I meet seems to have far less to do with Christian faith than with their own quest for cars, CDs, and immediate personal gratification.

Thank God there are Christian young people who are an exception to this overall pattern! But thus far I see little sign that mainliners and Catholics will be very successful in keeping their young people. Conservatives will be more success-ful in keeping the physical presence of their young, but they too seem to be losing their hearts to secularization.

A Church That Forgot to Count the Cost

In assessing the financial capacity of tomorrow's church to respond to tomorrow's global and national challenges, I find the prospects less than encouraging. I am particularly concerned about the swelling numbers of the poor in the Two-Thirds World. A financial commitment on a par with the post-World-War-II Marshall Plan will be needed to enable these people to escape their strangling poverty. But at a time when government, the private sector, and the church need to mobilize a much greater response, it looks as if almost everyone will do less. It is doubtful, therefore, that any such major compassionate initiative will be inaugu-rated in the nineties.

Governments are not likely, for instance, to contribute significantly more than they are already giving. The protracted debt crisis and the crushing needs of their own populations limit the self-help capabilities of Two-Thirds-World govern-ments. Western-European governments have already begun cutting back aid to poorer nations in the Southern Hemisphere in order to help jump-start the econo-mies of Eastern Europe. Canada has already cut back on its foreign aid due to ongoing economic difficulties.

And you can be sure that the United States, with our huge budget deficit, is not going to increase its investment in foreign aid. In particular, since we are no longer in a contest with the Soviets for the "hearts and minds" of people, Two-Thirds-World countries are no longer seen as strategic to the United States. As a consequence we will be less inclined to give them aid.

But how likely will the church be to increase its giving to meet the urgent needs of the nineties? Based on current trends, this picture is not encouraging, either.

First, as a direct result of graying and decline, the resource base of most mainline churches is at serious risk. Some mainline denominations haven't felt the economic crunch yet, but others are already cutting back. But remember, most of the wealth in both church and society is controlled by persons over fifty. As they pass from the scene in the next two decades, we can anticipate major economic crises in many mainline Protestant denominations. They will have to decide whether their shrinking resources will be used to maintain their bureaucracies or to support mission. And I am betting that the bureaucrats will win the day. Bottom line: in the decades to come, most mainline denominations will have fewer people, programs, and resources available to address the escalating needs of tomorrow's society.

Even though the Catholic church is growing demographically, it is having significant economic problems both internationally and in the United States. The Vatican has recently gone through a major economic scandal, involving fraud, showing a record deficit of $63.8 million in 1987.

This decline in the budget of the international church can be explained in part by changing giving patterns among American Catholics in the United States. In 1960, both Catholics and Protestants in the United States gave 2.2 percent of their income to their churches. Research indicates that twenty-five years later Catholics were giving only 1.1 percent—a 100 percent decline in giving. The recent closure of numbers of churches in Detroit and Chicago is evidence of the growing economic problems in the Catholic church.

Andrew Greeley, a leading Catholic sociologist, speculates that the decline in giving can be attributed primarily to an increased dissatisfaction with church policies.[45] While I am sure that dissatisfation with changes in church policy explains some of the decline, I suspect growing secularization of the membership is also to blame. But regardless of the reasons for the decline, the implications are the same. If Catholic giving continues on its present course, the Catholic church in the United States and worldwide is unlikely to invest significantly more in mission than it is doing now.

Conservative Protestants in the United States typically give a larger percentage of their resources to the church than their mainline counterparts. Many evangelicals still talk about mission, and some invest in it. But it is my experience that an increasing proportion of what is given in these churches typically goes for buildings, bureaucracy, and overhead. Conservatives, like mainliners, typically spend the bulk of their budgets providing for those within their own local church. And they both are involved in what I call "surrogate servanthood"— relying on paid help and hired guns instead of on lay volunteers to get the work done. If these giving and allocation patterns remain constant, I don't believe that conservative Protestants will be likely to increase their investment significantly in meeting tomorrow's needs, either.

Therefore, as physical and spiritual needs dramatically escalate at the threshold of the twenty-first century, it seems unlikely that church response will begin to keep pace with the mounting challenges. I sincerely hope I am wrong. I long to see an international renewal in the church and a mobilization of Christian resources to address these urgent needs. But unless a renewal takes place, the future looks very bleak.

Let me share some statistics behind my somewhat pessimistic projections. Between 1968 and 1985, Americans enjoyed a tremendous jump in disposable annual personal income—$2,511 in 1982 dollars. During this same period, however, total annual giving by church members increased only $49.[46] This pattern also reflects an overall decline in the percentage given during this same period—from 3.05 percent of income in 1968 to 2.79 percent in 1985.[47]

In 1990, the research group which originally released these statistics revised its estimates. Originally it had predicted that average giving would decline to 2.53 percent of members' income by the year 2002. However, now it projects it could be "as low as 1.94 percent in 2002, if the present trend holds constant."[48] This sharp decline in projected United States giving will obviously mean a significant reduction in resources available to invest in both domestic and international mission.

Ironically, research indicates that those who are poor tend to give a much higher percentage of their income than the affluent. Those with annual incomes under ten thousand dollars gave 2.8 percent of their household incomes. Those with annual incomes of seventy-five to one hundred thousand dollars contributed only 1.7 percent.[49] Particularly troubling is the recent report by the Independent Sector (another leading research firm) that indicates there has been a major shift in giving by Americans from the international to the domestic. It reported that while overall giving in the United States was up 20 percent from 1987 to 1989, giving to any kind of international organization was down 38 percent during the same period.[50]

If during a period of economic growth we saw a relative decline in giving, what is likely to happen if the recession we are in deepens or if the young are excluded from access to the economic bounty enjoyed by other generations? The giving patterns of the Baby Bust generation are already a cause for concern. Boosters aged fifty-five to sixty-four are the most generous, contributing $667 annually per household. Older Boomers aged thirty-five to forty-four contribute $478 annually per household. But those under twenty-five—the Baby Busters— contribute only $89.[51] And World Vision reports that in their child sponsorship program, those who are under thirty give fully 50 percent less than those who are over thirty. This is a much bigger differential then it has seen before.

Of course, the argument can be made that when these younger members are established, their giving patterns could match that of their parents and grandparents. I really don't believe that is likely. As shown in earlier chapters, the economic power of most of the younger Boomers and the Baby Busters is unlikely to come close to that of their parents. As a consequence, they will probably have much less discretionary time and money to invest in the work of the church than those who preceded them.

Even if this younger generation had the income, I seriously question whether as a group it will be more likely to invest its money in meeting the challenges of the future, especially in helping others. We have programmed the Christian young to expect to have everything economically that their parents had and a little more. But while their parents could typically buy the split-level and everything that goes with it on a single income, such a lifestyle today requires at least two incomes. Even then, most young people will never have as much economically as their parents have—but they will try. And in their efforts to get it all and have it all, they will have much less discretionary time and money to invest in the work of the church. My reluctant conclusion is that over the next three decades the Christian young will not even begin to match the present level of giving, let alone increase . . . and primarily because we sold them the wrong dream.

Remember, fewer and fewer young people are choosing to affiliate with the church. And a declining number of those who do affiliate are becoming seriously involved. "While 50 percent of those over thirty say they attended church in the past seven days," according to Gallup surveys, "only 28 percent of those under thirty report doing so." And George Gallup also reports that "by a 2 to 1 margin . . . religion is less important to them than it is to their parents."[52] With declining numbers, their ability to support the church will obviously further decline.

If we fail to begin reorienting the values of the young and to help them find another dream to which they can give their lives, I believe the future of the American church is in serious jeopardy. Not only will it be unable to address the challenges of the twenty-first century. We could also see the church in Canada and the United States follow the church in Europe into a post-Christian future.

A North-American Church in Need of Renewal

The purpose of this chapter, again, is to begin a very important conversation regarding how effective the church is likely to be in addressing tomorrow's challenges. My very cursory analysis leads me to conclude that much greater prayer and effort must be given to the renewal of the church and Christian life. Business as usual will not begin to prepare us to engage the escalating challenges of tomorrow's world.

As I will show in chapters to come, God is in the process of giving birth to a whole new order that will turn this world upside down. If we can reasonably take our declining involvement in serving and giving to the church as a barometer, it would appear that we are increasing our commitment to the present order, which is passing away. We appear to be spending more and more of our total life resources on conforming to the demands of our consumer culture instead of working for the inbreaking of the reign of God.

Let's reflect a moment on our stewardship responsibility as American Christians. We Americans constitute roughly 6 percent of the world's people, and we consume over 40 percent of the world's resources. What we need to address this inequity, however, isn't more guilt. What we need is to be awakened to a new global reality—that we live in an interdependent, interconnected world, and that if we use more than a fair share of what God has entrusted to us, someone else will go without.

David Barrett estimates that of the billion people living in absolute poverty (making less than $370 per person per year, with half the children not surviving to their fifth birthday), nearly 200 million identify themselves as members of the international body of Jesus Christ.[53] There is something desperately wrong in the body of Christ when some of us are living palatially and others are not able to feed their children.

In light of this reality, we in the Western Church must repent. We must unmask the powers in our lives, congregations, and the culture which has seduced us. We must be awakened to the reality that we are not called to advance the present order, but to be a part of the inbreaking of a radical new order. And essential to being part of this new order is the embracing of a new dream—a wild outrageous hope that the God who created all things will write the final chapter of the world and make all things new.

When we transfer our allegiance from working for the Western Dream to advancing the reign of God, one of the first things that will change is our priorities in the use of our time and resources. We will rediscover and embrace a theology of stewardship in which we recognize our responsibility to be caretakers of God's created order. We will take creative initiative to reduce how much of our time and resources we spend on our own lives and congregations so that we have much more of our total resources available to respond to the escalating challenges of tomorrow's world. And we will recognize that we are not autonomous believers or congregations, but part of a growing, international Christian movement. We will steward our resources, therefore, together with the international community of God's people, to cooperate in the birthing of something that looks more like the future that is of God than the Western Dream. And our transformation will only begin when we come to grips with the extent to which we have given ourselves to an alien dream and let ourselves be captivated by the values of a secular culture.

Questions for Discussion

1. How is Christianity likely to fare in relationship to the other world religions as we enter the twenty-first century?
2. How can Christians participate meaningfully in interfaith dialogue while maintaining the distinctiveness of the Christian faith?
3. How is the church in the Two-Thirds World likely to change in the future, and how will it be able to respond to the challenges of the coming decades?
4. How is the church in Western Europe, the Eastern Bloc, and in Australia-New Zealand likely to change in the future, and how will it be able to respond to the new challenges?
5. How is the church in North America likely to change in the future, and how ably is it likely to respond to the new challenges?
6. How is the character of religion in North America likely to change in the nineties and beyond?
7. How are the demographics of the church in North America likely to change as we enter a new century?
8. How are changes in demographics, changes in values, and changes in giving likely to impact the ability of the North American church to respond to the new challenges?
9. Why do the Christian young pose such a serious problem in terms of the church's ability to address tomorrow's challenges?
10. If we want to see a real change in the availability of resources to respond to the escalating challenges, where should we begin?

8

Waking Up to the Captivity of the Christian Mind

A scorching sun bore down on our Land Rover as we pulled into the city of Cayes in Haiti's southwest peninsula. We stopped to ask for directions. All around us, the heat was unrelenting, the poverty unbelievable, the friendly greetings of the people disarming.

We got underway again, our directions taking us up into the foothills above Cayes. The oppressive temperatures subsided. The poverty disappeared. All at once we found ourselves on a beautiful hilltop in a community of graciously landscaped three- and four-bedroom houses. Here the people didn't wave. They didn't even look up to acknowledge our arrival.

West Indies Missions had constructed this compound in this beautiful location decades earlier as a base from which to carry the gospel into the Haitian countryside. All the houses came complete with electricity, stereos, freezers—the works. It looked just like a typical stateside suburb—except for the idyllic climate and a view that would have commanded a dear price in Hawaii or Southern California. And the missionaries who lived in this American oasis also had Haitian servants who handled all domestic work and looked after the children.

As we walked to the far end of the compound, our hosts showed us, with evident pride, the newest house that had been built in their "City of Light." It was a large, elegant structure that the president of the Haitian Baptist Church had built with their help. He was the first Haitian invited to live in this all-white American compound.

Several months later, traveling in the back country, I saw the consequences of this missionary generosity. In at least three rural churches I happened upon, Christians were struggling, at tremendous sacrifice, to build homes for their pastors. They aspired to provide residences for their ministers that were as modern and as expensive as the ones their president and the missionaries lived in on the hilltop above Cayes.

Before this new standard had been raised, pastors had always lived in homes very much like members of their congregations. Typically, these are two- and three-room post-and-wattle residences with thatched roofs and glistening white-washed exteriors. Doors and windows are painted in festive pinks, bright blues, and subdued greens. A few have concrete floors, but most have dirt. None of them have plumbing or electricity. And most cost about five hundred dollars to construct.

When I arrived in one remote area, villagers were just putting the finishing touches on a concrete-block, metal-roofed house that towered over the more modest Haitian homes. To raise the more than ten thousand dollars needed to build this residence for their pastor, they had curtailed virtually all other church activities for a year and a half. Each church family had given sacrificially out of its very mar-ginal income (an average of two hundred dollars per person per year).

All of this took place in a community in which only 20 percent of the children can afford to go to school. The village cannot afford a health clinic. And this particular year, it didn't even have enough money for basic immunization of its children. While the villagers' willingness to sacrifice is certainly laudable, one wishes it could have been directed toward something other than affluent housing for their pastor.

To this day, I seriously doubt that the missionaries who lived in this mountaintop enclave have any idea of what they had done. I have no doubt their motives were sincere. But like most of us, they lived their lives and acted on their faith from largely unexamined assumptions. Most of us are loathe to ever take a good, hard, critical look at the assumptions on which we premise our lives or act out our mission. It is much easier to assume that because we are Christians, the visions and values to which we give our lives are Christian as well.

I am sure these missionaries came to Haiti highly motivated to advance the cause of Christ. But while they proclaimed the gospel of the kingdom of God with their mouths, they bore witness to a very different kingdom with their lives. And it looks like their witness for the American Dream may have been by far the most persuasive.

These missionaries unwittingly transplanted the values of modernization and the Western Dream into Haitian society. By building their American compound and by inviting the president of the Haitian Baptist Church to join their affluent inner circle, they planted an alien growth that is still spreading across the Haitian countryside with devastating effect.

Someone has written that the Western Dream has become the vision of a better future for virtually the entire planet. Regrettably, that seems to be true. Many are even interpreting the radical changes in the Soviet Union and Eastern Europe as a victory for the Western Dream and the expansion of the global consumer society. Tragically, the unquestioned commitment to modernization and the unrestrained quest of the Western Dream seem as pronounced among those who identify with the church as those outside it.

As we saw in the last chapter, one of the major reasons that the church is likely to fail to address the escalating challenges that fill our world is that our lives, resources, and institutions have been co-opted by an alien vision. We also saw that the prime seducers of the Christian young are not Eastern gurus or Marxist revolutionaries, but the sirens of the Great Consumer Society. I believe the principalities and powers have always sought to expand their influence not only over culture, but over the church as well. And regrettably, they seem in our modern world to be flourishing.

Many of us of all ages naïvely thought we could embrace modernization with all its affluence and benefits without ever being tainted by its values. Belatedly, a few seem to be waking up to the reality that when we welcome modernization into our lives, we unwittingly invite secularization into our souls as well.

Now, in assailing modernization, I am not for a moment arguing that we retreat to a premodern world or reject all forms of contemporary life and culture, including technology. But I am urging that we recognize that our form of modernization is premised on a set of value assumptions that are inherently in tension with biblical values. And this type of modernization aspires to little more than ever-expanding consumerism.

Walter Brueggemann charges,

> The contemporary American Church is so largely encultured to the American ethos of consumerism that it has little power to believe or to act. This enculturation is in some way true across the spectrum of church life, both liberal and conservative.[1]

It appears we Christians of all traditions are part of a vast parade, marching lockstep toward a post-Christian era. Those in Western Europe appear to be in the forefront of the parade, with Canadian and American Christians only a short distance behind. And I fear that as Christians in the Two-Thirds World increasingly embrace modernization and the Western Dream, they too will be seduced by the insidious values that go with them.

In this chapter we will strive to come to grips with why we Christians, particularly those of us living in North America, seem to be so unresponsive to the urgent challenges filling our world today and tomorrow. As we discussed in the first chapter, of course, part of our unresponsiveness comes from our failure to anticipate change.

However, I am strongly persuaded that the number one crisis facing the church today is a crisis of vision. When I use the term vision I am not referring to anything hyperspiritual. I simply mean the image of the preferred future we want for ourselves, those we care about, and the larger world.

Kenneth Boulding, speaking at a conference on the future, declared, "No people, society or organization can long exist without some compelling vision of the future that calls us forward into tomorrow." Stanley Hauerwas characterizes vision as the "hallmark" of the moral life.[2] And, of course, the Scriptures insist that "without a vision the people perish" (Prov. 29:18). Tragically, not only are we perishing; the people we are called to serve are perishing too, because we lack a biblically informed vision.

The intent of this chapter, then, is to enable readers to evaluate the extent to which the visions and values of secular culture have infiltrated our lives and churches and are likely to alter our future. And in so doing, we will intentionally seek an alternative to the "secular humanist" view of secularism which, as already mentioned, I find to be flawed both historically and biblically.

In our quest to find a basis of hope in a changing world, we will look at three very different visions for our common future. We will begin, in this chapter, by trying to understand something of the origin, character, and implications of modernization and the Western Dream. A growing number of people, in reaction to the Western Dream, are seeking to discover in our "organic" past an alternative vision for our future. We will try to understand something of the origin, character, and implications of the new organic visions for our future as well.

In the next chapter, we will look at a biblical vision. We will contrast it to both the Western Dream and the new organic visions to see if we can find a basis for life and action in a historic Judeo-Christian vision of the future.

Gibson Winter, a social ethicist at Princeton, has presented a helpful model for overviewing the history of human civilization and our approach to the world around us.[3] He suggests that history can be broken into two major periods, the "organic" period and the "mechanistic" period, each of which becomes a paradigm for a distinct set of attitudes and assumptions about creation, about human beings, and about our common future. By isolating our past into these two periods, Winter offers us the possibility of a "historical hermeneutic" through which we can more fully understand the human journey.

Further, Winter suggests that this analysis creates the potential for the emergence of a third paradigm—the artistic or the creative model. We will use that concept to discuss the biblical alternative in the next chapter. I have taken the liberty of borrowing Winter's helpful terminology to examine the origins and focus of these three very different visions for our common future.

Of each vision, we will ask four questions:

- What are the images of the preferred future in this vision?

- What are the images of God and the creation?

- What are the images of persons and community?

- What are the images of the pathway to the preferred future?

The reason I have chosen the word *image* in these two chapters instead of *idea* is that ideas are customarily seen as the property of intellectuals. Images, on the other hand, are really the possessions of all peoples. Images come to us through stories, songs, and faith. While ideas exercise the intellect, images engage us in the full range of human experience—including the intellect. In addition, images have the power to motivate us to act.

Kenneth Boulding states that images are "the basic bond of any society, culture, subculture or organization."[4] Mircea Eliade goes even further, asserting that "images bring [people] together more effectively and more genuinely than any analytic language. Indeed, if an ultimate solidarity with the whole human race does exist, it can be felt and activated only at the level of images."[5]

Since the mechanistic vision as expressed in the Western Dream is clearly the dominant model for much of today's world, we will look at that vision first. And we will examine the images that comprise that vision. Then we will examine how the images and values of the new organicists challenge the mechanistic model.

MECHANISTIC BEGINNINGS AND THE WESTERN DREAM

Our ancestors, operating from an essentially organic paradigm, found themselves victimized by natural forces over which they had little control—droughts, floods, fires, and disease. They were also victimized by spiritual forces they didn't understand. Increasingly, traditional peoples sought ways to achieve greater control of their environment. And they sought to increase their control not only through religion, but also through technology.

Out of this compelling desire to understand and master the natural world more fully, a new paradigm slowly emerged. A by-product of the Enlightenment, this mechanistic model proposed a strategy to subdue the natural realm and bring it under human control—to fashion a new and modern age.

This mechanistic paradigm is premised on very different assumptions than the essentially organic cultures that preceded it. And it is working for a very different notion of the better future. Gibson Winter writes:

From its inception, this [model] has been marked by a search for power over its world. . . . The passion for mastery led to advances in science, exploration of distant lands, conquest of and enslavement of peoples throughout the globe, and the development of techniques for mass production and distribution of goods.[6]

What Are the Images of the Preferred Future?

The mechanistic model is, of course, premised on a linear view of time. Out of a Judeo-Christian tradition, a linear view of time had been introduced into an organic world of seasons and cycles. Time was viewed as beginning in creation and ending in consummation. Jews, Christians, and Muslims all share this linear view of time.

In the Middle Ages, this linear view of time had a vertical dimension, with believers aspiring to the consummation of history and the establishment of God's kingdom on earth. In the Enlightenment, I believe, this vertical quest for God's promised consummation was turned on its side and became a horizontal, secular pursuit of progress—a quest to fabricate a terrestrial paradise. Leaders of the Enlightenment assured us that if we cooperated with natural law, our entire society would progress economically and technologically. We would achieve new levels of mastery over nature and erect a new, technological paradise.

Undoubtedly, the first vision of this technological paradise was presented in Francis Bacon's sixteenth-century work, *The New Atlantis*. Bacon reasoned,

> For man by the fall fell at the same time from his state of innocency and from dominion over creation. Both of these losses can in this life be in some part repaired; the former by religion and faith, the latter by arts and sciences.[7]

"Dominion over Creation" was both the goal of Bacon's life and the subject of *The New Atlantis*. Many have longed, as those who first bit into the fruit, to know as God knew in order to be powerful as God is powerful. The quest for power and control is at the center of the mechanistic vision for a better future. This quest for power has been increasingly separated from the reign of God and is being driven by the aspirations of the principalities and powers that are intent on undermining all that God purposes. In the mechanistic model, now and in Bacon's time, the powers found willing collaborators who also hunger for greater mastery and control.

In *The New Atlantis*, Francis Bacon described his vision for a technological paradise achieved through an aggressive science that subdues a passive creation for the benefit of humankind. As we enter Bacon's fictional island kingdom of New Atlantis, we are shown a realm of unprecedented affluence—richly draped walls, carpeted chambers and regal garments . . . and the possibilities of a new society of consumption on a grand scale.

Bacon envisioned technologies which would create artificial tastes and fragrances, preserve food, provide energy and offer advanced transportation and weapons systems. The central institution of this new advanced society wouldn't be the church; it would be a scientific research center.[8]

Theodore Roszak characterizes *The New Atlantis* as the earliest significant anticipation of the technocratic state.[9] And he goes on to point out that the Western Dream—the vision of an increasingly profitable future achieved through technology—is a fuller expression of Bacon's vision. Leaders of the Enlightenment built on Bacon's foundation to entrench the mechanistic model firmly at the center of modern thinking.

In the Western Dream, the better future has come to be seen as ever-increasing levels of economic growth, technological progress, and personal consumption. Someone has written, "Marxism says all there is is matter. Capitalism says all that matters is matter. But they are both inherently materialistic worldviews, lacking any sense of transcendence."

Futurist Barry Hughes, in summarizing the obvious benefits of the adoption of the Western Dream and the pursuit of modernization, points out not only that we have gained greater control over natural forces that often victimized our ancestors, but also that we are

> on the average better fed, better sheltered and healthier than at any time in history. If there is any doubt about the beneficial aspects of modern technology, a glance at mortality patterns should dispel it. Global life expectancy at birth is now sixty years. In the poorest forty-five countries, it is forty-eight years. In traditional societies it has seldom historically exceeded thirty.[10]

Undeniably, the Western Dream, modernization, and market-oriented economies have provided impressive material benefits. Even former Communist countries are belatedly acknowledging the superiority of the Western Dream and the market forces that drive it in terms of economic growth and the sheer capacity to produce enormous quantities of consumer goods. Nowhere has this dream proved more successful than in the United States. While Republicans and Democrats have somewhat different notions of how to keep America growing, they are singleminded in their commitment to the American Dream.

But to really understand this dream, it isn't enough to look at the pragmatic benefits; we must also look at the societal forces that drive it. The Western Dream is driven by the invented need for ever-increasing levels of stimulation.

John Rader Platt, a professor of physics at the University of Chicago, asserts that in this modern era we have invented the fifth need of humankind. In addition to the basic survival needs of air, water, food, and protection from climatic changes, "the fifth need is the need for novelty—the need throughout our waking life for continuous variety in the external stimulation of our eyes, ears, sense organs and all our nervous network."[11]

Our indoctrination to crave novelty, begun early in the century, has stepped up its pace in recent decades. A constant onslaught of advertising has conditioned us, instead of restricting our consumption to those things we need, to increasingly expand our wants and embrace products we never even considered before. And the result is the creation of a society whose economic health depends on constantly increasing consumer appetites, not only in the United States but around the world. Of course, it is precisely those expanding appetites that are creating our mountains of garbage; threatening our air, water, and land; and undermining our spirituality.

I believe the primary reason we have been seduced into becoming superconsumers is that we have bought into an image of the better future that equates happiness with acquisition. We have really come to believe that the more we accumulate in our garages, ring up on our charge cards, and invest in the newest novelties, the happier we will be. We all want what is best for our children, and we work long hours to provide for them. But even here we define "what is best" in largely economic terms, and we express our love by surrounding our children with all the artifacts of our consumer culture.

Lesslie Newbigin charges:

> The effect of the post-enlightenment project for human society is that all human activity is absorbed into labor. It becomes an unending cycle of production for the sake of consumption.[12]

The powers have persuaded us as a culture that our ultimate human purpose is to become successful consumers. And yet growing numbers are dissenting and looking for a more transcendent purpose.

In our founding papers for the United States we sanctioned, as a part of the American Dream, the individual "pursuit of happiness." Lesslie Newbigin observes that "happiness had no definition except what each autonomous individual might give to it."[13] And as we have seen, the pursuit of happiness with the Baby Boomers has been expanded to not only include material acquisition, but also self-actualization. Increasingly, both Christianity and the more Eastern spiritualities have sought to respond to this growing desire for self-actualization and self-mastery.

As we showed at the beginning of the chapter, Christians as well as non-Christians have embraced modernization, the Western Dream, and the individual pursuit of happiness as an unquestioned given. Although their approaches and concerns differ, mainliners and evangelicals alike seem also to have essentially accepted the materialistic aspirations of the Western Dream as their primary image of the preferred future.

Mainliners generally want to see the system operate more justly and with more economic opportunities for all, regardless of race, sex, or age. They are intent on trying to build an escalator into the Western Dream, even changing some of the structures of society so the poor get a taste of the "good life," too. But while mainliners sometimes criticize capitalism, rarely have I heard them critique modernization, the Western Dream, or the values on which the mechanistic model is premised. And ecumenicals seem largely indifferent to the fact that they are losing their young people to secularism, since it is often a secularism they share.

Evangelical Christians, in the main, have not only enthusiastically made the Western Dream their own; they often look at their material success as evidence of God's blessing on their lives. As a result, although they give to help the poor, they generally have little interest in seeing structures changed to make the American Dream operate more justly.

Evangelicals even tend to confuse the progress of the Western Dream with the advancement of God's kingdom. In reading most evangelical books on finance and career planning, one is left with the clear impression that the American economic system and the agenda of the kingdom are the same. They largely fail to recognize that our vocation is not the preservation and advancement of the present order, but cooperation with God in the inbreaking of a radical new one.

Apart from bandying about the superficial and inaccurate characterization of "secular humanism," few evangelical leaders offer a compelling critique of secularism either. Quite the contrary, most evangelical leaders in both their Christian pronouncements and their affluent lifestyles seem fully to sanction the Western Dream and all the values that go with it.

In many evangelical churches, for example, for all the talk about the lordship of Christ, the message to the Christian young regarding which agenda comes first couldn't be clearer. Agenda one is getting their careers underway, getting their houses in the suburbs, and getting their upscale lifestyles started. Then, with whatever time or resources are left, they are expected to serve Christ. And for the Christian young, as we have seen, the quest to do it all and have it all will leave them with significantly less to invest in the advance of the kingdom than their parents had.

As a result of this idolatrous elevation of the Western Dream to primacy in our lives, homes, and churches, we have seriously undermined our capability to address the escalating challenges of the twenty-first century. We are not only experiencing a crisis of vision. We have unthinkingly embraced secular values that are antithetical to values of God's kingdom—the values of self-seeking, individual-ism, and materialism that are endemic to the Western Dream. Of course, to the extent that these visions and values have captured our lives, neither our time nor our money will be available to invest in the advance of God's kingdom.

Therefore, the reason that neither mainline nor evangelical Christians nor their young are likely to rise to the challenges of a new century is that we have been captured by visions and values alien to the God we claim and the cause we seek. The principalities and powers have seduced us into following a fraudulent dream and embracing false values. And most of us are reluctant to unmask the powers or question the Western Dream.

What Are the Images of God and the Creation?

Against this backdrop of the Western Dream, what are the assumptions implicit in the mechanistic model regarding God and the larger created order? How do these assumptions affect our lives and shape our future?

Gibson Winter charges that too often Westerners have treated traditional cultures with disdain, dismissing people who are still a part of a more organic culture as "primitive." He adds that

> Western people have assumed that calculative thinking and organizing in their societies reflect "rational" or fully human development. On this evolutionary timeline, traditional peoples were thought of as ignorant or confused. The world of sacred and biological rhythms could be dismissed as a superstition that represented humanity's infantile period.[14]

Again, Francis Bacon was in the forefront of developing the metaphysical basis for this model. He made a historic distinction between the "Word of God" and the "Works of God." The "Word of God" in his view has to do with divine revelation and things religious. The "Works of God" involve the larger, natural world. By drawing a line between the natural and spiritual realms, Bacon fashioned a dualism that has remained with us to this day.

In that one act, Bacon unwittingly evicted God and any sense of divine purpose from the natural world. In that one act, Bacon repudiated

> Pantheism, Theism, imminence and transcendentalism. God as Being or Essence or Cause is neither imminent within his system of nature nor transcendental to it but lies altogether outside it.[15]

This remarkable declaration has significantly contributed to the desacralization of creation. Freed from any sense of divine presence or purpose, the natural realm is reduced to nothing but passive, malleable resources, the stuff out of which we erect our technological paradise. It is the place where we pump our oil and set up our campers. Unlike a historic Christian view, which regards the natural realm as inherently sacred, this model views nature in starkly utilitarian terms. And in this model even God is reduced to nothing but an impotent deity—a cultural hangover of a forgotten era and largely irrelevant to a modern world.

Bacon's primary tool for the construction of his technological paradise was objective knowledge: "Knowledge as power." He saw the potential power of empirically studying the phenomena of the natural realm in order to subdue that realm and to fashion a new world of technology and affluence for the benefit of humankind.

Clearly, Bacon's empiricism, as transmitted through our intellectual and scientific traditions, is still the standard window on the real world for modern society. We still seem to believe that it is possible to observe objectively and to understand empirically the world around us, even though quantum physics is beginning to challenge this bedrock assumption of the mechanistic worldview. However, "scientism" is still on the throne. And reductionistic positivism is still alive and well among many of those who subscribe to this viewpoint.

Today, we in the West still subscribe to a profoundly dualistic view in which the natural world is freed of any real sense of divine presence or purpose. Even many conservative believers tend to see the world this way—with God's activity largely confined to the spiritual realm. This God comes to prayer meetings and revival services but is largely impotent to do anything about the crises in Central America or the homeless in the United States—to in any way act in "secular" history until Christ returns.

I believe God seems even more remote and impotent in the belief of many mainline Christians. James Turner, in his very important work in American intellectual history, *Without God, Without Creed: The Origins of Unbelief in America,* suggests that as mainline churches increasingly adopted the rationalist values of their day, their God became increasingly powerless, and unbelief became distressingly widespread. He even suggests that mainline seminaries directly contributed to the growing attitude of disbelief in the United States.[16]

Lesslie Newbigin points out that liberal theology set the boundaries of what it was possible to believe, based on axioms of the Enlightenment. For example, modern scientific worldviews were accepted as the

> only reliable account of how things really are, and the Bible had to be understood only in terms of that account. This required a reconstruction of biblical history on the lines of modern historical science. It required the elimination of miracle. It dictated that while the crucifixion of Jesus could be accepted as a fact of real history, his resurrection was a psychological experience of the disciples.[17]

At any rate, the God of many ecumenicals does seem somewhat stuck in the backwash of history, unable to act in either the spiritual *or* the societal realm. And as a consequence, mainliners tend to assume it is *their* responsibility to act in God's behalf.

For a growing number of people in our modern world, regardless of their religious affiliation, the Creator God is no longer relevant to their lives, their society, or their future. They live in a world alienated from the God who created them—a world with no transcendent purpose, no meaning beyond the marketplace and the growing commercialization of our global society.

What Are the Images of Persons and Community?

When Bacon drew that historic line that severed the natural order from the spiritual, his scalpel unintentionally sliced through persons, dividing the natural from the spiritual dimensions of personhood. As the Enlightenment took precedence in the world of ideas, persons were no longer seen as image bearers of a Creator God, having innate worth and immortal life. Instead, persons were reduced to what could be empirically known about them. Over time, persons came to be seen by many as nothing but the sum of their organic core and their behavioral surface.

Not surprisingly, in this model we not only see the better future in largely economic terms, we also see persons that way. According to this view, human worth is not innate but derivative. It is our success as producer/consumers in the larger economic marketplace that determines our worth. We identify ourselves by where we work, where we live, the cars we drive. "The more we own the more we are."

Again, Christians are far from immune to this economic way of thinking. I find many Christians struggling to validate their existence through success in their jobs and their ability to consume, while at the same time struggling to nurture their spirituality.

This mechanistic model hasn't developed a cogent concept of evil. While society based on the mechanistic model may pay lip service to traditional views of morality, it really tends to define evil as anything that gets in the way of its advance. If the ultimate good is economic and technological expansion, then evil is pragmatically anything that undermines "progress," whether it is the attempt to preserve wetlands from development or the actions of a renegade dictator who threatens the international climate for commerce.

In the mechanistic model we find ourselves not only estranged from the creation and from the Creator, but from any real sense of human community. As we will see, Enlightenment thinker John Locke's ideas of radical individualism have become a dominant value in contemporary expressions of both the mechanistic and organic worldviews.

As Robert Bellah and his colleagues point out in *Habits of the Heart*, nowhere does this extreme autonomy find greater expression than in American society. And in the mechanistic model, the kind of individualism that is dominant is "utilitarian individualism" in which we individually pursue our own economic self-interest. It is rare in American society, including the church, to identify the kind of community that was an essential part of the more traditional cultures from which we have all come.

In fact, Paul L. Wachtel suggests that one of the driving forces behind our autonomous pursuit of material acquisition is the profound desire to replace the intimacy and the security we once knew in community. And yet it is evident that the substitute is not satisfying our deepest longings.[18] There is growing evidence that those of us who have succumbed to the novelties of modernization and the acquisitive impulses of the Western Dream are looking for new, community-based alternatives in which we can recover our humanity, our spirituality, and a sense of transcendent hope for the future.

What Are the Images of Pathways to the Preferred Future?

In the mechanistic model, the initiative for bringing about the better future rests in the hands of humankind alone. In no other model is the human quest for power, control, and mastery as great. And this is exactly the point at which the principalities and powers have seduced us.

It has increasingly become the responsibility not of God, but of rational planners, to make the mechanistic dream a global reality. Scientists, technocrats, economists, and politicians have the task of seeing that economic and technological growth continue unabated. Our responsibility as individuals is not only to produce an endless array of products and services, but also to develop a growing appetite to consume ever greater quantities of those goods and services. We are assured that pursuing our own economic self-interest will somehow work to the common good. Yet deep inside, we know the world doesn't really operate that way.

"The driving power of capitalism, as [Michael] Novak correctly emphasizes, is the desire of the individual to better his material condition. The name the New Testament gives to the force in question is coveteousness," Lesslie Newbigin charges. "The Capitalist system is powered by the unremitting stimulation of coveteousness."[19] But Christians of all stripes tend to embrace unquestioningly not only the basic premise of economic progress, but also the force that drives it.

As mentioned earlier, many mainline Christians want to see Western economic progress made more accessible to all peoples. And they want to see society operate more humanely with a greater regard for the created order. But they, too, see the initiative for the creation of a more inclusive Western Dream as resting in our hands, not God's.

Conservative Christians, on the other hand, remain solidly dualistic in their attitudes and assumptions. They truly believe that "God is in charge" of the heavenly future. But at the same time, most seem fully to sanction and work for the pursuit of the Western Dream, since it usually works well for them. Because of this dualism, conservative Christians, like their ecumenical counterparts, tend to see the initiative for the advancement of the Western Dream as largely up to humankind.

ORGANIC ROOTS AND ORGANIC VISIONS

Although the Western Dream is clearly at its zenith, there is a growing disenchantment among both Christians and non-Christians with its inherent alienation and reductionism. In fact, Lesslie Newbigin declares that

one of the most striking features of contemporary Western culture is the virtual disappearance of hope. The nineteenth-century belief in progress no longer sustains us. There is widespread pessimism about the future of "Western" civilization. Technology continues to forge ahead with more and more brilliant achievements; but the novels, the drama and the general literature of the West are full of nihilism and despair.[20]

As a result of this disenchantment, many are reaching into our organic past in an effort to recover a sense of purpose, meaning, and hope.

Gibson Winter characterizes the organic age of history as the period in which all of life was more fully integrated: "maintaining bonds with earth and sky, mortals and immortals."[21] Life was lived with a rhythm that was intimately related to the rhythms of the earth. Traditional peoples lived in a world of "more-than-human powers"[22] in which their concepts of life and their vision of the future were shaped by the ebb and flow of the natural world.

This general attitude of respect toward the earth and toward the larger spiritual/natural realm makes up what I call the organic worldview. It is of course the basic outlook for primitive peoples. It has been the source of periodic historical attempts to return to a simpler time. And it is behind the efforts of a growing number of people today who are attempting to fashion new, more hopeful visions for our future.

Because they are coming from so many different perspectives, the new organic visions are more disparate than the mechanistic ones. Since I am not an authority on the different expressions of the new organicism, I will offer only some brief impressions based on my reading and observation of this dynamic new movement.

What Are the Images of the Preferred Future?

People with an inherently organic worldview tend to view both time and the future in cyclical terms. For example, Native Americans are what Paul Tillich called a "thenomous culture," imaging the future in terms of the cycles of birth, death, and re-creation. In such a culture, a state of harmony with the natural/ spiritual order and with the tribal community, clan, or family is essential to well-being and even survival.

Of course, all peoples have their origins in a more organic communal culture that is intimately related to the natural/spiritual world and the cycles of that world. And the preferred future of the organic worldview typically has to do with living in harmony with nature and its cycles. There is typically little sense of linear progress to the achievement of some better age. Many in the more primitive societies, feeling they have little control of the larger natural/spiritual world, tend toward fatalism; they have little confidence that they can in any way shape or direct the future.

As Western civilization developed, the essentially organic view of the world and the future began to give way to a more linear view, first in the form of Greco-Roman civilization and then, especially, in the dominance of a Judeo-Christian view of history in Europe. Over the years, however, organic images have periodically reemerged—often in the form of a longing for return to some earlier, more ideal age. Such images of return appeared during the Middle Ages, the Renaissance, and even the Age of Reason. Eighteenth-century French Romantics such as Jean Jacques Rousseau, for example, extolled the idea of the "noble savage" and defined the ideal future as a return to a more primitive, natural existence.

Charles Sanford, in his seminal work, *In Quest of Paradise,* insists that even the period of Western exploration was motivated in part by images of return. Since the Middle Ages, the belief had persisted that the lost Eden not only existed, but could be recovered. It was sought after not only as the site of a more innocent spiritual past, but as a kind of terrestrial paradise filled with opulent wealth, medicinal herbs, and fountains of youth. Sanford states that even Columbus's venture to the new world was motivated in part by his hope of recovering the lost Eden.[23]

Nineteenth-century American philosopher, Henry David Thoreau, was an influential proponent of returning to a simpler way of life. He retreated to a cabin he built on the edge of Walden Pond to become more intimately reconnected to the larger natural world. Listen to what Thoreau saw and heard out the window of his cabin at Walden Pond:

> As I sit at my window this summer afternoon, hawks are circling about my clearing; the tantivy of wild pigeons by twos and threes athwart my view, or perching restless on the white-pine boughs behind my house, gives a voice to the air; a fish hawk dimples the glassy surface of the pond and brings up a fish; a mink steals out of the marsh before my door and seizes a frog by the shore; the sedge is bending under the weight of the reed-birds flitting hither and thither; and for this last half hour I have heard the rattle of the railway cars, now dying away and then reviving like the beat of a partridge, conveying travelers from Boston to the country.[24]

This engaging scene reminds us both of the inherent appeal of "back to nature" movements and the fact that Thoreau's latter-day organicism differs significantly from that of primitive cultures. Note, for example, that Thoreau encounters the unspoiled beauty of Walden Pond quite alone—in fact, withdrawing from society was part of his plan for achieving greater harmony with nature.

The twentieth century saw a number of attempts to find a better future by returning to a more organic past. Thoreau's retreat to Walden Pond was a partial inspiration for counterculture youth who took to the woods in the sixties. They sought to recreate a more natural, organic way of life that was more integrated with the rhythms of the larger natural/spiritual order. Sometimes, like Thoreau, they retreated alone. But more often they retreated in communities.

In the seventies, transformational futurists also embraced normative images for the preferred future that were drawn from an essentially more organic and more romantic worldview. Willis Harmon and Hazel Henderson, for example, envisioned a future in which human society arises like a phoenix from a decaying technocratic society, achieving a future of harmony, opportunity, and peace for all peoples. Their confident vision was based on an essentially beneficent view of nature.

The transformational futurists saw the natural realm not only as inherently good, but as a dynamic force shaping the course of human events. In their view, we will journey toward a harmonious future only by cooperating with the natural order. Believing that natural forces will inevitably bring about a new, transformed future, Willis Harmon listed, as his first strategy in the transition, "Promote awareness of the unavoidability of the transformation."[25]

The New Age movement which emerged in the eighties operates from a very similar set of assumptions. In contrast to historic Christian faith, New Agers have been influenced by Eastern thought to see the spiritual world as indistinguishable from the natural world. Their preferred future, therefore, is one in which humans reach greater individual harmony with the larger natural/spiritual world and, in the process, personal maximization as well. Like Thoreau, many New Agers believe they can achieve this harmony and optimization individualistically. Many New Agers also espouse a belief, drawn from Hindu philosophy, in reincarnation. They believe that if they fail to achieve their aspirations in this life, they have other lives and other futures.

Interestingly, I find that many conservative Christians, while aggressively attacking New Age spirituality, offer a brand of Christian spirituality that is often as preoccupied with personal optimization as anything New Agers present. Of course, theirs is offered within a Christian context, but it still has something of the aroma of the new organicism.

In the eighties we witnessed the birth of a new back-to-the-earth movement that was also based in part on an organic worldview. This movement, drawn not by religion but by a desire to reclaim greater intimacy with the natural order, is populated by environmentalists, organic farmers, and animal rights activists.

Belatedly, many Christians (usually those of ecumenical persuasion) have awakened to their responsibility to care for the created order. These Christians are joining forces with the new organicists all over North America to oppose the increasing negative impact of modernization on the environment. The problem is that many of these ecumenicals have joined forces not only in common cause, but increasingly in common philosophy as well. I find that growing numbers of mainliners, out of concern for the environment, are buying into a creational spirituality and theology that is more Hindu than Christian in its character.

What we are seeing more and more in mainline circles is the advocacy of a creational theology that repudiates the need for a redemptive theology. If we jettison a historic redemptive theology and adopt another view which sees God's initiative in Christ to redeem humankind and restore the created order as unnecessary, then Jesus Christ is no longer necessary, either.

Like that of the transformationalists and the New Agers, these Christians' image of the preferred future often has to do almost exclusively with preserving the natural world as it is now. And since in their view the spiritual already fully permeates the creation, they tend not to look forward to a future that significantly transcends what we are already experiencing. Apparently, their dream involves simply ensuring that the present created order is treated with greater respect and care and that human beings learn to live more harmoniously with that order.

What Are the Images of God and Creation?

Those who operate from an inherently organic worldview often tend to be animistic or pantheistic in their religious views. Those who are animists believe that all things animate and inanimate are possessed of spirits. Animists have historically operated with a great deal of fear of a natural/spiritual realm over which they have little control. Those who advocate a return to animistic religions, therefore, may unwittingly loose religious forces that could victimize their lives.

Pantheists hold that all things are part of a larger, impersonal supernatural realm that directly controls and influences their lives. C. S. Lewis observed,

> The religious options open to us are limited: We can believe in no God and be atheists. We can believe in one God and be theists. Or we can believe that all is God and be pantheists. Of these three, Pantheism has been humanity's major preoccupation through history—not because it is the final stage of enlightenment, but because it is the attitude into which the human mind falls when left to itself. In the absence of revealed religion, humanity gravitates towards natural religion.[26]

Mainline Christians who operate from an inherently organic paradigm often tend to be pantheistic in their view of the divine. For many of this pantheistic persuasion, the intimate God disclosed in the life and teachings of Jesus Christ is displaced by spiritual forces far less personal and engaging.

Those within the organic tradition tend to see the natural and the spiritual world as one and the same. And those within animistic cultures are particularly aware of the power of that larger spiritual realm. Many of their religious practices are attempts to exercise control over natural/spiritual forces. And a number in the New Age take this idea even farther. Not only do they see themselves as a part of a "cosmic consciousness"; they believe themselves actually to be divine.

The window through which the real is known in this model isn't empiricism, but personal subjective experience. Because they tend to be more open to the spiritual side of existence, people with an inherently organic worldview tend to place greater confidence in the intuitive and the subjective ways of knowing than in the scientific and empirical.

And because they hold a very high view of nature, the new organicists tend to treat the natural order with great respect. They regard nature not simply as a collection of passive resources to be exploited, but as a dynamic, active, directing force. Nature with a capital *N*—not a personal, transcendent Other—is the force to which they often look for direction and understanding, and they believe this force is essentially beneficent and trustworthy. For this reason, instead of relating to nature in detached, utilitarian terms, people with an organic worldview tend to nurture a more intimate relationship, picking up clues on how to cooperate with this active natural force.

One of the newest expressions of the organic worldview is a theory called the "Gaia principle," which regards the entire planet as a single living organism.[27] Subscribing to this theory, of course, dramatically alters how we relate to the planet. Followers of the Gaia principle tend to place much less emphasis on the well-being of the human population and much greater emphasis on the health of the planetary "organism" as a whole.

What Are the Images of Persons and Community?

Predictably, those working from an organic worldview see persons as integral parts of the larger natural order. In traditional organically based cultures, this included being an integral part of a tribe, clan, or community. Identity and self-worth were derived more from participation in the larger communal order than from singular individualistic accomplishments. As we have seen, however, in newer forms of organicism, autonomy is the rule and community the exception.

Since those with an organic view regard the natural order as inherently good and beneficent, and since persons are part of that order, organicists tend to see persons as inherently good also. As a consequence of this romanticism, these adherents often have serious difficulty explaining the presence of evil in human society. Rousseau saw evil as originating in "man devouring" cities. Mary Shelley (and others after her) saw evil emerging from the rapid expansion of modern technology. But few of this viewpoint have developed a clear, cogent explanation of how evil can exist in a society made up of persons who are innately good.

The original organic paradigm placed the well-being of the community above the interests of the individual. And subsequent centuries have seen periodic attempts to reawaken a more communitarian spirit. In the nineteenth century there were a number of utopian experiments, from New Harmony to Oneida Fellowship, that sought to establish new communities. In the sixties we saw another serious attempt to return to a more agrarian past and rediscover a more organic form of community. Communes sprang up all over the United States, particularly in the rural areas. But the sixties commune movement, like the nineteenth-century utopian movement, didn't last. Many of the communitarian experiments folded, and people rejoined the larger and more individualistic modern society. The ones that had staying power were the ones that were religiously grounded. A number of these, such as the Bruderhof Communities (described in Chapter 10), are still with us.

As we have seen, however, many of the organic models since the eighteenth century have stressed autonomy and individualism rather than community. This is certainly true of much of the New Age movement. The radical autonomy of John Locke, which pervades the mechanistic model, also finds forceful expression in these movements. Individuals are encouraged to follow their own inner spirit, "pull their own strings and push their own buttons." Individual self-actualization, not community advancement, is the goal of much of the new organicism.

Pollster Daniel Yankelovich concludes from his research that the pursuit of self-fulfillment has become a widespread goal throughout Western society. The dominant message of many evangelical and a growing number of mainline churches is, "How you can use your faith to become self-actualized." Increasingly, we are seeing the American church, influenced by this stream of the new organicism, become more inwardly focused and self-involved.

Mainline Christians, who are more creational in their theology, tend to have a broader social agenda and talk more about community than others who are a part of the new organicism. However, it is very rare to find mainline Christians of any stripe who actually participate in any significant expressions of common life or community. The declining presence and influence of the orders within Catholicism could result in Catholic Christians' also embracing a more autonomous faith in which the importance of community is minimized. And evangelicals do little better. Although some of their midweek prayer groups function as community support groups, their decision making tends to be as individualistic as anyone else's.

What Are the Images of the Pathway to the Preferred Future?

Essentially, those working from a more organic vision believe that the harmonious future they desire can be reached by cooperating with the larger natural/spiritual world. As we have seen, in traditional cultures this also means working within the structure of the tribe and clan. However, a number of those living within traditional animistic cultures feel themselves so victimized by the larger order that they really don't believe that a better future is possible. Organizations trying to do development among animistic people report that fatalism is often so entrenched in these people's thinking that they are extremely difficult to enlist in working to change their communities. When they embrace Christian faith, however, they become able to believe that their communities can be transformed as well.

Transformational futurists really believe that the larger spiritual/natural world is destined to transport us all to a new, transfigured future. In their view, therefore, the way to achieve a better future is simply to cooperate with the directions and impulses of that order. The same is true for those who see the better future almost exclusively in terms of their own self-actualization. They believe that cooperating with the natural/spiritual realm will help them achieve the sense of individual mastery they desire.

For New Agers, cooperating with that larger realm is also apparently at the heart of realizing the better future. Believing themselves to be gods, however, they don't look to a personal God beyond themselves. They look to channeling, crystals, and occult practices to assist their journey to their ideal future. And many New Agers believe they have a fallback position in reincarnation. If they don't achieve the ideal this time around, they can always try again in another life.

In general, members of the various Green movements, animal rights activists, and those embracing the Gaia principle aren't particularly interested in the self-actualization of human beings. Their concern is principally the preservation of the biosphere, sometimes regardless of what happens to the human species. Their pathway to the preferred future involves taking political and environmental action, sometimes including civil disobedience, to achieve their ends.

While the mechanistic model, therefore, relies on the power of the market-place and the prowess of science and technology to achieve its ideal future, the new organicists look principally to the beneficent guidance of the natural order. While the Western Dream is achieved through the power of human rationality, the visions of the new organicists rely much more on subjectivity, human intuition, and spirituality.

In our quest to find a basis for hope, a basis for response to the urgent and growing challenges of tomorrow's world, do either the mechanistic or organic visions fill the bill? I believe the mechanistic model is totally incapable of offering a vision that has any sense of transcendence. It is singularly limited to the here and now. And do we really believe we can trust our future to the magic of the market-place and prowess of science and technology?

While some of the visions of the new organicists do indeed offer a sense of transcendence, it is an impersonal transcendence. There is no Creator God who can be personally known in this paradigm. Are we really willing to trust our future to impersonal forces and subjective promptings of the new organic visions?

In the next chapter we will look at a third possibility—a creative vision for the future drawn from an ancient faith. In the meantime, however, there is growing concern that the dominant paradigm could collapse before anything else emerges to replace it. And the results could be enormously chaotic.

WAKING UP TO POSTMODERN CHAOS

The mechanistic model, with its technological confidence and materialistic outlook, has clearly won the day in the modern world. Despite periodic longings to return to a more organic past, mechanistic thinking still underlies the assumptions of modern culture today. And yet there is increasing evidence that the mechanistic age may be drawing to a close. The scientific discoveries of the last ten years indicate we may be on the threshold of an entirely different view of reality.

The mechanistic paradigm is premised on a Newtonian worldview, a fundamentally materialist outlook which saw the world as operating according to a set of predictable laws of cause and effect.

> In the world of Newtonian mechanics, the paths of particles and velocities of each particle are the determining causes. Discover the initial paths and velocities of each particle and you hold the key of every subsequent action and reaction in the universe. You could in theory explain everything.[28]

While this "billiard ball" view of causality provided a theoretical foundation for technological advancement, it also robbed the world of a sense of mystery. More to the point, in the past ten years the cause-and-effect theories of Newtonian physics have been scientifically demonstrated to be invalid. The findings of quantum physics have completely shattered the Newtonian worldview on which the mechanistic paradigm is based. Samuel Schweber, a Brandeis historian of science, calls this advance of quantum physics "the deep Revolution." Schweber says the revolution is "so deep that in some sense, in having affected so many areas of thought and intellectual life, we really have not assessed as yet the full impact of it."[29]

Some of the consequences of such a change are clear, however. No longer can we assume that we live in a materialistic cosmos in which everything is explicable. Once again we live in a world of dawning mystery—a world of unimagined new possibilities. That is why we are beginning to see the emergence of some of the new organic visions.

As we move into this postmodern world, there is the possibility of birthing something altogether new and creative—something that looks very much like the landscape of the biblical image of the City of God. We will examine that possibility in the next chapter.

But there is also another very real possibility. As we move from the security and structure of the modern world, we could see a rootless, unstructured society collapse in on itself in growing chaos and disorganization. David Harvey states, "post-modernism swims, even wallows in the fragmentary and chaotic currents of change as if that is all there is." Harvey continues, "post-modernism has a penchant for destruction bordering on nihilism, its preference for aesthetics over ethics, takes matters too far. It takes them beyond where any coherent politics are left."[30]

Undoubtedly, this is one reason the Baby Buster generation is so nihilistic. For many of the young, change is all there is. And there is a very real possibility that the alienated nihilistic young of today could become both the victims and the vandals of a chaotic tomorrow—one in which all structures and values are up for grabs. Never has it been more urgent for people of faith and people of concern to question the visions and values to which we have given our lives and to begin to dream new dreams while there is yet time.

Leon R. Kass insightfully observes that

> the project of Babel is making a comeback. Ever since the beginning of the seventeenth century, when men like Bacon and Descartes called mankind to the conquest of nature for the relief of man's estate, the cosmopolitan dream of the city of man has guided many of the best minds and hearts throughout the world.

Kass suggests, "Perhaps we ought to see the Dream of Babel today once again, from God's point of view."[31] And we need to reconsider that dream, I would add, because the foundation on which it is built is crumbling and the future it has created is at risk. Failing to give birth to a new dream, we are likely to inherit a postmodern future of growing chaos, alienation, and violence. In our arrogance and indifference, once again we may taste the fruits of Babel.

Questions for Discussion

1. Why is it so important that we understand the visions to which we have given our lives?
2. What is the basic image of the better future in the mechanistic vision, especially as it finds expression in the Western Dream?
3. What are the assumptions within that vision regarding: (a) God and creation? (b) persons and community? (c) the pathway to the better future?
4. What is the image of the better future in the new organicism?
5. What are the assumptions within that vision regarding: (a) God and creation? (b) persons and community? (c) the pathway to the better future?
6. Where have you seen people in the church embracing the vision and values inherent in the Western Dream?

7. Where have you seen people in the church embracing the vision and values inherent in the vision of the new organicists?

8. How have these allegiances affected the ability of Christians to respond to the escalating challenges of the twenty-first century?

9. What are some specific ways we can unmask the work of the principalities and powers in our lives, communities, and congregations?

10. If we move into the kind of postmodern future described in this chapter, what could be the societal consequences of the growing disorder and break-down of institutional structures?

9

Waking Up to the Birth of a New Creation

Giving birth! What imagery could remind us more compellingly of the agony of our journey or unleash such a wild hope within us for our common future? As we have anticipated the avalanche of change rushing toward us, it would be easy to focus on the pain, trauma, and ordeal of the birth process and never look forward to the birth of the new.

But where can we turn to find hope for the future? Where can we find any hint, any assurance that something new is being born? Where can we find a confident hope that helps us not only to make it through troubled times, but also to engage the emerging challenges of a new century creatively?

There seems to be a growing recognition among many that the Western Dream is in eclipse. I believe we can no longer premise our hope for the future on the productive capacities of the market or the remarkable innovations of modern science. While the market can, without question, produce an endless array of consumer delights and science can promise an endless spectrum of technological breakthroughs, modernization has absolutely no power either to envision a transcendent future or to transport us there.

As we seem to be moving toward a postmodern future, many are searching for a new paradigm—a new premise for hope. Growing numbers seem to be turning to one of a myriad forms of a new organicism we have discussed that are clearly at counterpoint to a mechanistic vision. But while these organic visions frequently offer some sense of transcendence, I find a number of people who are unwilling to bet their lives and futures on subjective impulses, a romantic view of the natural order, reincarnation, or latter-day animistic practices.

As we are scrambling to find a new paradigm, a new promise for hope, Gibson Winter suggests there is a third option beyond the mechanistic and organic paradigms. He describes this third model as an artistic or creative alternative. While distinctly different from the organic and mechanistic models, it draws upon both. I believe this paradigm emerges principally not from a scientific, economic, or romantic worldview, but rather from an ancient faith.

Is it possible that our hope for the future will not be found in the progress of the Western Dream or the beneficence of the natural order, but rather in the God who created all things? Is it possible that the Creator God is giving birth to a whole new order? Is it possible that much of the turbulence and change we are experiencing is in reality part of the birth process—and that somehow we could cooperate with the Creator in the birthing of the new?

Sheila Kitzinger, in her remarkable collection of childbirth case studies, describes her own experience of cooperating with the birth process in vivid and powerful prose:

> I have felt gathered up on waves as contraction has followed contraction with relentless power, and the birth of the baby has come as if on a tide which streamed through me.
>
> The wave surges toward me, rises in crescendo as I am enveloped by the walls of its pressure, and then sweeps back and away, leaving my body bounded by the little space . . . between contractions. The uterus works mechanically like the heart, without my willing or dictating what it shall do. Its muscle fibres contract and constrict . . . everything in the deep well of the pelvis is squeezed and trodden as if in a wine press.
>
> It comes again, with controlled power. Go with it. Breathe with it, up and over. The big contractions are the good ones. Skim over each, brushing the wings of pain. Soar above the raging waters, the swelling wonder of creation as the womb-fruit ripens, tilts, and feels almost bursting in its strength. . . . The contraction fades, the wave washes back. Down the slope into peace, the two minutes in which my boat is beached before it must set off again in the storm.
>
> The waves come faster, and I must go towards each with measured pace, keeping above them with my breathing. If I try to turn and run away, they will engulf me. . . . My body is like an island fretted by waves, like a widening bay filled by the swollen tide. . . . The widening bay turns warm, prickles with heat, as the tide urges toward it. My body has become a vessel from which life is poured.
>
> The child's head, like the hard bud in the middle of the peony, pushes forward. . . . [then] slides through and slips out, sweet and smooth . . . face puckered in displeasure at the world. Shoulders slither out, arms flailing,

finger fronds uncurling, rib cage working, tough little thighs and heels thudding, knees churning—my child's body glowing pink—and her mouth opens in a roar as, with a tearless cry, she greets life with innocent rage.[1]

It's no accident that many artists and writers describe their own creative endeavors—the power, the pain, the raw joy—in terms of childbirth. And it's no accident, either, that childbirth is a powerful biblical image for God's creative process of bringing about the new.

Madeleine L'Engle reminds us that the Creator God is intimately familiar with the powerful, loving experience of giving birth:

> the tearing violence of a birth. The Lord Himself, when the world first was spoken, took fistfuls of formless chaos, wrested sky, sea and our familiar earth from naught, so nothingness by Love was broken and it was good, and then God rested.[2]

And the good news of Scripture is that the Creator God who birthed creation isn't done. God is preparing for the birth of a new creation—a new heaven and a new earth. "We know that the whole creation has been groaning as in the pains of childbirth right up to the present time" (Rom. 8:21, NIV), exults the Apostle Paul.

> In my opinion whatever we may have to go through now is less than nothing compared with the magnificent future God has in store for us. The whole creation is on tiptoe to see the wonderful sight of the sons [and daughters] of God coming into their own. The world of creation cannot as yet see reality, not because it chooses to be blind, but because in God's purpose it has been so limited—yet it has been given hope. And the hope is that in the end the whole of created life will be rescued from the tyranny of change and decay, and have its share in that magnificent liberty which can only belong to the children of God! (Rom. 8:18–21, PHILLIPS)

Wild Hope is premised on the affirmation that the Creator God is at work within history to bring forth a future in which all things will be made new. For whatever reason, the Creator invites us to participate as collaborators—literally co-laborers—in birthing this new order in our lives, in our communities, and in the larger world. I believe this Wild Hope offers not only an alternative vision, but also a biblical base from which to engage the mounting challenges of tomorrow's world.

WAKING UP TO AN ALTERNATIVE VISION

If we are to be collaborators with the Creator in the birthing of the new, however, we must catch a glimpse of all that God purposes for our common future.

We must return to the biblical narrative and discover afresh the normative vision of a world made new.

As we have seen in the last two chapters, many of us have been seduced by other visions. In fact, as we have seen, the primary reason the church is failing both to flesh out God's kingdom and to respond aggressively to the escalating challenges of a new century is that we have been co-opted— mainliners, evangelicals, laity, and clergy alike—by the visions and values of our modern, secular society.

Many of us Western Christians have uncritically given our lives, resources, and institutions to visions and values that are inherently alien to the biblical vision. In fact, many of us have invested so heavily in the Western Dream that the last thing we really want is for God to break in with a new order and turn everything upside down. We have much too much to lose.

In particular, I think we fail fully to appreciate the pervasive impact that modernization has had on the entire fabric of our society. Os Guinness insists that

> modernization is not something simple, local, transient or inconsequential. At its most developed, it confronts us with such relentless power and pervasiveness it has been aptly described as an "iron cage" around human life (Max Weber), "a gigantic steel hammer" that smashes traditional institutions and traditional communities of faith (Peter Berger).[3]

As Guinness grimly shows, modernization will tolerate no deviation from its clearly defined agenda for human society and indeed the entire created order. The key reason I believe the future of the church is in serious jeopardy is that we so uncritically welcomed modernization into our midst. And we are belatedly discovering that we cannot embrace modernization and the Western Dream without also embracing the values that go with them.

The principalities and powers have seduced modern society into believing we are "regents of the world" who are able rationally to define the "ultimate" direction, happiness, and duty of life and do it with "ultimate" certainty. Tragically, we have too often let that deception permeate our most basic assumptions about ourselves, our communities, our world, and particularly our image of the better future.[4]

The purpose of this chapter, therefore, is to help us break free from our captivity to alien visions and recover some sense of God's loving intentions for the future. Only as we are captured by something of a biblical vision for the future is there any possibility that we can be creative collaborators in giving birth to a new future. In this chapter, I will attempt to sketch one expression of that vision, which stands in sharp contrast to both the mechanistic and organic views and yet is able to draw from both. I will briefly review something of God's intentions in the biblical narrative. Then I will pose the same questions that I asked of the organic and mechanistic visions:

- What are the images of the preferred future?

- What are the images of God and creation?

- What are the images of persons and community?

- What are the images of the pathway to the preferred future?

My intention in this chapter is not to offer a systematic theology of the kingdom of God. Instead, using a narrative approach, I will attempt to present some of the compelling biblical images of God's intentions and explore some of the values assumptions on which the biblical vision seems to be based—especially as these values contrast with those of the mechanistic and organic models. But I want to emphasize, again, that this is but one struggling attempt to articulate a biblical alternative.

WAKING UP TO THE FUTURE OF GOD IN THE STORY OF GOD

Where can we find a basis for hope as we journey toward a postmodern world? Where can we find a hope that enables us not only to approach the future with confidence, but also to address the new challenges creatively?

I find it curious that many of us who identify with a Judeo-Christian worldview, even some who are passionately religious, haven't seriously looked to our own faith tradition to find either hope or purpose. Of course, a number do look forward to a very privatistic, spiritualized hope "in the clouds." But rarely do I encounter Christians who live and act out of a vital hope that the God who created all things will author the final chapter and make all things new—a hope that permeates the biblical narrative.

The God Who Creates, Covenants, and Liberates

"In the beginning God." Out of nothing, God created everything:

In the beginning God created the heavens and the earth. The earth was without form and void, and darkness was upon the face of the deep; and the Spirit of God was moving over the face of the waters (Gen. 1:1–2, RSV).

In that primal creative act we are shown a Creator God who lovingly gives birth to a creation and pronounces it good.

Jürgen Moltmann, who has written some of the most provocative material on a theology of hope, suggests that creation is aligned toward the future because from the beginning God had a clear sense of purpose for all that had been created.[5]

Not only did God fashion a new creation and align it toward the future; God also chose to dwell in that creation. Moltmann explains that because God "is making it His own home, all created beings then find in nearness to Him the inexhaustible wellspring of their life, their home and rest in God."[6] From the beginning, the biblical story pictures God not only as transcendent and creative, but as personal and loving—fully present in the created order.

Even after the Fall, God's loving intentions, so compellingly expressed in creation, did not change. God did not give up on God's people or God's creation. God took redemptive initiative by establishing a new covenant with Abraham and Sarah:

> Go from your country and your kindred and your father's house to the land that I will show you. And I will make of you a great nation, and I will bless you, and make your name great, so that you will be a blessing. I will bless those who bless you, and him who curses you I will curse; and by you all the families of the earth shall bless themselves (Gen. 12:1–3, RSV).

"The family of Abraham left the history of expulsion and began the pilgrimage of promise,"[7] observes Walter Brueggemann.

Later, as we see this redeeming God call Israel out of slavery in Egypt, we discover that "the Creator of the world is the Creator and the Liberator of Israel."[8] The Exodus event makes it clear that God's intentions aren't just spiritual (as some conservative Christians believe), but social and political as well.

> And God said to Moses, "I am the Lord. I appeared to Abraham, to Isaac, and to Jacob. . . . I also established my covenant with them, to give them the land of Canaan, the land in which they dwelt as sojourners. Moreover I have heard the groaning of the people of Israel whom the Egyptians hold in bondage and I have remembered my covenant. Say therefore to the people of Israel, 'I am the Lord, and I will . . . deliver you from [the Egyptians'] bondage, and I will redeem you with an outstretched arm and with great acts of judgment, and I will take you for my people, and I will be your God. . . . And I will bring you into the land which I swore to give to Abraham, to Isaac, and to Jacob; I will give it to you for a possession'" (Exod. 6:2–9, RSV).

All of Israel's subsequent history was conditioned by the decisive Exodus experience. It was here Israel learned to hope in a God who acts redemptively in the world.

Not surprisingly, oppressed people of every century have identified strongly with the Exodus event. African Americans in the days of slavery, for instance, looked to God for their liberation, and they longed for the freedom and joy of the Promised Land. Black theology today still draws heavily on the Exodus narrative, as does liberation theology. The poor and dispossessed of this world are looking for a God who can not only save, but also deliver. That is certainly the God we see taking decisive action in the Exodus.

I think Brueggemann is right in asserting that this God who came to liberate Israel brought an "alternative consciousness" to that of Egyptian deities. The gods of Egypt fully sanctioned the existing political and economic order, which benefited a small ruling elite at the expense of the larger populace and a huge enslaved class. This God named Yahweh not only identified with a group of powerless slaves, but soundly condemned the way power was used in Egyptian society.[9]

However, to understand the appeal of the Exodus narrative for the poor and dispossessed, we must remember not only what Yahweh delivered them from, but what Yahweh promised to take them to: "a land flowing with milk and honey" (Exod. 3:8, RSV). Gustavo Guitierrez writes, "The Exodus is the long march towards the promised land in which Israel can establish a society free from misery and alienation."[10]

The God Who Creates a New People

There is more to the Exodus, however, than a condemnation of oppression and the restoration of an oppressed people to freedom and abundance. God's overarching intention was to be reconciled to the people of Israel in order that they might become a "holy nation," a foretaste of God's redemptive intentions for all peoples.[11] From the beginning, Yahweh was intent on creating a new community of people who would be reconciled to the God who created them.

But even though God acted in history to liberate the children of Israel from their captivity, liberation theologians sometimes fail to recognize that the redemption of the Israelites was not automatic. It was conditional, based on their behavior. This oppressed population was not *guaranteed* a relationship to God nor assured that they would inherit all that was promised simply because it was oppressed. The people of Israel had to maintain their covenant with God. They were told over and over that unless they obeyed God's commandments and trusted God's providence, they would neither know God's presence nor enter into all that had been promised. Yahweh insisted on new patterns of ethical, economic, and religious conduct that contrasted starkly to the patterns of surrounding nations:

> You shall therefore keep all my statutes and all my ordinances, and do them; that the land where I am bringing you to dwell may not vomit you out. And you shall not walk in the customs of the nation which I am casting out before you; for they did all these things, and therefore I abhorred them. . . . You shall inherit their land, and I will give it to you to possess, a land flowing with milk and honey. I am the Lord your God, who have separated you from the peoples (Lev. 20:22–24, RSV).

The children of Israel, of course, did not keep the statutes and the ordinances God had given them nor trust God for their future. And as a direct consequence, they didn't enter immediately into the Promised Land. Instead, they wandered aimlessly in the wilderness for forty years, having to learn the same lessons over and over. In spite of their recalcitrant behavior, however, God never abandoned Israel nor forgot the promises made to Israel's people.

> He is there with Israel. He enters into desolation with His people. He subjects Himself to the same circumstances as Israel. He also sojourns without rootage with His people enroute to the fulfilling land of promise.[12]

Even after the children of Israel finally entered into the land God had promised them, the struggle was not over. Even as God reluctantly granted them a king and gave them instructions for building a temple, their tragic lapses into idolatry, sexual immorality, and injustice toward the poor brought the repeated judgment of God. Eventually, everything they had fashioned collapsed around them. They found themselves forcefully evicted from the land of promise and taken into a galling captivity.

But even then, God didn't abandon Israel nor forsake the purposes outlined from the beginning. Through the prophets, God expanded the scope of those purposes. Even while pronouncing judgment on Israel's faithlessness and disobedience, God reaffirmed God's redemptive purposes and expanded their scope to include all peoples:

> This is the plan determined for the whole world; this is the hand stretched out over all nations. For the Lord Almighty has purposed, and who can thwart him? His hand is stretched out, and who can turn it back? (Isa. 14:26–27, NIV).

> Turn to me and be saved, all you ends of the earth; for I am God, and there is no other. . . . My mouth has uttered in all integrity a word that will not be revoked: Before me every knee will bow; by me every tongue will swear. They will say of me, "In the Lord alone are righteousness and strength" (Isa. 45:22–25, NIV).

Arthur Glasser, a noted evangelical spokesperson in world mission, suggests,

> One must ponder deeply the somber details of Israel's persistent apostasy and from this frame of reference review the hopes and expectations so vividly set forth by the prophets—that despite Israel's failure God would ultimately realize his consensual goal with his people.[13]

The God Who Gives Prophetic Vision

Perhaps none of the prophets more compellingly enables us to picture the imagery of God's intentions than the prophet Isaiah. I believe that within the composite images in Isaiah we can begin to discover not only something of God's intentions and a premise for hope, but also a basis from which to address tomorrow's challenges. Let's look at some of the compelling images of Isaiah.

From Isaiah to Revelation, the Scripture affirms that God intends to create "a new heaven and a new earth" (see Isa. 65:17–19, 2 Pet. 3:13, Rev. 21:1). Contrary to the popular understanding of some conservative Christians, the future of God is not in the clouds. Somehow that dimension in which God dwells—which we call heaven—and the created order in which we dwell will be fused into a single new realm in which God will dwell and reign with the people of God forever.

Brueggemann suggests that Isaiah's vision of a new heaven and a new earth "is an eloquent statement of an alternative reality which is the substance of hope."[14] It is born of a sacred discontent with the dominant reality. "The hope is in the overriding power of God to work a new will against the reality of the day. It is this act of hope that holds the present critically and loosely. Israel knows, in all those texts, that the purposes of God will finally move against the way things are."[15] And today we also know that God is still moving against the dominant reality—that God's kingdom will come and God's will be done "on earth as it is in heaven" (see Matt. 6:10).

Within the context of God's promise to establish a new heaven and a new earth, Isaiah shows us a compelling picture of what that new creation will be like. Picture yourself in a barren wasteland (a dominant image of the prophets) with not a single blade of living grass. All of a sudden, rising up out of that wasteland is a mountain that transcends all other mountains. On the furthest horizon we see small dots converging on that mountain. As they come closer, we see that they are people—people from every tribe and tongue and nation.

Listen to Isaiah's description:

> In the last days the mountain of the Lord's temple will be established as chief among the mountains; it will be raised above the hills, and all nations will stream to it.
> Many peoples will come and say, "Come, let us go up to the mountain of the Lord, to the house of the God of Jacob. He will teach us his ways, so that we may walk in his paths." The law will go out from Zion, the word of the Lord from Jerusalem. He will judge between the nations and will settle disputes for many peoples. They will beat their swords into plowshares and their spears into pruning hooks. Nation will not take up sword against nation, nor will they train for war anymore (Isa. 2:1–4, NIV).

As we join the international throng of people converging on the mountain of God, the earth shudders. Streams appear in the desert. The wastelands bloom. The transcendent mountain explodes with verdant life. And as the immigrants start up the mountain, something remarkable happens: the blind see, the deaf hear, the lame begin to run up the mountainside (see Isa. 35:1–10). At the summit of the mountain a huge feast is set—a lavish banquet. If the biblical images are to be taken seriously, the guests of honor will be the poor and the destitute (see Isa. 25:6–9, Luke 14:21).

The God Who Purposes a New Beginning

What does this very cursory recalling of the Old Testament narrative and Isaiah's prophetic images tell us about God's intentions for the future? From the very beginning, God intended to create a whole new order—a new community that was clearly at counterpoint to the nations around it. God's intentions are:

- to create a new peoplehood in which persons from every tongue and tribe and nation are reconciled to the living God.

- to establish a new community of righteousness in which there is no more sin, personal or structural.

- to fashion a new order of justice in which there is no more oppression of the poor.

- to build a new international community of peace in which the instruments of warfare are transformed into the implements of peace.

- to establish a new society of wholeness in which the blind see, the deaf hear, and the possessed are set free.

- to host a huge festival of celebration in which peoples from all ethnic and cultural backgrounds joyously celebrate the reign of God in our midst.

- to usher in a new future in which we are reconciled not only to our God and to one another, but to the entire created order.

Rosemary Ruether describes what this new way of life will look like: "We will neither exploit nor abandon what God has made. All creation—male and female, human and non-human—will enter into harmony and mutual support rather than antagonistic relations." We will aspire, in the imagery of Scripture, to "that 'good land' of Messianic blessedness which makes all things whole"[16]—the *shalom* of God.

The central vision of world history in the Bible, according to Brueggemann,

> is that all of creation is one, every creature in community with every other, living in harmony and security toward the joy and well-being of every other creation. Israel had a vision of all people drawn into community around the will of its God [Isa. 2:2–4].[17]

The God Who Takes on Flesh

Central to the realization of this promised future of God is the coming of the Promised One—the Messiah of God:

A shoot will come up from the stump of Jesse; from his roots a Branch will bear fruit. The Spirit of the Lord will rest on him—the Spirit of wisdom and of understanding, the Spirit of counsel and of power, the Spirit of knowledge and of the fear of the Lord—and he will delight in the fear of the Lord (Isa. 11:2, NIV).

The children of Israel hoped in the future of God and looked forward with anticipation to the coming of the Messiah. For more than four hundred years the children of Israel waited for the promised coming of the Messiah, who would embody the future of God. Years flowed into decades and decades into centuries, but the heavens were silent. But remembering the acts of God in their past, many maintained their hope in God and all that God had promised.

Asian theologian Kosuke Koyama's book, *Three Mile an Hour God,*[18] describes a God who moves at human speed. For those waiting for the Messiah, I am sure it must have seemed God was moving at a glacial pace.

James Michener's historical novel, *The Source,* tells of a rabbi who lived during the four hundred years of silence and yet maintained his hope and his faith in God's promises. Every week, as the Sabbath approached, his sense of anticipation began to mount. "Perhaps this is the Sabbath the Messiah will come." By the time each Sabbath morn approached, he became convinced that this would be the Sabbath of Advent. Every week he would take care to position himself in the synagogue by the door so that he would be the first to see the Messiah coming down the road. Of course, as each Sabbath ended he was always deeply disappointed. But somehow by the time the next Sabbath approached, his anticipation would build again. During those years of silence, I'm sure many Jews maintained their confidence in this God who seemed to move at glacial speed, waiting for God to fully be God.

In the fullness of time, the promise of God became a part of the history of God's people—again, through the miracle of birth. "The Word became flesh and made his dwelling among us," asserts the Gospel of John (1:14). God's future intentions were breaking into the world in a surprising way—a baby in a cow stall, a child in a small Palestinian village, a carpenter in a marketplace.

> As Leonardo Boff says, when we profess that "the word became flesh," we make a statement fraught with meaning. We are professing our belief that God is here, present absolutely, has come to stay, and is named Jesus of Nazareth. By means of this child, God tells the world and its human beings, once and for all: "I love you." This Word of divine love, now become flesh, does not remain indifferent to the world. No, everything in the world takes on a new meaning. Nothing is totally absurd, for God says, "I love." . . . God became a concrete, particular human being, and in fragile flesh.[19]

But this Messiah Jesus is not only the full disclosure of God's love, reconciling us to God. He is also an incarnational expression of all that God intends for the human future. Mary's song of adoration makes clear that in the coming of the

Messiah, God intended to give birth to a whole order that will have an impact not only on the spiritual realm, but on the economic and political structures of society as well. The present order will, by the power of God, be turned upside down forever, defeating the principalities and powers that victimize humankind and destroy God's creation.

> The Mighty One has done great things for me—holy is his name. His mercy extends to those who fear him, from generation to generation. He has performed mighty deeds with his arm; he has scattered those who are proud in their inmost thoughts. He has brought down rulers from their thrones but has lifted up the humble. He has filled the hungry with good things but has sent the rich away empty. He has helped his servant Israel, remembering to be merciful to Abraham and his descendants forever, even as he said to our fathers (Luke 1:46–55, NIV).

At the inauguration of his ministry in Nazareth, Jesus stands and reads from Isaiah 61:

> The Spirit of the Sovereign Lord is on me, because the Lord has anointed me to preach good news to the poor. He has sent me to bind up the broken-hearted, to proclaim freedom for the captives and release from darkness for the prisoners (Isa. 61:1, NIV).

And then he said to them, "Today is this Scripture fulfilled in your hearing" (Luke 4:21, NIV). Jesus chose to make God's purposes his purposes. The vision of God so powerfully communicated by Isaiah became the vocation of the Messiah Jesus.

Jesus Christ not only devoted his life to working for the purposes of God, and he not only announced that the future of God had broken into history, but he also incarnated that future. Every time Jesus heals the lame, sets free the oppressed and feeds the hungry, we are given a glimpse of the future of God. In fact, the evidence Jesus offers John that he is the Messiah of God is that "the blind receive their sight . . . the dead are raised up, the poor have good news preached to them" (Luke 7:22, RSV). In Jesus Christ the future of God has broken into our midst.

Ecumenical Christians are correct when they insist that God is particularly concerned for the poor and the marginalized. In the Gospels we repeatedly see God's love extended through Christ to those at the margins—helping, healing, lifting.

But evangelicals are also right when they insist that God wants people to be reconciled to God. Our deepest needs are not physical or economic; they are spiritual. Only as we are personally reconciled to the living God can we be a part of God's new community—working for God's purposes.

In addition, Pentecostals are right when they insist that God wants to set free those who are spiritually oppressed. Delivery from spiritual bondage was yet another characteristic of Jesus' earthly ministry (see Mark 1:21–28, 5:1–20, Luke 9:37). Many African churches, which are very aware of the activity of supernatural powers, consider such delivery very important. Such churches look to Jesus as Savior, healer, and liberator, and many Africans are delivered from spiritual oppression and the bondage of animistic religions in the Name of Jesus Christ.[20]

African theologian John Mbiti states, "For generations Africans [have orally recounted myths of] paradise lost, how death came about, how God and men were separated." Absent in traditional life, however, was a notion of paradise regained. "But in Jesus," states Mbiti, "all this falls into place; it makes sense, becomes a revelation, a hope, and a destiny to which the church and [salvation history] are moving."[21] Because, then, Jesus saves humankind from death and reconciles it to the Creator, the notion of Jesus as Savior is attractive to Africans.[22]

Of course, Jesus as Savior, Liberator, and Lord is attractive to peoples in *many* cultures. He is attractive because through this One we can both personally encounter the God who loves and begin to experience a new future of hope. Neither the organic nor the mechanistic paradigms can offer us a personal relationship with the Creator God who acts in Christ to make all things new.

This Christ came heralding the future of God. John Stott, an evangelical Anglican, points out that

> the kingdom of God He proclaimed and inaugurated was a radically new and different social organization, whose values and standards challenged those of the old and fallen community. In this way, his teaching had "political" implications. It offered an alternative to the status quo. His kingship, moreover, was perceived as a challenge to Caesar's and he was therefore accused of sedition.[23]

The God Who Is Crucified and Resurrected

The decisive act that ensured God's redemptive purposes would be realized and God's kingdom would come was the brutal crucifixion of the very One who embodied the future of God. The stark image of the cross reminds us of God's decisive initiative to reconcile all things to God's self, unmasking the principalities and powers. Listen to the words of the apostle Paul.

> In him we have redemption through his blood. . . . And he made known to us the mystery of his will according to his good pleasure, which he purposed in Christ, to be put into effect when the times will have reached their fulfill-ment—to bring all things in heaven and on earth together under one head, even Christ (Eph. 1:7–10, NIV).

Not only have we received redemption, forgiveness, and reconciliation through the brutal crucifixion of Christ on the cross, but God intends to reconcile all things in heaven and earth through Christ. And as indicated all through the biblical narrative, "all things" includes the spiritual, physical, relational, economic, and political. Jesus Christ will be Lord of all.

"At the crowning moments of divine revelation there has always been suffering: the cry of the oppressed in Egypt; the cry of Jesus on the cross (according to Mark); the birth-pangs experienced by the whole of creation as it awaits liberation."[24] But the cross of Jesus Christ is much more than a symbol of suffering. "It posits a new concept of God, and a revolutionary one. God does not appear here as resignation, or as a legitimation of a life of wretchedness, but as good news. The cross unleashes life and hope."[25]

Since God was fully incarnated in Jesus Christ, God fully participated in the pain, suffering, and death of the Messiah. God even tasted the bitter dregs of godforsakenness:

> He whose kingdom Jesus had proclaimed as being "near" becomes the forsaking God. The Son dies from the Father's curse. . . . The Son suffers death in dereliction. But the Father suffers death of the Son in the pain of His love. The Son endures the being forsaken by the Father, whose law of grace He had proclaimed.[26]

As a consequence, God is able to identify completely with those who suffer death, pain, and godforsakenness in every age. We can hope in God because God fully experienced in Christ all that we experience in this world.

> The manner in which God mediates His future through this particular one is the form of substitutionary suffering, sacrificial death and accepting love. If one looks from the future of God into the godless and godforsaken present, the cross of Christ becomes the present form of the resurrection. The cross is the negative form of the kingdom of God and the kingdom of God is the positive content of the cross.[27]

While the image of the cross, therefore, stands at the very center of the fulfillment of biblical promise, it is incomplete without the image of the empty tomb. Jürgen Moltmann, who premises his theology of hope on the redemptive power of the Cross, nevertheless holds emphatically that the "bodily resurrection of Jesus Christ is absolutely essential to my theology."[28] Moltmann sees Jesus Christ as the "hinge" of history:

> The kingdom of God has identified itself with Jesus in the resurrection of the crucified one. In His words and deeds Jesus anticipated the kingdom of God and has opened the coming of the kingdom. In the resurrection from the dead God has anticipated . . . his kingdom of "life from the dead" and herein . . . opened the future of the resurrection and life.[29]

Our confident hope is that because Christ rose we also will be resurrected—mind, body, soul, and spirit—to be a part of a new heaven and a new earth. In bringing Christ to life from the dead, God not only opened the kingdom and offered us the guarantee of our hope, but also defeated all those forces arrayed against us. God defeated the principalities and powers of this world that oppress the poor and exploit the innocent and victimize all of us. God brought an end to all suffering, pain, and godforsakenness. And, of course, the resurrection defeated the final enemy, which is death.

The God Who Creates an International Community

God's intention from the beginning was to create a new community, a community marching to a very different drumbeat than the culture around it. For centuries, God struggled with the children of Israel to create a countercultural community that would provide a small foretaste of the future God intended for all people. And then, forty days after the resurrection of Christ, during the festival of Pentecost, a new cross-cultural community appeared in a rush of wind, an igniting of flame, and the sound of many tongues (see Acts 2:1–13). This new messianic community—the church—didn't displace Israel as the focus of God's intentions, but rather extended God's loving intentions to all peoples. René Padilla explains,

> The church is the community of the kingdom in which Jesus is acknowl-edged as Lord of the universe and through which, in anticipation of the end, the kingdom is concretely manifested in history.
> "Messiah" and "Messianic community" are correlative terms. If Jesus was the Messiah, and indeed He claimed He was, then it is not at all strange that . . . He should surround Himself with a community that recognized the validity of His claim. Even a superficial analysis of the evidence leads us to conclude . . . that in His ministry He calls men and women to leave every-thing and follow Him. Those who respond to His call become His "little flock" to whom God desires to give the kingdom. They are His family closer to Him than His own brothers and mother.[30]

This new international family that Christ called to himself at Pentecost became infused with a new, supernatural power, filled with outrageous joy and united in a common purpose. Those early Christians understood what often seems lost to the church today: following the Messiah Jesus means that every member of the Messianic community must labor for the purposes of God, even as he did. It means every disciple's putting aside every lesser agenda and seeking God's kingdom purposes first, working for righteousness, justice, and peace in a rapidly changing world. It means committing ourselves not only to this radical new vision, but also to the radical values that go with it. Instead of adopting the values of our culture, we are to live out the right-side-up values of the kingdom in an upside-down world:

Because of His death and resurrection, Jesus Christ has been enthroned as Lord of the universe. The whole world has been placed under His lordship. The Church anticipates the destiny of all mankind. Between the times, therefore the Church—the community that confesses Jesus Christ as Lord and through Him acknowledges God as "both the creator and judge of all men"—is called to share His concern for justice and reconciliation throughout human society and for the liberation of men from every kind of oppression" (Lausanne Covenant, paragraph 5). Commitment to Jesus Christ is commitment to Him as Lord of the universe, the King before whom every knee will bow.[31]

This vision for the church is the natural extension of God's redemptive purposes as incarnated in Jesus and opened out to the whole world. As Brueggemann puts it:

In the New Testament, the church has a parallel vision [to the Old Testament vision] of all persons being drawn under the lordship and fellowship of Jesus (Matt. 28:16–20, John 12:32) and therefore into a single community (Acts 2:1–11). As if those visions were not sweeping enough, the most staggering expression of the vision is that all persons are children of a single family, members of a single tribe, heirs of a single hope.[32]

And the New Testament promise is that as Christ rose, we will also rise to be a part of this new family, tribe, and creation, celebrating with our God forever.

WAKING UP TO THE BIBLICAL ALTERNATIVE TO THE WESTERN DREAM

Clearly, the biblical narrative points us to an understanding and a hope that differ radically from the mechanistic and organic paradigms discussed in the previous chapters. And it is this alternative paradigm that gives us the basis for Wild Hope in a world of escalating challenges and crumbling belief systems. It is the affirmation of this chapter—and this book—that the God who created all things and who promised to make all things new will be faithful in bringing us to this better future. And we have the privilege of collaborating with that God in bringing that future to fruition. In the rest of this chapter, then, we will take a look at the images and values implicit in the biblical model and contrast them to the models we examined in the last chapter.

What Are the Images of the Preferred Future?

As we have seen, the biblical narrative bears witness to a Creator God who is intent on giving birth to a whole new order—a new heaven and a new earth. And this Creator God is intent on calling into being a new community—the people of God.

Clearly, God's new order and new community are at counterpoint to the dominant order. This vision does not intend to preserve the world as it is, but to transform it, by God's power, into what God intends it to become.

God purposes to turn the world upside down—pulling down the rich and the powerful and lifting up the poor and the marginalized. God intends to transform the weapons of war into the implements of peace. God intends to host a cross-cultural celebration from every tribe, clan, and nation. God intends for the blind to see, the deaf to hear, and the captives to be set free. God intends to fashion a new order in which all created life exists in harmony and *shalom*. And at the very center of this new future will be a new, inclusive community of persons who have been reconciled to the living God, with whom God will reign forever.

While this subversive new order is indeed turning the world upside down, somehow it is able to incorporate major elements of both modernization and organicism as a part of God's new creation. Like the Western Dream, for instance, the biblical vision embraces the material world—but it is never materialistic. And like the new organicists, it stresses living in greater harmony with the created order. But this vision also stresses that we must be reconciled to the Creator as well as to the created order.

Finally, like both the Western Dream and the new organicism, the biblical vision reaches out to incorporate the individual, but it certainly isn't individualistic. While self-interest is very much at the center of the Western Dream and of many visions of the new organicism, the biblical vision looks forward to a future that is festively corporate in its character.

This vision, obviously, will not be attained by the prowess of human rationality as expressed through our science and technology or the magic of the marketplace. Nor will it be achieved simply by cooperating with natural forces. This future will come into being through God's initiative and God's initiative alone. But for whatever reason, God has invited us to be involved in midwifing this new creation.

Tragically, the imagery of the inbreaking of God's kingdom seems largely absent from the consciousness of both ecumenical and evangelical Christians in North America. Both, of course, have images of the future of God. But I am not sure how biblically informed these images are.

For many conservatives, the future of God is divorced from this world and imaged as a wholly spiritual realm somewhere in the clouds. Strongly influenced by Greek philosophy, many conservatives really do believe that "this world is not my home; I am just passing through." As a consequence of this very narrow view of redemptive theology, they believe God is interested only in the spiritual realm of existence. This is the principal reason many conservatives have difficulty addressing issues of social justice or the environment. Since these issues don't concern God, why should they be concerned? It is also a reason many conservatives seem caught in a dualistic worldview—working hard to "get a piece of the rock" here on earth while looking forward to a future in the clouds . . . and failing to recognize that neither vision has much biblical support.

Ecumenicals, on the other hand, tend to be quite sure that this world is indeed their home and that they have responsibility to work for a better one. They often have more difficulty accepting the possibility that God's future will include, but also transcend, creation. Some mainline Protestants find it particularly hard to accept some of the more supernatural and spiritual aspects of faith. And they, too, fail to recognize that the biblical imagery of the future of God is not at all the same as their visions of the better future—something vastly different from getting the Western Dream to operate more justly and with more sensitivity toward the environment.

I personally reject the defeated fatalism of those dispensationalists who believe that it is impossible to see any change take place "in these last days"—that all we can hope for is "to rescue a few more souls before the end comes." But I also reject the naïve optimism of those postmillennialists who believe they can bring about the kingdom of God on earth through their own efforts. Neither view, I believe, is supported by the biblical vision.

What I believe we find in Scripture is an "inaugurated eschatology" which affirms that the reign of God has broken into history through the life, death, and resurrection of Jesus Christ. That kingdom is both present and coming, both now and not yet. Scripture seems to be clear that God's kingdom will not fully come until the second advent of Jesus Christ. And yet the Creator God remains actively at work in every tribe, culture, and nation, giving birth to the new.

For whatever reason, it appears that the Creator God has chosen to work through a new community of broken, recalcitrant human beings to help display and advance something of God's new order. I don't think any of us has fully grasped what God could do to manifest this new order within history if God could secure a little more cooperation from those of us who profess to be followers.

David Bosch, in his book, *Transforming Mission,* correctly insists that those who understand something of God's kingdom purposes will not be found sitting idly by, awaiting the consummation of God.

> Those who know that God will one day wipe away all tears will not accept with resignation the tears of those who suffer and are oppressed now. Anyone who knows that one day there will be no more disease can and must actively anticipate the conquest of disease in individuals and society now. And anyone who believes that the enemy of God and humans will be vanquished will already oppose him now in his machinations in family and society. For all this has to do with salvation.[33]

What Are the Images of God and Creation?

Against this backdrop of God's loving intentions for the future, what are some of the biblical images of God and the created order? And how do those images differ from those implicit in the mechanistic and organic visions?

To answer these questions, we need to answer another question first: Is there any room for mystery in our post-Enlightenment society? If the answer is no, as many of those who have subscribed to modernization would assert, we need go no further. You see, if we truly live in a world in which everything is fully explicable, mystery is an illusion, and the supernatural realm doesn't exist, then we live in a universe in which there is no room for God. Or at most, God exists as an abstract concept or a cultural archetype passed down from our ancient past. Obviously, such a God would be impotent to act, and we would have to look elsewhere to find a premise for our hope.

A brief vignette from an Australian film, *The Last Wave,* illustrates the point. A young attorney, played by Richard Chamberlain, has been asked to defend an aboriginal adolescent accused of killing another aboriginal. In the course of his investigation, the attorney receives more than he bargained for. He is plunged into aboriginal culture and discovers "dream time," the supernatural world of the aboriginal. One scene finds him in a semilit cave covered with aboriginal paintings. They depict a world he has never experienced before or even imagined. It is almost as though the pictures are reaching out for his life.

The next day, the young attorney confronts his stepfather, an Anglican priest: "Why didn't you tell me there is mystery in the world?"

"My son, tell you?" the priest responds, "I mentioned it in every sermon."

With measured words the young attorney charges, "You didn't mention it. You explained it away!"

Many in our society and, for that matter, the church, have made a vocation of explaining away mystery—discounting the supernatural and, as a consequence, reducing God to an impotent relic of our past while elevating our own sense of importance and rational control. Those who share this viewpoint tend to see the future as entirely in our hands and our hope as exclusively in our struggling human initiatives. As we saw in the last chapter, most Western people assume that the course of the future will be determined either by human rationality as expressed in our science and technology, by the invisible hand of the marketplace, or by beneficent inclinations of the larger natural world. Few in our modern world—Christians included—seem to believe that there really is a God who is able to act within history.

James Turner, in *Without God, Without Creed,* specifically indicts the church for the growing unbelief in modern society. He argues convincingly that our insistence on forcing God into our small rational categories of understanding has diminished our concept of God and significantly contributed to the rise of unbelief in the modern era.[34]

As we move toward a postmodern world, however, the tide seems to be turning toward making room for mystery. Anthropologists like Paul Hiebert at Trinity Seminary state that supernatural activities among both Christian and non-Christian communities can no longer be simply dismissed as so much primitive superstition. There is growing recognition of a larger spiritual realm that is beyond the reach of our senses, our science, and our understanding. People are dramatically healed from serious physical ailments. In some tribes, people die at the simple invocation of a curse. Other spiritual phenomena take place in animistic cultures and Pentecostal sects that are extremely difficult to rationally explain away.

Part of this growing recognition comes from leaving the graveyard of a Newtonian worldview, which arrogantly assumed we could rationally explain all phenomena. But with the coming of the new physics, scientists are among the first to recognize that we do indeed live in a world filled with mystery. (Of course, the new organicists are taking great comfort in this recognition.)

If we are willing to acknowledge the existence of mystery in the world and of a larger supernatural realm that we neither understand nor control, then can't we seriously consider the possibility of the existence of a God who is more than a cultural hangover from a prescientific world—a God who acts in history and can be known by us?

As we have seen in Scripture, the Creator God is one who acts with complete faithfulness and love toward the people of God and toward the created order. Yahweh's protection, guidance, unconditional love, and nurturing care are often compared to those of a parent. Even the root word for mercy and compassion in the Hebrew is *rechem,* or womb. God reaches out like a mother with "womblike" compassion to those who stray.[35] And Jesus, of course, referred to this parent God as Father.

It's important to remember that Scripture is not talking of a remote, impersonal deity like we find in much of the new organicism. This parent God whose fatherlike guidance and womblike love embrace a creation can also be known by us personally. This can however, be a very uncomfortable reality, as C. S. Lewis observed. He speculated what would happen if we could choose our own view of deity:

> An impersonal God—well and good. A subjective God of beauty, truth and goodness, inside our heads—better still. A formless life-force surging through us, a vast power we can tap—best of all. But God Himself, alive, pulling at the other end of the cord, perhaps approaching at an infinite speed, the hunter, king, husband—that is quite another matter.
>
> There comes a moment when the children playing at burglars hush suddenly: Was that a real footstep in the hall? There comes a moment when people who have been dabbling in religion ("man's search for God"!) suddenly draw back. Supposing we really found Him? We never meant to come to that! Worse still, supposing He had found us.[36]

One of the dominant characteristics of our post-Enlightenment culture is the need to maintain a very high level of control of our lives and societies through our own rationality. If we can keep God reduced to an abstract idea or a subjective impulse, then we can maintain control. The possibility of a real being at "the other end of the cord" who can make demands on our lives and world as God did with the children of Israel is a little terrifying. That's why C. S. Lewis has written elsewhere, "This God is good but not safe."

Clearly, the God of the Hebrew Scriptures is more than an abstract idea in the minds of some Jewish intellectuals. God is pictured as a living, directing, acting Being who faithfully acts in history on behalf of the people of God. This parent God disciplines the children of God, but also nurtures them tenderly and promises them a future of mercy and grace. And because this God is faithful, the children of Israel were able, in spite of their sins and often impossible circumstances, to steadfastly maintain their hope in God and all that God has promised.

As we have seen, this God chose to be personally revealed in a covenant relationship to the children of Israel. God sojourned with the people of God in the wilderness and brought them into the Promised Land—giving them a foretaste of a jubilant homecoming for all creation. Then, in due season, God sent the Promised One to both herald and incarnate the future of God. Through Jesus Christ, the Creator God became present in the creation, fully experiencing the joys of human life, the pain of brutal death, and the hope of resurrection.

In the biblical narrative, therefore, we see a God who participates fully in both the pain and the celebration experienced by the entire created order. And God's involvement has never ceased. Scripture affirms that, even now, God is actively at work within history.

Regrettably, many Western Christians seem to have lost sight of this personal, faithful, active God. Instead, their God seems to bear a striking resemblance to the impotent or absent God of the mechanistic model or the impersonal God of the organic model. Many mainline theologians, in a sincere effort to make God acceptable in the modern world, have rationalized the Creator into near oblivion. Many conservative theologians, on the other hand, have adopted the dualistic view that sees God as active in the spiritual realm but basically impotent to intervene in the larger "secular" realm, except to bring down the final curtain at the end of history.

The life and the action of the biblical God are the ground of Christian hope— and yet so many Western Christians seem to have lost sight of that God. Liberals rarely talk of a God who acts. Conservatives seldom talk of God who acts beyond their own subjective spiritual experience and their personal relationships.

Only a modest number of theologians, such as Jürgen Moltmann, describe God as both a Promiser and an Actor. Moltmann reminds us that as we live between promise and fulfillment, we can have complete confidence that the God revealed in the Bible and embodied in the life, death, and resurrection of Jesus Christ will be faithful to all that has been promised. Our wild, outrageous hope is premised above all on the love and faithfulness of the biblical God.

The biblical view of the faithful Creator God inescapably shapes the biblical view of the created order. And this view contrasts markedly with the other dominant models we have discussed.

The biblical story certainly repudiates the starkly utilitarian, reductionist view of the created order found in the mechanistic model. In Scripture, creation is clearly characterized as much more than a grab bag of passive resources from which we produce an ever-expanding glut of consumer products and swelling waste.

Neither does Scripture characterize the created order as a "directing beneficent force." With all due respect to the new organicists, it is the Creator and not the created order that is directing the tide of history. We live in the sea of the presence of the eternal God—the God in whom "we live and move and have our being" (Acts 17:28, RSV). And yet nowhere within Scripture have I found any passages that confuse the Creator with the created. While God's presence pervades everything, God is clearly distinct from the created world.

In the biblical story, the creation is seen as innately sacred because God created it. It is pervaded by the presence and the purposes of the living God. Christ became a part of it, and God intends to redeem it. If we choose to embrace the biblical vision of a world made new, therefore, we must also commit ourselves to developing a new sense of reverence for all created life. We must be in the forefront of those working for the restoration of the created order.

In embracing the biblical vision, we don't jettison the rational, predictable world we have inherited from modernization, as some postmodernists would do. Nor do we unquestioningly turn to the subjectivism of many of the new organicists. Our vision is drawn from an ancient story that we claim as true. And in that context, we draw on both rational understanding and subjective intuition to live responsibly in our rapidly changing world.

What Are the Images of Persons and Community?

If we make the assumption that God exists—and that God acts within history to bring about God's purposes—all our other assumptions begin to change as well. And this includes not only our vision for the future and our images of the created order, but our view of humankind.

In embracing the biblical vision, we are forced to repudiate the modern reductionist view that persons are nothing but the sum of their organic core and their behavioral surface. Instead, we believe we are created as immortal beings who will be resurrected by our God to be a part of God's new heaven and new earth. Our identity and self-worth are not derived from our success in the marketplace as producers or consumers. Scripture affirms that since we are image bearers of the Living God, our worth is innate.

And in the biblical vision, autonomy is not an option. We are a part of a larger story and a larger community—a new international order. As we have seen, it was God's intention from the beginning to create a new community. The children of Israel were to be different from the surrounding nations, not only in the God they worshiped and the moral values they lived by, but in their political and economic systems and the way they treated the poor in their midst. What particularly distinguished and motivated the children of Israel was the fact that they were a people who lived in hope of a new future.

The first thing Jesus did at the inauguration of his ministry was to form a new community. He made it clear this new community expanded the circle of family beyond those who were biologically related. And again, this new community was distinguished by the vision for which its people labored—the inbreaking of the reign of God. More than that. At some level, they understood that following Jesus meant they were supposed to flesh out, in community, something of the right-side-up values of that kingdom in an upside-down world.

Today, following Christ still means abandoning our autonomous, self-interested agendas and becoming a part of a new international community of those who are intent on advancing God's kingdom. That means we must repudiate the "utilitarian individualism" that is obsessed with the acquisitive aspirations of the American Dream. But it also means we must forsake the organicist's "expressive individualism" that is preoccupied with self-actualization and personal mastery. We are invited to get ourselves off our hands, to replace our autonomous aspirations with new, collective aspirations of working and praying for the inbreaking of the reign of God.

This kind of community is not totally foreign to today's church, of course. Historically, the Catholic and Orthodox orders have demonstrated one model of Christian community. Thirty thousand Hutterites living with their families in residential communities in Canada and the United States have presented us with another model. A number of lay orders and alternative Catholic and Protestant communities are scattered all over North America, and a few ecumenical and evangelical Christians participate in small-group networks in their churches.

But for most ecumenicals and evangelicals, the idea of being part of a small group in which you are known, loved, and held accountable is a foreign concept. The idea of actually setting aside one's own autonomous aspirations and working with others to advance God's kingdom would seem abhorrent to many. But according to the biblical narrative, that is a normative expectation of what it means to follow Jesus Christ. We are supposed to be a part of some expression of a new community where we can be truly known, nurtured in our faith, held accountable in our lives and corporately involved in both incarnating God's new order and working for its realization.

Stanley Hauerwas and William Willimon persuasively argue that our first call as Christ's followers is to be the church, "a colony of resident aliens."

> A colony is a beachhead, an outpost, an island of one culture in the middle of another, a place where the values of home are reiterated and passed on to the young, a place where the distinctive language and lifestyle of resident aliens are lovingly nurtured and reinforced.[37]

To become a part of this new community, we are called to repent—to turn away from the evil of this age and turn toward the living God. As we have seen, however, evil is a bit of a problem for both the modernists and the new organicists.

As Charles Colson points out in his book, *Against the Night,*[38] modern society has gravitated away from any sense of moral absolutes to a growing sense of moral relativity. I believe that part of the reason we are slipping into a postmodern world is that the moral foundations of our society have been seriously eroded. With each succeeding generation, we see our young increasingly left with the impossible task of creating their own ethical premise for life, because so little has been passed along.

The only serious "evil" many modernists are concerned with is anything that interferes with the advancement of the Western Dream. And the new organicists have extreme difficulty explaining the presence of evil in a beneficent natural order. Some, like the New Agers, simply contend evil doesn't exist—it is an illusion. Others blame the structures of society while insisting that those who comprise those structures are inherently good.

In the biblical view, humanity is seen as a part of a larger cosmic struggle between God and the forces of evil that places both the larger created order and human society at risk. We are in a life and death struggle "not with flesh and blood, but with principalities and powers."

Richard Mouw suggests that the "powers" easily become objects of idolatry for any of us:

> Fallen humanity, having chosen to redirect the allegiance that properly belongs to the Creator, turns to various dimensions of the creation in order to find substitute objects of loyalty and trust. Some absolutize a moral code, others a political ideology. A nation or a race can become an object of ultimate loyalty, as can sexual enjoyment, humanitarian pursuits or even a religious commitment. Our devotion to them becomes an instrument of rebellion and we are separated from the love of God.[39]

And fundamental to our separation is insistence on our own autonomy . . . our individual pursuit of our own self-interest that places us on a collision course with the global interests of the Creator God.

Far from being inherently good, therefore, we all find ourselves, by our own self-interested longings and desires, drawn away from the God who created us. And often we find that, in seeking to satisfy those desires, we not only alienate ourselves from God and from others, but also undermine our own best interests and even jeopardize our personal futures.

Those of us from Western culture only have to read our own literature— Dostoevsky, Kafka, or Shakespeare—to be reminded that evil is real and that it pervades all human societies. One has only to recall contemporary political regimes that were almost demonic in their expression of evil—those of Adolph Hitler or Idi Amin or the Khmer Rouge—to be reminded that evil is no illusion. And even some of those who aspire to cure deviant or destructive human behavior through science have confronted the reality of evil that cannot be explained away by their modern theories.

One of these is psychologist M. Scott Peck, author of *People of the Lie*.[40] Peck's own therapeutic work has led him to conclude—reluctantly at first—that there are forces at work even in our "enlightened" society for which the standard scientific therapies are impotent and useless. There is, Peck argues, a larger spiritual realm connected to our observable world of the senses, a world we have all experienced but little understand—and a part of that world is evil. And yet we find little in our modern world that helps us either to understand or to ameliorate the evil pervading human society.

The biblical view, as Lesslie Newbigin reminds us, holds that evil is both a present reality and an enemy defeated. On the cross, Jesus Christ once and for all disarmed the powers arrayed against God, but he has not yet fully destroyed them. In this in-between time, therefore, we must continue to wrestle against evil in all its personal and structural manifestations:

> The principalities and powers are real. They are invisible and we cannot locate them in space. They do not exist as disembodied entities floating above this world, or lurking within it. They meet us as embodied in visible and tangible realities—people, nations and institutions. And they are powerful.[41]

Until God fully establishes the new order and Christ's reign is fully established, those powers remain inextricably entwined with the human personality and human institutions. Evil is an integral part of human society. But as we give our allegiance to the realm of God, we are empowered to begin overcoming evil in our lives and communities, as well as working against structural evil in our world.

What Are the Images of the Pathway to the Better Future?

As we have seen, the biblical vision of the birthing of a new heaven and a new earth is radically different from the essentially economic aspirations of the Western Dream. While the Western Dream can provide a bounty of consumer delights and technological novelties, it is incapable of providing a transcendent hope.

And the new organicism also envisions the world as continuing very much as it is, only with greater harmony in the natural order and greater individual self-fulfillment. There is generally no expectation of a radical reordering of society. While the biblical vision also emphasizes the need for us to learn to live in greater harmony with the created order, it differs by insisting that we must first be reconciled to the Creator before we can be reconciled to the created order.

Not surprisingly, since these three visions differ so vastly in their character and are premised on such very different assumptions about God, creation, and humanity, the pathways they offer to the better future differ vastly as well.

For example, since the Western Dream was first generated during the Enlightenment, it has looked to human initiative and not God's initiative to achieve its version of the better future. The Western Dream is a vision absolutely obsessed with the use of power—technological, economic, military, and personal.

The new organicists have, in part, fashioned their vision for the better future in part as a reaction against the power-driven, hierarchical, acquisitive mentality of the Western Dream. Many are trying to cultivate a vision that has some elements of transcendence without God. Of course, they don't look to empiricism, rationalism, and the magic of the marketplace to achieve their image of a preferred future. Most see the natural/spiritual realm as taking the initiative to bring about the better future; they simply seek to cooperate with this initiative.

In the biblical vision, the initiative for change comes from neither humankind nor the natural order, but from the Creator God. It is God who is giving birth to a whole new order. And as we know, birth doesn't take place without a great deal of pain and trauma.

God experienced the pain of the birth process as God journeyed with the children of Israel toward the Promised Land. God experienced the pain in Jerusalem in the torture, crucifixion, and death of Jesus Christ. And God experiences the pain today in the suffering of children of South Africa, the torture of church workers in El Salvador, and the spiritual alienation of teenagers on American streets.

And yet, although it is God who brings about God's future, we have a role to play as well. Our role doesn't involve taking power, leveraging the market, or pursuing our own self-interest. It comes through relinquishing our own agendas and placing God's agenda first. It comes through suffering love and sometimes even through death. It comes through our cooperating with the Creator in the birthing of a whole new order.

Jesus Christ stands at the threshold of a new era, inviting us to follow him into the future. He invites us to lay down our lives and pick up his cross. He invites us to lose our lives in order to find life. He invites us, like the mustard seed, to fall into the ground and die so that we may be part of a great tree extended into a chaotic world.

The biblical paradoxes make little sense to either the modernists or the new organicists. Everything within their respective philosophies repudiates the notion that relinquishment could be the pathway to a new future. Dying to our own personal aspirations in order to join the Creator God in the birthing of a new future for the whole creation is incomprehensible to those outside of faith and outside of God's new community.

Such a community, as G. B. Baird points out, is the only effective means of countering the evil that infects every element of human society:

Christ's method of dealing with evil must be our method also—we must be ready to absorb all that the powers of evil can do to us, and to neutralize it with forgiving love. "Be not outwardly conformed to this age, but be transformed by the renewing of your mind—recompense no man evil for evil—avenge not yourselves but give place to wrath—if your enemy is hungry feed him; if he is thirsty give him drink. Do not be overcome by evil, but overcome evil with good." Any other method of meeting evil means being conformed to this present age, which is under the domination of the principalities and powers. Any other method of meeting evil means being severed from Christ. Any other method of meeting evil is a reversion to the weak, beggarly elements from whose bondage Christ has set us free."[42]

We live as people in anticipation. The whole creation struggles in massive labor. And as part of that creation, we labor as well. Like those in the throes of childbirth, we are both participants and awed observers of the magnificent new creation God is bringing forth.

As we approach the threshold of the twenty-first century, the needs, challenges, and opportunities are all increasing. The Western Dream is in apparent eclipse. The search is on for a new metaphor or a new vision. And one of the options is rediscovering an ancient story—a biblical vision of God bringing forth a whole new order. In compassionate response to the challenges of an uncertain future, we are invited to join this Creator God in the birthing of a new future:

> The giant wave rises to a peak
> Breathstopping
> And the world splits open.
> Waters flow
> And on their salt flood
> A child
> Presses deep, stinging sweet
> And urgent for birth.[43]

Questions for Discussion

1. What seem to be God's purposes for the future as disclosed in creation, covenant, and the vision of the prophets?
2. How did Jesus Christ relate his life and vocation to the purposes of God?
3. What was Christ's singular message of hope?
4. How did the death and resurrection of Christ relate to the promised future of God?
5. How did that first community of Jesus relate to God's purposes for the future?
6. What images of the preferred future do we find in the biblical story, and how do they compare to the mechanistic and the organic visions?
7. What images of God and creation are implicit in the biblical vision, and how do they compare with the visions we discussed in the last chapter?
8. What are the images of persons and community in the biblical vision, and how do they compare with those in the mechanistic and the organic visions?
9. What are the images of the pathway to that better future, and how do they differ from those in the Western Dream and the new organicist visions?
10. How can those who embrace the biblical vision for the future help birth the new order in response to the challenges of tomorrow's world?

part two

Unleashing
a Wild Hope

10

Unleashing a Wild Hope in Our Personal Lives, Families, and Communities

"Atallah whispered in conspiratorial tones to his younger brother, Elias, 'Father is going to buy a lamb.' A lamb! Then it must be a special occasion. But why? It was still a few weeks until the Easter season . . . ."[1]

Elias immediately went searching for his father in the village of Biram to find out what the celebration was all about. He was unable to find him in the olive orchard, the crowded village square, or even at home. And Elias was bursting with curiosity. Finally, his father came home to the family, and they began their evening meal.

Elias was just about to explode. Finally, his father set aside his plate and said, "Come here, children, I have something special to tell you. . . ." Years later, Elias would recall what he had to say:

> "In Europe," he began, and I noticed a sadness in his eyes, "there was a man called Hitler. A Satan. For a long time he was killing Jewish people. Men and women, grandparents—even boys and girls like you. He killed them because they were Jews. For no other reason. . . . Now this Hitler is dead . . . but our Jewish brothers have been badly hurt and frightened. They can't go back to their homes in Europe, and they have not been welcomed by the rest of the world. So they are coming here to look for a home."[2]

When the Zionist soldiers arrived, Elias's father killed and roasted the lamb and blessed the feast and the men. His mother served them plates heaped full with lamb, vegetables, and bread. But Elias remembers that the men were somber and the meal never really became the celebration he had anticipated.

A week later, something totally unexpected happened. The military commander of these soldiers called the village elders of Biram together. He told them he had some alarming confidential news. "Our intelligence sources say that Biram is in serious danger. . . . Fortunately, my men can protect you. But it would risk your safety to stay in your homes. You're going to have to move into the hills for a few days. Lock everything. Leave the keys with us. I promise nothing will be disturbed."[3]

The villagers of Biram, including Elias and his family, compliantly left the village and decided to camp in an old olive grove nearby. After nearly two weeks, the elders decided not to wait for the commander's signal to return. They climbed the hill back to Biram. A short time later, they came running back to the encampment in the olive grove, their faces filled with confusion and fear. The soldiers had ordered them out of the village and told them never to return. Others went back and tried to reason with these armed soldiers but discovered they were powerless to get their homes and lands back.

"The betrayal cut like a knife," Elias remembers. "A few of the men were bitterly angry, seething with the thought that we had been tricked out of our village by these European men we had trusted. Others were simply bewildered. Pain etched every face."

And yet, even after the family had been refugees from their own home for almost two years, barely surviving on stray sheep, small stores of grain, and produce from small gardens, Elias's father continued in an attitude of love and forgiveness:

> He faithfully continued our times of family prayer and never failed to pray for those who had made themselves our enemies. Night after night I would lean my head against my Mother, fingering the fish and doves on her necklace, and hear Father pray: "Forgive them, oh God. Heal their pain. Remove their bitterness. Let us show them your peace."[4]

Elias Chacour and his family survived this traumatic period in Palestine's history as a new Israeli state was born. But clearly their strength was in something more than their own survival. Their strength was in their faithfulness to the Christ who called them to turn the other cheek and go the second mile. This is what the Wild Hope of God looks like in practical terms—living out the paradoxical values of the future of God in a world exploding with change.

Learning to Live Authentically in a Changing World

The assessment of this book should, by now, be abundantly clear. As we approach the twenty-first century, we are facing an unprecedented array of challenges. Our institutions in general and the church in particular are doing little either to anticipate or to mobilize resources to address the many new issues that will confront us as we enter a new century.

If we, the church, are to participate with God in giving birth to a new order, then we must respond both with greater authenticity in our lives and greater investment in our mission. We need to double and quadruple our response. But as we have seen, given the present demographic and giving trends in the North American church, we will do well to hold our own. Indeed, as the Christian young take over leadership, every indicator I have found suggests they will not even be able to sustain present levels of investment and mission. Again, this is principally because their elders have sold them the wrong dream and nurtured them in the wrong values—not to mention letting their own lives and spirits be secularized.

How can the church in North America begin, in partnership with the church worldwide, to engage these troubling trends? How can we see the church of Jesus Christ captured by a new biblical vision for the future? How can we more authentically live out the faith we claim? How can we, out of a new vision, significantly increase our capacity to engage the escalating challenges of the twenty-first century?

The journey begins, as I have indicated, by repenting—by turning our back on the seductions of culture, unmasking the powers, and embracing a new vision. But it continues in the struggle to flesh out that vision in a changing world.

Earlier, we defined the mission of the church as both "word and deed," "proclamation and demonstration." But I want to clarify. I don't believe the first call of the gospel of Jesus Christ is to proclamation. I don't believe the first call of the gospel is to social action. I strongly believe the Scripture affirms that the first call of the Gospel is to *incarnation.*

Only as we attempt to flesh out the vision and values of the new order of God in this world can we have any authentic basis on which to speak or to act. Like the Chacour family, we must struggle to live out with integrity the paradoxical values of our faith, recognizing they will likely make little sense to the larger secular society in which we find ourselves.

Such a call to incarnation will, in all likelihood, be difficult for both mainline Protestants and evangelical Protestants to hear since both groups are so activist in their character. It is in the Orthodox and Catholic traditions of spirituality, charism, and community that this call is more fully understood. And such a call will require that we all embrace a more radically biblical form of discipleship that will reorder our entire lives. Anything less will not fit us to live authentically and effectively in a new century.

The intent of this chapter, therefore, is to suggest some creative ways we can begin in our personal lives, families, and communities to flesh out more authentically the visions and values of the Wild Hope of God.

To live authentically in a changing world, first we must understand something of how the world is changing and something of what faith demands. Therefore, the format of the chapter reflects the following progression:

First, I will outline specific practical ways we as individuals can become better informed, learning to anticipate the new needs, challenges, and opportunities that are likely to confront us in coming decades. Then I will propose some starting points for how we can:

- become liberated from our cultural captivity,

- flesh out something of the future of God,

- discover a new rhythm for our lives,

- reorder our priorities and lifestyles, and

- create new incarnational communities of hope.

It would be easy to be overwhelmed by all the projected changes raised to this point. But as a New Zealand Christian film I saw years ago suggests, "we need to learn to grasp the problems at the near edge." Obviously, none of us in our lives, churches, and institutions can begin to respond to all the changes filling our world. But part of the problem is that many of us are making no effort to engage the emerging challenges at all. I believe all of us can find the "near edge" of one problem and engage it for the kingdom.

The proposals in this chapter are not definitive. But I hope they will stir some passionate conversation on how we can live more authentically, responsibly, and compassionately in a rapidly changing world.

LEARNING TO BE HORIZON WATCHERS

The journey toward more authentic living begins by more fully understanding the world of which we are a part and gaining a better sense of how that world is changing, paying attention to the "signs of the times" (Matt. 16:3, RSV). It is evident from the issues we discussed earlier in this book that our world is changing at blinding speed. To live responsibly in such a world, we must learn to take the future seriously in our personal lives. To do this, we must become much more informed.

How can we learn to take the future seriously? How can we learn to live at the horizon? First, we must recognize that we are headed into a much more transnational, cross-cultural future. One way to get in touch with that future is to begin to immerse ourselves and our families in the rich cultural opportunities that fill our communities and world.

I encourage every individual and family who wants to gain a little broader picture of how our world is changing to make a point of getting to know people from other ethnic groups and national cultures. If we are going to get ready for the twenty-first century, we must get to know people who experience life very differently from the way we do. We need to have them in our homes, visit their celebrations, fully share in their lives.

This all needs to be done with sensitivity and with an openness to reevaluating our Christian faith, our cultural values, and our political viewpoints on the basis of what we learn from others. You could give your children no better gift or preparation to live in an increasingly cross-cultural future than to live in a different cultural environment for a couple of years or even a few months.

Horizon watchers need, as resources allow, to make excursions into other cultural settings on a regular basis, whether this means attending a Greek or Hispanic festival in their hometown, visiting inner-city ministries, or traveling overseas. I don't meaning taking tours. Many affluent Americans travel overseas all the time but learn very little about the culture because they stay in such insulated, Westernized environments. Staying in the homes of nationals, at the sites of mission projects, or in local inns rather than American enclaves will save money and also boost the local economies. And it will help Americans learn more about the local culture and their own values as well.

The Church of the Saviour in Washington, D.C. has inaugurated a new program in servanthood education in which individuals live for a short time among the homeless of the city, then undergo a time of "debriefing" and reflection to assimilate what God is teaching them.

If we are serious about anticipating the new challenges and opportunities, we must set aside regular time in our schedule to read about how our world is changing and about the issues that fill the future. I recommend that, in addition to your local newspaper, you subscribe to the *New York Times* or the *Christian Science Monitor*; both provide much more comprehensive international reporting than most United States newspapers. Listening to National Public Radio news broadcasts, either morning or evening, is helpful and relatively easy for busy people. These broadcasts generally do a much more thorough job on both domestic and foreign news than the highly abbreviated sound bites we get on the six o'clock news. "The MacNeil-Lehrer News Hour" on public television, coverage on the CSPAN cable network, and some TV news specials are often very instructive as well.

Finally, I encourage individuals to go to the best library in their community at least once a month. Select a spectrum of publications, including those from other cultures, that reflect a broad range of different political and religious viewpoints. Spend four hours devouring the stack and photocopying what you want to keep.

Of course, it is also important to make a regular discipline of reading both nonfiction and fiction literature to broaden our scope. One to two books a month is a good beginning. Those in the professions will of course keep up on reading in their field. I encourage Christians to subscribe to at least two major religious publications that deal seriously with contemporary issues—such as *Christian Century, Sojourners, Christianity Today,* and *Christianity and Crisis*. Evangelicals for Social

Action puts out an informative newsletter that works hard to avoid political party lines of right and left in discussing today's issues.[5]

Finally, in monitoring the future, there is tremendous value in not doing it alone. Families can set aside time to discuss, with their children, what is happening in this world—teaching them to anticipate the new challenges and opportunities. Some may want to organize a horizon-watch group in their church or with their friends. *The Futurist* magazine helps organize chapters of the World Future Society to provide a forum to learn about our changing world.

It is not enough, however, simply to read and collect information. We must also make the effort to interpret what all this information *means* for our lives and the world. One simple way to do this is to make a habit of asking, "What might be the consequences?" of major events that are reported. Another helpful idea is to maintain a running list of issues that have particular significance for our careers, our families, our communities, our churches—and particularly those in need. Identifying possible consequences of major events and monitoring major issues will give us greater lead time to respond and enable others to respond. Then, in our lives, families, and communities, we will have an opportunity to be proactive instead of reactive in manifesting something of the realm of God.

FLESHING OUT THE KINGDOM IN CONFESSING COMMUNITY

As important as it is to take the future seriously, it is even more important to discover and embrace a biblical vision for the better future. Next to our relationship to God, nothing is more important than discovering a compelling vision for the future to which we can devote our lives, families, and communities.

Regrettably, this does not seem to be a strongly felt need in most of our churches. As mentioned earlier, we seem completely content, silently sanctioning the Western Dream and all the baggage that goes with it. Ecumenical Christians and evangelicals alike seem to have embraced both the vision and the values of the secular culture as an unquestioned given. Then things of faith must be worked in around the edges of the cultural agenda as though they all go together—and, of course, they don't.

How can we as the church define who we are in a way that challenges the seduction of secular culture? Stanley Hauerwas and William Willimon suggest there are at least three possible models of what it means to be the church, only one of which seriously addresses the seduction of culture.

Hauerwas and Willimon suggest that the first of these models, the *activist church,*

is more concerned with building a better society than with the reformation of the church. Through the humanization of social structures, the activist church glorifies God. The difficulty . . . is that the activist church appears to lack theological insight to judge history for itself. Its politics becomes a sort of religiously glorified liberalism.[6]

And the reason for this, I believe, is that the activist church has unquestioningly embraced not only modernization, but the liberal political values that accompany it. This model is found most frequently in mainline denominations.

"On the other hand," Hauerwas and Willimon continue, "we have the *conversionist church*," which

argues that no amount of tinkering with the structures of society will counter the effects of human sin. The promises of secular optimism are, therefore, false because they attempt to bypass the biblical call to admit personal guilt and to experience reconciliation to God and neighbor. Because this church works only for inward change, it has no alternative social ethic or social structure of its own to offer the world.[7]

The conversionist church, by privatizing faith, unwittingly trivializes it so that it deals only with inward personal change. It is left to modern culture and conservative political ideology to establish values and priorities that define the Christian's relationship to the larger society. Of course, this model is found most often among evangelical Protestants.

Hauerwas and Willimon suggest that we consider a third possibility—the *confessing church*. They explain,

The confessing church is not a synthesis of the other two approaches, a helpful middle ground. Rather, it is a radical alternative. Rejecting both the individualism of the conversionists and the secularism of the activists, the confessing church finds its main political task to lie, not in the personal transformation of individual hearts or the modification of society, but rather in the congregation's determination to worship Christ in all things.[8]

Hauerwas and Willimon go on to emphasize,

The confessing church, like the conversionist church, also calls people to conversion, but it depicts that conversion as a long process of being baptismally engrafted into a new people . . . a counter-cultural social structure called church. It seeks to influence the world by being something the world is not and can never be, lacking the gifts of faith and vision, which is ours in Christ. The confessing church seeks . . . a place clearly visible to the world, in which people are faithful to their promises, love their enemies, tell the truth, honor the poor, suffer for righteousness, and thereby testify to the amazing community-creating power of God. The confessing church has no interest in withdrawing from the world, but it is not surprised when its witness evokes hostility from the world. The confessing church moves from the activist church's acceptance of the culture with a few qualifications, to rejection of the culture with few exceptions. The confessing church can participate in secular movements against war, against hunger and against other forms of inhumanity. But it sees this as a part of its necessary proclamatory action. This church knows that its most credible form of witness is the actual creation of a living, breathing, visible community of faith.[9]

This definition of the church as a confessing community reaffirms, in more motivating terms, the premise of this chapter—that the first call of the gospel is neither to social activism nor to proclaimation, but to *incarnation*, to fleshing out something of God's new order.

Orlando Costas reminds us, in addition, that disciple making is central to preparing people to be a part of a biblical church. Disciple making means calling people into a radically new community that would manifest God's kingdom in history by redirecting our ambitions, transforming our values, and altering our lifestyles.[10]

Ecumenical Christians tend to talk little of disciple making. Evangelicals, on the other hand, focus a great amount of attention on disciple making, but evangelicals typically offer a privatized, compartmentalized notion of discipleship that tends to fully embrace the American culture and is often disengaged from the larger issues of our world.

If our primary calling as followers of Jesus Christ is to flesh out God's new order, how do we begin? How do we become disciples not just in one aspect of our lives, but in all of our experience? Doesn't the journey begin with becoming liberated from our cultural captivity, by dreaming new dreams and creating new communities?

The entire Old Testament narrative makes it clear that God expected the community of Israel to live in hope of a very different future and to base its common life on a very different set of values than the people around it. And when Christ called that first band of disciples to follow him, he called them to a hope and a set of values that were radically different from those of the dominant culture. One cannot read the Gospels as a whole or the Beatitudes specifically without realizing that the call to follow Jesus Christ is the call to become a part of a new countercultural community, working for a new dream.

Listen to British theologian Michael Green's description of that earliest Christian community:

They made the grace of God credible by a society of love and mutual care which astonished pagans and was recognized as something entirely new. It lent persuasiveness to their claim that the new age had dawned in Christ. The

Word was not only announced but seen in the community of those who are giving it flesh.

The message of the kingdom became more than an idea. A new human community had sprung up and looked very much like the new order to which the evangelist had pointed. Here love was given daily expression; reconciliation was actually occurring; people were no longer divided into Jew and Gentile, slave and free, male and female. In this community the weak were protected, the stranger welcomed. People were healed, the poor and dispossessed were cared for and found justice. Every thing was shared. Joy abounded and ordinary lives were filled with praise.[11]

RECAPTURING THE BIBLICAL VISION

How do we break free from the captivity of culture? How do we, like those first disciples, become a new community? One possible place to begin is to invite Scripture to help us critique and evaluate the culture that is too much with us.

Moving toward a biblical vision, however, can be as fraught with difficulty as the children of Israel's journey toward the Promised Land. As I intimated earlier, even many of the theologians who intellectually understand a theology of the kingdom don't seem to be personally caught up in the Scripture's remarkable imagery and what it represents for our lives and our world.

As a consequence, church leadership seems to be doing little to communicate a vision of the kingdom of God that is both comprehensible and compelling. I believe that most of the material on the kingdom of God is much too cerebral and abstract for laity. Somehow, it needs to be translated into terms that capture our hearts and our allegiance as well as our intellect. We need to have the imagery of Scripture translated into new celebrations, liturgy, music, and rituals.

While speaking at Fuller Theological Seminary a few years ago, I proposed an extended retreat on the kingdom of God. The purpose of the retreat would be to bring together theologians who write about the kingdom with artists, dramatists, and musicians. The retreat would have a single purpose: to translate the powerful biblical imagery of God's loving intentions for the future into song, dance, and dramatization that could touch our hearts and win over our allegiance. Somehow the rich tapestry of images for the Wild Hope of God which spill through both Old and New Testaments need to be translated into contemporary, living images that could flood our consciousness and capture our imaginations today.

However, we dare not wait for someone to convene such a retreat. Time is too short. I would encourage us instead to go back to the Bible and begin to discover the stirring imagery afresh. The Book of Isaiah is especially rich in imagery and offers a good place to start, although you can find similar breathtaking images throughout the Scripture. And a study of the Gospel of Luke and the Book of Acts presents a compelling picture of God's kingdom work in action.

If we were to embrace the biblical image of the better future, how would our lives be altered? How would the biblical vision change our life direction, transform our values, and reorder our priorities? How would it alter our notion of what the "good life" is? A hint is given in that scene when Jesus Christ, at the inauguration of his ministry, committed his life to working for the purposes of God:

> The scroll of the prophet Isaiah was handed to him. Unrolling it, he found the place where it is written:
>
> > "The Spirit of the Lord is on me,
> >   because he has anointed me
> >   to preach good news to the poor.
> > He has sent me to proclaim freedom for the prisoners
> >   and recovery of sight for the blind,
> > to release the oppressed,
> >   to proclaim the year of the Lord's favor."
> >
> > Luke 4:17–19, NIV

What the Scripture seems to imply is that, for Jesus, being the Messiah of God meant quite simply devoting his life to working for the purposes of God. If there are any doubts, all we have to do is read ahead to Luke 7, in which John sends his disciples to learn if Jesus is the One they are expecting or not. Christ responds to John's inquiry:

> "Go back and report to John what you have seen and heard: The blind receive sight, the lame walk, those who have leprosy are cured, the deaf hear, the dead are raised, and the good news is preached to the poor." (v. 22, NIV)

One doesn't have to read much further to discover that, for Jesus' disciples, following Christ meant not only committing their lives to God, but also working for the purposes of God in the world. I believe that's why so many of them radically reordered their lives, quitting jobs and leaving homes. They committed themselves to a new vision and a new vocation that had priority over their own aspirations, economic security, relationships, societal expectations, or anything else. They understood, as we don't seem to understand today, that following Jesus Christ is a whole-life proposition which requires our commitment to a new sense of purpose.

FOLLOWING CHRIST INTO REORDERED LIVES

How are we to reorder our lives so we can be actively involved in bringing release to the captives, sight to the blind, and good news to the poor? For some it could mean changing jobs or changing living situations. For many it will mean changing our "timestyles" and our priorities to clear at least one evening a week to work with abused children, share faith with international students, or care for housebound seniors. There are as many possibilities as there are persons.

And not only will we ask God to transform our life direction from seeking life to finding ways to give life away, we will also invite God to transform our values from the values of the dominant culture to the values of the kingdom of God. In concert with other sisters and brothers, we will commit to living out the right-side-up values of the kingdom in an upside-down world. We will open ourselves to allowing God to create within us and in our communities a foretaste of that new future.

But building this kind of right-side-up community will require a renaissance of creativity. If we are to live out the Wild Hope of God in a rapidly changing world, we must seek to burst the wineskins of the conventional and, with God's help, to find the new and creative.

For the past seventeen years I have been leading creativity workshops. And I believe one of the greatest untapped resources in the church today is the imaginations of its members. I have discovered over and over again that people have tremendous potential to imagine whole new possibilities for their lives and God's world.

For example, during a creativity workshop at Hollywood Presbyterian Church in Los Angeles, three young men created a new approach for Christians struggling with how to manage their time. They stood up to present their proposal to the entire group and performed a brief skit:

"Hi, my name is Brad. I am a time-addicted Christian, and I really need your prayers,"

"Hello, my name is John. My time schedule is chronically screwed up and I need your help."

"Hi, I am Larry and I'm a busyness freak, and I need prayer."

There was immediate laughter of recognition as these guys began their presentation. They outlined a very imaginative "twelve-step program" to help time-addicted Christians become liberated from their frenzied lives and regain control of their time schedule. And frankly, even though they had only spent an hour creating their proposal, it looked very feasible.

The journey toward a life that more fully embraces God's vision of a world made new begins with developing our spirituality and altering the rhythms of our lives. The dominant culture has not only largely defined the future for which many of us labor and the values we subscribe to. More than we recognize, the culture also has a great deal to do with the timestyles we adopt—the busyness that many of us succumb to. We have been seduced into believing that our worth is determined largely by our activity and our busyness.

I find that most of us middle-class Americans are absolutely manic in our use of time. Typically, we are booked every evening of the week. If we get a free evening, we immediately book something else in that space and then complain about how busy we are—as if someone else did it to us. No one else did it to us. We do it to ourselves.

Transforming the Rhythm of Our Lives

The young men from Hollywood Presbyterian are right. Most of us are time-addicted Christians, living in denial. We all seem to need help in this area. And I don't think time management seminars are the answer. They simply teach us how to squeeze more into what we are already doing. They don't typically teach us how to reorder our priorities and seriously order the rhythm of our lives.

We need God's help in fundamentally transforming our life rhythms. As we examine Genesis, we see a rhythm established for work and rest. We also see God institute a certain rhythm for the land in the teaching of the sabbatical year where the land is to lie fallow on the seventh year. Of course, in the more rural cultures the rhythms of life are largely determined by the cycles of the seasons.

In the New Testament, Jesus introduced a new dimension to the rhythm of life. While keeping the rhythm of Jewish Sabbaths and feast days, his commitment to the kingdom of God profoundly affected how he used his time. In the New Testament, we typically find Jesus in one of two places. He is either with people, visiting, teaching, healing, and celebrating, or he is with God alone. He appears to have had little time for anything else. And yet he never seemed hurried.

The most self-evident characteristic of Christ's prayer life, a characteristic I have seldom heard mentioned in a Protestant church, mainline or evangelical, is that he went on extended prayer retreats. Part of the new rhythm of life he modeled for us was not only taking time to be fully present with others, but taking time to be fully present with the God he knew with such remarkable intimacy.

The beginning point of the transformed life is learning, like the One we follow, to center our lives in prayer. The place where we most fully encounter God and most completely participate in the birth process with God is in the life of prayer. Henri Nouwen reminds us that prayer is the very center of incarnational living: "The paradox of prayer is that it asks for serious effort while it can only be received as a gift. We cannot plan, organize or manipulate God. But without careful discipline we cannot receive him either."[12]

A few years ago, I was struggling unsuccessfully with my time-addicted life. I found I had extreme difficulty fitting into my life the two things for which Jesus had the most time—God and others. Then I spent a few weeks working on a project in rural Haiti. I got to know people who had a rhythm to their life that looked very much like what I read about in the Gospels. They were hard-working people, many of them farmers who had to work more than eight hours a day, six days a week. But they always had time to stop their work and visit with passers-by. Though working more total hours than most people in the United States, they never seemed harried.

I know these people spent more time in prayer than I did, so constantly were they confronted with imminent issues of life and death. In the evenings they would routinely drop in unannounced on neighbors. On many warm Haitian evenings during my sojourn we would visit the homes of friends. They would open their homes to us and serve us food and drinks. We would spend a whole evening telling stories, laughing, singing, and playing with the children to the flicker of kerosene lamps.

I came back from that trip determined to begin changing the rhythm of my life so that I had more time for people. I thank my Haitian friends for helping me discover a more biblical approach to my time. More recently I have been learning from Catholics and Episcopalians about how I can reorder my timestyle through a life of prayer, periodic prayer retreats, and following the rhythm of the liturgical calendar.

Out of these experiences—and the changes they have made in my life—I am convinced that it is possible to be set free from our time-addicted lives. In *Why Settle for More and Miss the Best?* I outlined a strategy by which we can begin our journey toward a new timestyle. I will briefly outline it here as well.[13]

We begin by clearing the decks—freeing up as much time in our schedule as possible. This may include getting rid of "good" activities as well as "empty" ones. It may mean getting off church committees, cutting back on club involvements, saying no to unnecessary busyness.

Next comes taking a little time to savor the newfound freedom—making a point of not filling in the spaces. Then, I would suggest scheduling a prayer retreat. If Jesus Christ needed periods of quiet alone with God, we surely do. I encourage singles and couples to go on prayer retreats at least twice a year; four times a year would be better. Taking at least a day and a half or two days to pray and seek God's guidance can enable us to recenter our lives and recall our vocations. A Bible and a journal are all we really need to take.

Once again, I encourage people to begin by meditating on the imagery of the future of God as pictured in Scripture, trying to visualize what the coming of God's kingdom would mean for the urgent issues that fill our world. What would release to the captives, sight to the blind, and good news to the poor mean in our world or our community if the Wild Hope of God were fully unleashed?

Then comes a time of active listening, focusing on our own personal lives and asking two questions:

- How does God want to use my life, my gifts, my time for the purposes of the kingdom? and

- How does God want to revolutionize my lifestyle to more authentically flesh out, in community with others, the visions and values of God's kingdom?

It is important to recognize that if we ask these two questions with complete openness and availability, the Creator God could do as God has done with so many others: turn our lives upside down. Or God might just help us sharpen our focus for our ministries, our vocations, our marriages, and our family lives.

In either case, we will return from our retreat, hopefully, with some struggling new sense of direction and priority that is informed by our understanding of God's kingdom. This should enable us to begin to reorganize our time schedule. In light of new insights we have gained by prayer and active listening, we need to ask ourselves specific questions:

- How much time do I need to set aside for daily prayer and biblical study?

- How much time do I need to set aside for family and those I care about?

- How much time do I need to set aside to be in worship Sunday morning and to be in a small group in which I experience Christian community?

- How much time do I need to set aside every week to be explicitly working for God's purposes in response to the needs of others and the creation?

- How much time should I spend reading and monitoring a changing world?

- How much time do I need to set aside for celebrating relationships and the goodness of God's creation?

- How much time should I invest in my occupation and in maintaining the basic life systems?

As we recover our center in a life of prayer, regain some sense of the natural rhythms of our organic past, renew our lives in the seasons of the liturgical year, and refocus our lives around the visions and values of God's kingdom, then we can begin our lives over again. Then, with the help of the Holy Spirit, not only will we be set free from the frenzy of the rat race and the obsessions of the American Dream. We will also be enabled to create ways of life for ourselves and those we care about that are more festive and celebrative than anything the consumer culture can offer. We will then have time and energy to invest in all that God is doing to make the world new.

Beyond the Tithe: Rediscovering Whole-Life Stewardship

I run into people all over the country who want to be set free, who long to live life with a new sense of purpose and a new rhythm. I believe that many are looking for creative ways we can steward our whole lives in promoting the purposes of God's new order.

Most of our churches, evangelical and ecumenical, tend to emphasize a compartmentalized or tithe view of stewardship. While understanding the Old Testament origins of the tithe, a growing number of biblical scholars, like John

Howard Yoder, insist the tithe is not normative in the New Testament.[14] Instead, the Gospels seem to call us to jubilary or whole-life stewardship.

Whole-life stewardship is premised on the biblical proposition, "the earth is the Lord's." If the earth is indeed the Lord's, then it is no longer a question of "how much of mine do I have to give up?" If the earth is the Lord's, then the question becomes, "How much of God's do I get to keep?" in a world where even Christians are struggling to survive.

Rarely does one hear either evangelical or ecumenical churches advocating whole-life stewardship—challenging their members to reorder their life priorities fundamentally in order to place the visions in order the values of God's kingdom first.

Few of the evangelical writings on stewardship question the consumptive preoccupations of secular culture, and many seem to sanction them. Typically, they insist we can even purchase all the luxury consumer goods we want—second homes, expensive autos, and recreational vehicles—as long as we don't get a materialistic hangup. And evangelicals have apparently been remarkably successful in avoiding materialistic hangups!

But the issue involves more than an attitude problem. What many evangelical leaders fail to recognize is that we live in an interdependent, interconnected world in which there is only so much to go around. If we use more than a fair share of what God has entrusted to us, someone else will go without.

Ecumenical Christians, on the other hand, often seem very aware that we live in an interdependent world filled with inequity and distributive injustice. But I have found, in speaking to ecumenical gatherings, that when I suggest our quest for social justice should begin by adopting more just personal lifestyles, the audience seems to develop an acute hearing loss. And as I have mentioned before, those who talk the most about social justice and the poor consistently seem to give the least.

We can't begin to be a part of God's compassionate response to escalating need with our present levels of investment. That's why it is so essential that we recover a biblical theology of whole-life stewardship that enables us to reorder our use of both time and money.

Whole-life stewardship begins by asking how we can give our lives and families new focus—becoming much more intentionally a part of what God is doing to give birth to a new creation. In other words, our life's mission is no longer to preserve the present order, but to intentionally be a part of what God is doing to give birth to a whole new order.

I think we will discover that with a growing sense of purpose in our lives and a growing quality of intimacy in our relationships, we will be less inclined to turn to consumerism to meet these needs. In addition, our identity and self-worth will no longer be derived from our success as either producers or consumers.

What does whole life stewardship look like? It looks like a doctor in Denver who sold half of his medical practice. He supports his family very comfortably on a twenty-hour a week income. And he spends his other twenty hours running an inner-city health clinic for the growing numbers who can no longer afford access to even basic levels of health care.

Whole-life stewardship looks like eight young people in Seattle who have devoted their lives to enabling a community of fifty Laotians to become economically self-reliant by starting an agricultural project. The young people found that by living together in shared housing they could shelter and feed themselves for only two hundred fifty dollars per person per month. They could support themselves at this modest rate with part-time jobs, thus freeing up generous portions of their time to work with the Laotians.

A growing number of seniors with time on their hands are discovering they can have a second career for the kingdom in their retirement years. Some are working in homeless shelters in the United States. Others are doing short-term veterinary work with rural farmers in Africa through Christian Veterinary Mission (a part of World Concern).

What these people have done, along with thousands of others, is to realign their lives to catch the tempo of a different dream. No longer driven by the autonomous impulses of our acquisitive culture, they are discovering, in community with others, a more integrated, satisfying way of life in which they find creative ways to free up time and resources to invest in the advancement of God's kingdom.

UNLEASHING NEW POSSIBILITIES IN ALTERNATIVE HOUSING, NONTRADITIONAL VOCATIONS, AND ETHICAL RESPONSES

Once we have begun to realign our lives and families in the direction of the kingdom, the creative possibilities are unlimited. We will discover we can take charge of our own lives and create a better way of life than anything the rat race offers.

One of the major stewardship decisions facing any American Christian is the issue of housing. As we have shown, the single-family detached dwelling has proven increasingly elusive for many younger Boomers and for those from the Baby Buster generation. People are looking for alternatives, and many are discovering new possibilities.

A number of Inter-Varsity Christian Fellowship staff who are working both with college students and the urban poor in southern California have met their shelter needs by living cooperatively in rented houses. A growing number of Christian young people involved in mission are likely to settle for rental and cooperative living situations instead of devoting their lives to working for a mortgage company. They remind us that we are sojourners living in a transitional time and that we dare not become too encumbered.

Others, like Jon and Pam in Redmond, Washington, have let their commitment to the kingdom influencehow they approached home owership. By building their modest two-bedroom, split level home themselves, they were able to keep costs to a minimum. They completed construction in 1989 for the cost of $25,000 in front end cash.

What's the difference between paying $25,000 up front and paying nearly a half-million dollars over thirty years for a $100,000 house? The difference is a whole lot of two people's lives. Without a mortgage payment, Jon and Pam no longer need two incomes. They not only have more time for their kids, but more time to address the needs of others.

In the nineties, the church will need to make a heroic effort to enable the Christian young to shelter themselves less expensively. Failing to do this, we could lose a whole generation to the American obsession with the single-family detached home.

A number of Christians who are already homeowners are placing God's purposes first in other ways. Some are selling large homes to purchase more modest dwellings, hoping to free more time and resources to invest in the advance of God's new order. A growing number are opening their homes to foster children, single-parent families, and seniors in need. As the numbers of homeless continue to increase, it will be essential that every Christian homeowner look seriously at his or her responsibility to share available housing in the nineties.

Yet another innovative approach is the Langley Assistance Mortgage Plan (LAMP), developed by a group of Christians in Langley, British Columbia. These women and men studied biblical principles about usury. Then they developed a covenant community and pooled their economic resources to enable members of the community to pay off mortgages sooner and then invest the money and time they save in the work of the kingdom. Reportedly, all members of this cooperative, to their own amazement, were able to pay their mortgages off within seven years.[15]

Not only in housing, but in every area of life, whole-life stewardship forces us to ask the important question, "How much is enough?" How much do we really need to spend on housing, transportation, wardrobe, recreation and vacation in a world of growing need? If we can creatively reduce how much we spend on ourselves, then we don't have to spend such a large portion of our waking hours working for income. We will have more time and money to invest in addressing the growing needs of others and in the restoration of God's creation.

In Seattle, I recently ran into Joe Dominguez, who started an organization called the Road Map Foundation. In a cassette series he talks about the myths of money, two of which he identifies as (1) "Everybody has to make a living," and (2) "It is unseemly to retire financially independent at an early age."

Joe, a former Wall Street broker, has proven both these myths wrong. He and his wife significantly reduced their economic needs so that they could retire early and use their lives to make a difference in society.

I interviewed two women who are living in the same household with the Dominguezes. By following the nine-step process Joe developed, they were both able to retire five years after they started the process. The way they did it was to significantly reduce their lifestyle costs and save seventy-five thousand dollars over a period of five years. They invested the seventy-five thousand dollars in United States treasury bonds, and now they live off the interest of some six thousand dollars a year. Through this strategy, they were able to quit working at income-producing jobs and begin investing their time in working for projects they really care about. One of them, for example, is working with Habitat for Humanity.

I am not sure I could live on six thousand dollars a year, even in a shared household. But the principle is still valid. Nothing in Scripture suggests we have to work forty hours a week for income. If we can find creative ways to reduce our economic needs, become economically self-reliant, and retire early, then we can more fully take charge of our lives. We don't have to be chronically dependent on an employer, working at jobs that are often irrelevant to the new order that God is birthing. And we can make the best hours of the day available to advance God's kingdom.

Of course, there are any number of professions where the work can be directly aligned to our sense of the intentions of God. Sadly, however, I find very few career-guidance programs in Christian colleges that seem to recognize this. Rather than helping students locate work that is clearly aligned to God's purposes, they tend to point students toward those jobs that have the best perks, "bennies," and starting salaries—just like secular institutions.

There are a number of ways we can intentionally put our educations to work for God's kingdom. Some Christians are starting small businesses among the poor; others are using their legal training to work in the field of domestic reconciliation or victim-offender reconciliation. And there are rapidly expanding opportunities for those with backgrounds in computer science to work with the disabled.

With a little creativity, any training or profession can be given a specific kingdom application. But if we can't find a way to become economically self-reliant so we can focus the best hours of our day in working for God's cause, or if we can't find a way to align our occupation to promote the purposes of God's new order intentionally, then we need to free some of our discretionary time, as we discussed earlier, to be of service to others. Most people could free up one evening a week to work for God's purposes.

Regardless of where we work, there is another issue at stake: integrity in the workplace. Some, like Inez Austin, may even be called upon to put their job on the line for higher principles. Inez Austin, an eleven-year employee of Westinghouse at a nuclear site at Hanford, Washington, made a decision that reflected a great deal of integrity but came at a very high cost:

> Inez Austin refused to sign a report last June that would have allowed Westinghouse Hanford Company to start a pumping operation that could cause nuclear waste tanks containing tons of deadly radioactive chemicals to explode.
> Her caution was later supported by a U.S. Government report. Once a highly rated employee, she said her boss threatened to fire her, her work was

taken away, she was told to see a company psychologist, her office mail stopped coming for two months and she was moved repeatedly. "If it costs me my job, this one was worth saying no to."[16]

In business, engineering, and law journals and in the daily press, I have read many such accounts—stories of workers who have put their jobs on the line to call attention to practices that endangered human safety or the environment or violated ethics. I have yet to read in the religious press a single account of such whistle blowing.

In the nineties we will have a growing responsibility to report on ethical violations and to support those who are taking a stand. We also will need to help Christians faced with serious ethical dilemmas in the workplace to find a position that is congruent with biblical principles. This is likely to be particularly difficult for conservative Christians who are conditioned to be submissive to all in positions of authority and who seem able totally to divorce their personal morality from the morality of the place where they work.

In our rapidly changing future, most of us will probably need help learning how to live with greater integrity in our private lives—in the ways we shop, invest, and relate to God's created order. And several excellent resources are available to provide us with information we need in this regard.

The Council on Economic Priorities, for example, has published *Shopping for a Better World*[17] to help us learn where and under what circumstances products are made so we can shop with a greater sense of integrity—intentionally seeking products that are made without exploiting the poor or fouling God's creation.

In their important book, *Ethical Investing,*[18] Amy L. Domini and Peter D. Kinder maintain that every investment has an "ethical dimension" and help the reader develop ethical criteria to guide his or her investments. Of course, the criteria could cover anything from withholding investments in mutual funds that invest in South Africa, the tobacco industry or weapons of mass destruction to purposefully investing in companies that engage in affirmative hiring or employee profit-sharing plans. The authors insist that those operating from an ethical criteria can enjoy profits at levels equal to those who have no criteria at all.

In preparation for Earth Day 1990, Earthworks Press in Berkeley, California, published *50 Simple Things You Can Do to Save The Earth*. It is filled with creative ideas for ways we can intentionally change our lifestyles to live more lightly and responsibly on the earth.

UNLEASHING POSSIBILITIES FOR THE CHRISTIAN YOUNG

As we begin to live out the vision of God more responsibly and creatively, we will begin to provide members of the younger generation with what they need most—alternative models. We will show them what fleshing out God's new order is like. But to do this, we need to create new models of family life, community life, alternative vocations, and celebrative lifestyles.

In spite of all the Christian books and broadcasts on family life, I believe there is a glaring oversight. I asked a local church, "What is it that the American Christian family does together more than anything else?" After a pause, someone said, "We consume together." And she was right. Like their secular counterparts, our Christian families find most of their bonding in consuming sitcoms and Big Macs and making trips to the mall. I rarely find churches that actively encourage families—parents and kids—to be bonded together in service to others.

Whole-life stewardship means placing God's purposes— "sight to the blind, release to the captives and good news to the poor"—at the center of family life, too. One glimpse of what that might look like is parents and children visiting nursing homes once a week and having the kids tell stories. Another is working together in a community garden that provides food for the poor. Yet another is parents working in an English as a Second Language program while their children play with the children of the students. Unless we begin early in raising children to look beyond their own needs to the needs of others, we are not likely to have a generation who has any interest in what God is seeking to bring into being.

Involving young people in whole-life stewardship also stretches to include the way we entertain ourselves. We need to help not only the young, but Christians of all ages, learn that they can do better than Ninja Turtles, MTV, and Trivial Pursuit. They can create their own good times. We can take any historical or biblical imagery to create new celebrations. If you were going to create a celebration around the kingdom of God as a wedding banquet, what would you include? How might you create new rituals and rites of passage for the young that reflect the values of the new order?

And whole-life stewardship certainly means helping young people wrestle with some of the most important questions that are likely to shape their future: (1) What is ultimately important? (2) What is the good life? and (3) Where are we likely to find it? As I travel the country, I find few churches, Christian schools, or youth programs that provide forums in which the young are challenged to examine issues of life direction in light of the purposes of God.

If we don't want the young simply to go with the flow, we must place much greater emphasis on the visions and values to which they give their lives and on helping them live responsibly and creatively. It is particularly important to expose them to a much broader cross-cultural environment as well as a broader array of options for housing, cooperative living, creative lifestyles, celebrations, and nontraditional vocations. Only then will they realize they have alternatives and can actually take charge of their own lives.

Rediscovering Community

The only way any of us at any age can hope to be successful in reordering our lives and begin to flesh out something of God's future is in community. In Century

One, community wasn't optional; it was normative. One could not claim to be a follower of Jesus Christ without being a part of a community in which he or she was known, loved, and held accountable. Today, because of the invidious influence of our individualistic culture, it is rare to find believers who participate in any expression of Christian community.

Ecumenical Christians will, at times, serve on committees, but many have little experience with being a part of a small group in which they are expected to be vulnerable and accountable to others. Evangelicals and charismatic churches have a history of midweek Bible studies and prayer meetings, but generally these groups don't become places in which people are truly known, committed to one another, or held accountable for the stewardship of their lives.

As we conclude this chapter, I will examine a selection of models of Christian community in North America. And I will argue that if we are to authentically incarnate something of God's new order in the nineties, we must create some wholly new models of what Christian community will look like. Our largely autonomous American Christianity simply will not be up to the challenges of the twenty-first century.

For most of us, community will probably mean being a part of a small home group from our church that meets weekly to pray, study Scripture, and get caught up with one another's lives. Some small groups also enable participants to identify their vocations and equip them for mission.

Assembly Mennonite Church in Elkhart, Indiana, has broken its congregation down into small face-to-face groups that meet weekly for mutual support. But this church does something else that is unique. Twice a year, each member in each small group brings his or her household budget and time schedule to the small-group meeting. Group members openly share how they are trying to steward their lives in light of the purposes and values of the kingdom of God. Then they seek discernment from the community on how God might have them reorder their priorities. Every autonomous nerve bristles at such disclosure, but this is really very similar to the kind of openness and accountability that apparently was practiced in the earliest church.

In the Bruderhof Communities, autonomy is subject to even sterner medicine. The Bruderhof Community I visited in Woodcrest, New York, which has nearly three hundred members, is a common-purse community. That means that all the profits from the Bruderhof's company, Community Playthings, go directly to the community. There are no individual salaries. Everyone is provided with what he or she needs for shelter, food, clothing, and other necessities. None of the members has his or her own spending money or really any possessions except a few personal effects. As a result of this arrangement, the community must pay only about two hundred dollars per person per month in living costs.

But more remarkable than the way the Bruderhof members handle finances is their spirit, their love, and the way they raise children. The Bruderhof is the oldest

Protestant community in the United States, transplanted here from Germany almost a century ago. Its members haven't forgotten their first love or why God called them together. They are deeply devoted in their common life to following the radical call to be disciples of Jesus Christ and to trying to manifest some of the values of his kingdom.

Nowhere in my travels in North America have I seen children more lovingly raised than at Woodcrest. First, there is no addiction, fragmentation, or abuse in this community. Second, everyone—older children, singles, seniors, not just the parents—is involved in loving and raising the children. And instead of inundating kids with consumer goodies—stereos, phones, TVs, VCRs, video games, and cars—the environment of the Bruderhof celebrates the goodness of relationships. And that's not just relationships in the community. Families regularly work with the homeless in New York City and visit the prison near their community.

The advantage of communities in which people live together residentially is that they have the opportunity to live out the values of God's kingdom much more intentionally. As a result, they are often a much stronger sacramental presence in society. During the eighties, there was a gradual decline in Christian communities of all kinds, from Catholic orders to Protestant communes. But as we began to turn the corner into the nineties, there were some unexpected but welcome signs of renewal. A new wind seems to be blowing. And new communities are being birthed again.

John R. Stott, an Anglican priest and an elder statesman of British evangelicalism, has stated that if he were a young Christian beginning his discipleship again, he would be inclined to start a monastic order calling other young men to the vows of celibacy, poverty and peace. Perhaps new lay orders could compensate for the decline in traditional orders that have been so integral to the Catholic, Episcopal, and Orthodox traditions.

Senate Chaplain Richard Halverson, speaking in 1988 to members of the Bruderhof and other Hutterites, said, "Something 'cataclysmic' is in the air." To be responsive to what is happening, evangelicals will have to move away from materialism "which has badly infected the whole evangelical community" and toward the kind of simplicity so evident in the Bruderhof.

Richard Mouw, the provost at Fuller Theological Seminary, has said that the church would benefit from a "remonasticization," creating smaller lay orders within the church, and "calling the entire church to a clearer and more radical witness."[19]

I would go further than Mouw. I believe that a return to a radical idea of Christian community is essential to the renewal and the survival of a vital church in the Western nations. The only way we can win the battle against the encroaching waves of modernization is to launch a counteroffensive in both mainline and evangelical churches to establish lay orders, radical Christian communities, and base communities.

Thankfully, the new movement has already begun. Some mainline churches are starting base or basic Christian communities modeled after those in Latin America:

> Base communities are permanent gatherings of Christians committed to being the church on a small scale. They meet at least every three weeks, reflect on Scripture, share their experiences of God working in their lives, challenge each other to live out the call to put the gospel into action and support each other in a life of service. . . . they appear counter-cultural because they are. Deep reflection on the gospel message calls into question our consumer, waste-prone, shortsighted society. Because they cannot be controlled, these communities are a threat to those in control.[20]

Other expressions of this new movement are in evidence as well. Richard Rohr, a Franciscan brother, works with a charismatic Catholic community in Albuquerque, New Mexico, that is energetically addressing the urgent needs in its community. A group of Lutherans started St. Martin's community in Minneapolis in 1985. They are a community who all live in geographical proximity in a transitional neighborhood. In addition to coming together regularly for eucharistic worship, they are also heavily involved in working with the poor in their neighborhood and helping run the "overground railway" transporting Central American refugees to Canada.

Servants with the Poor is calling small groups of Christians to relocate into communities of poverty, taking a vow to live at the same economic level as those in their community. This organization's intention is to enable these small groups to become an integral part of a specific neighborhood, then to begin working with other community members to restore that neighborhood for the love of God.

Musician John Michael Talbot has started a new contemporary Catholic lay order modeled very directly after Third-Order Franciscans. Music and celebration as well as service to others characterize this community.

Even though the larger church doesn't seem to recognize it, something new is being birthed. Even older communities like Reba Place outside Chicago, which was started in the sixties, are feeling fresh breezes filling their sails.

What is missing, though, are some interim models of community that don't require a lifelong or a common-purse commitment like the Bruderhof or necessitate relocating into communities of poverty like Servants with the Poor. Alvin Toffler suggested in *Future Shock*[21] that we need to develop "enclaves of the future." Never has that been truer. We need a whole spectrum of models of what the Wild Hope of God might look like as expressed in communities that are clearly at counterpoint to the dominant culture.

As long as we simply participate in the agenda of modern culture and become involved in the activities of a local church, we will not be a match for the new challenges coming at us from the future. We need some new models of residential communities that are not communal and are within reach of middle-class people.

One possible departure point might be an adaptation of the cohousing movement in Europe. For the past two decades, people in Denmark and other Scandinavian countries have been experimenting with creating cohousing communities. People in

Northern Europe have created these nonreligious settlements to both increase their sense of community and reduce their costs of living. One of the most recent books on the movement, simply entitled *Cohousing*, describes eight established cohousing arrangements in Denmark.[22]

In the cohousing model, land is used much more conservatively than in our typical single-family, detached dwelling. Housing units of all different sizes are clustered together. Some are even designed with flexible space that can be traded back and forth between adjoining families. Clustering the units together achieves a significant reduction in land use. Typically, cohousing planners plan any green space remaining for a children's play area, a garden area for adults, and an open "commons" area. In addition, people who live in the cohousing projects often share meals in the evening, child care in the daytime, and gardening activities on the weekends. Such an arrangement offers promising possibilities for using land and resources more responsibly as well as freeing time and money for kingdom service and making community more feasible.

Most of all, if Christians in North America could create such communities, they would provide an excellent setting in which both evangelical and ecumenical Christians could struggle together to flesh out something of God's kingdom more authentically .

Unleashing New Possibilities for Century Twenty-One

If we could enable the Christian young and others in the United States to find a viable alternative to the single-family detached home and the mortgage trap and a values alternative to the American Dream, we might be able to give birth to a new generation of Christian leadership. What would that alternative look like? Let me describe one possible model, based on the idea of combining less expensive cluster housing (like that used in cohousing), alternative financing, and assistance in creating covenant communities in these enclaves.

Where zoning permits, a group of Christians could cooperatively build a small cohousing model with six units. While the single-family detached home in the Seattle area starts at about $125,000 (but actually costs more like a half-million over thirty years), you can construct units in a multiplex unit (investing some of your own labor) for around $50,000 a unit in the Seattle area.

Next, I propose that wealthy Christians could be persuaded to invest $300,000 to provide interest-free loans for five years. This would be enough to enable each of six couples to purchase one of the $50,000 units in the multiplex unit. In other words, instead of paying a half-million dollars over thirty years for a $125,000 home, these six couples would only have to pay $50,000 over five years for a $50,000 home—a savings of $450,000 per couple or $2,700,000 for all six couples!

Written into the contract for this arrangement would be a stipulation that a certain generous share of the time or money freed up by such an arrangement would be directly invested in the work of God's kingdom. For example, the couples could make mortgage payments for an additional two years, which would amount to almost $150,000. According to LeRoy Troyer, a member of the board for Habitat for Humanity, that would be enough to build six homes for the poor in the United States or a hundred homes in the Two-Thirds World.

That would mean the Christian investors would get a double whammy out of their investment. By allowing $300,000 of their money to work for the kingdom, interest free, the investors would not only enable six couples to escape the mortgage trap and invest more of their lives in kingdom work, but would also provide housing for a number of the poor who otherwise wouldn't be able to afford it. And at the end of five years, the investors would have their $300,000 back.

Once the young Christian couples have paid off their five-year mortgages, they could each support themselves on a single income. That means that one could work full time while the other devotes time to raising the kids and helping others. Or both could work half-time jobs so that both could be involved in raising their children and working together for the purposes of God.

Do you begin to see the possibilities of actually achieving the kind of radically altered timestyle mentioned earlier in this chapter? Couples who were gifted with this kind of opportunity would, at the end of five or seven years, have much more of their lives, their time, and their money to invest in the advance of God's kingdom. And clearly, addressing tomorrow's challenges will require this kind of availability.

But even more important than the kind of resources this model frees up is the possibility it creates for the creation of Christian community. Instead of simply seeking to live out the suburban rat race in a new box, participants in this model would have the opportunity to create an example of what the reign of God could look like in one small community.

For example, before the six young couples ever moved into their less expensive cohousing experience, they could meet with leaders in their church to hammer out a covenant statement. In this covenant statement they would

- express how they would, as a community, seek to live out the values of the kingdom instead of the values of modern culture,

- establish how they would hope to nurture one another in discipleship,

- outline how they would support one another in Christian vocation,

- set up new models for parenting their kids that are based upon biblical and not cultural values,

- establish priorities for how, through retreat and prayer, they would orchestrate their use of time and resources around the impulses of God's kingdom,

- create imaginative ways to fashion a more festive, celebrative way of life than anything the rat race can offer,

- set a regular weekly time to meet together for prayer and nurture as well as periodic prayer retreats and family celebrations.

LeRoy Troyer and the Troyer Group, an architectural firm in Goshen, Indiana, have drafted a preliminary sketch for one model of a cooperative sixplex. For a copy or more information about the model or this type of cooperative living, see the Notes.[23]

I am convinced that if we North American Christians, living in the final decade of the twentieth century, are to have any hope of engaging the challenges of a new century and participating with our God to birth a new future, we must radically change our way of life. No longer will we be able to give primacy to the agenda of culture and simply work faith in around the edges. We must abandon the idolatries of our consumer society and rededicate our lives both to the God who created us and to God's agenda of a world made new. We must learn to take the future more seriously, anticipating tomorrow's needs, challenges, and opportunities. We must become informed, cross-cultural, discerning world Christians.

But even more important than taking the future seriously is learning to take the future of God seriously. In the nineties we will need a confessing church that bears witness in its common life to the advent of a whole new order.

This will require the creation of a host of new intentional communities and lay orders in which we seek with others to incarnate a flavor of God's new realm much more authentically. We will find in these communities the support we need to become whole-life stewards freeing up both time and money to much more intentionally invest in the work of God's kingdom. And in the process of being liberated from our captivity and finding a new center in the life of prayer, I think we will also discover the kind of celebration God has always intended for the people of God.

The good news is that there are Christians from Soweto to Bucharest who are not simply imagining but are actively involved with the Creator God in giving birth to the new—some at a very high cost. The question is: Will significant numbers of Christians in North America be willing to set aside lesser agendas to be much more intentionally involved in God's conspiracy of hope.

Listen to the strong affirmation of hope from our sisters and brothers in South Africa as they give themselves without reservation to the inbreaking of God's future:

At the very heart of the Gospel of Jesus Christ and at the very center of all true prophecy is a message of hope. Jesus has taught us to speak of this hope in the coming of God's kingdom. We believe God is at work in our world turning hopeless and evil situations to good so that God's kingdom may come and God's will may be done on earth as it is in heaven.[24]

Questions for Discussion

1. What are specific ways we can learn to anticipate change in the world around us?

2. What steps can we take to embrace more fully and flesh out more authentically something of God's intentions for the future in our lives and families?

3. How can we reorder our lives and priorities around God's intentions for the future, giving greater place to a life of prayer, service, and celebration?

4. How can we through whole-life stewardship create a range of new possibilities for vocation, housing, and celebration?

5. How can we live our lives with a greater sense of ethical integrity in the workplace, as consumers, and in relationship to the created order?

6. How can we enable the young to create new possibilities for their lives?

7. In what specific ways could participating in Christian community enable us to flesh out more authentically something of the future of God and help us reorder our priorities?

8. How would the construction of new living arrangements, like the sixplex discussed in this chapter, enable believers to give greater place in their lives for the advancement of God's kingdom?

9. Make a list of some specific ways you can, in community with others, give greater expression to the Wild Hope of God in your lifestyle, spirituality, outreach, and celebration.

10. Write down some innovative ways the church can motivate individuals and families to consider changing their values, lifestyles, and priorities for the sake of God's kingdom.

11

Unleashing a Wild Hope in Our Churches, Society, and the Created Order

The hot Haitian sun broke from behind the menacing clouds, causing the white presidential palace to glisten brilliantly in the sunlight, like a bride waiting for her intended. Throngs pressed jubilantly through the streets and alleys of Port-au-Prince, filling the air with the powerful blasts of conch shells, the rhythmic beating of drums, and shouts of liberation.

Inside the National Assembly Hall, a historic event was taking place: the inauguration of the first democratically elected president in Haiti's two-hundred-year history. By an overwhelming margin, the people of Haiti had elected Jean-Bertrand Aristide, a thirty-seven-year-old Roman Catholic priest who had devoted his life to working among the poor of Port-au-Prince. Now, in the presence of both national and international leaders (including President Jimmy Carter, who had provided oversight for the election), the young president stood to speak. Everyone's attention was riveted on him.

> With thousands of slum dwellers whose cause he has championed raucously chanting his name outside, Father Aristide wiped tears from his face with both hands and bowed his head as the ceremony began. Opening the inauguration, the president of the newly elected Senate, Eudrice Raymond,

said this event represented "the overthrow of systems of repression and darkness."

After taking the oath of office, Father Aristide, a slight, shy-looking man, stepped slowly to the podium and accepted the red-and-blue presidential sash from an elderly peasant woman. One by one, he embraced four boys from the orphanage he has run for the last several years. . . .

Addressing the nation from the balcony of the gleaming white presidential palace, a smiling Father Aristide engaged the crowd in a rousing call and response during a prayerful speech filled with Creole parables.

"It took 200 years to arrive at our second independence," he said referring to his election on December 16. "At our first independence we cried 'Liberty or Death!' We must now shout with all our strength, 'Democracy or Death!'"[1]

Although the battle for justice in Haiti is far from over, the historic election in early 1991 represents a monumental triumph. And it isn't the triumph of a single man, but of thousands upon thousands of people who have prayed, struggled, and even sacrificed their lives to bring about this day of peace and the just rule of their country. Most of the stories of these courageous ones will be lost to the historians. But I want to tell you about one of these whom God is using behind the scenes to nurture this small flame. His name is Chavannes Jeune.

As a very young child, the son of a rural Haitian pastor, Chavannes Jeune turned his heart toward God. Even though his family was very poor, somehow they found resources to send Chavannes to school. He worked hard and did very well in school—so well, in fact, that when he graduated he was sent to France to be trained as a civil engineer.

When I first met Chavannes in 1977, he had just been hired as codirector for a rural development project in Haiti sponsored by World Concern. From the first time I met him, I sensed there was something unusual about this young man. And as I got to know him, I learned what that "something" was. Chavannes is one of those rare people who have committed their lives not only to God, but to the purposes of God.

Chavannes brings together a remarkable array of attributes. Through his education, he has learned to monitor trends, to anticipate and respond to change in his country. Perhaps his most distinctive characteristic is his receptivity to a vision God is giving him for the restoration of a nation and the salvation of a people. It is a vision that touches every element of Haitian society. As he shared it with me, I *saw* the vision stirring within him. And over the years I have seen Chavannes find creative ways to act it out as he responded to the emerging needs of his church, his community, and his nation.

Recently Chavannes was promoted to one of the top leadership positions in the Haitian Baptist Church. As national momentum began to develop for constitutional elections, he was asked to serve with five others on an interim National Council. Sensing that this presented a historic opportunity, he organized the first national day of prayer that has ever been held in Haiti. All the presidential candidates, diplomats, and military leaders were present, as well as those from the business community and the Catholic and Protestant churches. They spent a full day praying that God's justice and peace would come to Haiti and that they would be united, whatever the outcome of their first democratic election.

When Father Aristide was elected, Chavannes immediately arranged to meet with him. They have known each other for many years and share a common compassion for children and for the poor and dispossessed. Chavannes challenged Aristide to make the Word of God the premise of the new democracy. A short time later, Father Aristide went on nationwide television to thank people for their overwhelming support during the election. And he announced that the new government in Haiti will be premised on two foundations: the Constitution and the Word of God.

This compelling new beginning for the nation of Haiti has all the telltale marks of a Creator God who is determined to defeat the powers that oppress and give birth to the new. And clearly, Christians like Jean-Bertrand Aristide, Chavannes Jeune, and thousands of others, through their prayers, receptivity, and action, are collaborating with their Creator in the midwifing of this historic new era in the nation of Haiti.

This chapter will focus on what God is doing to change the world and how we, like our friends in Haiti, can be much more fully a part of it. I believe God is looking for a new generation of leaders who are willing to set aside their own aspirations, interests, and security to give primacy to the agenda of God.

When I use the term *leadership*, however, I mean servant-leadership. And I'm not just talking about people in significant positions. I also mean leadership that emerges from the grassroots—women and men from different cultures working together as a team guided by the Spirit of God, not seeking to maximize their own positions, but cooperatively striving to advance God's kingdom. We need to make a major commitment to nurturing a new generation of servant-leaders, particularly those who are attentive to the dreams of God.

The model of leadership we find in Jesus Christ has never, to my knowledge, been fully expounded in a book. But it seems clear that Jesus led by giving away power, by teaching his disciples to do everything he did, by living with the poor, by telling stories, by playing with children. He led by lifting the fallen, washing the feet of his co-laborers, and laying down his life for the kingdom of God. He is our model of a radical new form of servant-leadership that will be essential to lead the church into a new century.

The purpose of this chapter, therefore, is to suggest specific, practical ways we can enter into servant-leadership with the international community of God's people to see something of God's new order birthed in the world. I will argue, however, that anyone who would provide leadership for a new century must struggle to address three crises that are facing the contemporary church:

- a crisis of anticipation,

- a crisis of vision, and

- a crisis of creativity.

In response to these three crises, therefore, this chapter will outline some ideas for how the church and those leading the church can

- anticipate the needs, challenges, and opportunities of tomorrow's world more effectively;

- discern something of God's vision and articulate that vision more clearly, and

- create new strategies to implement that vision in response to the anticipated challenges in the church, the larger society and God's created order.

This chapter, in other words, will not seek to answer all the issues raised earlier in the book. Instead, it will suggest some specific methodologies Christian leaders can use both to anticipate change and to respond to it. But let me begin with a note of clarification.

While working with ecumenical leaders at Maryknoll headquarters in New York several years ago, I discovered that many people tend to blur together very different views of the future. I asked these ecumenical leaders, "What are some of the challenges you anticipate the church could face in the nineties?" And many of them, in response, began sharing their dreams for a world filled with justice and peace. While these dreams were stirring, they didn't answer my question. I hadn't asked them for their dreams, but for their anticipation of future challenges.

To clarify the misunderstanding I outlined for them three different ways we can think about the future:

(1) *First, we can attempt to predict what we believe the likely future will be.* I call this an "anticipatory" view of the future. Some would call this probabilistic forecasting.

(2) *Second, we can share a vision or dream—our ideal of what we want the future to be.* I call this a "normative" or preferred view of the future.

(3) *Finally, we have the capacity to imagine how we would act out our normative vision* in a way that responds to tomorrow's anticipated challenges. I call this a "creative" approach to the future.

Throughout this book we have been discussing the future in these three different ways. First, we anticipated the probable future based on current environmental, technological, economic, political, and demographic trends. We also anticipated the church's likely response to these developments, based on current trends in commitment and giving. (As you remember, my assessment wasn't terribly optimistic.)

Next, we examined the primary vision to which most of us, Christians included, have given our lives—the Western Dream of consumerism, status, and power. And we have contrasted that vision with a normative vision of the future of God which permeates Scripture.

Finally, we have begun a dialogue about how the biblical vision can be creatively integrated into our lives—how we in our personal lives, our families, and our communities can begin to flesh out something of the Wild Hope of God. In this final chapter, we will focus more specifically on how God's Wild Hope can be more fully unleashed in our churches, our society, and the larger created order.

A CRISIS OF ANTICIPATION

We have already established that most religious organizations make little effort to anticipate change within either their institutions or the larger world. As a result, our Christian organizations and those leading them tend to be chronically surprised by change.

Virtually all Christian organizations do long-range planning. But the irony is they do it as though the future is static, as though the future is simply going to be an extension of the present. Rarely do I find denominations, Christian organizations, or local congregations that attempt to incorporate any forecasting in their planning.

Thankfully, there are a few exceptions. In 1990, for example, Peggy Shriver coordinated an important process for the National Council of Churches that has enabled leaders to study and analyze a broad spectrum of issues on the future. Reportedly this process has been quite valuable for those who participated. But it isn't clear how this process will affect the planning of the participating mainline denominations.

I often find that when ecumenical Christians do futuring, they tend to see it as a mind-stretching exercise. They rarely use their forecasts in institutional planning. And rarely do I find any evangelical organizations that do any futuring at all, with the possible exception of those doing church planting.

I will attempt to make a convincing case for the importance of anticipatory planning and outline some of the specific methodologies that might aid the church to meet its crisis of anticipation.

ANTICIPATORY LEADERSHIP FOR THE TWENTY-FIRST CENTURY

Dr. Burt Nanus, a professor in the graduate school of business at the University of Southern California, insists that tomorrow's leaders must "constantly anticipate how forces, current trends and society's momentum may play out."[2] In his book, *The Leader's Edge,* Nanus reminds decision makers that change is accelerating and that global systems are becoming more interdependent, interactive, and complex. If leaders in all sectors, including the church, are to operate responsibly in such a world, they must make a much greater effort to anticipate how the contexts in which we are operating are likely to change. Anticipating change will be necessary not only for effective strategic planning, but for day-to-day management:

> As the pace of change accelerates due to these forces, organizational tempos speed up; lead times are reduced. Instead of solving problems, the leader is more often called upon to steer the organization through dynamic and perilous situations. All of this puts a premium on the leader's ability to anticipate, monitor and manage.[3]

Of course, the corporate world is interested in anticipating change in order to capitalize on it, protecting market advantage or initiating new areas of corporate venturing. Those of us in the church have a very different reason to take the future seriously. Our purpose in anticipating the future isn't to increase our market share, but to respond more compassionately and effectively to the new needs and challenges of our common future. If we can anticipate even a few new areas of human need before they arise, then we will have lead time to create new responses. Instead of simply reacting to change, as we have done too often in the sixties, seventies, and eighties, we will have an opportunity to be proactive—to provide "foresightful" leadership as we enter the twenty-first century.

Anticipating Internal and External Change

If the church is going to faithfully engage the challenges of a new century, we will need a new brand of leaders who learn to live on the frontiers of tomorrow, calling and enabling the church to serve in a radically different world. First, we will need to do a much more responsible job of anticipating change within our churches and religious organizations. For example, how is the demography of your religious organization likely to change over the next ten years? What are likely to be the new needs of your changing population? Given the changing demographics and levels of income of your constituency, how able will they be to support your organization as we enter a new century?

As shown in chapter 7, Roof and McKinney document the graying and declining of mainline denominations in the United States. Reginald Bibby does the same thing for mainline churches in Canada. But I have yet to find a single denomination that has taken the next step and asked, "How is the aging and decline of our membership likely to change our economic support base ten to fifteen years from now?" Since, as we have established, most of the wealth in North America is possessed by those over fifty, the impact of these demographic changes could be more serious than anyone realizes. The only way to find out is to do an analysis of changing demographics and projections of likely changes in giving patterns.

But it isn't enough for leaders to learn to monitor change within their organizations. They also need to make a much greater commitment to anticipating how the larger global, national, and regional arenas in which they minister are likely to change. They may even need to consider securing staff researchers or using the services of a futures research organization to help keep them aware of how the larger context is changing and what new challenges these changes are likely to present. Whatever steps are taken, the emerging challenges of the twenty-first century are, for the church, emerging opportunities to express the Wild Hope of God.

An Anticipatory Tool Kit

This business of trying to anticipate change isn't a science. It is a very messy art, and any number of authors can catalog the failures. As the world's peoples become more interdependent and interactive, the number of variables increases. And as the variables increase, so does the number of ways that change in any one area can interact with change in other areas. All our efforts to anticipate change, certainly including this book, need to be done with a great deal of humility. In spite of our best efforts, sometimes we will totally miss the mark. And we will always be surprised by change.

But as I pointed out at the beginning of this book, we really only have two choices. We can either allow ourselves to be totally surprised by change (as church leadership has done too often). Or we can make our best efforts to anticipate some of the change that is likely to fill tomorrow's world, so that we have lead time to respond.

Over the past four decades, the corporate community has done most of the pioneering in the field of forecasting and strategic planning. And let me hasten to acknowledge that planning in general and forecasting in specific are a part of the modernization of human society. But as I mentioned before, I believe we can borrow with integrity from both modern culture and our organic past if we are clear about how our borrowing can be incorporated in advancing God's agenda. Instead of using various forms of anticipatory planning to maximize our advantage over others, like corporations do, we can use the same tools to improve our ministry to others.

In the following pages, I will outline a selection of the more common methods that are used to anticipate change. Some of these methodologies lend themselves to use in larger organizations, but some can also be used by local congregations. They can be used to begin monitoring change both within your organization and within the larger external environment.

(1) *Trend extrapolation.* One of the easiest forms of forecasting is trend extrapolation—to use known data to project possible future trends. An application

of this method would be analyzing current demographic data in order to determine how the population either within your organization or in the community you serve is likely to change. Even a local church will generally have someone in the congregation who can develop such a projection.

If we can anticipate how a given population is likely to change, we can usually anticipate what some of the needs of that emerging population are likely to be. For example, I asked the members of Brentwood Presbyterian Church in Los Angeles during a futures workshop to identify one of the most rapidly increasing population groups in their neighborhood. They responded, "Single-parent families." I asked, "Typically what are the needs of single-parent families?" They replied, "Day care, emotional and support systems—perhaps economic help." Having done this bit of forecasting, workshop participants created an innovative program to respond to the needs of this emerging population group.

Those of us at Mustard Seed Associates are currently using demographics to enable Presbyterian churches in North Puget Sound to anticipate how their congregations and their communities are likely to change over the next ten years. We are doing this to enable these congregations to anticipate what the emerging needs are likely to be in the next ten years in order to get a little jump on change.

While doing a futures consultation with executives from World Vision International, a Christian relief and development agency, I asked, "Since the rate of population growth is almost 4 percent a year in Kenya, who is likely to make up the major part of the Kenyan population in ten years?" They answered, "Children and mothers with young children." I asked, "What are the special needs of children and mothers with young children?" Their response: "Maternal and infant child care, immunization, nutrition, education." By anticipating this important demographic change, this agency has ten years in which to gear up for these emerging challenges.

Of course, trend extrapolation is only as valid as the data you use. And it is important to remember that trend extrapolation is a simple, straight-line projection. Anything that interrupts that straight line—a famine in Kenya, for instance—can invalidate the projections. For this reason, trend extrapolation, to be of value, needs to be used in conjunction with other forecasting methods.

(2) *Consequence forecasting.* This type of forecasting involves working in a group to anticipate the possible consequences of any projected external event—local or global. For example, what are the likely consequences—positive and negative—of a shopping mall's being built across from your church? Or, if the government decided to devalue the dollar 25 percent against all major world currencies, what would be the likely consequences for United States missionary salaries overseas or for the ability of Christian colleges to bring students from foreign countries to their campuses?

The basic process of consequence forecasting is very simple. It involves listing all the possible positive and negative consequences of a particular event, present or anticipated, then attempting to identify the implications of the positive and negative consequences. Those who want to use consequence forecasting more methodically often develop "consequence trees," diagramming positive and negative consequences to the second, third and fourth order.

Like trend extrapolation, consequence forecasting really can't stand alone. It needs to be used together with other tools. It is simply a way to anticipate the possible consequences of change.

(3) *Analogue forecasting.* With analogue forecasting, an organization that is at the threshold of making a major change simply tries to find a similar organization that has recently gone through an analogous situation. For example, a group that was going to plant a church in a very high-growth suburban community in Washington state would look for and learn from a group that had recently planted a church in a similar locale.

Obviously, analogue forecasting is only as good as the analogue that is found. But it can be a very helpful technique in anticipating both new opportunities and constraints as an organization manages the transition into a new situation.

(4) *Delphi forecasting.* Delphi forecasting is a technique designed by Norman Dalkey of the Rand Corporation to secure expert opinion on the future of a specific field. It has been used successfully in fields ranging from health care to higher education.

Essentially, Delphi forecasting works by asking experts in the selected field to fill out a survey form about the future of their field at least three times. Before each round (after the first) the participants are shown the combined responses of all the other respondents on the previous round. This enables them to change their responses after reading the combined responses of their colleagues—to change their opinions without losing face.

Typically, on the next-to-last survey, those with extreme positions are asked to explain their positions. (In the area of health care, for example, an expert who insists there will never be an artificial kidney and another who says one will be developed within a year might be asked to explain their reasons for these predictions.) After reading the explanation of the extreme views, the participants fill out their response forms one last time, and a final report is drawn up. Those working on the Catholic education futures project, which used a Delphi survey to solicit views on the challenges facing religious education as we approach a new century, found it was a useful tool.

Delphi forecasting is basically a consensus tool; it leads experts to reach a fairly high level of consensus about projections for the future. But even though it tends to skew individual opinion toward consensus, it is still an effective way to solicit expert opinions about the future.

(5) *Issues management.* Issues management is a fairly new approach to forecasting. Essentially, it involves putting together a research team to anticipate ten to twenty key issues that are likely to have the greatest impact on a corporation, a state, a university, or a religious organization during a coming period of time.

For example, the state of Florida might list, as one of the top ten issues, the possible passage of new federal wetlands legislation that would totally upset state land-use planning policies. Or a church-affiliated university might list the passage of a new tax law that would affect its tax-exempt status.

Issues management is particularly useful in identifying areas of potential constraint or threat to an organization, as well as in identifying new opportunities. It is already being used by the Southern Baptist Sunday School Board as a tool for anticipating issues that could affect the denomination. The Southern Baptists have an issues-analysis team that holds a quarterly one-day meeting. Issues areas are research-ed in advance. A range of issues is identified at each meeting, and attention is focused on one or two. Then the team develops a careful issues statement for in-house use.

Issues management is oriented less toward anticipating new opportunities and more toward identifying changes that could have a potentially negative impact on an organization. As a consequence, this is a form of forecasting that has limited application.

(6) *Intuitive forecasting.* This isn't as much a methodology as it is an openness to a more intuitive or subjective sense of how the future may change. Corporate futuring tends to be linear and "left brain," relying heavily on quantifiable data and measurable trends. But a growing number of organizations are beginning to recognize that people with more intuitive capabilities are able to see more possible relationships and new opportunities.

Not surprisingly, new organicists and transformational futurists place much more emphasis on intuitive forecasting than on most corporate futurists. However, Faith Popcorn and her organization, Brain Reserve, operate with a highly intuitive flair in forecasting societal change for a broad array of corporate clients. Popcorn accurately predicted the coming of home media rooms and salt-free products and the advent of "cocooning" (centering activities around home), for example.

Of course, working intuitively without a responsible data base is simply speculation and very unreliable. But intuitive forecasting when used in conjunction with other foresight systems can provide some of those creative linkages that more linear approaches to forecasting would never provide.

(7) *Information/scenario futuring.* Information/scenario futuring makes deliberate use of those with intuitive talents. It involves researching data on current changes, then giving this data to a single creative writer or team of writers with instructions to produce a set of alternative scenarios for the future.

I used this methodology successfully with the New Business Division of the Weyerhaeuser Corporation several years ago. My team and I collected information and trends on how the state, national, and global context were changing. Then I contracted with science-fiction writer Frank Herbert, the author of *Dune,* to construct three distinctly different scenarios, using this information, for ten years into the future.

Once Herbert was finished, we proceeded to walk the New Business ventur-ing staff through each scenario, describing in detail the characteristics of each possible future. Then we assigned them the creative task of identifying where the new business opportunities were likely to emerge in each scenario, how they would market their products in each case, and where they would secure resources.

In a Christian organization, we would ask a different set of questions regarding the different scenarios: Where are the human needs to which we can respond? Who will collaborate with us? And where will we secure resources to respond to the new challenges?

The benefit of information/scenario futuring is that it enables decision makers to develop contingency-planning capabilities. It teaches them to draw on their intuition and helps them become much more flexible in their planning. In addition, if the future begins to go in the general direction of any one of the three scenarios, the groundwork has been laid for advanced planning. Leaders will find it easier to move decisively and to address the new challenges because they have already given some thought to an alternative.

(8) *Prophetic insight.* This form of anticipating is closely related to intuitive forecasting but is spiritually premised. It involves spiritual insights about how the future might unfold. Sometimes such insights come during religious gatherings; at other times during times of personal inspiration or Scripture study. God sometimes seems to gift us today, as in biblical times, with a brief glimpse of the future so that we can be more responsive to these emerging challenges.

However, I must add that this area of forecasting carries serious risks. Most of us know of instances in which alleged divine insights and messages have been used to manipulate individuals or entire congregations. Prophetic insights need to be checked against Scripture, confirmed in the community of believers, and used cautiously along with other methods to anticipate tomorrow's needs and challenges.

(9) *Innovation assessment.* One of the by-products of the first environmental movement was a field of study called technology assessment. I taught students about the possible uses of technology assessment as part of the courses on ethics and the future I taught for Social Management of Technology, an interdisciplinary program in the University of Washington School of Engineering. My students learned to anticipate not only the potential environmental impact of technology, but the possible human impact as well. For example, I asked them to anticipate the likely human impact of engineering a freeway through an urban African-American community, dividing the community in half.

Innovation assessment is a variation on this theme. It attempts to anticipate the consequences of any new plan or process we might initiate. This type of forecasting is often used in business, but is rarely applied to innovation in societal or religious planning. If we are to be responsible about planning in a radically changing world, however, we must try to anticipate the positive and negative consequences of whatever intervention we may do.

Ideally, the innovation assessment forecast should precede the final decision about whether to proceed with a project—and could even result in cancellation of the plan. But even if the decision is to proceed, the innovation assessment process can indicate ways either to ameliorate some of the unintended negative consequences of the innovation or to take advantage of positive ones.

(10) *Futures positioning.* Although futures positioning isn't really a forecasting method, an institution can benefit from doing it once it has completed its use of other forecasting methods. After any kind of environmental scanning of the future, it can be very helpful to ask, "How should we position our institution in a changing context or environment that is likely to look very different in five to ten years?"

In the corporate world, positioning is used to enable businesses and corporations to place themselves strategically to outdistance their competitors. Here again, I think it is possible for the church to redeem a concept and breathe new meaning into it. Obviously, the last thing we want is to heighten any sense of competition among various churches or religious organizations. And we certainly shouldn't be pursuing a "power advantage" over others. But positioning can achieve another goal . . . enabling Christian organizations to work together more effectively by sharing their areas of strength and their resources in common mission. In the nineties, we will need to see much more collaboration to address the mounting challenges.

Positioning requires clarifying and sharpening the organization's sense of purpose—in the case of a Christian organization, its sense of kingdom vocation. (We will be describing how to do this in greater detail in the next section). An organization that wants to position itself effectively must have a clear understanding of its unique mission.

In addition, positioning means that decision makers need to determine where their changing organization fits best in ministry to a changing world. Just as no one corporation can meet all consumer needs, no single Christian organization can begin to address all the needs and challenges facing the church as we enter a new century. Positioning enables an organization to select those emerging challenges it can address most effectively, given a clear sense of institutional mission and an understanding of institutional strengths and deficits. Positioning thus enables churches and Christian organizations, in cooperation with others, to focus their mission more strategically and effectively in a changing world.

Resources for Anticipatory Planning

Preparing for the future may require enlisting outside help. However, while some three dozen organizations provide futures research and consultation to corporations and governments, very few organizations service the church. Let me list some services that may be of use.

(1) *Princeton Religion Research Center,* PO Box 389, Princeton, NJ 08542, phone: (609) 921-8112. George Gallup started this center to serve the church. PRRC can be commissioned to conduct surveys. It also provides research on broader societal trends.

(2) *Church Information Development Services,* 3001 Redhill Avenue, Suite 2-220, Costa Mesa, CA 92626, phone: (800) 442-6277. CIDS specializes in providing demographic research that is particularly valuable in the planting of new churches. It also provides resources to help synods, districts and local congregations plan in light of changing demographic projections.

(3) *Barna Research Group,* PO Box 4152, Glendale, CA 91222-0152, phone: (818) 241-9684. BRG provides research that particularly relates to marketing, not only for the church and Christian organizations, but for secular agencies as well.

(4) *Mustard Seed Associates,* PO Box 45867, Seattle, WA 98145, phone (206) 545-SEED. Mustard Seed Associates provides services to the church in three areas:

- forecasting, including demographic forecasting; research on global, national, and regional trends; and an issues-and-trends database,

- "visioning" and enabling Christian organizations to develop mission statements and operational theologies of mission,

- creating new mission responses through use of a database on innovative mission and creativity workshops.

Our organization is particularly committed to enabling the church to respond more creatively to tomorrow's challenges.

A CRISIS OF VISION

Although I am very concerned about how few leaders make any effort to anticipate change, I am even more concerned at how few take seriously the importance of vision. As I stated earlier, I firmly believe the number-one crisis in the church today is a crisis of vision.

Most churches I work with seem to be afflicted by what I call "chronic randomness." Typically, different groups in the church go in different directions with little larger sense of integrated vision or mission. I find most Christian organizations also operate from what I call a set of "immaculate assumptions." These assumptions regarding institutional mission are not written down; they are not discussed. If they were, people within these institutions might find they don't agree with them. And yet we tend to operate as though we had reached consensus within our Christian organizations regarding our direction and the assumptions on which our organizations are premised.

To fight this tendency toward chronic randomness, every Christian organization needs an operational theology of mission which clarifies its direction and makes explicit the assumptions on which it operates.

Evangelical organizations typically have a credal statement, often patterned after one developed by the National Association of Evangelicals, which affirms their biblical orthodoxy. Larger ecumenical organizations frequently focus on biblical themes such as social justice and peacemaking at their conferences. But seldom do I find any Christian organizations that have actually drafted an operational theology of mission—a statement of the organization's mission and the assumptions on which it is premised.

Without this, our religious institutions not only often lack a clear sense of direction; they tend to operate from unstated assumptions that often have more to do with the quality of the American Dream than the character of the kingdom of God. For example, we have uncritically embraced the institutionalized, hierarchical, and systematic Western organizational model as a given without seeming to recognize that it is loaded with all the same values that brought us modernization and the secularization of Western culture.

The Western organizational model is essentially patterned after the machine. Efficiency of production too often becomes the primary good—and this happens even in Christian organizations. When that happens, the welfare of persons easily becomes secondary to the efficiency of the operations.

Stop and think about the value assumptions that underlie the Western organizational model: efficiency, routinization, conformity, rationalization of action, expediency, and pragmatism. Then ask yourself how different the values underlying our so-called Christian colleges, Christian hospitals, or parachurch organizations are from their secular counterparts?

I am not suggesting that all religious organizations abandon the Western bureaucratic model of organization. But I do believe it is well past time to examine the values on which this model is premised in light of biblical values. I am persuaded that the gospel calls us to incarnate the values of God's kingdom not only in our personal lives and communities, but in our institutional forms as well. And too often, I fear, our Christian organizations are premised on values that repudiate the very gospel we advocate.

What would happen if a new Christian organization started out by drafting an operational theology of mission, clearly articulating the values and assumptions on which it was based? What values would be listed? And what would the new organization look like? I suspect it would look very different than most of our contemporary religious organizations. If we took the trouble to clarify our purposes and assumptions before setting up our institutions, I believe we might create new organizational forms that would look more like an extended family or that first band of Christian followers than like a bureaucracy or a machine. (As resources become more restricted, I believe we will be forced to create models that are also much less cost intensive than our current bureaucratic organizations.)

If we want to engage the challenges of a new century faithfully, everything we do needs to be critically evaluated in light of Scripture—including how we organize ourselves. If our Christian organizations are to have any part in advancing the cause of God's kingdom, then we need to evaluate both the values on which they are premised and the visions to which they are committed.

William Scott and David Hart, in their book, *Organizational America,*[4] insist that the primary mission of any bureaucratic organization is to preserve itself, to maintain its own survival. Aren't our Christian organizations called to a higher mission than organizational maintenance and institutional survival? Aren't we called, like the One we follow, to be ready to lay down both our lives and our organizations to advance the cause of God's new order?

VISIONARY LEADERSHIP FOR THE TWENTY-FIRST CENTURY

As we move into the twenty-first century, we will need a new brand of leaders who are not afraid to criticize the values implicit in their organizations and to lead with a more compelling sense of biblical vision. John Gardner, author of the classic book, *Excellence,* writes, "The first task of a leader is to keep hope alive."[5] Somehow our Christian organizations must be linked to a larger sense of purpose or hope beyond themselves—hope that is premised on the confidence that God is acting within history and we can be co-creators with God.

But Burt Nanus also reminds us that "a true vision must provide a clear image of the desirable future, one that represents an achievable, challenging and worthwhile target toward which people can direct their energies."[6] In Christian institutions, that "clear image of the desirable future" must be derived from a sense of biblical vision.

And that is where I believe leadership needs to begin in its quest for a more compelling sense of vision. We need leaders like Jean-Bertrand Aristide and Chavannes Jeune—men and women who are particularly receptive to the vision of God. Let's look at several ways Christian leaders can go about cultivating vision for a new century.

Listening for a Vision through Scripture Study

Not long ago, World Concern asked those of us from Mustard Seed Associates to help it develop a theology of mission to undergird its work. We designed a process in which both those overseas and those in the Seattle office studied Scripture together and worked cooperatively to develop an operational theology of mission. With the able assistance of an Old Testament theologian, Steve Hayner, and a New Testament theologian, Eugene Lemcio, we then began developing drafts of a mission statement. The resulting operational theology of mission didn't just confirm what World Concern was already doing; it began to change the agency's direction.

Always before, World Concern had considered that its mission was simply to do agricultural or community-health projects among the poor overseas. As a result of the study, it realized that one of God's intentions is to develop strong churches that minister wholistically wherever they are planted. As a result of this insight, World Concern has developed curriculum to be used in a Bible School in El Salvador. The curriculum teaches young pastors how to plant churches that minister wholistically, addressing not only spiritual needs, but physical and economic needs as well. It teaches them how to start economic co-ops, agricultural development projects, and community-health programs through the church, so that Western development agencies like World Concern need never come to their community. If World Concern hadn't done the hard work of hammering out an operational theology of mission, it never would have developed this form of empowering ministry.

Listening for God's Vision in Local Congregations

It's not only the larger Christian organizations who need to listen to one another and study Scripture to develop a vision statement and an operational theology of mission. Local churches need to go through the same process. Luther Place congregation in Washington, D.C., did exactly that in the early seventies. In the process, this group of Christians overcame the chronic randomness that is so common in many churches.

Luther Place had been an established church in an older section of Washington, D.C., that began to go through dramatic changes in the late sixties. The area around the church was hit by protests and civil unrest, and the neighborhood began to rapidly deteriorate. Some members of Luther Place moved away. And predictably, the remaining members of the church set a date to vote on whether to sell their building and relocate the church to the suburbs.

When the day for voting rolled around, people came praying. And when the votes were tallied, amazingly, the members of Luther Place congregation had voted to stay put in their neighborhood. Suddenly they realized that if they were going to have to stay in this very difficult location, they would have to have a reason to be there—a sense of purpose. It was no longer enough simply to be a Lutheran church in a particular location. They needed to find their vision.

So the members of Luther Place began studying Scripture together and listening to one another in an effort to discover a clearer sense of purpose. Out of their study of the Gospels came a strong sense of vocational call which they reflected in their vision statement: "As Christ welcomes you to his table in bread and wine of the Eucharist, so you are to be the hospitality of Jesus Christ in a broken and needy community."

As a direct result of this vision statement, the Christians of Luther Place scrapped a lot of their in-house programs for members and instead developed a number of ministries to the urban poor—all integrated around their vision to act out the hospitality of Christ in their needy community. Because this congregation found a sense of integrating vision, its members have been able to make a positive impact on the community.

A major Christian organization once asked me to do a critique of a proposal it had developed for carrying out urban mission in the United States. The proposal talked about meeting employment needs, housing needs, educational needs, nutritional needs, and other typical needs of a poor urban population.

But wouldn't it be possible, I asked, to meet all the physical needs in a given community and still have an inherently pathological community? As a Christian organization, doesn't our vision include more than meeting needs—as important as that is? Don't we really want to see—in an urban, suburban, or rural community—the establishment of the reign of God so that relationships are transformed, so that people start looking out for one another instead of victimizing each other? If that kind of transformation were to take place, it would no longer be necessary to have outside agencies endlessly delivering services to "meet needs."

What I am suggesting is that if we are serious about doing the work of God in a world of exploding need, we must recover a compelling biblical vision not only for our personal lives and communities, but for our churches and Christian organizations as well. We must discover a clear sense of direction based upon what we discover in Scripture to be the purposes of God.

Listening for a Vision through the People of God

If leaders are to facilitate the drafting of an operational theology of mission, it isn't enough that we listen to God's call through scriptural study, as important as that is. We also need to listen to the vision God has placed within the community of God's people.

Too often, especially in conservative circles, vision is seen as emerging primarily from a charismatic leader or a ruling elite. But if we sincerely believe God speaks to all members of a body of believers, then we need to find ways to discover the vision God is giving everyone in that body. In our churches and organizations, therefore, we need to create ways to listen for the sense of vocation and vision God is giving every individual as well as the group as a whole.

When Chavannes Jeune and I started working together in Haiti in 1977, we met with community leaders in the Plaisance Valley to discuss a community development project. We began by asking the people of the valley what their vision was. Someone from the team had already asked the valley leaders what their "felt needs" were, and the response had included tractors, buildings, and roads. The question we asked as valley leaders came together for the first planning meeting was, "What are your dreams? What are the dreams God is giving you for your families and your community?" And when we asked that question, we got a very different response. People began sharing their dreams for how they wanted to see broken relationships in their community restored, the entire valley renewed by the power of God's Spirit, and all the children given an opportunity to go to school.

If we start with the theological assumption that God is alive and well and at work in a community, doesn't it follow that we will ask the members of that community, "What dreams is God giving you for your future?" Shouldn't we begin by trying to discover what visions God has been growing within them?

We will need leaders for the third millennium who know how to receive something of God's vision for their lives and mission through a life of prayer, biblical study, and societal sensitivity. But we will also need leaders who are able to discern the vision in other people's lives and to help implement that vision.

A CRISIS OF CREATIVITY

If we are to lead and serve responsibly in a changing world, we must not only attempt to anticipate coming challenges and to articulate a biblical vision; we must also find creative ways to implement that vision. That requires that we move beyond the kind of nonreflective incrementalism that characterizes too much of institutional planning.

Corporations find that they must constantly struggle to find the creative edge in order to maintain a market advantage. Churches and religious organizations not operating in a competitive market environment are seldom motivated to seek that creative edge. In fact many organizations seem content simply to implement the same activities over and over, regardless of whether they work or not. And as I have shown, our present programs don't have a prayer of successfully addressing tomorrow's challenges.

In the nineties and beyond, we will need a renaissance of Christian creativity to make a difference in a world of need. Please understand—I am not advocating innovation for innovation's sake. Mindless innovation is no more helpful than mindless incrementalism. And I am certainly not recommending that Christian organizations use their creativity to establish advantages over other groups or to manipulate members. But I am recommending that Christian leaders and Christian groups take deliberate steps to develop and use their God-given creativity . . . in order to develop imaginative new ways to address the escalating challenges of a new century.

CREATIVE LEADERSHIP FOR THE TWENTY-FIRST CENTURY

Management specialist Burt Nanus uses the term *futures-creative leadership* to describe the kind of innovative leadership tomorrow will require. And he is of the opinion that "futures-creative leadership is, by and large, absent in

America. . . . Some doubt that many leaders even understand what is going on, let alone have a clear idea of how to create a better future for their organizations."[7] And I believe there is a particular dearth of imagination among church leaders, both ecumenical and evangelical. Highly institutionalized religious organizations have a particularly difficult time bursting old wineskins and creating the new. But this must change if we are to have any hope of addressing the unprecedented challenges of the coming century.

Nanus insists, "The futures-creative leader not only imagines the preferred future but works to create it."[8] In the context of the church, this means not only helping people anticipate new challenges and clarify their vision, but also setting their imaginations free for the kingdom of God.

Beyond Autocracy: Creating a Space for Imagination

Christian leaders can enable their congregations and staffs to become more creative by designing an environment that encourages and rewards creativity. This will probably mean abandoning top-down autocratic management models in favor of more horizontal models that encourage ownership and participation by all involved. It may also mean disposing of all strictures and structures that are not absolutely essential to the mission of the organization. (This will probably reduce overhead costs as well.) Most important, individual members—both staff and congregation—must feel they are trusted and their ideas valued.

Creativity in a church or Christian organization will be closely connected with a clear and compelling vision. A futures-creative leader will strive to create an environment that not only reminds people of the challenges ahead, but that calls them to a compelling vision for the future. All those involved in creating the new must be sensitive to the reality that they are collaborating with the Creator and must constantly check their creative work against that grander vision.

Beyond a Budget-Limited Mentality: Becoming Creative Christian Scroungers

After we genuinely learn to listen for and envision more keenly all that God is bringing to pass, then we need to assess the resources out of which we will fashion the new. Too often, I have heard leaders announce the death knell of an innovative idea with those infamous words: "It's not in the budget; we can't do it!" To have any hope of creating the new, then we must begin by burying this "budget-limited mentality," which stifles innovation. If we limit our resources to those funds that are a part of our organizational budgets, we will live and work in an atmo-sphere of constant constraint.

As we approach a new century, we will need not only a renaissance of Christian imagination, but an army of creative Christian scroungers who are marvelously imaginative in doing more with less. What I am suggesting is that before any brainstorming or specific planning takes place, futures-creative leaders should encourage their team to inventory all underutilized resources within their organization itself and in their sphere of mission.

Some people from Longview Community Church in Washington state came up with an interesting approach to this problem during a creativity workshop I conducted. They decided to interview every one of their four hundred active members in order to uncover underutilized resources of time, talent, and materials. They designed a questionnaire to help them learn who could do child care, teach the book of James, or fix plumbing—and which hours these people were available. Before the workshop was over, someone had donated an Apple computer to provide easy access to this invaluable information.

A Baptist church in a suburban community in Portland discovered its large front lawn was an underutilized resource. The members dug up the lawn and planted a huge vegetable garden to provide vegetables for the urban poor.

During a creativity workshop on urban mission at a conference sponsored by the Seminary Consortium in Urban Pastoral Education (SCUPE) in Chicago, another example of creative Christian scrounging was born. I asked a small group to find something that had been thrown away in the city and to use it to create something new for the kingdom.

When the paticipants returned forty minutes later, I asked, "What do you have?" They responded, "vertical gardening." They went on to explain that old tire casings were to be found littering urban areas such as St. Louis and Washington D.C. Their idea was to collect the old tires and stack them nine tires high. Then they would fill the tires with dirt and the dirt with seed potatoes. They would water the stack from the top, and the sprouts would grow out from between the tires. At harvest time, they would simply tip over the tires, pick up the potatoes, and sweep up the dirt.

Even in very poor countries, there are always underutilized resources that can, with a little imagination, become building blocks of the kingdom. For example, Ben Bryant, a professor in forest products at the University of Washington, conceptualized a way to take sugar-cane fiber, which is burned or discarded in many Asian countries, and create socially beneficial products. In his model, a basic oil-drum technological process could be used to convert a throwaway resource into an alternative to corrugated metal roof material, sewer tile, and wallboard. This would not only mean transforming sugar-cane waste into useful products, jobs, and money for the local economy, but also creating an economic engine in a poor community that can help fund other forms of Christian mission to those in need.

Beyond Incrementalism:
Creating New Possibilities for a New Century

Once Christian leaders have designed an environment that enhances creativity and have inventoried underutilized resources, they can take specific and deliberate steps to spark creativity among staff and congregation members. In the past seventeen years, I have conducted many creativity workshops with leaders in denominations, Christian organizations, and local churches. Let me share one of the processes I have found very effective in helping these organizations inject a little more creativity into their planning and strategizing.

First, well in advance of planning, I recommend setting aside time for an "idea-storming" session. This will help participants break out of the incremental mind-set that limits most planning efforts. The idea-storming session could involve everyone in the organization or a representative cross-section. I suggest holding a one- or two-day session in a large open room set up with small tables and chairs for participants.

In advance of the idea-storming session, the organizer of the session should draw up a list of eight to twelve specific "creativity tasks"—challenges for specifically addressing the needs that have been uncovered in previous futures research. *The goal of the entire idea-storming process is to enable participants to create imaginative new responses to tomorrow's challenges in ways that use underutilized resources to implement the organization's biblical vision.*

I often begin idea-storming sessions with some type of group process that frees people up a bit and gives them an opportunity to use their imaginations, such as drawing a picture of their ideal personal future ten years from now. It is important to emphasize to the group that we are all gifted with creativity, but that creativity for some may be a "muscle" that hasn't had frequent exercise. (The more we call on people to exercise their imaginations, the easier it is for them to effectively participate in the process.)

After the group creativity exercise, I review with the group the results of efforts that have preceded the idea-storming session:

- *The results of futures research.* The compelling needs, challenges, and opportunities which have been uncovered will become the targets toward which the creativity process is directed. Participants should be reminded that anticipating these needs ahead of time gives us lead time to create new responses.

- *The operational theology of mission.* This statement will help serve as a criterion in determining which of the emerging needs should be addressed. It will also inform the kinds of responses that are created, ensuring greater congruence between what is being done and the way it is done.

- *The list of underutilized resources.* These will become available resources to incorporate in the creativity process.

- *The list of creativity tasks* that has been drawn up before the session.

Then I invite participants to select one of the creativity tasks from the list and to meet in groups with others who have chosen that task. Idea-storming groups should consist of three to eight participants. One member of each group should be a facilitator (selected ahead of time). This person should have a clear sense of the creativity task and some background in group process.

In idea-storming, like brainstorming, the facilitator encourages everyone in the group to participate. Participants are asked to share as many ideas on their assigned task as they can come up with, and all ideas are listed without criticism on large sheets of newsprint. Thirty to sixty minutes should be allowed for this segment.

Next, participants in each group are asked to select and focus on one idea or a cluster of ideas that they find particularly compelling. Often I ask groups to give the new idea they are working with a creative name or acronym. The simple act of naming the new idea tends to give it a stronger sense of identity and integrity. During this segment, participants will also be asked to outline a few goals and strategies to begin fleshing out their ideas. An additional thirty to sixty minutes should be allowed for this phase of the process.

The first round of the idea-storming process concludes with each group's sharing a brief but "electric" two-minute summary of its new ideas. (It helps to have someone keep time in order to limit the length of the presentations.)

After a break, participants are invited to participate in a second round of idea-storming, in which they select a new creativity task and work with a new group. The second round is identical to the first except, of course, that participants have had some experience with the process.

After the second round of idea-storming, all groups gather together in a plenary discussion to evaluate the ideas that have been generated. Evaluation should be based on the following criteria:

- How responsive are the new ideas to the anticipated needs, challenges, and opportunities identified earlier?

- How fully do the new ideas reflect both the intention and the values of the operational theology of mission?

- How effectively do the new ideas incorporate the utilization of underutilized resources?

Those ideas that rank highest according to these criteria will then be referred to those who have the primary responsibility for strategic planning. After the plenary sessions and perhaps a time of fellowship and relaxation, the preplanning idea-storming session is complete.

After the planners review the ideas generated by the preplanning idea-storming sessions, I recommend that they go through the same process themselves immediately before planning. Doing this helps the planning process to be more open, more creative, more responsive to new challenges, and more congruent with the biblical vision and its attendant values.

Mustard Seed Associates is using this process in our work with North Puget Sound Presbyterian, trying to help these twelve congregations, in a pilot project for the Alaska and Northwest synod of the Presbyterian church, to create new responses to emerging needs in their communities. In working with this group, we have been amazed once more at the remarkable creativity that is available in local congregations yet rarely called upon. In fact, I am convinced that the greatest untapped resource in the church today is the imagination and creativity of its adherents.

Samples from the Creative Edge

Let me share with you what some of our creative new responses to tomorrow's challenges might look like if we burst the constraints of the conventional and took our biblical vision and values more seriously. I want to share some local and transnational examples of what imaginative responses to specific areas of need might look like.

(1) *Creative evangelism and church planning.* Ichthus Fellowship in London represents the creative edge of what evangelism and church planting could look like in the future. This remarkable church of some two thousand members is growing at a rate of about 4 percent a year through relational evangelism, church planting, and social action projects in some of the poorest parts of London. New members are immediately incorporated in small, nurturing home groups, which meet together in larger congregational groupings several times a month. Once a month, the entire body rents a school and comes together for a celebrative time of charismatic worship.

Ichthus Fellowship is a thriving repudiation of the homogeneous principle—bringing together Pakistanis, Bengalis, Nigerians, working-class Brits, and even a few professionals in a festive Christian fellowship. This congregation is a wonderful, celebrative alternative to the gigantic consumer churches discussed earlier. This is a church-planting model within the reach of the poor as well as the affluent.

The reason these Christians have chosen not to invest their money in a church building is that they want their focus as a growing congregation to be outward. And having visited them, I would estimate that at least half of their time and resources is invested in mission to their various communities. They work with street kids trapped in prostitution, with the unemployed, and with the destitute, as well as starting mission projects in the Middle East. They are becoming what all of our churches in the nineties must become . . . a church for others.

(2) *Worship and celebration.* The creative church of tomorrow will also be transformed in its worship and community life. In the process, it will become more connected to the past as well as more responsive to the future. Gertrude Mueller Nelson writes,

The dawning of a renewed faith to which I see people striving to go forward is one which connects us to our forebears, to our ancient roots, to all those who went before us and to all who will come after us in the development of our human existence. Celebrating binds us together with a common symbolic form, a unique identity and a tradition in which to be founded. To celebrate as a church community, to commit ourselves to the realities in its history, to its traditions, to its forms, to its leadership, is also to commit ourselves to its reformations and growth.[9]

The way that we reconnect ourselves more fully to the past is not only to reclaim our ancient story, but to find new ways to retell that story through creating imaginative new rituals, celebrations, and worship. The renewal of the church begins with the renewal of its worship and celebration. We need new rituals that enable us to celebrate not only our past, but also our future . . . the festival of God.

(3) *Addressing the needs of the urban poor in the United States.* Tomorrow's innovative church will need to come up with whole new approaches to address the mounting problems of caring for the poor in inner-city areas. I don't believe the liberal approach of institutionalizing an entire system of care provides an adequate answer. Neither does simply dispensing handouts to the poor. Both systems fail to empower the poor, and both tend to foster dependency.

Chicago community organizer John McKnight, when asked at an urban missions conference in the late 1980s what would happen if poverty was ended in Chicago tomorrow, responded, "It would throw thousands of middle-class social workers out of jobs!"

John reported that twenty-four thousand dollars a year is allotted for every poor person in Cook County, but that only eight thousand of those dollars actually go to the poor people. Where does the rest go? That's right—to the service bureaucracy that provides the assistance. McKnight pointed out that service-industry specialists are regularly involved in identifying deficits among the people in the inner city in order to justify new programs. And the lion's share of the funding in these programs typically goes to the providers, not to the poor.

John McKnight urged the church to avoid getting involved in the institutionalization of services and to find other, more creative ways to empower the poor. He recommended a community organization approach, which is a low-cost, low-bureaucracy, and much more organic way of addressing problems. Instead of hiring a "director of urban ministry," for example, a church could hire a community organizer. This organizer could be charged with helping people learn to use their own power and resources to solve their own problems.

John asked what would happen if the full twenty-four thousand dollars spent on each poor person in Chicago was given to the poor so they could solve their own problems. What would happen if, instead of telling the poor what their defects were, we helped them identify their capabilities so they could work with others in their neighborhood to solve their own problems?

A group of young people at Hollywood Presbyterian, who participated in a creativity workshop I conducted, came up with a new idea for responding to the needs of inner-city kids through organizing them to take charge of their lives more fully. These young people envisioned an inner-city arts program that focuses on children's gifts and abilities rather than their deficits. Through drama, visual arts, and music, such a program could enable kids from blighted neighborhoods to develop self-confidence through developing their artistic abilities. Research for actually carrying out this program is in progress.

(4) *Raising awareness of need in the world.* Just standing up and talking about the challenges in the world—or even writing a book—isn't the most effective way of raising awareness of the challenges facing us and motivating people to act on them. I predict that the creative church of the future will, instead, develop people-to-people programs to help North American Christians experience firsthand the reality of need and the call of mission.

I have seen several churches become international congregations overnight by becoming partners with Two-Thirds-World churches to work on missions projects. A similar partnership could be set up between suburban congregations and ethnic, inner-city churches to start programs of inner-city empowerment such as computer education. I am certain that both congregations would receive more than they ever expected from this type of people-to-people initiative, but I believe the North American suburban congregations would learn the most.

(5) *Educating people for tomorrow.* Increasingly, Christian leaders from the Two-Thirds World and from North American inner-city churches will be called on to speak prophetically to the struggling middle-class church in the United States. The influence of these transnational and ethnic churches may hold out the best hope for the renewal of the church in North America. But we must reallocate resources to train these leaders—in the Two-Thirds World, the Soviet Union, the ghettos, and the barrios—to lead their churches into the twenty-first century. We must particularly seek out those who, like Chavannes Jeune, are receptive to the vision of God.

But the creative church of tomorrow will need to do more than train Two-Thirds-World and ethnic leaders. A radical reformation of Christian higher education and theological education in North America will be necessary to prepare a new generation to engage the new issues of the twenty-first century.

Frankly, much of Christian higher education seems devoted to preparing the Christian young to fit into this present world, not to change it. Many Christian schools seem to be preparing the young to fit into middle-class professions and lifestyles rather than involving them in a vision that can turn our world upside down. Instead, we need educational systems that focus on preparing students to live and serve in a world that will be radically different from today's world.

This means, in part, that the study of the future must be incorporated in *all* curricula in both colleges and seminaries. And this study of the future must be global in scope. The Association of Theological Schools in the United States and

Canada has called for "the internationalization of theological education to educate a generation of pastors and scholars who will be sensitive to the fact that the context for ministry and scholarship in their future is global."[10]

(6) *Transforming structures.* Creatively addressing needs is a vital part of addressing the mounting challenges of our nation and our world. But just meeting needs won't be enough. We must also find creative new ways to work together for the transformation of oppressive government and corporate structures.

Gerald Barney, who headed up the *Global 2000* study for President Carter, has made a wonderfully imaginative proposal for the church to engage the growing environmental challenges that fill our world. Barney, a Lutheran layman, has proposed to the bishops of the Evangelical Lutheran Church of America that they sponsor a "third millennium project." Barney explains that the purpose of such a project would be

> to give the world, on the occasion of the 2000th anniversary of the birth of Christ, a vision of how we Christians think God would like the planet earth managed during the Third Millennium. It would include a detailed country-by-country analysis of the likely future if present trends and policies continue and also of the possible futures if nations pursue alternative policies and programs. It would also include an assessment of global consequences of all of the individual national actions. In this way, we, the human part of creation, might enter the Third Millennium "having the eyes of our hearts enlightened" (Ephesians 1:18).[11]

Patterns of Creativity

Again, it has not been the purpose of this chapter to respond to all the issues that have been raised in this book. Rather, I have outlined some specific, practical ways that Christian leaders can be much more a part of the new order God is birthing by:

- *anticipating*—paying much more careful attention to how the world is changing,

- *visioning*—discovering and clarifying the specific mission to which God is calling us, our congregations, and our organizations,

- *creating*—learning to use the powers of imagination that God has placed within us to collaborate in unleashing the Wild Hope of God.

While I haven't sought to resolve all the issues involved in leading the church into the future, certain patterns seem to suggest themselves. Our attempts to collaborate in the advance of God's kingdom will likely require less expensive, less bureaucratic approaches. God's vision also seems to suggest that our responses need to have more of an organic, community-based, people-to-people character. And yet, with a little care, I suspect that even satellite technology can be redeemed for God's purposes.

The mounting challenges of the twenty-first century will require a new ecumenicity of mission, in which the Catholic church, the World Council of Churches, and the Lausanne Commission, and the World Evangelical Fellowship begin cooperating together to advance the kingdom of God. Only as we jointly seek to unmask the principalities of this age and to reclaim a biblical vision can we offer the world a compelling hope.

Lesslie Newbigin asserts that

> if the Gospel is to challenge the public life of our society, if Christians are to occupy the "high ground" which they vacated in the noon-time of "modernity," it will not only be by movements that begin with the local congregation in which the reality of a new creation is present, known, and experienced, and from which men and women will go into every sector of public life to claim it for Christ, to unmask the illusions which have remained hidden and to expose all areas of public life to the illumination of the Gospel. But that will only happen as and when local congregations renounce an introverted concern for their own life, and recognize they exist for the sake of those who are not members, as sign, instrument and foretaste of God's redeeming grace for the whole life of society.[12]

Only as the Wild Hope of God is unleashed in our lives and churches can we be a part of what God is doing to unleash it in the larger world. And Newbigin is right. The only way we can be a foretaste or an instrument of this hope is by realizing we exist not for ourselves, but for others. The future does indeed belong "to those who offer it hope."

Questions for Discussion

1. Why is it important for Christian leaders to learn to take the future seriously?
2. What are specific methodologies that leaders can use to anticipate how the larger context, as well as their own organization, is likely to change?
3. Which of these methodologies might have the most beneficial application within your organization and how could they be incorporated in your planning process?
4. Why is it important for leaders to enable their organizations to develop clear, compelling biblical visions to direct their organizational mission?
5. What are some specific ways leaders can enable their organizations to develop a clear, compelling, biblical statement of mission that actually directs the organization?
6. Why is it important for leaders to enable their churches or Christian organizations to begin to much more fully use their creativity in addressing tomorrow's challenges?
7. What are some creative ways that underutilized resources in your organization or spheres of mission could be transformed into tools for the kingdom?
8. What are some creativity processes your organization could use to create imaginative ways to implement your biblical vision in responding to the challenges of tomorrow's world?
9. Idea-storm some imaginative new ways your organization can more fully respond to the anticipated needs of those in your sphere of mission as we approach a new century.

12

Unleashing a Wild Hope in Your Own Future

The final chapter of *Wild Hope* hasn't been written. This is an ongoing saga. And the Creator God invites us all to set aside lesser agendas and participate in what God is doing to make a world new.

It is in that spirit that I invite you to coauthor the final pages of this book.

As a beginning, I invite you to write a futures history. Writing futures histories isn't easy, but it can be very rewarding. What you do, essentially, is to imagine in detail what some segment of your family, congregation, or the larger society would be like in ten years if something of God's new order really broke into our midst. Describe a specific scene. Then work back from that scene and describe the series of events that might be necessary over the next ten years to realize the transformation you described. You can write a futures history as though it were an article in a newspaper, a personal diary entry, or a TV documentary—ten years in the future.

Obviously, to write a compelling futures history you will need to:

- give a good deal of thought to how the world is changing.

- be very clear concerning your assumptions about what a preferred, normative future would look like and the values it would reflect.

- unleash your creativity to write a compelling, provocative narrative that would give a fresh vision of the future that engages some of the anticipated challenges.

I am convinced that writing a futures history will provide an innovative way for you to integrate all we have discussed in this book into your own vision and leadership. It might also provide the larger Christian community with fresh, imaginative ways we could more fully give expression to the Wild Hope of God and more effectively engage the growing challenges of the twenty-first century.

If you respond to my challenge, this may turn out to be the first interactive book on the future. At any rate, I would be most interested in reading what you write. I invite you to send me your futures histories. I will read them and seek to publish several of the best in a Christian magazine or perhaps a small book. I will, of course, give all authors full credit for their work, and all royalties will be given to Habitat for Humanity. I won't be able to return manuscripts, but I will let you know if your futures history has been selected for publication.

The ball is in your court now. What do you plan to do with the issues raised in this book and Scripture's strong call to seek first the kingdom of God? It is up to you to write the final chapter not only in a futures history but, more importantly, in your own life, the church, and the larger world. It is up to you, in collaboration with the Creator God and in community with millions of other sisters and brothers all over the world, to help midwife God's new order. And I would also be interested in learning how you seek to collaborate with others in unleashing something of the Wild Hope of God in your life, organization, and community. My address is: Mustard Seed Associates, P.O. Box 45867, Seattle, WA 98145.

I am looking forward to seeing your version of the final chapter of this book. I am as intrigued as you are by seeing how the Creator God continues to give birth to this new order within history, in anticipation of that day when Christ returns and all things are made new.

And so, looking forward to that day, we conclude this book as we began it, with a reminder from the prophet Isaiah regarding the unswerving purposes of the Creator God who has promised to make all things new:

> The Lord Almighty has sworn,
> "Surely as I have planned, so it will be,
>   and as I have purposed, so it will stand . . . .
> [The] yoke will be taken from my people,
>   and [the] burden removed from their shoulders."
> This is the plan determined for the whole world;
>   this is the hand stretched out over all nations.
> For the Lord Almighty has purposed, and who can thwart Him?
>   His hand is stretched out, and who can turn it back?
> Isaiah 14:24–27, NIV

notes

CHAPTER 1

1. Jeffrey L. Sheler, "A Revelation in the Middle East," *U.S. News and World Report,* 19 November 1990, 67.

2. Henri Focillon, *The Year 1000* (New York: Frederick Ungar, 1969), 53–59.

3. Richard Erdoes, "The Year 1000," *Psychology Today,* May 1989, 44–45, reprinted from *AD 1000: Living on the Brink of the Apocalypse* (San Francisco: Harper & Row, 1989).

4. Lester R. Brown, ed., *State of the World 1990: A Worldwatch Institute Report on Progress toward a Sustainable Society* (New York: W. W. Norton, 1990), xv.

5. "Third Millennium: Time toward Home," *The Religion and Society Report,* September 1988, 5 (no. 9):1.

6. Linda DeStefano, "Looking Ahead to the Year 2000: No Utopia, but Most Expect a Better Life," *Gallup Monthly Poll,* January 1990, 18.

7. Tony Hendra and Peter Ebling, ed., *A History of the 1990s before They Happen* (New York: Koppel and Scher, 1989), 8.

8. Council on Environmental Quality and the Department of State, *The Global 2000 Report to the President: Entering the Twenty-First Century* (Washington, D.C.: Government Printing Office, 1978). Out of this study, President Carter has established Global 2000, Inc., as a part of the Carter Center, to help improve health and agricultural services in poorer countries.

9. For further information, contact Mustard Seed Associates, Box 45867, Seattle, WA 98145; phone: (206) 545-SEED.

10. John Naisbitt and Patricia Aburdene, *Megatrends 2000: Ten New Directions for the 1990s* (New York: William Morrow, 1990), 30.

11. Marvin Cetron and Owen Davies, *American Renaissance: Our Life at the Turn of the Twenty-First Century* (New York: St. Martin's, 1989), 7.

12. Peter F. Drucker, *The New Realities: In Government and Politics, in Economics and Business, in Society and World View* (New York: Harper & Row, 1989), 13.

13. Willis W. Harmon, *Global Mind Change: The Promise of the Last Years of the Twentieth Century* (Indianapolis: Knowledge Systems, 1988).

14. Hal Lindsey, *The Late Great Planet Earth* (Grand Rapids, MI: Zondervan, 1970); John R. Walvoord, *Armageddon, Oil and the Middle East Crisis* (Grand Rapids, MI: Zondervan, 1990).

15. Robert McAfee Brown, *Elie Wiesel: Messenger to All Humanity* (Notre Dame, Univ. of Notre Dame Press, 1983), 4.

16. Hendrik Berkhof, *Christ and the Powers* (Scottsdale, PA: Herald, 1962), 13–33.

17. Berkhof, *Christ and the Powers*, 13–33

CHAPTER 2

1. Bill Dietrich, "Many Hope This Is the 'Decade of the Environment,'" *Seattle Times,* 28 January 1990, 1.

2. *Environmental Progress and Challenges: EPA's Update,* United States Environmental Protection Agency, 1 August 1988, 3–4.

3. Tom Sine, *The Mustard Seed Conspiracy: You Can Make a Difference in Tomorrow's Troubled World* (Waco, Texas: Word, 1981), 47.

4. Julian Simon, *The Resourceful Earth* (Princeton, NJ: Princeton Univ. Press, 1981), 4.

5. Thomas A. Sancton, "Planet of the Year," *Time,* 2 January 1989, 26–27.

6. Daniel B. Wood, "National Geographic Begins Its Second Century with a Warning," *Christian Science Monitor,* 1 December 1988, 1.

7. Sancton, "Planet of the Year," 26–27.

8. Louis Harris, *Inside America* (New York: Vintage, 1987), 24.

9. Harris, *Inside America,* 246–49.

10. Daniel B. Wood, "Aerial Crusaders," *Christian Science Monitor,* 14 July 1988, 16–17.

11. Melinda Beck with Mac Margolis, "Chronicle of a Death Foretold: Murder and Ecological Tragedy in the Amazon," *Newsweek,* 9 January 1989, 62.

12. Kristin Helmore, "Strength from a Stillness Within," *Christian Science Monitor,* 12 January 1989, 19.

13. Tyler Bridges, "Trees Fall, Protests Rise over the Future of the Amazon," *Christian Science Monitor,* 22 September 1988, 7.

14. World Commission on Environment and Development, *Our Common Future* (New York: Oxford Univ. Press, 1987), 151.

15. "Hotter, Drier Amazon Seen in Study," *New York Times,* 5 December 1989, C-10.

16. Lester R. Brown and Christopher Flavin, "The Earth's Vital Signs," in *State of the World 1988: A Worldwatch Institute Report on Progress toward a Sustainable Society,* ed. Lester R. Brown (New York: Norton, 1988), 15.

17. William K. Stevens, "Study Supports Global Warming Prediction," *New York Times National,* 14 December 1989, A36.

18. Roberto Suro, "Bush Defends Blocking of Environmental Plans," *The New York Times,* 12 July 1990, A10.

19. Melinda Beck with Mary Hager, "More Bad News for the Planet," *Newsweek,* 28 March 1988, 3.

20. Beck with Hager, "More Bad News for the Planet," 63.

21. Malcolm W. Browne, "Ozone Fading Fast, Thatcher Tells World Experts," *New York Times,* 28 June 1990, A4.

22. Lloyd Timberlake, *Only One Earth: Living for the Future* (New York: Sterling Publishing Company, 1987), 19.

23. Joe Paddock, *Soil and Survival: Land Stewardship and Future American Agriculture* (Washington, D.C.: Sierra Club, 1986), 1.

24. Sandra Postel, "Controlling Toxic Chemicals," in *State of the World 1988,* 119–25.

25. Larry Tye, "Pollution Knows No Boundaries," *Seattle Times,* 30 January, 1990, 1.

26. Bruce Piasecki and Peter Asmus, "Radioactive Challenge to Nature's Resilience," *Christian Science Monitor,* 15 November 1988, 14.

27. "Buried Alive," *Newsweek,* 27 November 1989, 67.

28. Peter Tonge, "All That Trash," *Christian Science Monitor,* 9 July 1987, 16–17.

29. Amy Brooke Baker, "A Cleanup Still Waiting to Happen," *Christian Science Monitor,* 22 September 1988, 16–17.

30. Philip Shabecoff, "Military Is Accused of Ignoring the Rules of Hazardous Waste," *New York Times Science,* 14 June 1988, 16.

31. Piasecki and Asmus, "Radioactive Challenge," 14.

32. Robert C. Cowen, "Rapid Rise in Methane Gas May Speed Worldwide Climatic Changes," *Christian Science Monitor,* 15 March 1988, 17.

33. Alvin Toffler, *The Third Wave: The Book That Makes Sense of the Exploding Eighties* (New York: Bantam, 1980), 89.

34. Byron Chepesiuk, "From Ash to Cash: International Trade in Toxic Waste," *E: The Environment Magazine,* 2 (no. 4): 30.

35. Sine, *Mustard Seed Conspiracy,* 47.

36. Steve Tripoli, "Costa Rica Saves a High Dry Forest," *Christian Science Monitor,* 9 January 1989, 12.

37. World Concern, Box 33000, Seattle, WA 98133.

38. Carl Woestendiek, "Recycling Plastics," *PCC Sound Consumer,* September 1988, 1.

39. Loren Wilkinson, ed., *Earthkeeping: Christian Stewardship of National Resources* (Grand Rapids, MI: Eerdmans, 1980).

40. Wesley Granberg Michaelson, *Worldly Spirituality* (San Francisco: Harper & Row, 1984).

41. Grace Halsell, *Prophecy and Politics: Militant Evangelists on the Road to Nuclear War* (Westport, CT: Lawrence Hill and Company, 1986), 8.

42. Halsell, *Prophecy and Politics,* 42.

43. Peter Hebblethwaite, "Vatican Statement on Ecology Possible, Overdue," *National Catholic Reporter,* 4 November 1988, 4.

44. Hebblethwaite, "Vatican Statement Possible," 4.

45. Clyde Haberman, "John Paul Rebukes Lands That Foster Environment Crisis, *New York Times,* December 1989, A7.

46. Arthur Jones, "Pained Cry of the Planet Exclaimed As World Christians Gather in Seoul," *Independent Catholic News Weekly,* 23 March 1990, 1.

47. Calvin B. DeWitt, "Seven Degradations of Creation,"*Perspectives,* February 1989, 4.

48. Wesley Granberg Michaelson, "Renewing the Whole Creation," *Sojourners,* 19 (February/March 1990):13.

49. Interview with Wendel Berry, *Radix,* 19:3.

CHAPTER 3

1. Charles L. Sanford, *The Quest for Paradise: Europe and the American Moral Imagination* (Urbana, IL: Univ. of Illinois Press, 1961), 127.

2. Sanford, *Quest for Paradise,* 157–64.

3. Andrew S. Berky and James P. Shenton, eds., *The Historian's History of the United States,* vol. 1 (New York: Capricorn Books, 1972), 490–95.

4. Harry L. Shipman, *Space 2000: Meeting the Challenge of a New Era* (New York: Plenum Press, 1987), 386.

5. "Living in a World of Your Own," *Life,* February 1989, 91; "Not Your Average Terrarium," *Newsweek,* 1 June 1987, 60.

6. Robert C. Cowen, "Space Trash: Falling Satellites, Orbiting Junk," *Christian Science Monitor,* 28 September 1988, 3.

7. "Special Interest Colonies for Oceans and Space," *Futurist,* January/February 1987, 42.

8. World Commission on Environment and Development, *Our Common Future,* (New York: Oxford Univ. Press, 1987), 137.

9. World Commission on Environment and Development, *Our Common Future,* 138.

10. John Liston, "Seafood Information Needs of the Third World," *Life League for International Food Education,* 20 (February/March 1987):2.

11. Robert C. Cowen, "Mining Ocean Floor Mineral Ore," *Christian Science Monitor,* 4 August 1987, 17.

12. "Water Dirtiest on the Surface," Future Scope, *Futurist,* May/June 1988, 5.

13. David Clark Scott, "Treaty Opens Up World's Last Untouched Continent to Mining," *Christian Science Monitor,* 7 June 1988, 9.

14. Scott, "Treaty Opens Up Continent," 9–10.

15. Arthur Unger, "Antarctica's Prospects Clouded by Treaty's Impending End," *Christian Science Monitor,* 17 August 1987, 23.

16. Grant Fjermedal, *The Tomorrow Makers: A Brave New World of Living Brain Machines* (Redmond, WA: Tempus Books, 1986), 220.

17. "Tomorrow in Brief," *Futurist,* January/February 1988, 3.

18. Stewart Brand, *The Media Lab: Inventing the Future at M.I.T.* (New York: Penguin, 1987), 18.

19. Alvin Toffler, *The Third Wave: The Book That Makes Sense of the Exploding Eighties* (New York: Bantam, 1980).

20. Marilyn Garner, "Burning Up the Highway," *Christian Science Monitor,* 2 June 1988, 23.

21. Tom Sine, *The Mustard Seed Conspiracy: You Can Make a Difference in Tomorrow's Troubled World* (Waco, TX: Word Books, 1981), 60.

22. "Don't Jump into Designer Genes," *Christian Science Monitor,* 24 April 1988, 15.

23. "With Billions in the Balance Many Moral Questions Remain," *World Press Review,* August 1988, 28–29.

24. Nathan E. Angier, "Team Cures Cystic Fibrosis by Gene Insertion," New *York Times,* 1 September 1990, 1.

25. Robert C. Cowen, "Playing Fast and Loose with Genetic Engineering Research Rules," *Christian Science Monitor,* 25 August 1987, 17.

26. "Life, Death and DNA: Shaking the Family Tree," *Atlanta Journal and Constitution,* 26 April 1987, 2.

27. Joseph Fletcher, *The Ethics of Genetic Control: Ending Reproductive Roulette* (New York: Prometheus Books, 1988), 56.

28. "Feats to Concoct the Flawless Being," *Insight on the News,* 11 July 1988, 3.

29. Jeremy Rifkin, "The Social Implications of Mapping the Human Genome," speech given by Jeremy Rifkin in 1989, 1.

30. Fjermedal, *Tomorrow Makers,* 209–10.

31. Fletcher, *Ethics of Genetic Control,* 71.

32. Paul Bagne, "High Tech Breeding," *Mother Jones,* August 1983, 23–26.

33. Marcia Angell, "The Right to Die in Dignity," *Newsweek,* 23 July 1990, 9.

34. Harriet Goetz, "Euthanasia: A Bedside View," *Christian Century,* 21–28 June 1989, 620.

35. Rita L. Marker, " 'Aid-in-Dying': The Last 'Pro-Choice' Frontier," *Our Sunday Visitor,* 8 December 1987, 21.

36. Owen Thomas, "Ethics Tries to Keep Pace with Medical Technology," *Christian Science Monitor,* 29 March 1988, 1, 32.

37. "The Organ Grinders," *South,* April 1989, 78.

38. Colm Keena, "Ban on 'Trading' of Human Organs," *Irish Press,* 19 December 1987, 1.

39. Stephen Post, "Fetal Tissue: A 'Gift' for Transplanting?" *Christian Century,* 7 December 1988, 1120.

40. Mark Clayton, "Artificial Intelligence," *Christian Science Monitor,* 17 February 1987, 23.

41. Tom Athanasiou, "Artificial Intelligence: Cleverly Disguised Politics," in *Compulsive Technology: Computers As Culture,* ed. Tony Solomonides and Les Levidow (London: Free Association Books, 1985), 32.

42. Raj Reddy, "Foundations and Grand Challenges of Artificial Intelligence," 1988 American Association for Artificial Intelligence presidential address, Winter 1988, 11.

43. Clayton, "Artificial Intelligence," 18–20.

44. Paul Bracken, *Command and Control of Nuclear Forces* (New Haven, CT: Yale Univ. Press, 1983).

45. Fjermedal, *Tomorrow Makers,* 193–94.

46. Catherine Foster, "Can-Do Technology, 'Smart' Devices Help to Liberate Disabled People," *Christian Science Monitor,* 26 July 1988, 19.

47. T. A. Heppenheimer, "Microbots," *Discover,* March 1989, 78–84.

48. Fjermedal, *Tomorrow Makers,* 193–94.

49. Sandra Postel and Lori Heise, "Reforesting the Earth," in *State of the World 1988: A Worldwatch Institute Report on Progress toward a Sustainable Society,* ed. Lester Brown (New York: W. W. Norton, 1988), 90.

50. Gary Paul Nabhan, "Seeds of Renewal," *World Monitor,* January 1989, 17.

51. Glen S. Grow, "Gene Bank Keeps Building Blocks of Wonder Crops," *Christian Science Monitor,* 29 December 1987, 19.

52. "Fill'er Up with Methyl," *Newsweek,* 1 May 1989, 67.

53. Jacques Ellul, *The Technological Society* (New York: Vintage Books, 1964), xxv.

54. Ellul, *Technological Society,* 8.

55. Ellul, *Technological Society,* xxx.

CHAPTER 4

1. E. F. Schumacher, *Small Is Beautiful: Economics As If People Matter* (New York: Harper & Row, 1973).

2. Richard J. Barnet and Ronald E. Muller, *Global Reach* (New York: Simon and Schuster, 1974), 30–33.

3. "Japan Builds a New Power Base," *Business Week,* 10 April 1989, 42.

4. James Fallows, "Getting Along with Japan," *Atlantic Monthly,* December 1989, 56.

5. "Where the Jobs Are," *Newsweek,* 2 February 1987, 42–52.

6. "An Unhealthy Trade," originally published in *Asian Week,* reprinted in *World Press Review,* July 1988, 47.

7. "Outside Looking In," *World Press Review,* January 1989, 22.

8. Louis Vchitelle, "East Europe Tries a Mild Capitalism," *New York Times,* 11 December 1989, C1.

9. "Altar of a Broken Idea," *U.S. News and World Report,* 3 April 1989, 38.

10. "500 Days," *Business Week,* 10 October 1990, 139–45.

11. John Kenneth Galbraith, "Can the Russians Reform?" *Harper's,* June 1988, 54.

12. Paul Kennedy, *The Rise and Fall of the Great Powers* (New York: Random House, 1987), xxiii.

13. David M. Abshire, "The Nature of American Global Leadership in the 1990s," in *The Global Economy: America's Role in the Decade Ahead,* ed. William Brock and Robert Hormats (New York: W. W. Norton, 1990), 176.

14. Alfred L. Malabre, Jr., *Beyond Our Means: How Reckless Borrowing Now Threatens to Overwhelm Us* (New York: Vintage, 1988), 3.

15. Lester R. Brown, ed., *State of the World 1990: A Worldwatch Institute Report on Progress toward a Sustainable Society* (New York, W. W. Norton, 1990), 7–8.

16. Susan F. Rasky, "Substantial Power on Spending Is Shifted from Congress to Bush," *New York Times,* 30 October 1990, 1.

17. "Banks in Trouble: Sweaty Brows and Slippery Fingers," *Economist,* 8 September 1990, 21.

18. Marvin Cetron and Owen Davies, *American Renaissance: Our Life at the Turn of the Twenty-First Century* (New York: St. Martin's, 1989), 1–20.

19. "The Recession Isn't Ready to Pull Out," *Business Week,* 11 March 1991, 33.

20. David R. Francis, "Low Wages and Social Discontent," *Christian Science Monitor,* 14 April 1989, 9.

21. "Do We Live As Well As We Used To?" *Fortune,* 14 September 1987, 42.

22. Gregg Easterbrook, "The Revolution," *Newsweek,* 26 January 1987, 50.

23. Christian Community Health Fellowship, P. O. Box 12548, Philadelphia, PA, 19151–0548.

24. "Where the Most Richest Are," *Forbes,* 25 July 1988, 91.

25. Myron Magnet, "The Money Society," *Fortune,* 6 July 1987, 26–27.

26. Magnet, "Money Society," 26.

27. "Greed on Sesame Street?" *Newsweek,* 20 July 1987, 38–39.

28. Magnet, "Money Society," 26.

29. Robert Reich, "Secession of the Successful," *New York Times Magazine,* 1 January 1991, 16–44.

30. Tom Sine, *Mustard Seed Conspiracy: You Can Make a Difference in Tomorrow's Troubled World* (Waco, TX: Word Books, 1981), 51.

31. Jonathan Kozol, *Rachel and Her Children: Homeless Families in America* (New York: Fawcett/Columbine, 1988), 52.

32. Kozol, *Rachel and Her Children,* 9.

33. David T. Ellwood, *Poor Support: Poverty in the American Family* (New York: Basic Books, 1988), 81–100.

34. Ellwood, *Poor Support,* 238.

35. Sine, *Mustard Seed Conspiracy,* 30.

36. Lester R. Brown and Sandra Postel, "Thresholds of Change," in Lester R. Brown, *State of the World 1987: A Worldwatch Institute Report on Progress toward a Sustainable Society* (New York: W. W. Norton, 1987), 5.

37. World Bank, *World Development Report 1989* (Oxford: Oxford Univ. Press, 1990), 214–15.

38. World Commission on Environment and Development, *Our Common Future* (Oxford: Oxford Univ. Press, 1987), 235–37.

39. Carl Haub, "Population Time Bomb," *San Francisco Chronicle,* 14 September 1988, 5.

40. "U.N. Agency Sees Third World Sliding Back into Misery," *Seattle Times,* 20 December 1988, A3.

41. Curtis J. Sitomer, "Justice for the World's Children," *Christian Science Monitor,* 22 December 1988, 17.

42. Robert Hey, "Banning Child Sweatshop Imports," *Christian Science Monitor,* 23 October 1987, 3–4.

43. P. G. "Paul" Lewis, "World Bank and Other Agencies Pledge to Increase Aid to Poor Children!" *New York Times,* 29 September 1990, 6.

44. Lori Heise, "The Global War against Women," *Washington Post,* 9 April 1989, 1.

45. R. Bernard, "End June 1989 Global Status of Reported AIDS Cases to the World Health Organization and 1986–1992 WHO/GPA Estimates for Sub-Saharan Africa," speech given in Geneva, Switzerland, 15 July 1989.

46. Susan Okie, "1.3 Billion Sick, Malnourished in World Report Says," *Seattle Times,* 25 September 1989, 4.

47. John W. Helmuth, "World Hunger amidst Plenty," *USA Today* magazine, March 1989, 48.

48. David C. Korten, *Getting to the 21st Century: Voluntary Action and The Global Agenda* (West Hartford, CT: Kumarian Press, 1990), 216.

49. Arthur Simon, *Bread for the World* (New York: Paulist Press, 1987), 42.

50. Penny Lernoux, "In Common Suffering and Hope," *Sojourners,* December 1987, 25.

51. Andrew Baker, "A New Lease Is Life: Building Communities with Creative Investing," *Jubilee: Social Concerns and the Episcopal Church* 6 (Spring 1980):1–13.

52. David Neff, ed., *The Midas Trap* (Wheaton, IL: Victor Books, 1990), 125.

53. Lay Commission on Catholic Social Teachings and the U.S. Economy, *Toward the Future: Catholic Social Thought and the U.S. Economy: Lay Letter on Catholic Social Teachings and the U.S. Economy* (New York, 1984), 50.

54. Sine, *Mustard Seed Conspiracy,* 29.

55. Ron Sider, *Rich Christians in an Age of Hunger* (Dallas: Word, 1990), 112–14.

56. Amy L. Sherman, "Christians and Economic Development," *First Things: A Monthly Journal of Religion and Public Life,* March 1990, 46.

57. Michael Novak, *The American Vision: An Essay on the Future of Democratic Capitalism* (Washington, D.C.: American Enterprise Institute for Public Policy Research, 1982), 24.

58. Horatio Alger, *Ragged Dick and Mark the Match Boy* (New York: Collier Books, 1962), 24–25.

59. Francis Fukuyama, "The End of History," *National Interest,* Summer 1989, 3–18.

60. M. Douglas Meeks, *God the Economist: The Doctrine of God and Political Economy* (Philadelphia: Fortress, 1989), 1.

61. National Conference of Catholic Bishops, *Pastoral Letter on Catholic Social Teaching and the U.S. Economy,* 2nd draft, Washington, D.C., 5 June 1986, 13.

CHAPTER 5

1. Javier Perez de Cuellar, "The Future and the United Nations," *International Review,* Winter 1989, 8.

2. Zbigniew Brzezinski, *The Grand Failure: The Birth and Death of Communism in the Twentieth Century* (New York: Scribner's, 1990), 3–6.

3. Brzezinski, *Grand Failure,* 7.

4. Brzezinski, *Grand Failure,* 2.

5. Richard Barnet, "The Challenge of Change," *Sojourners,* June 1989, 17.

6. Quoted in Anne Hope, ed., *Torch in the Night* (New York: Friendship Press, 1988), 83.

7. Frank C. Laubach, *The World Is Learning Compassion* (Westwood, NJ: Revell, 1958).

8. Robert O. Keohane, *After Hegemony: Cooperation and Discord in the World Political Economy* (Princeton, NJ: Princeton Univ. Press, 1984), 49.

9. Keohane, *After Hegemony,* 1–49.

10. Joseph S. Nye, *Bound to Lead: The Changing Nature of American Power* (New York: Basic Books, 1990).

11. David M. Abshire, "The Nature of American Global Leadership in the 1990s," in *The Global Economy: America's Role in the Decade Ahead,* ed. William Brock and Robert Hormats (New York: W. W. Norton, 1990), 175.

12. Jean J. Kirkpatrick, "Beyond the Cold War," *Foreign Affairs,* 69 (1990):3.

13. Allen Lynch, "Does Gorbachev Matter Anymore?" *Foreign Affairs,* 69 (1990):19.

14. "An Inside View of the Soviet Future," *World Press Review,* June 1990, 38.

15. J. Bryan Hebir, "Papal Foreign Policy," *Foreign Policy,* Spring 1990, 41.

16. Vaclav Havel, "The Chance That Will Not Return," *U.S. News and World Report,* 26 February 1990, 30.

17. Tom Sine, *The Mustard Seed Conspiracy: You Can Make a Difference in Tomorrow's Troubled World* (Waco, Texas: Word, 1981), 47.

18. Efraim Karsh and Martin Navias, "Iraqi Military Power and Its Threat to Regional Stability," *Harvard International Review,* Winter 1990–91, 12–14, 60.

19. Christopher S. Wren, "De Klerk Asks Repeal of Racial System's 'Cornerstone,'" *New York Times,* 2 February 1991, 1.

20. Desmond Tutu, *Hope and Suffering: Sermons and Speeches* (Grand Rapids, MI: Eerdmans, 1984), 102.

21. Mark O. Hatfield, "Beyond Containment" *Christianity Today,* 18 June 1990, 29–34.

22. David R. Francis, "World Military Spending Peaking?" *Christian Science Monitor,* 13 June 1989, 9.

23. Alvin Toffler, *Power Shift* (New York: Bantam, 1990), 346.

24. "There's Got to Be a Better Way," *Newsweek,* 22 October 1990, 24.

25. "Out of Order," *U.S. News and World Report,* 22 October 1990, 31.

26. Sine, *Mustard Seed Conspiracy,* 52.

27. Meg Greenfield, "How The West was Lost" *Newsweek,* 23 July 1990, 70.

28. Kevin Phillips, "Taxes Will Rise and the Republicans Will Fall," *Fortune,* 26 March 1990, 144.

29. William Kaufmann, "A Plan to Cut Military Spending in Half," *Bulletin of the Atomic Scientists,* March 1990, 37.

30. Jack Beatty, "A Post Cold War Budget," *Atlantic Monthly,* February 1990, 74–82.

31. John Davis, "Time for This State to Begin Beating Swords into Ploughshares," *Seattle Times,* 23 March 1990, A-7.

32. James W. Skillen, "Justice for the Unborn," an APJC position paper (Washington, D.C.: Association for Public Justice, n.d), 5.

33. "State By State," *Newsweek,* 1 May 1989, 38.

34. Interview with Dennis R. Kasper, Attorney at Law, Los Angeles, California, 10 March 1990.

35. "FBI Report Confirms Sharp Rise in Violent Crime," *New York Times,* 6 August 1990, A10.

36. Michael deCourcy Hinds, "Number of Killings Soars in Big Cities across the U.S.," *New York Times,* 18 July 1990, 1.

37. Stanley Hoffman, "A New World and Its Troubles," *Foreign Affairs,* Fall 1990, 118.

38. G. William Domhoff, *Who Rules America Now?: A View for the '80s* (New York: Simon & Schuster, 1983), 222–23.

39. Harris, *Inside America* (New York: Vintage, 1987), 33.

40. Michael Oreskes, "Alienation from Government Grows," *New York Times,* 16 September 1990, A15.

41. Oreskes, "Alienation from Government," A15.

42. Robert Parry and Peter Korn Bluh, "White House Manipulated U.S. Public Opinion Using CIA and NSC," *Seattle Times,* 25 September 1988, A17.

43. *Violations of the Laws of War by Both Sides in Nicaragua 1981–1985,* An Americas Watch Report (New York: Americas Watch, 1985), 61. The address and telephone number of the Americas Watch organization are 485 Fifth Avenue, New York, NY 10017, (212) 972-8400.

44. John Conyers, "When the FBI Is Looking through the Keyhole," *Christian Science Monitor,* 31 March 1988, 13.

45. Conyers, "FBI through the Keyhole," 13.

46. "Is America Becoming a 'Surveillance Society'?" *Seattle Times,* 21 September 1987, A8.

47. "A Diminished Ron, A Refurbished Jimmy," *Newsweek,* 2 April 1990, 36.

48. "Carter Earns Mixed Ratings for His Role as a Peace Broker," *Insight,* 30 April 1990, 28.

49. Interfaith Council for Corporate Responsibility, Room 566, 475 Riverside Drive, New York, NY 10115.

50. Jubilee Partners, PO Box 68, Comer, GA 30629.

51. Taken from a public relations brochure put out by Jubilee Partners.

52. Charles Colson, "Of Mice and Men," *Eternity,* March 1987, 11.

53. Colson, "Of Mice and Men," 11.

54. *National and International Religion Report,* 4 (12 February 1990):1.

55. Jonathan Marshall, *Drug Wars, Corruption, Counter-Insurgency, and Covert Operations in the Third World* (Forest Hill, CA: Cohan and Cohen, 1991); see also Chadwick Healey, *Iran-Contra Affair National Security Archives,* available in microform (Alexandria, VA: Government Printing Office, 1990).

56. Richard Neuhaus, *The Naked Public Square* (Grand Rapids, MI: Eerdmans, 1984).

57. John Richard Burkholder, *Mennonites in Ecumenical Dialogue on Peace and Justice,* Mennonite Central Committee Occasional Paper #7 (Akron, PA: Mennonite Central Committee, 1988), 16.

58. Glenn Tinder, "Can We Be Good without God?" *Atlantic Monthly,* December 1989, 70.

CHAPTER 6

1. U.S. Bureau of the Census, *Statistical Abstract of the U. S.* 110th ed. (Washington, D.C.:1990), 9.

2. U.S. Bureau of the Census, *Historical Statistics of the United States, Colonial Times to 1970, Part I* (Washington, D.C., 1989), 9.

3. Signe I. Wetrogan, *Projections of the Population of States by Age, Sex and Race: 1988 to 2010,* prepared for the U.S. Bureau of the Census (Washington, D.C.: 1988), 13.

4. Ken Dychtwald, *Age Wave: The Challenges and Opportunities of an Aging America* (Los Angeles: Jeremy Tarcher, 1989), 9.

5. Population Reference Bureau, *America in Twenty-First Century,* 9.

6. William A. Henry III, "Beyond the Melting Pot," *Time,* 9 April 1990, 28.

7. Rafael Valdivieso and Cary Davis, *U.S. Hispanics: Challenging Issues for the 1990s,* no. 17 (Washington, D.C.: Population Reference Bureau, December 1988), 1–4.

8. William P. O'Hare, *Assimilation and Socioeconomic Advancement of Hispanics in the United States* (Washington, D. C.:Population Reference Bureau, 1989).

9. Wetrogan, *Projections of the Population,* 10.

10. Population Reference Bureau, *America in Twenty-First Century,* 10.

11. National Urban League, *The State of Black America 1989* (New York: National Urban League, 1989), 4.

12. National Urban League, *State of Black America,* 121–29.

13. Population Reference Bureau, *America in Twenty-First Century,* 9–10.

14. U.S. Bureau of the Census, *1980 Census of Population,* vols. 1–2 (Washington, D.C.: 1981).

15. Elinor Abramson, "Projections 2000," *Occupational Outlook Quarterly,* Fall 1987, 1–10.

16. Jim Wallis, "America's Original Sin," *Sojourners,* November 1987, 17.

17. Tom Sine, *Mustard Seed Conspiracy: You Can Make a Difference in Tomorrow's Troubled World* (Waco, TX: Word, 1981), 56.

18. Wallis, "America's Original Sin," 17.

19. Wallis, "America's Original Sin," 16.

20. Cheryl Russell, *100 Predictions for the Baby Boom: The Next 50 Years* (New York: Plenum, 1987), 29.

21. Russell, *100 Predictions,* 29.

22. George Gallup, Jr., and Jim Castelli, *The People's Religion: American Faith in the 90s* (New York: Macmillan, 1989), 4–8.

23. Michael Reese and Jennifer Foote, "California American Dream, American Nightmare," *Newsweek,* 31 July 1989, 23–27.

24. Louis Harris, *Inside America* (New York: Vintage, 1987), 8–10.

25. Dychtwald, *Age Wave,* 72–73.

26. Dychtwald, *Age Wave,* 267.

27. Population Reference Bureau, *America in Twenty-First Century,* 3.

28. Population Reference Bureau, *America in Twenty-First Century,* 3.

29. Jolie Solomon and Gilbert Fuchsberg, "Great Number of Older Americans Seen Ready to Work," *Wall Street Journal,* 26 January 1990, B1.

30. "The Graying of the Campus," *Newsweek,* 6 June 1988, 56.

31. "Ailing Parent: A Woman's Burden Grows," *New York Times,* 14 November 1989, A15.

32. Erik Eckholm, "Haunting Issue for the U.S.: Caring for the Elderly Ill," *New York Times,* 22 March 1990, 12.

33. Dychtwald, *Age Wave,* 55.

34. Paul C. Light, *Baby Boomers* (New York: W. W. Norton, 1988), 9.

35. Daniel Yankelovich, *New Rules: Searching for Self-Fulfillment in a World Turned Upside Down* (New York: Bantam, 1981), xv–xvi.

36. Light, *Baby Boomers,* 28.

37. Robert N. Bellah, Richard Madsen, et al., *Habits of the Heart: Individualism and Commitment in American Life* (New York: Harper & Row, 1985), 47.

38. Light, *Baby Boomers,* 30.

39. James F. Engel and Jerry D. Jones, *Baby Boomers and the Future of World Missions* (Orange, CA: Management Development Associates, 1989), 51.

40. Light, *Baby Boomers,* 147–151.

41. Population Reference Bureau, *America in Twenty-First Century,* 6.

42. *Clarion-Ledger,* Jackson, MS, 3 June 1990, 9A.

43. Russell, *100 Predictions,* 18–19.

44. Jerrold K. Footlick, "What Happened to the Family?" *Newsweek,* Winter/Spring 1990, 18.

45. Jean Seligmann, "Variations on a Theme," *Newsweek,* Winter/Spring 1990, 38.

46. Footlick, "What Happened to the Family?" 17.

47. Ginny NiCarthy, *Getting Free* (Seattle: Seal Press, 1986), 277.

48. Herb Boyd, "The Crisis of Affordable Housing," *Crisis,* 96 (May 1989):11–16.

49. William Dunn, "Too Rushed to Relax," *USA Today,* 18 January 1990, 1.

50. Dychtwald, *Age Wave,* 20–21.

51. Geoffrey Cowley with Mary Hager, "Can Hormones Stop the Clock?" *Newsweek,* 16 July 1990, 66.

52. Dychtwald, *Age Wave,* 21–22.

53. Matthew Greenwald, "Bad News for the Baby Boom Generation," *American Demographics,* February 1989, 34–37.

54. J. C. Barden, "Poverty Rate Is Up Sharply for Very Young, Study Says," *New York Times,* 16 April 1990, A7.

55. J. C. Barden, "Toll of Troubled Families: Flood of Homeless Youths," *New York Times,* 5 February 1990, 1.

56. Pete Axthelm, "Somebody Else's Kids," *Newsweek,* 25 April 1988, 65.

57. Paul Clancy, "Child Sex Abuse: Crime of the '90's," *USA Today,* 29 September 1989, 3-A.

58. Harris, *Inside America,* 70.

59. Harris, *Inside America,* 61–66.

60. Michael Josephson, "Young America Is Looking Out for No. 1," *Los Angeles Times,* 16 October 1991, 37.

61. Gallup and Castelli, *People's Religion,* 27.

62. Kenneth L. Woodward, "Young beyond Their Years," *Newsweek,* Winter/Spring 1990, 57.

63. Tim Stafford, "Great Sex: Reclaiming a Christian Sexual Ethic," *Christianity Today,* 2 October 1987, 24–46.

64. James Scott, "Diseases Transmitted through Sex Escalating," *Seattle Times,* 15 October 1989, A9.

65. "AIDS: the Next Ten Years," *Newsweek,* 25 June 1990.

66. Woodward, "Young beyond Their Years," 54.

67. Population Reference Bureau, *America in Twenty-First Century,* 18.

68. "Demographic Issues for the 1990s," *Futurist,* March/April 1990, 11.

69. Steven A. Holmes, "School Reform: Business Moves In," *New York Times,* 1 February 1990, C1.

70. Sidney Hook, "Books: The Closing of the American Mind, An Intellectual Best Seller Revisited," *American Scholar,* Winter 1989, 127.

71. Connie Leslie, "Lost on the Planet Earth," *Newsweek,* 8 August 1988, 31.

72. Leslie, "Lost on Planet Earth," 31.

73. David Cohen, "Tribal Enterprise," *Atlantic Monthly,* October 1989, 32–34.

74. Daniel B. Wood, "A Refuge for Abused Children," *Christian Science Monitor,* 19 July 1989, 14.

75. H. Richard Niebuhr, *Christ and Culture* (New York: Harper & Row, 1951).

76. Tim LaHaye, *Battle for the Mind* (Old Tappan, NJ: Revell, 1980).

77. Aleksandr I. Sozhenitsyn, *A World Split Apart: Commencement Address Delivered at Harvard University, 8 June 1978* (New York: Harper & Row/Torch, 1978), 51.

CHAPTER 7

1. Eric Hoffer, *True Believers* (New York: Harper & Row, 1951).

2. Carol Ostrom, "A Study of Fundamentalism," *Seattle Times,* 24 March 1990, A10.

3. Ann Levin, "Jewish Baby-Boomers Give Rise to a Kosher Craze," *New York Times,* 11 November 1990.

4. David B. Barrett and Frank Kaleb Jansen, *The World in Figures,* handbook for the Lausanne II conference (Manila: Lausanne Commission, 1989), 13–1 to 13–35.

5. Barrett and Jansen, "World in Figures," 13–1 to 13–35.

6. Paul G. Hiebert, "World Trends and Their Implications for Mennonite Brethren Missions," *Mission Focus,* December 1988, 16 (no. 4):75.

7. James A. Scherer, *Gospel, Church and Kingdom: Comparative Studies in World Mission Theology* (Minneapolis: Augsburg, 1987), 48.

8. Harvey Cox, "Many Mansions or One Way? The Crisis in International Dialogue," *Christian Century,* 17–24 August 1988, 732–33.

9. "AD 2000 Movement at Lausanne," *Daily News,* official newspaper of Lausanne II (Manila: 20 July 1989) 1.

10. Ralph Winter, "Countdown 2000," *World Evangelization,* November/December 1988, 7.

11. Eugene L. Stockwell, "Evangelicals and the WCC: Bringing Down Walls, Putting Up Bridges," *World Christian,* December 1989, 18–21.

12. Scherer, *Gospel, Church and Kingdom,* 40–41.

13. However, the only way evangelicals and mainliners can work together is to start building trust and desist from writing lopsided caricatures of one another like Ernest W. Lefever's *Nairobi to Vancouver: The World Council of Churches and the World, 1975–87* (Washington D.C.: The Ethics and Public Policy Center, 1987).

14. Lesslie Newbigin, "Cross-Currents in Ecumenical and Evangelical Understandings of Mission," *International Bulletin of Missionary Research,* October 1982, 148.

15. Paul E. Pierson, "9 Trends For the 90s," *Latin American Evangelist,* April/June 1990, 6.

16. Hiebert, "World Trends and Their Implications," 79.

17. Clara Germani, "Pope Visits Latin America as Church Faces Tougher Times," *Christian Science Monitor,* 8 May 1988, 10.

18. Germani, "Pope Visits Latin America," 10.

19. Penny Lernoux, "The Fundamentalist Surge in Latin America," *Christian Century,* 20 January 1988, 51.

20. Lesley Gill, "Bolivia: Pentecostals Fill a Gap," *Christianity and Crisis,* 7 November 1988, 395.

21. Flora Lewis, "Straight Talk by an African to Africans," *International Herald Tribune,* 3 October 1988, 6.

22. "Gap between Rich and Poor Is Threat to Church Unity, Nababan Says," *Lutheran World Information,* August 1989, 5.

23. "Will Success Spoil the South Korean Church?" *Christianity Today,* 20 November 1987, 36.

24. "Church of Berlin-Brandenburg Looks to Unified Future," *Lutheran World Information,* May 1990, 5.

25. Brian Carrell, "Re-evangelization of New Zealand," *World Evangelization,* July/August 1989, 21.

26. "Understanding New Age Conspiracy Theories," *The Door,* March/April 1989, 9–23.

27. Don Latin, "Mythologist's Sudden New Appeal," *San Francisco Chronicle,* 15 August 1988, A4.

28. Latin, "Mythologist's Sudden Appeal," A4. See also Douglas Groothuis, "Myth and Power of Joseph Campbell," *Radix* 19 (September 1990), 13–16.

29. Peter L. Berger, *The Sacred Canopy* (Garden City, NY: Doubleday, 1967), 132–33.

30. Wade Clark Roof and William McKinney, *American Mainline Religion: Its Changing Shape and Future* (New Brunswick, NJ: Rutgers Univ. Press, 1987), 88.

31. Robert Wuthnow, *The Restructuring of American Religion* (Princeton, NJ: Princeton Univ. Press, 1988).

32. Linda-Marie Delloff, "New Roles, New Power for Women in the Church," *Progressions: A Lilly Endowment Occasional Report,* 2 (January 1990):14.

33. Paul Wilkes, "The Hands That Would Shape Our Souls," *Atlantic Monthly,* December 1990, 60.

34. R. Gustav Niebuhr, "Mass Shortage," *Wall Street Journal,* 13 November 1990, 1.

35. Reginald W. Bibby, *Fragmented Gods: The Poverty and Potential of Religion in Canada* (Toronto: Irwin Publications, 1987), 11.

36. Bibby, *Fragmented Gods,* 5.

37. David Heim, "Looking for the Mainline with Roof and McKinney," *Christian Century,* 1 June 1988, 545.

38. Lyle E. Schaller, "The Changing Face of the Passing Parade," *The Lutheran,* 3 January 1990, 16.

39. Heim, "Looking for the Mainline," 545.

40. Michael McManus, "Troubled Council of Churches Must Find New Ways to Spur Ecumenical Cooperation," *Seattle Post-Intelligencer,* 12 November 1988, 4.

41. Stanley Hauerwas and William H. Willimon, *Resident Aliens* (Nashville: Abingdon, 1990), 29.

42. Heim, "Looking for the Mainline," 233.
43. Roof and McKinney, *American Mainline Religion,* 21.
44. Roof and McKinney, *American Mainline Religion,* 22.
45. Peter Steinfels, "Church Message for This Season: Erasing Debt by Giving More," *New York Times,* 14 November 1988, 12.
46. *A Composite: A Comparison of the Growth in 31 Denominations' Total Contributions with U.S. Per Capita Income 1968–1985* (Champaign, IL: Empty Tomb, 1988), 1.
47. Sylvia Ronsvalle, *Protestant Giving As a Function of United States Per Capita Income 1916–1985* (Champaign, IL: Empty Tomb, 1989), 3.
48. Ronsvalle, *Stewards into Consumers* (Champaign, IL: Empty Tomb, 1991), 2.
49. *Giving and Volunteering in the United States,* 1988 edition (Washington, D.C.: Independent Sector, 1988), 6.
50. *Giving and Volunteering in the United States: Findings From a National Survey,* 1990 edition (Washington, D.C.: Independent Sector, 1990), 15.
51. Bureau of Labor Statistics, *Consumer Expenditure Survey, Integrated Survey Data* (Washington, D.C. 1989), 1.
52. George Gallup, Jr., and Jim Castelli, *The People's Religion: American Faith in the 90s* (New York: Macmillan, 1989), 27, 127.
53. David Barrett, "Silver and Gold Have I None: Church of the Poor or Church of the Rich?" *International Bulletin of Missionary Research,* October 1983, 147.

CHAPTER 8

1. Walter Brueggemann, *The Prophetic Imagination* (Philadelphia: Fortress, 1978), 11.
2. Stanley Hauerwas, *The Presence of the Kingdom: A Primer for Christian Ethics* (Notre Dame, IN: Univ. of Notre Dame Press, 1983), 23.
3. Gibson Winter, *Liberating Creation: Foundations of Religious Social Ethics* (New York: Crossroad, 1981).
4. Kenneth Boulding, *The Image* (Ann Arbor: Univ. of Michigan Press, 1971), 64.
5. Mircea Eliade, *Images and Symbols: Studies in Religious Symbolism* (New York: Sheed and Ward, 1961), 20.
6. Winter, *Liberating Creation,* x.
7. *Frances Bacon: A Selection of His World,* ed. Sidney Warhaff (New York: Odyssey Press, 1965), 21.
8. *Bacon: A Selection,* 19–25.
9. *Bacon: A Selection,* 14; Theodore Roszak, *Where the Wasteland Ends: Politics and Transcendence in Post Industrial Society* (Garden City, N.Y.: Doubleday, 1972), 147.
10. Barry B. Hughes, *World Futures: A Critical Analysis of Alternatives* (Baltimore: Johns Hopkins Univ. Press, 1985) 27–28.
11. Stuart Ewen, "Waste a Lot, Want a Lot: Our All-Consuming Quest for Style," *UTNE Reader,* September/October 1989, 81.
12. Lesslie Newbigin, *Foolishness to the Greeks: The Gospel and Western Culture* (Grand Rapids: Eerdmans, 1986), 30.
13. Newbigin, *Foolishness to the Greeks,* 26.
14. Winter, *Liberating Creation,* 22.

15. F. H. Anderson, *The Philosophy of Francis Bacon* (Chicago: Univ. of Chicago Press, 1948), 298.

16. James Turner, *Without God, Without Creed: The Origins of Unbelief in America* (Baltimore, MD: Johns Hopkins Univ. Press, 1985), 49–202.

17. Newbigin, *Foolishness to the Greeks,* 45.

18. Paul L. Wachtel, *The Poverty of Affluence: A Psychological Portrait of the American Way of Life* (New York: Free Press, 1983), 61.

19. Newbigin, *Foolishness to the Greeks,* 113.

20. Lesslie Newbigin, *The Gospel in a Pluralistic Society* (Grand Rapids, MI.: Eerdmans, 1989), 232.

21. Winter, *Liberating Creation,* 103.

22. Winter, *Liberating Creation,* 2.

23. Charles Sanford, *Quest for Paradise: Europe and the American Moral Imagination* (Urbana, IL: Univ. of Illinois Press, 1961), 39.

24. Henry David Thoreau, *Walden and Civil Disobedience* (New York: W. W. Norton, 1965), 77.

25. Willis W. Harman, *An Incomplete Guide to the Future* (Palo Alto, CA: Stanford Alumni Association, 1976), 141.

26. Robert Burrows, "Americans Get Religion in the New Age," *Christianity Today,* 16 May 1986, 17–23.

27. Frank Barnaby, ed., *The Gaia Peace Atlas: Survival into the Third Millennium* (New York: Doubleday, 1988), 10.

28. Rushworth M. Kidder, "How Might Quantum Thinking Change Us?" *Christian Science Monitor,* 17 June 1988, 3.

29. Kidder, "How Might Quantum Thinking," 3.

30. David Harvey, *The Condition of Post-Modernity: An Enquiry into the Origins of Cultural Change* (Cambridge: Basil Blackwell, 1984), 44, 116.

31. Leon R. Kass, "What's Wrong with Babel?" *American Scholar,* Winter 1989, 59–60.

CHAPTER 9

1. Sheila Kitzinger, *Giving Birth: How It Really Feels* (New York: Noonday Press, 1989), 45–46.

2. Madeleine L'Engle, "Charlotte Rebecca Jones, 22nd August, 1969," in *The Weather of the Heart* (Wheaton, IL: Harold Shaw, 1978), 64.

3. Os Guinness, "Mission in the Face of Modernity: Nine Checkpoints on Mission without Worldliness in the Modern World," plenary address given at the Lausanne II conference, Manila, 11–20 July 1989.

4. Hendrik Berkhof, *Christ and the Powers* (Scottsdale, PA: Herald, 1977), 39.

5. Jürgen Moltmann, *The Future of Creation: Collected Essays* (Philadelphia: Fortress, 1979), 118.

6. Jürgen Moltmann, *God in Creation: A New Theology of Creation and the Spirit of God* (San Francisco: Harper & Row, 1985), 5.

7. Walter Brueggemann, *The Land: Place as Gift, Promise and Challenge of Biblical Faith* (Philadelphia: Fortress, 1977), 18.

8. Gustavo Guitierrez, *A Theology of Liberation: History and Politics of Salvation* (Maryknoll, NY: Orbis, 1973), 156.

9. Walter Brueggemann, *The Prophetic Imagination* (Philadelphia: Fortress, 1978), 1–21.

10. Guitierrez, *Theology of Liberation,* 157.

11. Guitierrez, *Theology of Liberation,* 157.

12. Brueggemann, *The Land,* 43.

13. Arthur F. Glasser and Donald A. McGaupan, *Contemporary Theologies of Mission* (Grand Rapids, MI: Baker, 1983), 34.

14. Walter Brueggemann, *Hope within History* (Atlanta: John Knox, 1987), 82.

15. Brueggemann, *Hope within History,* 84.

16. Charles Scriven, *The Transformation of Culture: Christian Social Ethics after H. Richard Neibuhr* (Scottsdale, PA: Herald Press, 1988), 108–109.

17. Walter Brueggemann, *Living toward a Vision: Biblical Reflections on Shalom* (New York: United Church Press, 1982), 15.

18. Kosuke Koyama, *Three Mile an Hour God* (Maryknoll, NY: Orbis, 1979).

19. Jon Sobrino, *True Church and the Poor* (Maryknoll, NY: Orbis, 1984), 49–50.

20. Kofi Appiah-Kubi, "Indigenous African Christian Churches," in Kofi Appiah-Kubi and Sergio Torres, ed., *African Theologies en Route: Papers from the Pan-African Congress of Third-World Theologians, December 17–23, 1977* (Maryknoll, NY: Orbis, 1979), 118–19.

21. Kofi Appiah-Kobi, "Indigenous African Christian Churches," 118–19.

22. Josiah V. Young, *Black and African Theologies: Siblings or Distant Cousins* (Maryknoll, NY: Orbis, 1986), 74–75.

23. John Stott, *Involvement: Being a Responsible Christian in a Non-Christian Society,* vol. 1 (Old Tappan, NJ: Revell, 1985), 31.

24. Sobrino, *True Church,* 59.

25. Victorio Araya, *God of the Poor: The Mystery of God in Latin American Liberation Theology* (Maryknoll, NY: Orbis 1987), 66–67.

26. Jürgen Moltmann, "Theology as Eschatology," in *The Future as Hope: Theology as Eschatology,* ed. Frederick Herzog (New York: Herder and Herder, 1970), 31.

27. Moltmann, "Theology as Eschatology," 31.

28. Moltmann, in a personal interview held in his office in Tübingen, Germany, 1985.

29. Moltmann, "Theology as Eschatology," 23.

30. René Padilla, "The Mission of the Church in Light of the Kingdom," *Transformation,* April/June 1984, 1 (no. 2):17.

31. Padilla, "Mission of the Church," 17.

32. Brueggemann, *Living toward a Vision,* 15.

33. David Bosch, *Transforming Mission* (Maryknoll, NY: Orbis, 1991), 400.

34. James Turner, *Without God, Without Creed: The Origins of Unbelief in America* (Baltimore, MD: Johns Hopkins Univ. Press, 1985).

35. Rosemary Radford Ruether, *Sexism and God Talk: Towards a Feminist Theology* (Boston: Beacon Press, 1983), 56.

36. John Beversluis, *C. S. Lewis and the Search for Rational Religion* (Grand Rapids, MI: Eerdmans, 1985), 21.

37. Stanley A. Hauerwas and William H. Willimon, *Resident Aliens* (Nashville, TN: Abingdon, 1989), 12.

38. Charles Colson, *Against the Night: Living in the New Dark Ages* (Ann Arbor, MI: Servant, 1989).

39. Richard J. Mouw, *Politics and the Biblical Drama* (Grand Rapids, MI: Baker, 1976), 89.

40. M. Scott Peck, *People of the Lie: The Hope for Healing Human Evil* (New York: Simon & Schuster, 1983).

41. Lesslie Newbigin, *The Gospel in a Pluralist Society* (Grand Rapids, MI: Eerdmans, 1989), 204–7.

42. G. B. Baird, *Principalities and Powers: A Study in Pauline Theology* (Oxford: Clarendon, 1956), 100.

43. Kitzinger, *Giving Birth,* 12.

CHAPTER 10

1. Elias Chacour with David Hazard, *Blood Brothers* (Grand Rapids, MI: Chosen, 1984), 11–21.

2. Chacour, *Blood Brothers,* 11-21.

3. Chacour, *Blood Brothers,* 21-37.

4. Chacour, *Blood Brothers,* 33-49.

5. Evangelicals for Social Action, 10 Lancaster Ave., Wynnewood, PA 19096.

6. Stanley A. Hauerwas and William H. Willimon, *Resident Aliens* (Nashville, TN: Abingdon, 1989), 44–45.

7. Hauerwas and Willimon, *Resident Aliens,* 45.

8. Hauerwas and Willimon, *Resident Aliens,* 45.

9. Hauerwas and Willimon, *Resident Aliens,* 46–47.

10. Orlando E. Costas, *The Integrity of Mission: The Inner Life and Outreach of the Church* (New York: Harper & Row, 1979), 13–14.

11. Quoted in Jim Wallis, *The Call to Conversion: Recovering the Gospel for These Times* (San Francisco: Harper & Row, 1981), 15.

12. Henri Nouwen, *Reaching Out* (New York: Doubleday, 1975), 10–40.

13. *Why Settle for More and Miss the Best?* (Waco: Word, 1987) makes an excellent congregational study book to enable members to creatively reorder their lives.

14. John Howard Yoder, *The Politics of Jesus* (Grand Rapids, MI: Eerdmans, 1972).

15. LAMP, Langley Mennonite Fellowship, 19774 56th Ave., Langley, British Columbia V3A 3X6.

16. Eric Naider and Elouise Schumacher, "Breaking the Code," *Seattle Times,* 2 December 1990, 1.

17. Council on Economic Priorities, *Shopping for a Better World* (New York: Ballantine, 1991).

18. Amy L. Domini and Peter D. Kinder, *Ethical Investing* (Reading, MA: Addison-Wesley, 1986).

19. Rodney Clapp, "Remonking the Church,"*Christianity Today,* 12 August 1988, 20.

20. Thomas W. Sweeter, "The Parish of the Future: Beyond the Programs," *America,* 10 March 1990, 239.

21. Alvin Toffler, *Future Shock* (New York: Random House, 1970).

22. Kathryn McCamant and Charles Durrett, *Cohousing: A Contemporary Approach to Housing Ourselves* (Berkeley: Habitat Press, 1988).

23. Mustard Seed Associates, Box 45867, Seattle, WA 98145.

24. "From the Kairos Document," in *Torch in the Night,* ed. Anne Hope (New York: Friendship Press, 1988), 116.

CHAPTER 11

1. Howard W. French, "Haiti Installs Democratic Chief, Its First," *New York Times,* 8 February 1991, A3.

2. Burt Nanus, "Futures-Creative Leadership," *The Futurist,* May–June 1990, 13–15.

3. Burt Nanus, *The Leader's Edge: The Seven Keys to Leadership in a Turbulent World* (New York: Contemporary Books, 1989), 40–43.

4. William Scott and David Hart, *Organizational America* (Boston: Houghton Mifflin, 1979).

5. John W. Gardner, "Leadership and the Future," *The Futurist,* May–June, 1990.

6. Nanus, "Futures-Creative Leadership," 17.

7. Nanus, *Leader's Edge,* 54.

8. Nanus, "Futures-Creative Leadership," 13.

9. Gertrude Mueller Nelson, *To Dance with God: Family Ritual and Community Celebration* (New York: Paulist Press, 1986), 7.

10. Norman E. Thomas, "From Missions to Globalization: Teaching Missiology in North American Seminaries," *International Bulletin of Missionary Research,* July 1989, 105.

11. Gerald O. Barney, "Letter to the Bishops, Executives, Chairs and leaders of the ELCA," from Gerald O. Barney Institute for 21st Century Studies (Arlington, VA: February 1989), 15.

12. Lesslie Newbigin, *The Gospel in a Pluralist Society* (Grand Rapids, MI: Eerdmans, 1989), 233.

index